TCP/IP
for Windows® 2000

ISBN 0-13-028160-3

90000

9 780130 281609

PRENTICE HALL PTR MICROSOFT® TECHNOLOGIES SERIES

TCP/IP
for Windows® 2000

Dave Houde

Tim Hoffman

Prentice Hall PTR, Upper Saddle River, NJ 07458
www.phptr.com

Library of Congress Cataloging-in-Publication Data

CIP Data available

Editorial/Production Supervision: *Mary Sudul*
Acquisitions Editor: *Mary Franz*
Marketing Manager: *Dan DePasquale*
Manufacturing Buyer: *Maura Goldstaub*
Cover Design: *Anthony Gemmellaro*
Cover Design Direction: *Jerry Votta*
Interior Series Design: *Gail Cocker-Bogusz*

 © 2001 by Prentice Hall PTR
Prentice-Hall, Inc.
Upper Saddle River, NJ 07458

Prentice Hall books are widely used by corporations and government agencies for training, marketing, and resale.

The publisher offers discounts on this book when ordered in bulk quantities. For more information, contact Corporate Sales Department, phone: 800-382-3419; fax: 201-236-7141; email: corpsales@pren-hall.com
Or write Corporate Sales Department, Prentice Hall PTR, One Lake Street, Upper Saddle River, NJ 07458.

Product and company names mentioned herein are the trademarks or registered trademarks of their respective owners. The Electronic Commerce Game™ is a trademark of Object Innovations. Inc.

Printed in the United States of America

10 9 8 7 6 5 4 3 2 1

ISBN 0-13-028160-3

Prentice-Hall International (UK) Limited, *London*
Prentice-Hall of Australia Pty. Limited, *Sydney*
Prentice-Hall Canada Inc., *Toronto*
Prentice-Hall Hispanoamericana, S.A., *Mexico*
Prentice-Hall of India Private Limited, *New Delhi*
Prentice-Hall of Japan, Inc., *Tokyo*
Pearson Education Asia Pte. Ltd.
Editora Prentice-Hall do Brasil, Ltda., *Rio de Janeiro*

In memory of Bernice and Hervé Houde who left us during the writing of this book. They're greatly missed.

CONTENTS

ACKNOWLEDGMENTS

This book was written for the technical student. Several dedicated professionals at Prentice Hall and The Alida Connection coordinated the input to create the final product. Dave and Tim want to acknowledge the guidance, support, and watchful eyes of acquisitions editor Mary Franz, and our taskmaster, development editor Jim Markham. Together we encourage the student to learn as much as possible about the technology and wish you well with your career.

INTRODUCTION

When Microsoft launched Windows 2000 in February 2000, it sharply altered the way we're required to support local network operations. While earlier versions of Windows products can communicate on the local area network (LAN) using simple broadcast level protocols (e.g., NetBEUI), Windows 2000 and its Active Directory add a new dimension of capability and complexity to networking. A Windows 2000 network administrator must be comfortable and familiar with Transmission Control Protocol/Internet Protocol (TCP/IP) and the Domain Name System (DNS) just to get the Active Directory to function on his or her LAN. The reward for his or her effort in successfully creating a Windows 2000 networking environment is a robust Windows 2000 Active Directory domain with unparalleled scalability, extensibility, and interoperability.

This book begins with the basics of TCP/IP—information that would apply to any TCP/IP installation on any platform. Following a discussion of the TCP/IP protocol suite, we discuss key issues such as TCP/IP *networks*, *subnetting*, *routing*, and *name resolution*. We provide a primer on the Windows 2000 Active Directory and launch into Windows 2000 specific implementations of *Windows Internet Name Service*, *Dynamic Host Configuration Protocol*, and *DNSystem*. The coverage of these Windows 2000-specific network services will provide the background to effectively plan and manage a Windows 2000 network on the LAN, over a wide area network (WAN), through a company intranet, and on the Internet.

Chapter 14 provides very comprehensive coverage of the Windows 2000 *Internet Protocol Security* and *Routing and Remote Access Service*. These advanced subjects will permit the administrator to provide *routing*, *virtual private networking*, and *dial-up access* to his or her Windows 2000 network while ensuring tight network security.

The book concludes with a good look at *heterogeneous connectivity* and *troubleshooting*—two more areas that apply to TCP/IP on Windows 2000 or any other TCP/IP-based platform.

If you need to learn about the inner workings of TCP/IP or if you want to update your TCP/IP knowledge to ensure you can be fully functional in today's robust and flexible Windows 2000 environment, mastery of the subjects covered in this book is essential. Good reading!

Introduction to TCP/IP

In this chapter we will look at the terminology of TCP/IP, its history and perspectives. We will speak about installation of TCP/IP on a Windows 2000 computer and briefly cover major TCP/IP utilities that are used to test the installation. We will also discuss Microsoft Network Monitor, which helps you diagnose and troubleshoot many TCP/IP related problems.

TCP/IP Basics

TCP/IP stands for Transmission Control Protocol/Internet Protocol and it's an industry-standard suite of protocols designed for wide area networks (WANs). Since the Internet is an example of a WAN, we can say that TCP/IP is the protocol suite for the Internet also. The most common mistake is to think that TCP/IP is one protocol or two (TCP and IP). As we will see, the TCP/IP abbreviation implies several protocols. Among them are some that you might already have heard about: HTTP (Hypertext Transfer Protocol) which is used to navigate World Wide Web, FTP (File Transfer Protocol) protocol that provides reliable file transfer over the Internet, and SMTP (Simple Mail Transfer Protocol) which supports email communications. Some of the protocols that are included in the TCP/IP suite are quite exotic, for example ICMP, SNMP, and TFTP.

Although many of the ideas associated with TCP/IP are quite new, the technology itself has been with us for a relatively long time.

Table 1.1 presents some of the major milestones in TCP/IP technology.

TABLE 1.1	*TCP/IP History*

Year	Event
1969	The Department of Defense Advanced Research Projects Agency (ARPA) creates an experimental network called ARPANET. This network provides a test-bed for emerging network technologies. ARPANET originally connected four universities and enabled scientists to share information and resources across long distances. ARPANET continued to expand, connecting many more sites throughout the 1970s and 1980s.
1972	The National Center for Supercomputing Applications (NCSA) develops the *telnet* application for remote login, making it easier to connect to a remote computer.
1973	FTP (File Transfer Protocol) is introduced, standardizing the transfer of files between networked computers.
1974	The Transmission Control Protocol (TCP) specified in detail. Later revised in RFC 793.
1981	The IP standard specified and published in RFC 791.
1982	Transmission Control Protocol (TCP) and Internet Protocol (IP) established as the TCP/IP Protocol Suite.
1983	The TCP/IP suite of networking protocols, or rules, becomes the only set of protocols used on the ARPANET. This decision sets a standard for other networks, and generates the use of the term "Internet" as the network of networks which either use the TCP/IP protocols or are able to interact with TCP/IP networks. To keep military and nonmilitary network sites separate, the ARPANET splits into two networks: ARPANET and MILNET.
1984	Domain Name System (DNS) elaborated and introduced.
1985-86	The National Science Foundation (NSF) connects the nation's six supercomputing centers. This network is called the NSFNET, or NSFNET backbone.
1990	The ARPANET is dissolved.
1993	The European Laboratory for Particle Physics in Switzerland (CERN) releases the World Wide Web (WWW), developed by Tim Berners-Lee. The WWW uses Hypertext Transfer Protocol (HTTP) and hypertext links, changing the way information can be organized, presented, and accessed on the Internet.

Standards and How They Appear

As you can see, TCP/IP has a rich history. Today, TCP/IP is often associated with the Internet. Its architecture and design are closely bound with Internet advances and growth. Since, however, there is no organization that owns the Internet, you might ask how this whole system is controlled. There are organizations that are responsible for setting up standards and controlling the advance of the TCP/IP technologies. Some examples are The Internet Society and The Internet Architecture Board.

INTERNET SOCIETY (ISOC)

The **I**nternet **SOC**iety (http://www.isoc.org/) is a professional membership society with more than 150 organizational and 6,000 individual members in over 100 countries. It provides leadership in addressing issues that confront the future of the Internet, and is the organization home for the groups responsible for Internet infrastructure standards, including the Internet Engineering Task Force (IETF) and the Internet Architecture Board (IAB). ISOC's members are bound by a common stake in maintaining the viability and global scaling of the Internet. They comprise the companies, government agencies, and foundations that have created the Internet and its technologies as well as innovative entrepreneurial organizations contributing to maintain that dynamic. The Society is governed by its board of trustees elected by its membership around the world.

INTERNET ARCHITECTURE BOARD

The IAB is a technical advisory group of ISOC. Some issues discussed during IAB meetings are:

- The future of Internet addressing
- Architectural principles of the Internet
- Management of top level domains in the Domain Name System
- International character sets
- Charging for addresses

The IAB governs the Internet Engineering Task Force (IETF) (http://www.ietf.cnri.reston.va.us/), Internet Assigned Number Authority (IANA) (http://www.iana.org/), and Internet Research Task Force (IRTF) (http://www.irtf.org/).

REQUESTS FOR COMMENTS

You may wonder how the groups' decisions are documented. Requests for Comments (RFCs) are a series of notes, started in 1969, about the Internet (originally the ARPANET). The notes discuss many aspects of computing and computer communication focusing on networking protocols, procedures, programs, and concepts, but also include meeting notes, opinion, and sometimes humor. TCP/IP standards are always published as RFCs.

Warning   Although TCP/IP standards are always published as RFCs, not all RFCs specify standards. Some of them have *Limited use* or even *Not recommended* status.

When a document is published, it is assigned an RFC number. The original RFC number is never updated, but when changes are required, a new RFC is issued with a new number. Therefore, when you are looking for information in RFCs, be sure that you have the most recent one.

Note   You can find the text of the RFCs at www.cis.ohio-state.edu/htbin/rfc. You can also find links to RFC sites as well as a wealth of Internet information at www.internic.net.

Advantages of TCP/IP

As TCP/IP has become the industry standard protocol suite, many software vendors have included TCP/IP support in their products. Let's take a closer look at the Microsoft implementation of TCP/IP. Because of its myriad advantages, TCP/IP is the default protocol for Windows 2000. This text will explore the advantages that drove Microsoft to select TCP/IP for that role.

Modern networks are large and complex. They are connected with routers and need reliable protocols to communicate. Implementing TCP/IP in a corporate network gives you a standard, routable environment. Since TCP/IP offers robust, scalable architecture, you can easily expand your network. This is why most of today's large networks rely on TCP/IP.

Imagine a large enterprise network with hundreds of computers, many of which work under different operating systems such as Microsoft Windows NT, Windows 2000, UNIX, and Novell NetWare. The typical problem is to connect all these computers so users can seamlessly exchange information. Obviously, this situation requires common protocols as well as connectivity utilities and tools to access and transfer data. Since TCP/IP is supported by all modern operating systems, it has become the logical choice when connecting dissimilar systems. In addition to a common network protocol, however, compatible applications are needed on both ends. Microsoft TCP/IP includes useful utilities that provide access to foreign hosts for data transfer, monitoring, and remote control. For example: FTP, tracert, and telnet.

Remember, also, that the Internet is based on TCP/IP. The TCP/IP protocol running on a Windows 2000 computer allows it to gain Internet access (assuming, of course, it has physical connectivity to the Internet).

Finally, Microsoft TCP/IP offers the Windows Sockets Interface, which can be used for developing client/server applications that can run on Windows Sockets-compliant stacks from other vendors. By using Sockets, TCP/IP provides a robust, scalable, cross-platform client/server framework.

To summarize:

- TCP/IP is an industry-standard suite of networking protocols.
- TCP/IP is a routable transport for Windows 2000 networks.
- TCP/IP provides the ability to share information with non-Microsoft network TCP/IP-based hosts.
- TCP/IP provides the ability to log on to remote TCP/IP-based hosts from a Windows 2000 computer.
- TCP/IP adheres to Internet-community standards, providing access to thousands of networks worldwide.

TCP/IP Utilities and Services

We have already seen that the Microsoft implementation of TCP/IP provides a way to access foreign hosts, tune the TCP/IP configuration, and troubleshoot connectivity problems. This is achieved through a number of tools and utilities. Knowing how to use the utilities often helps you to solve network-related problems. To get started, we'll identify the purpose of the most important Microsoft TCP/IP utilities (we will cover them in greater detail later in the book).

Microsoft TCP/IP utilities can be logically divided into groups based on their purpose: data transfer utilities, remote execution utilities, printing utilities, and diagnostic utilities.

DATA TRANSFER UTILITIES

These tools allow you to transfer data between two computers. The computers can be located anywhere as long as there is a TCP/IP connection between them.

TABLE 1.2   *TCP/IP Data Transfer Utilities*

Utility	Function
File Transfer Protocol (FTP)	Provides bidirectional file transfers between two TCP/IP hosts. One host is acting as an FTP server, while another is acting as a client.
Trivial File Transfer Protocol (TFTP)	Provides bidirectional file transfers between two TCP/IP hosts where one is running TFTP server software.
Remote Copy Protocol (RCP)	This connectivity command copies files between a Windows 2000 computer and a system running **rshd**, the remote shell server. The **rshd** server is available on UNIX computers, but not on Windows 2000, so the Windows 2000 computer can only participate as the system from which the commands are issued.

REMOTE EXECUTION UTILITIES

These utilities provide the ability to launch applications and processes on remote hosts.

TABLE 1.3	*TCP/IP Remote Execution Utilities*
Utility	**Function**
Telnet	Provides terminal emulation to a TCP/IP host running Telnet server software. When you connect, your computer acts as if your keyboard were attached to the remote computer. This means that you can run programs on a computer on the other side of the world, just as if you were sitting in front of it.
Remote Shell (RSH)	Runs commands on remote computers running the RSH service. Runs commands on a UNIX host.
Remote Execution (REXEC)	This connectivity command runs commands on remote hosts running the **REXEC** service. **REXEC** authenticates the user name on the remote host by using a password, before executing the specified command.

PRINTING UTILITIES

TCP/IP printing utilities provide a way to submit, receive, and manage print jobs in a TCP/IP environment. TCP/IP printing utilities allow, in particular, Microsoft-based clients to submit print jobs for printers connected to UNIX computers.

TABLE 1.4	*TCP/IP Printing Utilities*
Utility	**Function**
Line Printer Remote (LPR)	LPR lets a client application on one computer send a document to a print spooler service on another computer. The client application is usually named LPR and the service (or daemon) is usually named LPD.
Line Printer Queue (LPQ)	This diagnostic utility is used to obtain the status of a print queue on a host running the LPD server.
Line Printer Daemon (LPD)	A line printer daemon (LPD) service on the print server receives documents from line printer remote (LPR) utilities running on client systems. With LPD installed, a Windows 2000 Server can receive print jobs from UNIX-based computers.

DIAGNOSTIC UTILITIES

In addition to the data transfer utilities we've already discussed, Windows 2000 provides tools for diagnosing TCP/IP related problems. Table 1.5 describes the major diagnostics utilities that are included in the Microsoft TCP/IP implementation.

TABLE 1.5 *TCP/IP Diagnostic Utilities*

Utility	Function
Finger	Displays information about a user on a specified system running the Finger service.
Address Resolution Protocol (ARP)	Displays and modifies the cache of locally resolved IP addresses to Media Access Control (MAC) addresses.
NBTSTAT	Displays protocol statistics and current TCP/IP connections using NetBIOS over TCP/IP. This utility is also used to determine the registered NetBIOS name and to view the local name cache.
Packet InterNet Groper (PING)	Verifies the availability of the remote host by sending the echo request and analyzing replies.
TRACERT	Traces the route for packets from local hosts to the specified remote host.
IPCONFIG	Displays current TCP/IP configuration including IP address(es) and DNS and WINS addresses.
HOSTNAME	Returns the local computer's host name. You can use it in logon scripts for identification.
NSLOOKUP	Displays information from DNS name servers about a particular host or domain. You can also use this utility to check the availability of the domain name.
NETSTAT	Displays protocol statistics and current TCP/IP network connections.
ROUTE	Views and modifies the local routing table.

Installing Microsoft TCP/IP on Windows 2000

Now that you're sold on TCP/IP, let's see how TCP/IP can be installed on your computer. Before we proceed, we need to decide on parameters.

TABLE 1.6	TCP/IP Parameters

Parameter	Description
IP address	An IP address is a logical 32-bit address that is used for the unique identification of a TCP/IP host. For your convenience the 32-bit value is divided into 4 octets, 8 bits in each, and written in the decimal form. An example of an IP address is **137.200.0.10**. Each computer running TCP/IP must have a unique IP address.
Subnet mask	A subnet mask is used to determine the network ID. When TCP/IP hosts communicate the subnet mask is used to determine whether the destination host is located on a local or remote network. An example of a subnet mask is **255.255.0.0**. Each computer running TCP/IP must have a subnet mask.
Default gateway	If your network consists of two or more segments connected by routers the default gateway address must be provided in order to access the other segment(s). TCP/IP packets, destined for remote networks, are sent to the default gateway if there is no route configured on the local host. Although this parameter is optional, communication will be limited to the local network segment if the default gateway address is omitted.

Automatic Configuration

If your network supports a *dynamic* TCP/IP configuration, an automatic TCP/IP configuration takes place when Windows 2000 is installed. A dynamic configuration, based on the Dynamic Host Configuration Protocol (DHCP), is usually used if another computer on your network is installed as a DHCP server. The DHCP server can provide the IP address, subnet mask, default gateway (IP router), DNS domain name, DNS server, and WINS server configuration information.

The Windows 2000 *Media Sense* feature permits the network interface card to detect when it is physically moved from one network segment to another (assuming the card supports this feature). The computer uses Media Sense to effect a reconfiguration of dynamic network parameters without rebooting.

It is possible to configure TCP/IP for automatic addressing after Windows 2000 is installed. You must be logged on as an administrator or a member of the administrators' group in order to complete this procedure:

1. From the **Start** menu open **Settings** and launch **Network** and **Dial-up Connections**.
2. Right-click the network connection that you want to configure, and then click **Properties** (see Figure 1-1).

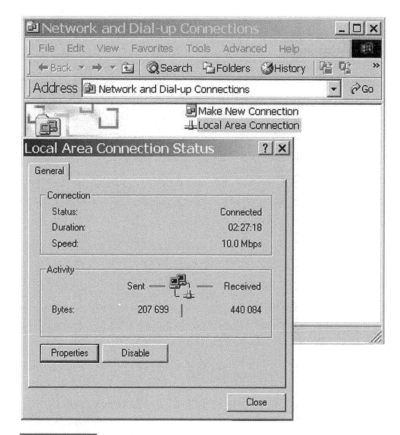

FIGURE 1-1   *Configuring TCP/IP for automatic addressing (Steps 1 and 2)*

3. On the **General** tab (for a local area connection) or the **Networking** tab (all other connections), click **Internet Protocol (TCP/IP)**, and then click **Properties**.
4. Click **Obtain an IP address automatically**, and then click **OK** (see Figure 1-2).

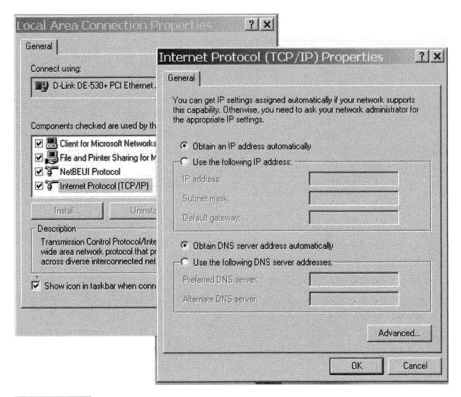

FIGURE 1-2   *Configuring TCP/IP for automatic addressing (Steps 3 and 4)*

Manually Configuring TCP/IP

You also have the opportunity to install TCP/IP after Windows 2000 is operational. To set up TCP/IP manually you need to define the IP address and subnet mask. Be sure to keep track of the assigned parameters.

Important   IP addresses and subnet masks cannot be assigned arbitrarily. The process of assigning TCP/IP parameters requires planning and following certain rules. For now, we may assume we've already calculated these parameters. We will learn all about them in the following chapters.

Once you have decided on an IP address and subnet mask, you are ready to install TCP/IP. You must be logged on as an administrator or a member of the administrators' group in order to complete this procedure.

1. From the **Start** menu point to **Settings**, and then click **Network and Dial-up Connections**.

Tip   You can quickly launch the **Network and Dial-up Connections** dialog box by right-clicking the **My Network Places** icon on the desktop and choosing **Properties**.

---

2. Right-click the network connection for which you want to install and enable TCP/IP, and then click **Properties**.
3. On the **General** tab (for a local area connection) or the **Networking** tab (all other connections), if **Internet Protocol (TCP/IP)** is not in the list of installed components, then do the following (see Figure 1-3):
   a. Click **Install**.
   b. Click **Protocol**, and then click **Add**.
   c. In the **Select Network Protocol** dialog box, click **Internet Protocol (TCP/IP)**, and then click **OK**.

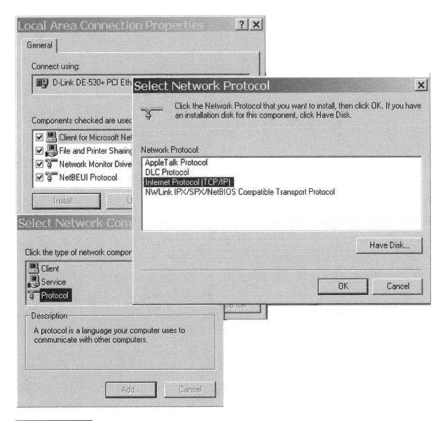

FIGURE 1-3   *Manually installing TCP-IP on Windows 2000*

4. Verify that the **Internet Protocol (TCP/IP)** check box is selected, and then click **OK**.
5. Launch the **Internet Protocol (TCP/IP) Properties** dialog box (see Figure 1-4.) Type your IP address, subnet mask, default gateway address, and DNS server in the corresponding boxes. (At this point we assume you already have an IP address, DNS server, subnet mask, and default gateway assigned. We will learn how to calculate them ourselves a bit later in the text.)
6. Click **OK**.
7. After the computer recalculates the network bindings the **Network** Dialog Box will appear, prompting you to restart the computer. Click **Yes** and wait until the computer restarts.

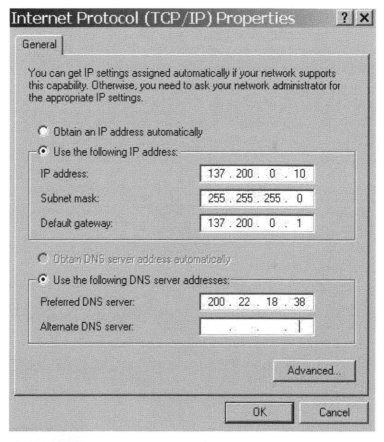

FIGURE 1-4   *Internet protocol TCP/IP properties*

After the computer restarts, it will have your TCP/IP settings.

Changing TCP/IP Parameters

In some cases you need to change existing TCP/IP parameters—for example when you move the computer to another building. In order to change the TCP/IP parameters for the existing installation perform the following steps:

1. From the **Start** menu open **Settings** and launch **Network** and **Dial-up Connections**.
2. Right-click the network connection that you want to configure, and then click **Properties**.
3. Choose the **Internet Protocol** (TCP/IP) and click **Properties**.
4. The TCP/IP properties dialog box appears.
5. Make the appropriate changes to the IP address, subnet mask, DNS server, and default gateway boxes.
6. Click **OK**.

Testing the TCP/IP Configuration

After you have successfully installed TCP/IP on Windows 2000, it's a good idea to verify you have set the TCP/IP parameters properly. You can perform the following steps as the basic troubleshooting tool.

USING THE IPCONFIG UTILITY

To verify the TCP/IP configuration parameters, including the IP address, subnet mask, and default gateway, use the IPCONFIG utility. This utility is provided as a part of the Microsoft TCP/IP installation. IPCONFIG is useful in determining whether your parameters have been initialized or what values these parameters received.

IPCONFIG is a command line utility, and the simplest way to use it is to type the following at the command prompt:

```
ipconfig
```

If the TCP/IP configuration is initialized, the assigned IP address, subnet mask, and default gateway (if configured) appear. For example:

```
C:\WINDOWS>ipconfig
Windows 2000 IP Configuration
Ethernet adapter Elnk31:
 IP Address. . . . . . . . . : 137.200.0.10
 Subnet Mask . . . . . . . . : 255.255.255.0
 Default Gateway . . . . . . : 137.200.0.1
```

USING THE PING UTILITY

While the IPCONFIG utility is used to test the configuration parameters on a local computer, the PING utility will test connectivity with other computers.

PING is a diagnostic tool that can report basic TCP/IP problems such as connection failures or router problems. For example, you can use the PING utility to verify that contact can be established between the client and server.

The work of the PING utility is based on the Internet Control Message Protocol (ICMP). PING sends ICMP echo packets to the host and listens for echo reply packets. PING waits up to one second for each packet sent and prints the number of packets transmitted and received. Each packet is validated against the transmitted message.

PING is a command line utility. Its syntax is:

```
ping IP_address, where IP_address is the IP address of the
destination host.
```

The successful PING returns a sequence of replies as follows:

```
C:\WINDOWS>ping 137.200.0.1
Pinging 137.200.0.1 with 32 bytes of data:
Reply from 137.200.0.1: bytes=32 time<10ms TTL=128
Reply from 137.200.0.1: bytes=32 time<10ms TTL=128
Reply from 137.200.0.1: bytes=32 time<10ms TTL=128
Reply from 137.200.0.1: bytes=32 time<10ms TTL=128
```

If communication problems exist, for example the destination node is powered down, the PING output may look like this:

```
C:\WINDOWS>ping 137.200.0.2
Pinging 137.200.0.2 with 32 bytes of data:
Request timed out.
Request timed out.
Request timed out.
Request timed out.
```

This listing may indicate a problem with a router:

```
C:\WINDOWS>ping 137.200.3.1
Pinging 137.200.3.1 with 32 bytes of data:
Destination host unreachable.
Destination host unreachable.
Destination host unreachable.
Destination host unreachable.
```

Some specific IP addresses are reserved for special purposes. For example the IP address 127.0.0.1 is the loopback address. You can use **ping 127.0.0.1** to check if TCP/IP is loaded correctly on your computer.

As you may have noticed, by default the PING command sends four 32-byte packets and waits for four replies. The following syntax will cause PING to continuously send packets until interrupted with a CTRL-C:

```
ping -t IP_address
```

TCP/IP Testing Sequence

Using the PING and IPCONFIG utilities you can perform basic testing and troubleshooting tasks.

To verify a computer's configuration and check router connections perform the following steps:

1. Use the IPCONFIG for the verification of the TCP/IP initialization. At the command prompt type:

   ```
   ipconfig
   ```

2. Ping the loopback address, to verify that TCP/IP is installed and bound to the network adapter. Type:

   ```
   ping 127.0.0.1
   ```

3. Ping the IP address of your own host, to verify that TCP/IP was added correctly. Type:

   ```
   ping your_IP_address
   ```

   If the previous steps fail, you most likely have an IP addressing problem.

4. Ping the IP address of your default gateway, to ensure that it is operational. Additionally, a successful ping to the default gateway indicates that you can connect to hosts in your local subnet. Type:

   ```
   ping default_gateway_IP_address
   ```

5. Finally, ping the IP address of the remote host to verify that you can connect through a router. Type:

   ```
   ping remote_host_IP_address
   ```

   If this step fails, you may have an incorrect subnet mask, or an incorrect default gateway. It can also indicate the failure of a WAN link or malfunctioning router.

Important   If you go directly to Step 5 and can successfully ping the remote host, it guarantees all previous steps would have been successful.

Microsoft Network Monitor

Sometimes network problems become too complex to solve by means of simple diagnostic tools such as IPCONFIG and PING. In this case Microsoft Network Monitor, the tool which can capture network traffic, may be helpful. Network Monitor is able to capture and display frames (also called packets) in order to detect and troubleshoot problems on a local area network (LAN).

Network Monitor is particularly useful in diagnosing hardware and software problems when two or more computers cannot communicate. If the problem is too complex, you can capture network activity and send the capture file to a support organization or network analyst for assistance.

Microsoft Network Monitor configures the network card to capture all incoming and outgoing frames. You can define capture filters and capture triggers to capture only specific data. For security reasons the version of Microsoft Network Monitor that is shipped with Windows 2000 is limited to capturing only data originating from or destined to the computer running network monitor, as well as broadcast and multicast messages. Microsoft Systems Management Server (SMS) includes a version of Network Monitor that can also capture frames sent to or from any computer on the network, edit and transmit frames on the network, and capture frames remotely. The SMS version achieves this by setting the network adapter card to the so-called promiscuous mode.

Note

You can use the SMS version of Network Monitor to capture frames remotely from Network Agents installed on Windows 2000 computers, Windows NT Workstations, and Windows 95 computers.

Installing Microsoft Network Monitor

You must be logged on with Administrator or Power User privileges to install Microsoft Network Monitor in Windows 2000.

To install Network Monitor (see Figure 1-5), follow these steps.

1. Click **Start**, point to **Settings**, and then click **Control Panel**.
2. Double-click **Add/Remove Programs**.
3. Click **Add/Remove Windows Components**.
4. Click **Management and Monitoring Tools**, and then click **Details**.
5. Select the **Network Monitor Tools** check box and click **OK**.
6. Select **Network Monitor Tools** and click **OK**.
7. You may be asked to provide the path to the Windows 2000 Setup files. Type the full path to the Windows 2000 distribution point and click **Continue**.

Now you can use Microsoft Network Monitor.

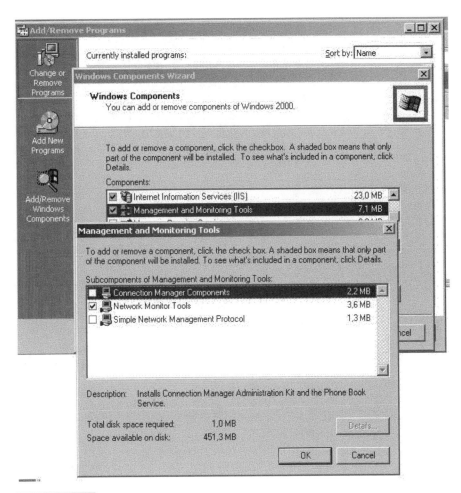

FIGURE 1–5   *Installing Microsoft Network Monitor on Windows 2000*

Using Microsoft Network Monitor to Capture and View Data

When the Microsoft Network Monitor is installed you can access it in the Administrative Tools (Common) folder in the Start menu. Figure 1-6 illustrates the layout of the Microsoft Network Monitor Window.

The typical procedure for using Network Monitor is:

1. Start capturing
2. Generate network traffic to capture
3. Stop capturing
4. View captured data

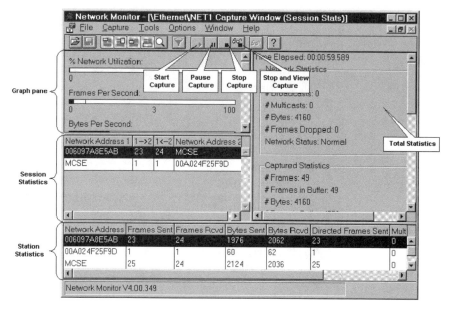

FIGURE 1-6   *Microsoft Network Monitor window*

STARTING A CAPTURE

To start capturing network traffic, use the **Start Capture** button on the tool-bar (you can also use the **Start** command from the **Capture** menu or press **F10**). Captured frames are stored in the capture buffer. When the buffer over-flows, new frames replace the oldest ones. You can control the buffer size with the **Buffer Settings** option in the **Capture** menu. When you are captur-ing, the information panes display capture statistics. The meaning of the panes is described in the Table 1.7.

TABLE 1.7   *Microsoft Network Monitor Panes Capture View*

Pane	Displays
Graph	A graphical representation of the activity currently taking place on the network, including network utilization and broadcast level.
Session Statistics	Statistics about individual sessions currently taking place on the network.
Station Statistics	Statistics about the sessions in which the computer running Network Monitor participates. They include bytes and frames sent and received.
Total Statistics	Summary statistics about network activity detected since the capture began.

GENERATING NETWORK TRAFFIC

To generate network traffic you wish to analyze, use a network-based application such as Microsoft Internet Explorer or the PING command.

STOPPING AND VIEWING THE CAPTURED DATA

To stop the capture, use the **Stop Capture** button (see Figure 1-6), the **Stop** command from the **Capture** menu, or **F11**.

To view the captured data, use the **Stop and View** command from the **Capture** menu if you are currently capturing or the **View** command from the **Capture** menu if the capture has been stopped.

When opening a capture window, a **Frame Viewer** window appears (see Figure 1-7). The Frame Viewer window shows each captured frame. It contains a frame number, the time the frame was received, source and destination addresses, protocols contained in the frame, and other information. To get more detailed information about the particular frame, double-click the frame.

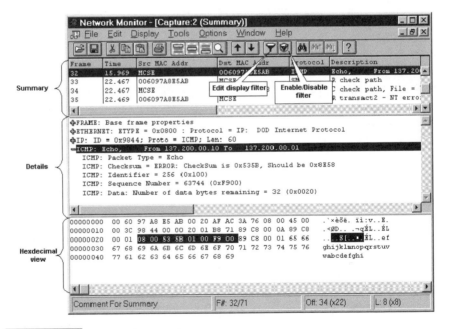

FIGURE 1–7   *Microsoft Network Monitor capture view*

The Frame Viewer window includes the panes shown in Table 1.8.

TABLE 1.8	Microsoft Network Monitor Panes Frame View
Panes	**Displays**
Detail	The frame's contents, including the protocols used to send it.
Hex	A hexadecimal and ASCII representation of the captured data.
Summary	General information about captured frames in the order in which they were captured.

You can save the capture to hard disk for later analysis. To do this, choose **Save As** from the **File** menu.

As we use Microsoft Network Monitor in the labs following this chapter, you will become familiar with its more advanced features.

Summary

In this chapter we discussed the basics of TCP/IP. You learned that TCP/IP is not just one or two protocols, but a set of protocols that have different purposes and properties. We covered the main advantages of using Microsoft TCP/IP such as its industry standard routable environment, its compatibility with modern operating systems, its connectivity with dissimilar systems, and its ability to provide access to the Internet. You also learned how to install Microsoft TCP/IP on Windows 2000. Finally, we looked at a number of network analysis tools and procedures to include IPCONFIG, PING, and Microsoft Network Monitor, the tool that can be used to capture network traffic and analyze network-related problems.

Test Yourself

1. Which protocol provides bidirectional file transfers between TCP/IP hosts?
   A. FTP
   B. ARP
   C. IP
   D. PPTP

2. Which application allows your keyboard to act as if it were attached to a remote computer?

   A. Ping

   B. Telnet

   C. LPR

   D. FTP

3. What does the Ping utility do?

4. What is Microsoft Network Monitor used for?

Windows 2000 Active Directory Overview

Although not actually a part of Windows 2000 TCP/IP, the Active Directory is the engine that makes a domain-based Windows 2000 network operate. In a Windows 2000 domain, the functions of TCP/IP and the Active Directory are inexorably linked—each depends on the other to perform its job. Understanding the Active Directory is critical to understanding how TCP/IP functions in the Windows enterprise network.

Directory Services and the Active Directory

In the context of a computer network, a *directory* is a structure that stores information about *objects* on the network. Objects include shared resources such as servers, shared volumes, printers, network user and computer accounts, domains, applications, services, security policies, and just about everything else in your network. A network directory, for instance, might store a user's name, password, email address, phone number, and so on.

A *directory service* differs from a directory in that it is both the directory information source and the services making the information available and usable to administrators, users, network services, and applications. Ideally, a directory service makes the physical network topology and protocols transparent so a user can access any resource without knowing where it's located or how it's connected. It is the directory service that lets authorized users access stored directory information (such as an email address) about the user account object.

Directory services can support a wide variety of capabilities. Some directory services are integrated with an operating system, and others are applications such as email directories. Operating system directory services, such as the Windows 2000 Active Directory, provide user, computer, and shared resource management. Directory services that handle email, such as Microsoft Exchange, enable users to look up other users and send email.

Installing Active Directory on a computer running a Windows 2000 Server operating system (Windows 2000 Server, Advanced Server, or Data Center Server) is the act that transforms the server into a domain controller. In other words, a domain controller is a computer running Windows 2000 Server that has been configured using the Active Directory Installation wizard, which installs and configures components that provide Active Directory services to network users and computers. Domain controllers store domainwide directory data (such as system security policies and user authentication data) and manage user-domain interactions, including user logon processes, authentication, and directory searches.

User Management with Active Directory

A great part of network administration involves managing users, computers, and groups. A successful operating system must ensure that only properly authenticated users and computers can log on to the network and that each network resource is available only to authorized users. In the Windows 2000 operating system, the Active Directory service plays several major roles in providing security. Among these are the efficient and effective management of user logon authentication and user authorization. Both are central features of the Windows 2000 security subsystem and both are fully integrated with Active Directory.

Active Directory *user authentication* confirms the identity of any user trying to log on to a domain and lets users access resources (such as data, applications, or printers) located anywhere on the network. A key feature of Windows 2000 user authentication is its single logon capability. This permits a user to access resources throughout the network using only a single user name and password.

Active Directory Features

Let's take a brief look at some of the Active Directory's features:

- **Integration with DNS.** Active Directory uses the Domain Name System (DNS). DNS, covered in Chapters 12 and 13, publishes Active Directory domain names as well as the names of computers within the domain. DNS also publishes information concerning the services available from network servers to permit computers and users to find resources throughout the Active Directory.

- **Extensibility.** Active Directory is extensible, which means that administrators can add new types of information to the directory to meet network needs. For example, you could add a Purchase Authority attribute to the User object and then store each user's purchase authority limit as part of the user's account.

- **Policy-based administration.** Group Policies are configuration settings applied to computers or users as they are initialized. The settings determine access to directory objects and domain resources, what domain resources (such as applications) are available to users, and how these domain resources are configured for use.

- **Scalability.** Active Directory includes one or more domains, each with one or more domain controllers, enabling you to scale the directory to meet any network requirements. Multiple domains can be combined into a domain tree and multiple domain trees can be combined into a forest. In the simplest structure, a single-domain network is simultaneously a single tree and a single forest.

- **Information replication.** Active Directory uses multimaster replication, which lets you update the directory at any domain controller. Deploying multiple domain controllers in one domain provides fault tolerance and load balancing. If one domain controller within a domain slows, stops, or fails, other controllers within the same domain can provide necessary directory access, since they contain the same directory data.

- **Information security.** Management of user authentication and access control, both fully integrated with Active Directory, are key security features in the Windows 2000 operating system. Active Directory centralizes authentication. Access control can be defined not only on each object in the directory, but also on each property of each object. In addition, Active Directory provides both the store and the scope of application for security policies.

- **Interoperability.** Because Active Directory is based on standard directory access protocols, such as Lightweight Directory Access Protocol (LDAP), it can interoperate with other directory services employing these protocols. Several APIs—such as Active Directory Service Interfaces (ADSI)—give developers access to these protocols.

Quality of Service

Windows 2000 Server Quality of Service (QoS) technology integrates with the Active Directory to ensure the availability of network bandwidth for designated services or users. QoS permits the administrator to set policies to allocate a particular amount of bandwidth to a specific function at a predetermined time. By doing so, he/she can guarantee applications requiring QoS delivery are given the bandwidth they need when they need it, without exceeding predefined bandwidth limitations. Windows 2000 supports several QoS mechanisms such as the Resource Reservation Protocol (RSVP), Differentiated Services (DiffServ), IEEE 802.1p, and ATM QoS.

Summary

The backbone of any large Windows 2000 network, the Active Directory must always be considered when working with Windows 2000 networking. TCP/IP and the Active Directory work hand-in-hand to locate and identify critical network resources. We saw that a *directory* is simply a structure to store information about network *objects*, which we defined as users, computers, printers, and the like. Directory Services, we decided, was the combination of the directory and a means to publish it. The Windows 2000 Active Directory is a directory service that provides both resource locations and user authentication. When Active Directory is installed on a Windows 2000 server computer, that machine becomes a domain controller capable of authenticating users to allow them access to network resources.

The Active Directory is fraught with features that sharply improve network operation. Its integration with DNS enables it to publish information about available network and domain services through this industry standard service. Furthermore, the Active Directory permits the Windows 2000 domain to be scalable and extensible. Policy-based administration allows you to control the function of the domain and network through Active Directory. The Active Directory is comprised of industry standard protocols and services to permit extensive interoperability with other network operating systems. The integration of Active Directory and QoS technologies allows a network administrator to ensure the right network bandwidth is available to specific applications or users when needed.

Test Yourself

1. Active Directory must be installed on what type of machine?
2. Which of these is an advantage of MS Active Directory?
   A. Scalability
   B. Interoperability
   C. Extensibility
   D. All of the above

3. Network administration involves managing:
   A. Users
   B. Groups
   C. Computers
   D. All of the above

4. The Active Directory permits a user to access resources throughout the network using:
   A. An account created at each computer
   B. A single user name and password
   C. A single user name but multiple passwords
   D. Recursive authentication

5. Active Directory uses _____ replication.

TCP/IP Architecture

In this chapter we will take a look at the TCP/IP protocol stack to help us better understand how TCP/IP functions in the network.

We'll look at the Department of Defense (DoD) protocol layers and the Open Systems Interconnect model to help us better understand how the protocols and utilities function at the various layers. We'll discuss the protocols that comprise the TCP/IP suite of protocols and look at some TCP/IP configuration and troubleshooting information.

ISO/OSI and DoD Overview

TCP/IP is clearly more than just Transmission Control Protocol over Internet Protocol. When we speak of TCP/IP we're really talking about several protocols and utilities that work together to permit interoperability of hosts on a network (local, metropolitan, or wide area network). These protocols and utilities provide the means by which machines can connect to share information.

The Open Systems Interconnect Model

The Open Systems Interconnect (OSI) model was developed by the International Standards Organization (ISO) and helps to identify how the functions of the protocols relate to each other. By showing how the functions relate, we'll define how the parts of the protocol stack connect to permit machines to effectively communicate. As we look at the OSI model, remember it is just a concept—we don't actually see it when two hosts work together. The model, however, *is* the standard and to communicate we must adhere to it. If both computers trying to establish communications are configured according to the standard, communications will take place. If they're not, you may end up getting error messages, failure to initialize services, or no communications at all.

The OSI Model contains seven layers:

- Application Layer
- Presentation Layer
- Session Layer
- Transport Layer
- Network Layer
- Datalink Layer
- Physical Layer

Figure 3-1 compares the layers of the ISO-OSI model to the layers of the DoD model. These models give us a sense of how communication is expected to take place. Moving from the highest layers down to the wire, we see the application needs to be able to operate without being concerned about identifying all of the lower-level hardware and maintaining drivers for each device.

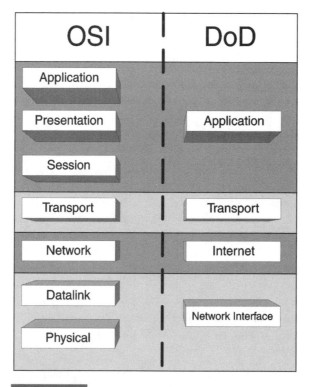

FIGURE 3-1   *Comparison of OSI and DoD models*

In the OSI model, the Application, Presentation, and Session Layers provide services useful to applications in general. These services are separate from similar but distinct functions that take place at the lower levels. Error detection and correction, for instance, may take place at two different points in the protocol stack.

The Application Layer provides support to end user applications by providing the application programming interfaces (sets of procedure calls) that provide the engines that drive actual user applications. This layer is responsible for working with the originated data stream and communicates with the lower layers. Some examples of applications programming interfaces (APIs) would be Mail API (MAPI), MS FAX API (FAPI), Telephone API (TAPI), and Internet Server API (ISAPI).

The Presentation Layer provides platform-to-platform translation of syntax for the purpose of data exchange. Modification of data according to a common set of rules is done at this layer. Compression and encryption, for instance, are accomplished here.

The Session Layer provides for the establishment, maintenance, and recovery from failures that occur between applications. When two computers establish a session to share data, control of the flow and direction, and the recovery of missing or corrupt data, is the responsibility of this layer. Depending on the type of application, you might see a simplex, half-duplex, or full-duplex data flow. Simplex is a one-way data flow. Half duplex is the same as simplex but implies that there is a duplex channel to permit full duplex if so configured. Full duplex provides two-way data flow. By providing appropriate checkpoint methods, the wire between the two computers can stay full of data and only the data that does not make it properly to the distant end need be retransmitted.

The Transport Layer guarantees that the data is delivered in the right order and in a reliable manner. Here again, we consider error checking and correction as a means to put the information in the right order and to make certain the whole message is received.

The Network Layer provides routing between internetworks and shields the layers above from the details of the lower layers (the physical topology for example). It is at this layer that we first find addressing (example: IP address).

The Datalink Layer provides reliable transfer of data across the physical link. The Datalink Layer functions to provide formatting, error detection, link management, and data flow control. Again we find addressing—this time at the Hardware Layer (example: hardware address of the Network Interface Card).

The Physical Layer accepts data from the Datalink Layer and puts it in the right format for the physical medium. This layer specifies the requirements for the wire such as the voltage levels (electrical properties), connector types (mechanical specifications), and handshake (procedural specifications of how to connect).

DoD Four-Layer Model

More than one theory can be used to identify how the components in the TCP/IP protocol stack connect dissimilar systems. The DoD four-layer model was the original example. Let's take a look at how each Microsoft TCP/IP component or utility fits this model.

The DoD four-layer mode contains:

- Network Interface Layer
- Internet Layer
- Transport (also known as Host-to-Host or Transmission) Layer
- Application Layer (known earlier as the Process Layer)

Starting with the place where the signals go (the wire) and working our way up the protocol stack we find:

NETWORK INTERFACE LAYER

The lowest layer in the model is responsible for the putting frames on the wire and pulling frames off the wire. In order to get information to the next higher level, which is where the routing and switching take place, there must be information that permits computers to find each other on the subnetwork or subnet. This is the hardware address of the network card. The Network Interface Card (NIC) contains a hardware address that is mapped to and used by higher level protocols to pass the information up and down the stack and back and forth across the wire.

TCP/IP can be used in a wide variety of LAN, WAN, and dial-up environments. Supported LAN types include: Ethernet, Token Ring, Fiber Distributed Data Interface (FDDI), and ARCnet. Supported WAN types include serial lines and packet-switched networks such as X.25, Frame Relay, and ATM. (Dial-up is supported by Routing and Remote Access Service on Windows 2000 computers and will be discussed later in this book.) Metropolitan Area Network (MAN) types of topologies supported using TCP/IP are the same as the previously mentioned WAN types.

Each of the LAN, MAN, WAN, and dial-up types have different requirements for cables, signaling, data encoding, and so on. The network interface layer specifies the requirements equivalent to the Datalink and Physical Layers of the OSI Model as we noted in Figure 3-1.

INTERNET LAYER

The Internet Layer protocols provide three specific services:

- A connectionless delivery service.
- A mechanism to break the data up into individual packets or frames on the transmitting side and to put them back together on the receiving side (fragmentation and reassembly).
- The routing functions necessary to interoperate with other networks.

Five protocols are implemented at this layer:

- The Internet Protocol (IP), which addresses and routes packets.
- The Address Resolution Protocol (ARP), which determines the hardware address of the hosts.
- Reverse Address Resolution Protocol (RARP), which provides reverse address resolution at the receiving host. (Although Microsoft does not implement the RARP protocol, it is found on other vendors' systems.)
- Internet Control Message Protocol (ICMP), which sends error messages to the IP when problems crop up.
- Internet Group Management Protocol (IGMP), which informs routers of the availability of members of multicast groups.

These protocols do their job by encapsulating packets into Internet *datagrams* and running all the necessary routing algorithms (a datagram is a connectionless or one-way communication—it is sent with no confirmation of arrival, much as when you send a letter to someone). The user data originates in one of the higher level protocols and is passed down to the Internet Layer. The router, then, examines the IP address of the datagram to determine if the destination is local or remote. If both machines are on the same network (local), the datagram is forwarded directly to the destination host. If the destination host is on a different network (remote), the datagram is forwarded to the default gateway (locally attached gateway—router—to remote networks).

When a network joins the Internet, the administrator must apply for and receive a valid IP network and host number from the Internet Information Center (InterNIC). The hosts carry out the functions mentioned here through the use of these numbers, which, when combined, is known as an IP address.

TRANSPORT LAYER

Transport protocols provide communications sessions between connected computers. The desired method of data delivery determines the transport protocol. The two transport protocols provided within TCP/IP are the Transmission Control Protocol (TCP) and the User Datagram Protocol (UDP). TCP provides the virtual circuit service to make the end-to-end connection for user applications. Data transfer is made reliable through the use of connections and acknowledgements. The UDP provides delivery but does not use connections or acknowledgements so it is less reliable but faster. Such connectionless protocols are termed "unreliable" to indicate they do not provided receipted delivery. (A connectionless protocol is like a telegram—you send a message but you can't be sure it reached its intended recipient. A connection-oriented protocol, on the other hand, is like a telephone call where you can ensure the person on the other end has received and, possibly, understood the message.)

The terms Host-to-Host or Transmission Layer are used interchangeably with the Transport Layer. The Transport Layer is responsible for error detection and correction in the DoD model and is analogous to the Transport Layer in the OSI model.

APPLICATION LAYER

Microsoft implements two program interfaces at the Application Layer to allow the applications to utilize the services of the TCP/IP protocol stack. These are Windows Sockets and NetBIOS.

The Windows Sockets interface provides a standard API under Microsoft Windows to many transport protocols such as IPX and TCP/IP. This open standard library of function calls, data structures, and programming procedures permits Windows applications to take advantage of TCP/IP. This enables Windows 2000 to exchange data with foreign or non-NetBIOS systems.

NetBIOS provides a standard interface to protocols that support NetBIOS naming and message services such as TCP/IP and NetBEUI. NetBIOS is used in Microsoft products to permit application communication with the lower protocol layers as well. Three TCP ports provide NetBIOS support. These exist as port 137 for NetBIOS Name Service, port 138 for Datagram Service, and port 139 for Session Service.

Several standard TCP/IP utilities and services exist at the Application Layer. For example:

- File Transfer Protocol (used for transferring large files between remote machines)
- Simple Mail Transfer Protocol (used by mail servers to exchange mail)
- Standard Network Monitoring Protocol (used by network monitoring machines to determine the health and status of the network)
- Telnet (used by your machine to connect to a remote host and use its services)

What Is Encapsulation?

The way information is handled under the OSI or DoD models is often referred to as *encapsulation*. Encapsulation is the process of adding a header to the data accepted from a higher level protocol. When the application *originates* the data or sends a request to *get* data, the data or request moves down through the protocol stack and at each level a new header is added. This increases the total size of the information until it reaches the wire. The individual zeros and ones are sent via the wire to the remote computer where each of the headers is opened and peeled off, much like peeling the skin and layers off an onion. The header information is stripped off at each layer and the information is sent upward to reach, finally, the intended application.

The Microsoft TCP/IP Protocol Suite

Now that we've seen the theoretical models that comprise the network standards that define the use of the elements of the TCP/IP protocol suite, let's take a look at the *functionality* of the Microsoft TCP/IP protocol suite.

Address Resolution Protocol

The purpose of ARP is to permit the successful mapping of an IP address to a hardware address. The process starts where one host sends a local broadcast to obtain a hardware address and puts the resulting information into a cache for future reference.

Let's suppose you try to ping a particular IP address. The first action in this procedure is a query to the existing ARP cache. If no match for the IP address is found in the cache an ARP broadcast is sent. The target machine answers the broadcast with its hardware address and the calling machine stores the information in its cache. Once the calling machine has the target's hardware address, it can use directed communications from that point on. (When we say "directed communication," we're talking about a communication to a particular machine versus a "broadcast" to all machines on the local network.)

RESOLVING A REMOTE IP ADDRESS

If a host tries to resolve a remote host's address to its hardware address there is a need to traverse a router. IP routers do not permit ARP broadcasts to go from one subnet to another to minimize network and Internet traffic in general. How then does a remote IP address get resolution? This is what happens when Host 1 initiates communication with a computer for which it does not have a hardware address (host *X*):

1. Host 1 initiates a command using an IP address for host *X*.
2. TCP/IP determines the destination host is on a remote network.
3. Host 1 checks its internal route table for a route to the destination network via an available gateway. (If no entry is found for the remote host network, Host 1 the uses the IP address of its properly configured default gateway.)
4. Host 1 broadcasts an ARP request to resolve the gateway's IP address.
5. The gateway sends an ARP reply to Host 1's request, which updates the ARP cache on both machines.
6. Now that it knows the gateway's hardware address, Host 1 sends a request for the destination host to the gateway.
7. The gateway starts with Step 2 and the process is repeated until a router on host *X*'s local network is able to resolve the hardware address.

OVERVIEW OF THE ARP CACHE

The ARP cache on each host consists of static and dynamic entries that map IP addresses to hardware addresses. The static entries remain in the ARP cache until the computer is restarted or until they're manually deleted. An entry will be dynamically changed if the host receives an ARP broadcast for an IP address that is already in the cache but with a different hardware address than the existing entry. An address can be added manually to the ARP cache by typing: `arp -s IP_address hardware_address` (e.g., `arp -s 172.13.3.1 00-10-4B-86-76-3D`). To delete an entry type: `arp -d IP_address` (e.g., `arp -d 172.13.3.1`). To view the information in the ARP cache, type: `arp -a`.

The dynamic entries are added and deleted from the ARP cache based on the exchange of information between local and destination hosts. If a dynamic entry is not used within a two-minute period, it is deleted from the cache. If it *is* used within two minutes, the Time to Live (TTL) is extended to ten minutes.

ARP Packet Structure

The ARP Packet Structure is designed for IP address resolution. This structure can be adapted, however, to other types of address resolution. The actual packet structure is outlined in Table 3.1.

TABLE 3.1   *ARP Packet Structure*

Field	Function
Hardware Type	Indicates the type of hardware being used
Protocol Type	Indicates the protocol that is being used for the resolution. Uses the EtherType value of 0x08-00 for IP
Hardware Address Length	Length (in bytes) of the hardware address. For Ethernet and Token Ring, it is 6 bytes.
Protocol Address Length	Number of bytes of the protocol address. For IP, it is 4 bytes.
Operation Code (OPCODE)	Indicates the operation being performed
Sender's Hardware Address	Source hardware address (ARP requester)
Sender's Protocol Address	Source protocol address (ARP requester)
Target Hardware Address	Destination hardware address (ARP Responder)
Target Protocol Address	Destination protocol address (ARP Responder)

Internet Control Message Protocol (ICMP)

ICMP is responsible for handling the errors that occur when data packets are transmitted across a network. Ping, as well as other utilities, uses ICMP to operate. If a host fails to respond to a `ping` request, ICMP notifies the originator that the transmission was unsuccessful. ICMP messages are datagrams and considered to be unreliable.

ICMP PACKET STRUCTURE

While their length may vary, all ICMP packets use the same structure as defined in Table 3.2

TABLE 3.2	*ICMP Packet Structure*
Field	**Function**
Type	Uses 8 bits to indicate the type of ICMP packet. Types include Echo Request and Echo Reply.
Code	Uses 8 bits to indicate one of multiple functions within a specific type. If there is only one function specified, the value is set to 0.
Checksum	Uses 16 bits to verify the ICMP portion of the packet is not corrupt.
Type-Specific Data	Additional data that can vary depending on the ICMP type.

ICMP SOURCE QUENCH MESSAGES

Sometimes, during normal communications, hosts will send information faster than the routers, gateways, and links between them can handle it. Some routers can send an ICMP source quench message to request that a host transmit at a slower rate. A Windows 2000 TCP/IP host will accept source quench messages and comply by lowering its transmission rate. A Windows 2000 computer that is being used as a router, however, will drop datagrams that cannot be buffered because it is not able to send source quench messages to the sending host. Note that Source Quench is an elective ICMP message and is not commonly implemented.

Internet Group Management Protocol

IGMP is used to inform routers that a host or group of hosts, designated as members of a specific multicast group, are available on a given network. A multicast group is a set of hosts that are identified by a single destination address. Using IGMP, each router that supports multicasting is made aware of which host groups are on which networks. IGMP packets are sent as UDP datagrams, which makes the IGMP packets unreliable.

IGMP PACKET STRUCTURE

The IGMP packet structure is defined in Table 3.3.

TABLE 3.3	*IGMP Packet Structure*
Field	**Function**
Version	The version of IGMP. This value is fixed at 0x1.
Type	Type of IGMP message. A type of 0x1 is called a Host Membership Query and is used by a multicast router to poll a network for members of a specified multicast group. The type 0x2 is called a Host Membership Report and is used to declare membership in a specific group or to respond to a router's Host Membership Query.
Unused	Field filled with the value of zero by the sender and ignored by the receiver.
Checksum	Uses 16 bits to verify the IGMP portion of the packet is not corrupt.
Group Address	Used by the hosts in a Host Membership Report to store the IP multicast address. In the Host Membership Query, the group address is set to a value of all zeros and the hardware multicast address is used to identify the host group.

Internet Protocol

The IP provides several necessary functions such as the addressing and routing of packets to and from destination hosts. If the packets need to be fragmented and reassembled, the IP provides for this.

IP is considered connectionless which means that it does not expect nor need to be connected to the other side in order to do its job. There is no session established when IP is used by itself. Because there is no positive response from the target computer when it receives a communication, there is no *guarantee* that the communication will take place and a "best effort" is used to get the information to the other side. Because of this, data can sometimes be lost or received out of sequence and neither the sending nor receiving host know about it. In this case, acknowledgement for the receipt of packets, and the sequencing of the received packets to place them in the correct order, is the responsibility of a higher layer transport protocol, such as TCP.IP.

PACKET STRUCTURE

The IP Packet consists of a variable length header that prefixes the IP data. The information contained in the header is outlined in Table 3.4.

| **TABLE 3.4** | *ICMP Packet Structure* |

Field	Function
Version	Uses 4 bits to indicate the version of IP. (The current version is IP version 4.)
Header Length	Uses 4 bits to indicate the number of 32-bit words in the IP header. Minimum header size is 20 bytes; the smallest header length is 0x5. IP options can extend the minimum IP header size by 4 bytes at a time. If an IP option does not use all 4 bytes of the Option field, remaining bits are completed with zeros so the IP header is 32 bits (4 bytes).
Type of Service	Uses 8 bits to indicate the quality of service desired for delivery through routers across the IP network. The 8 bits contain specifics like precedence, delay, throughput, and reliability.
Total Length	Uses 16 bits to indicate the total length of the IP datagram.
Identification	Uses 16 bits to identify the specific IP packet. If the IP packet is fragmented, all of the fragments need to have the same original identification scheme so the packets can be reassembled at the destination.
Fragmentation Flags	Only two of the three potential bits for this field are used. One flags whether IP datagrams can be fragmented and the other indicates whether more fragments are to follow.
Fragment Offset	Uses 13 bits as an offset counter to indicate the position of the fragment relative to the IP Payload. If no fragmentation is present, the fragment offset will be 0x0.
Time to Live	Uses 8 bits to indicate the amount of time or number of hops that an IP packet can travel before being discarded.
Protocol	Uses 8 bits to identify the "client" protocol—this is the protocol that provided the payload (data) for this packet and is used to break the packet down to yield the transmitted information.
Header Checksum	Provides error detection on the IP header only.
Source Address	Uses 32 bits to store the IP address of the machine that originated the message.
Destination Address	Uses 32 bits to store the IP address of the target computer.
Options and Padding	Stores IP options in multiples of 32 bits. If this information does not use an even multiple of 32, the remaining bits are padded with zero to arrive at a total of 32 bits.

IP ON THE ROUTER

When it traverses a router, the following happens to an IP packet:

1. The packet's TTL is decremented for each second inside the router (a minimum decrement of 1 is always required).
2. Packets that are too large to be pushed on to the next network segment (due, for instance, to differing network standards) get broken into smaller fragments and are numbered.
   - A new header for each new packet along with a packet flag to indicate its sequence is created along with a fragment ID and fragment offset.
3. A new checksum is calculated and applied.
4. The hardware address of the next router is determined.
5. The packet is forwarded.

Transmission Control Protocol

TCP is *connection-oriented*, meaning the remote computer is expected to be "connected to" the remote host before exchange of data takes place. TCP guarantees a more reliable method of delivery of information through use of sequence numbers, acknowledgements, and a three-way handshake.

TCP uses byte stream communications, which is where the data elements are handled as a sequence of bytes without any boundaries. Each segment of data is assigned its own sequence number so the data can be reassembled at the receiving end. To ensure that the data is received as transmitted, the receiving host must send an acknowledgement or ACK within a specific period of time. If the ACK is not received, the segment is retransmitted. If a segment is received in a corrupt or unusable condition, the host on the receiving end simply sends it to the bit bucket without sending an ACK. In the absence of an ACK, the sending station knows to resend the information.

TCP functions through numbered ports to provide specific delivery locations. Any port with a number of less than 256 is considered a "commonly used port." Table 3.5 shows some of TCP's commonly used ports.

TABLE 3.5	TCP Ports
Port	**Description**
21	FTP
23	Telnet
53	Domain Name Server (DNS)
139	NetBIOS Session Service

What Is a Three-Way Handshake?

A three-way handshake is simply the way two hosts ensure they've exchanged accurate and complete data. To do so, they must make sure they're properly synchronized to send and receive portions of the data, that they each know how much data the other can receive at one time, and that they've established a virtual connection. The handshake takes place in the following three steps:

1. The machine that wishes to start the communication sends a data segment with the synchronization (SYN) flag set to *on*.

2. The target machine sends a segment with SYN on, with a sequence number to indicate the starting byte for the next segment (if any) it will send, and an ACK that includes the sequence number of the next segment it expects to receive.

3. The first machine returns a segment that contains the acknowledged sequence number and an acknowledgement number.

TCP PACKET STRUCTURE

The TCP packet consists of a TCP header with the TCP data attached. The header consists of the ten fields outlined in Table 3.6.

TABLE 3.6	*TCP Header Fields*
Field	**Function**
Source Port	TCP port of the transmitting machine
Destination Port	TCP port of the target machine—the "delivery address" for the communication
Sequence Number	Sequence number for the segment—used to reassemble the data and to ensure all bytes have been received
Acknowledgment Number	The sequence number of the next byte the machine expects to receive
Data Length	The size of the TCP segment
Reserved	For future use
Flags	Indicates type of information in the segment
Window	Indicates available space in the TCP window
Checksum	Verifies the header is not corrupt
Urgent Pointer	If urgent data is being transmitted, it will be indicated in the *Flags* field. This pointer points to the end of the urgent data in the segment.

SLIDING WINDOWS

To ensure the most efficient communications, TCP employs a technique called *sliding windows* to keep data streams full of send and receive data. Each machine involved in data communication maintains two buffers (sliding windows), one for sending and one for receiving data. Each of these windows is sized in relation to the amount of data the computer can buffer. The entire process is relatively simple:

1. When TCP receives outbound data, it places it in its outbound window and (after affixing the appropriate header information) passes it to IP for transmission.
2. The data remains in the outbound window until an ACK is received from the destination (if an ACK is not received within a specified amount of time, the data is retransmitted).
3. When the destination computer receives the packets, they are placed in the receive window and are put in the proper sequence. As the packets are properly sequenced, the receiving computer acknowledges their receipt and reports its current window size.
4. When the transmitting computer receives the acknowledgement, its send window slides to data that is waiting to be transmitted and repeats the process.

User Datagram Protocol

UDP is a "connectionless" protocol that does not establish a session nor provide for guaranteed delivery. By connectionless, we mean the UDP packets are sent out over the network very much like a telegram—the receiving computer does not send an acknowledgement. The message is sent and we must assume it has been received. This is distinct from a telephone call where we are able to establish two-way communication to ensure the person on the other end of the line has received and understood our message. Much like IP, UDP neither guarantees delivery nor the proper sequencing of delivered packets. If these are important to the application using UDP, the application or a higher-level protocol must supply an additional level of checking. While UDP does utilize a checksum for error checking, this is an optional field and not enforced by the protocol.

UDP is most often used in one-to-many communications of small amounts of data. Later in this book, we'll discuss broadcast "messages," especially in relation to the resolution of NetBIOS names to IP addresses. Normally when we talk of "broadcasts" in the context of TCP/IP, we're referring to UDP traffic.

UDP functions through distinct UDP ports. Although TCP and UDP may use the same port number in some instances, these numbers do not represent the same port. A UDP port is a 16-bit address that exists only to transmit datagram information to the correct location above the transport layer of the protocol stack—simply a location for sending messages. UDP ports can receive more than one message at a time and are identified by "well-known" port numbers. Before it can use UDP, an application must supply an IP address and port number for the target of its message. Table 3.7 defines the "well-known" UDP Port numbers.

TABLE 3.7	UDP Ports

Port	Keyword	Description
15	NETSTAT	Network Status
53	DOMAIN	Domain Name Server
69	TFTP	Trivial File Transfer Protocol
137	NETBIOS-NS	NetBIOS Name Service
138	NETBIOS-DGM	NetBIOS Datagram Service
161	SNMP	SNMP Network Monitor

UDP PACKET STRUCTURE

The UDP packet consists of an 8-byte UDP header with the UDP data appended. The header consists of the four fields outlined in Table 3.8.

TABLE 3.8	UDP Header Fields

Field	Function
Source Port	UDP port of machine transmitting the UDP. This is an optional value, which is set to zero if not used.
Destination Port	UDP port of target machine—the "delivery address" for the UDP communication.
Message Length	The size of the UDP message. The minimum size is the header length (8 bytes).
Checksum	Verifies the header and data are not corrupt—this is an optional field.

Ports and Sockets

Our protocol discussion has, thus far, taken us from the wire, through the network interface card, all the way up to the Transport Layer of the DoD model. The only remaining step is to see how the data flows to and from the applications that use and create it. The vehicles to accomplish this last step are *ports and sockets*. Figure 3-2 provides an overall view of where they fit into the data transmission picture.

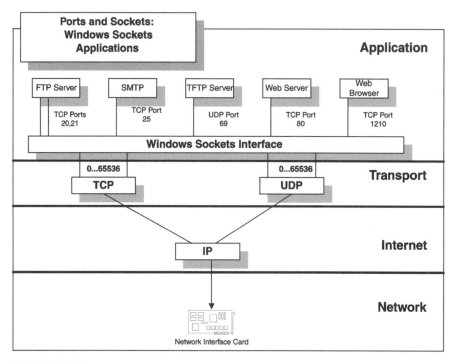

FIGURE 3-2   *Ports and sockets*

A port provides a location for sending messages. It functions as a multi-plexed message queue, which means that it can receive more than one message at a time. Ports are identified by a numerical value between 0 and 65,536. The port numbers for client-side TCP/IP applications are assigned dynamically by the operating system when a request for service is received. The port numbers for well-known server-side applications are assigned by a group called the Internet Assigned Numbers Authority (IANA) and do not change. These well-known port numbers are documented in RFCs 1060 and 1700. You can find the port numbers in the ASCII text file: \WINNT\system32\drivers\etc\services.

A socket is a bidirectional "pipe" for exchanging data between net-worked computers. The Windows Sockets API is a networking API used by Windows programmers in building windows applications that will communi-cate over a network. The API consists of a set of calls that perform defined functions and pass information back and forth to the lower protocol layers. An application creates a socket when it specifies the IP address of an intended host, the type of service requested (TCP for connection-based requests, UDP for connectionless-based requests), and the port that the particular application will use. Sockets are identified within a host through the use of unique protocol port numbers.

Summary

In completing this chapter you should have developed a good background understanding of the parts and functions of TCP/IP to help you better understand the material we will present in this text's subsequent chapters.

We saw the TCP/IP protocol was developed as computer networking grew to become today's Internet and that it was TCP/IP, in fact, that made the Internet possible. To better understand how data flows through the TCP/IP components, we reviewed the seven-layer OSI model and the four-layer DoD model and saw that data moves between layers during its journey from the application to the wire. We learned that, as data moves throughout the layers, header information is added (for transmission) or removed (for reception).

We, then, took a close look at the basic protocols that make up the TCP/IP suite. We found that ARP finds a computer's hardware address when the IP address is known. We learned that ICMP reports errors in the transmission of network data and that IGMP supports multicasting. The IP was found to be a connectionless protocol that operated at the layers between those concerned with physical transmission and those concerned with the transport functions. We saw that IP can pass data to two transport protocols: TCP for connection-oriented communication and UDP for connectionless communication. Finally, we saw that the data handled by TCP or UDP makes its way to and from the application through ports and sockets.

Test Yourself

1. Which of the following is NOT a layer of the OSI model?
   A. Application
   B. Presentation
   C. Transport
   D. Network
   E. Directory
   F. Physical

2. Which layer of the OSI model is concerned with IP addressing?

3. Which protocol is used to determine a machine's hardware address?
   A. ICMP
   B. IGMP
   C. ARP
   D. IP

4. When you send a message using TCP over IP, the IP protocol is responsible for providing delivery verification.
   A. True
   B. False

5. A TCP/IP socket is:
   A. A multiplexed message queue
   B. A combination of an IP address and a port number
   C. The place where you attach the network wire
   D. A connectionless communication

IP Addressing

*I*n this chapter you will learn about the differences between the three main address classes (Class A, Class B, and Class C), as well as the ins and outs of network IDs and host IDs. We will discuss how to plan IP addressing and how to assign IP addresses to computers. You will be able to determine what devices need IP addresses. We will also look carefully at the subnet mask and default values for various IP address classes.

Before implementing TCP/IP on your network, you should carefully plan your actions and develop a comprehensive working plan. To enable you to do this, we will devote a great deal of attention to planning. This chapter has many real world examples that will help you better grasp the IP addressing picture. While you'll find some examples to be extremely easy, others will be real brainteasers.

Defining IP Addresses

In Chapter 1 we mentioned that each system attached to an Internet Protocol (IP)- based network must be assigned a unique, 32-bit IP address value. As you already know, the administrator assigns the IP address to the computer. IP addresses are neither built into the operating system, nor are they part of the network adapter interface. Configured by the administrator, the IP address provides the logical identification number of a computer connected to an IP-based network.

To gain a basic understanding of what an IP address is, it is convenient to draw an analogy between the IP address and a street address. Just as the street address uniquely identifies a house on a particular street, the IP address points to the computer on a network.

Dotted Decimal Notation

We have already discussed that IP addresses are 32-bit binary numbers, but for your convenience the 32-bit value is divided into four 8-bit fields, called octets (see Figure 4-1). Octets are written in the decimal form and separated with periods—this style of writing the IP addresses is called *dotted decimal notation*.

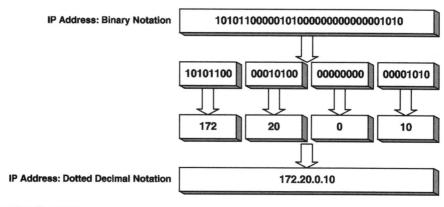

FIGURE 4-1   *Binary and dotted decimal notation of the IP address*

Although you will normally work with IP addresses written in dotted decimal form, you should be able to convert the binary form to decimal. This is essential for planning and troubleshooting.

You may already know that in binary notation each bit that is set to 1 has an assigned decimal value. The bit that is set to 0 has a zero value. In an octet, the rightmost bit represents the decimal value of 1; the next bit represents 2, the next one 4, up to the leftmost bit, which represents the decimal value of 128. To get the decimal result, sum all the bit values (see Figure 4-2).

Note that each octet represents a decimal number ranging from 0 (00000000 binary) to 255 (11111111 binary). Thus the IP address 172.315.16.3 is invalid by inspection, because the second octet is greater than 255 (all bits are set to 1). Table 4.1 illustrates some examples of how the numbers in one octet are converted from binary form into a decimal value.

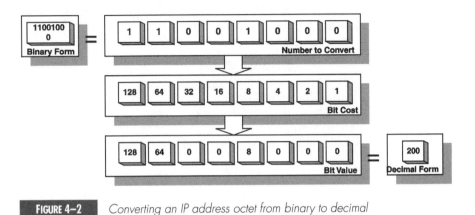

FIGURE 4–2   *Converting an IP address octet from binary to decimal*

TABLE 4.1   *Examples of Converting One Octet from Binary to Decimal*

Binary Code	Bit values	Decimal value
00000000	0	0
00000001	1	1
00000011	2+1	3
00000111	4+2+1	7
00001111	8+4+2+1	15
00011111	16+8+4+2+1	31
00111111	32+16+8+4+2+1	63
01111111	64+32+16+8+4+2+1	127
11111111	128+64+32+16+8+4+2+1	255
11111110	128+64+32+16+8+4+2	254
11111100	128+64+32+16+8+4	252
11111000	128+64+32+16+8	248
11110000	128+64+32+16	240
11100000	128+64+32	224
11000000	128+64	192
10000000	128	128

Tip   You can use the Windows 2000 calculator to convert decimal numbers to binary and vice versa. In order to do this, switch the calculator into the scientific view.

Practical Application

1. Convert the following binary numbers to decimal format:
    10000001   _____
    11100000   _____
    00011111   _____
    00100000   _____
    10101010   _____

2. Convert the following decimal values to binary format:
    255   _____
    21   _____
    192   _____
    240   _____
    150   _____

Network ID and Host ID

Let's consider another example. IP addressing can be compared to the telephone numbering system, consider the number (722) 151-1936. In this example it is obvious that 722 is the area code, 151 the local telephone exchange, and 1936 is the telephone number within the particular exchange. Things become less obvious, if we omit the parentheses and hyphen and write the same telephone number as 7221511936. Now you have to take some time to distinguish the area code from the exchange and number. The same applies to the IP addresses.

Just as the telephone number contains two parts—the area code and the telephone number within area—the IP address is composed of two parts as well. These parts of an IP address are called *Network ID* and *Host ID*. The border between the network ID and the host ID lies somewhere in the middle. Note that there is no visual boundary between the network ID and the host ID. It's like writing a telephone number with no hyphens and spaces.

Note	In recent years, the network ID field has been often referred to as "network prefix."

Let's look at the IP address 172.20.0.10. The network ID and the host ID are both there but not easily distinguishable (see Figure 4-3). In this case we may assume that the border is between the second and the third octet. (Later we will learn how to determine its exact position.) In this example the network ID is like an area code and the host ID is like a local telephone number.

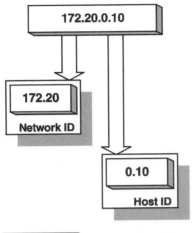

Network ID and host ID

The network ID identifies the systems that are located on the same physical segment just as the area code identifies telephone subscribers located in a particular area. All systems on the same physical segment must have the same network ID. The host ID identifies a workstation, server, router, or other TCP/IP device within the network segment. The host ID must be unique within the given network ID just as the local telephone number must be unique within the area code. Figure 4-4 shows three computers with different IP addresses.

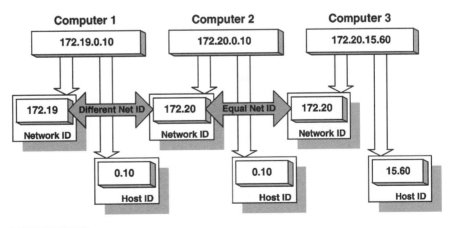

Computers with similar but unique addresses

Computer 2 and Computer 3 must be located in the same physical network, because the network ID of their IP addresses is the same. On the other hand, it is apparent that Computer 1 and Computer 2 are located in different network segments since their network IDs are different. Although, Computer 1 and Computer 2 have identical host IDs, there are no network problems, because these computers are located in different networks. This latter case is analogous to two people with the same telephone number but in different area codes.

Defining Address Classes

Earlier, we said all TCP/IP hosts within a particular network segment must have the same network ID, but different host IDs. It is reasonable to ask how many host IDs are available within a specific network. To answer, we must determine where the border between the network and host portions of the IP address lies. Knowing this, we can determine how many bits are devoted to the network ID and host ID and thus calculate the maximum number of hosts in the network segment.

Different networks require different amounts of available host IDs. Large companies need to set up thousands of computers while smaller companies may require only a few computers on their network segment. In order to provide the flexibility required to support different size networks, the designers of the TCP/IP protocol have decided that the IP address space should be divided into several different address classes. The address classes that are available for use are *Class A*, *Class B*, and *Class C*. This approach is often referred to as *classful* addressing.

Each class fixes the boundary between the network ID and the host ID. In other words, the class of the address defines how many bits are devoted to the network ID and how many bits are used for the host ID. This indirectly defines the possible number of networks in the given class and the number of hosts per network.

Class A

Class A addresses are useful for organizations with an extremely large number of hosts. The first octet (first eight bits) is devoted to the network ID. Accordingly the last three octets (24 bits) are host ID bits (see Figure 4-5).

One of the fundamental features of classful IP addressing is that each address contains a self-encoding key that identifies the dividing point between the network ID and the host ID. Let's look at how it works.

The high-order bit of a Class A address is set to zero. This serves as the self-encoding key by which Class A addresses can be identified from other

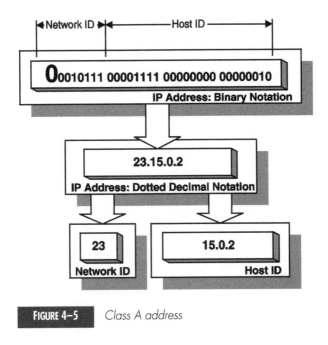

FIGURE 4–5   *Class A address*

address classes. The next seven bits in the first octet complete the network ID. If the IP address is written in dotted decimal notation, you can distinguish a Class A address by looking at the first octet. If the first octet of the IP address is between 1 (**0**0000001 binary) and 126 (**0**1111110 binary), it is a Class A IP address.

Note

You may ask, what happened to 127, since it also has the leading bit set to zero. Remember all IP addresses beginning with 127 are special case IP addresses. They represent the loopback address and thus can not be assigned to a real host.

Another example: your computer has been assigned the IP address 50.6.210.8. The question is what is the network ID, host ID, and how many other computers can exist in the same network? We can see that this is a Class A IP address, because the first octet is 50 (between 1 and 126). Since it's a Class A IP address it has 8 bits for the network ID (50) and 24 bits for the host ID (6.210.8). The possible number of hosts in the same network segment is about 2^{24} or more than 16 million.

Other examples of Class A IP addresses would be: 30.24.5.0, 15.0.0.1, and 120.6.0.3.

How many Class A networks are there? Obviously, 126—exactly as many as the first octet variations allow. Each Class A IP network allows more than 16 million hosts. That's why small or medium organizations do not require a whole Class A network.

Altogether, Class A IP addresses cover 50 percent of the total IP address space.

Class B

Class B addresses are assigned to medium-sized organizations. The network ID occupies two octets. This time the first two bits of the IP address are fixed to be 10 binary. These two bits are the self-encoding key for Class B addresses, and the remaining 14 bits complete the network ID. The host ID is 16 bits in length (see Figure 4-6).

You can also identify a Class B address by the decimal value of the first octet. If the first octet is between 128 (**10**000000 binary) and 191 (**10**111111 binary), you have a Class B address. The total number of Class B networks is 16,384—which is how much the 14 available bits in the network ID allow. The remaining two octets allow approximately 65,000 hosts per network.

For example, if your computer has been assigned an IP address of 172.20.0.10, it's in Class B—because the first octet of the IP address is 172, which is greater than 128 and less than 191. In this case the network ID is 172.20 and the host ID is 0.10.

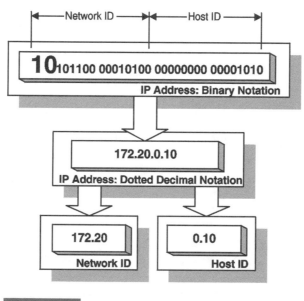

FIGURE 4–6   *Class B address*

Altogether, Class B IP addresses cover 25 percent of the total IP address space.

Note   The range of Class B IP addresses from 169.254.0.1 through 169.254.255.254, is reserved by the Internet Assigned Numbers Authority (IANA) and used for Automatic Private IP Addressing. Any IP addresses within this range are not used on the Internet.

Class C

Class C addresses are used by small organizations. This standard defines three octets for the network ID and one octet for the host ID. The three high-order bits in a Class C IP address are set to binary 110. The next 21 bits complete the network ID. This allows 2^{21} Class C networks with 254 hosts per network (see Figure 4-7).

Written in dotted decimal notation the first octet of the Class C address ranges from 192 (**110**00000 binary) to 223 (**110**11111 binary). Some examples of Class C IP addresses are: 207.46.130.139 and 194.226.192.23.

Altogether, Class C networks occupy 12.5 percent of the total IP address space.

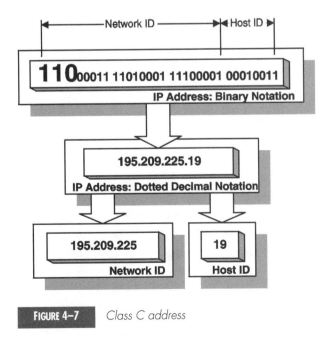

| **FIGURE 4-7** | *Class C address* |

Class D

Class D is special. Class D addresses are used for multicast group usage. The multicast group may contain several hosts. The four high-order bits in Class D are set to binary 1110. The remaining bits designate the specific group in which computers participate. No network and host IDs are defined in Class D addresses. Class D IP addresses can be recognized by the first octet between 224 (**1110**0000 binary) and 239 (**1110**1111 binary). Class D addresses are used by some applications, such as Microsoft NetShow™ and WINS.

Class E

The rest of the IP address space is Class E. Class E is used for experimental addresses and it is not available for general use. The four high-order bits in the Class E IP address are set to binary 1111. In decimal form the first octet of the Class E IP address is greater than 240 (**1111**0000 binary).

To summarize: IP addressing space has been divided into several address classes. Some of the classes (Class A, Class B, and Class C) are available for assignment, while others (Class D and Class E) are special addresses that can not be used to configure a computer. Figure 4-8 displays the address class summary.

Number of Networks	Number of Hosts per Network	First Octet (Binary)	Range of the First Octet (Decimal)	
126	16 777 214	0 * * * * * * *	1 - 126	Class A
16 384	65 534	1 0 * * * * * *	128 - 191	Class B
2 097 152	254	1 1 0 * * * * *	192 - 223	Class C

FIGURE 4–8   *Classful IP addressing summary*

Practical Application

1. Write the address class to each IP address:

   10.0.0.1   _____
   9.255.255.0   _____
   200.0.56.1   _____
   192.15.67.3   _____
   127.0.0.1   _____
   191.233.42.3   _____

2. Which of the following IP address pairs have the same network ID?

   10.0.0.1 and 10.45.2.6   _____
   192.56.2.6 and 192.56.1.6   _____
   131.107.2.1 and 131.107.3.1   _____
   200.0.0.1 and 200.0.0.254   _____
   191.18.3.9 and 191.18.44.3   _____

3. Your network consists of 5,000 computers. Which network classes satisfy your needs?
   _____ and _____

IP—The Next Generation (IPng)

The structure of the IP packet has not been changed since the 1970s. This, of course, is a tribute to its original design. Over the past few years, however, the Internet has experienced an unprecedented growth heralding the eventual exhaustion of available IP address space. The current version of IP, also known as IP version 4 (IPv4), defines a 32-bit host address, which means that there are only 2^{32} (approximately 4 million) addresses available. Remember not all IP addresses are available for assignment—the finite number of IP addresses will eventually be exhausted and a new version of IP needed. *IPng* is a proposed new Internet Protocol to replace IPv4. The formal name for IPng is *IPv6* (6 being the new version number). IPv6 is defined in RFCs 1883, 1884, 1885, 2147, 2373, and others. [You can review these (and other RFCs) at www.cis.ohio-state.edu/htbin/rfc.]

What's new in IPv6? IPng is not just an IPv4 upgrade. You may consider IPv6 a whole new protocol. Its addresses and headers are different. It provides more options and supports auto-configuration. Some of the new features of IPv6 are:

- Extended address space

  IPv6 addresses are 128 bits long. They can identify individual nodes and sets of nodes. IPng addresses can be unicast (single node), anycast (a group of nodes where the packet is delivered to one of the nodes—typically the nearest one) or multicast (group of nodes where the packet will be delivered to all nodes in the group) addresses. 128 bits can express over 3×10^{38} possible combinations. Unlike IPv4, IPv6 addresses are written in hexadecimal form like:

  ```
  3A3F:BE67:F890:56CD:3412:AE52:9011:FA03
  ```

IP — The Next Generation (IPng) (continued)

- Simplified header

  In IPng the header has been greatly simplified. Many of the current IPv4 fields have been omitted, while many others have been made optional. The cost of processing packets has become as low as possible. In spite of a greatly increased address size, the headers are only twice as big as those in IPv4. Anything that is not included in the IPv6 header can be added through IPv6 extension headers.

- IPng's Automatic Network Configuration

  This feature is one of the key changes in IPng. It aims to ease the creation of new networks. This will allow network devices to find and claim their own network address as soon as they are installed on the network.

- Flow control

  In order to support applications, which requires some degree of consistent throughput, delay, and jitter, a new field was added in the IPv6.

Windows 2000 supports the current development version of IPv6 with the addition of the Microsoft IPv6 stack. This may be downloaded from www.research.microsoft.com/msripv6. The Windows 2000 DNS is capable of supporting IPv6 without modification.

Although IPv6 will make life in the TCP/IP world much easier, it's time to return to current reality. All the concepts discussed in the rest of the text correspond to the IP version 4 and should not be directly applied to IPng.

Assigning IP Addresses

Windows 2000 can participate as a Dynamic Host Configuration Protocol (DHCP) client to automatically obtain IP addressing from a DHCP server. It can also use Automatic Private IP Addressing to find an IP address. While both of these features are convenient, it is important to understand how IP addressing works. Before we try IP addressing the easy way (see Chapter 7), we need to learn how to do it manually.

Choosing a Network ID

As you remember, the network ID groups the TCP/IP hosts connected to the same network segment. The first and most basic rule of assigning IP addresses to devices is:

- All hosts located on the same physical network must be assigned the same network ID to communicate with each other.

  If you are not connected to the Internet and never plan to be, you can technically take any valid network ID and plan your network with it. It is highly recommended, however, that you use one of the special case network IDs for private networks. The IANA has reserved the following three blocks of the IP address space for *private networks*:

TABLE 4.2	*Private Network IP Addresses*		
	From	**To**	
Small Networks	10.0.0.0	10.255.255.255	1 Class A network
Medium Networks	172.16.0.0	172.31.255.255	16 Class B networks
Large Networks	192.168.0.0	192.168.255.255	256 Class C networks

Note

The addresses described in Table 4.2 are only for hosts that do not require access to any other hosts on the Internet or any other network not under their control, or hosts that need access to only a limited set of outside services (e.g., hosts behind firewalls).

If you plan to connect directly to the Internet, you must obtain the network ID portion of the IP address from the InterNIC (http://internic.net). This guarantees the uniqueness of your IP addresses across the Internet. An enterprise that requests IP addresses for its external connectivity will never be assigned addresses from the private blocks defined above.

Selecting the Right Amount of Network IDs

Corporate networks often consist of several network segments connected by routers. Some companies use WAN links to connect branch offices. In this case the following rule has to be applied:

- Every physical network segment separated by routers requires a unique network ID. This also applies to each wide area connection.

Note

Separate network segments connected by repeaters, bridges, and switches normally do not require a separate network ID. In most cases you need as many separate network IDs as *broadcast domains* your network has.

Let's consider the following example. The "Horns&Hoofs" corporation has the network illustrated in Figure 4-9.

Network 1 and Network 3 are connected by routers and a wide area network (WAN) link. Obviously Networks 1 and 3 should have dedicated network IDs. In addition, Network 2 requires a separate network ID, so that the interfaces between two routers can be assigned corresponding host IDs.

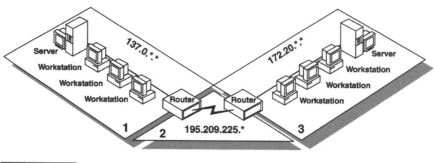

FIGURE 4–9   *Assigning network IDs*

If Horns&Hoofs decides to add another network segment, but will use a bridge instead of a router (see Figure 4-10), it does not require an additional network ID.

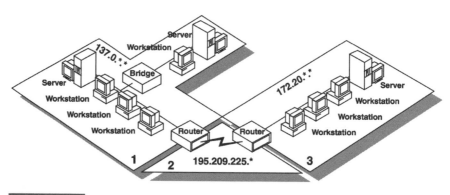

FIGURE 4–10   *Assigning network IDs to a network with bridges*

In this example we used arbitrarily chosen network IDs. If Horns&Hoofs plans to connect its networks to the Internet, it must obtain the network ID portion of segments 1 through 3 from the InterNIC to ensure IP address uniqueness.

Choosing the Host ID

Once the network IDs are assigned you should develop host IDs for your computers. In contrast to network ID assignment, host ID assignment requires no InterNIC registration. You can assign host IDs within your network as you like but must comply with the following rule:

- Within a network, all TCP/IP hosts, including computer network adapter cards and router interfaces, require unique host IDs.

Note   Generally speaking, the IP address is not the computer's attribute, but an attribute of the network adapter card to which TCP/IP is bound. If your computer has two network interfaces, you need two IP addresses, one for each card.

Figure 4-11 shows how it can be implemented for the Horns&Hoofs.

Please note:

- Every TCP/IP host has a unique host ID within its network. (Host IDs are marked in bold in Figure 4-11.)
- Routers each have two or more IP addresses assigned. Each router interface has the IP address from the corresponding network.

Once you have the IP addresses assigned to your computers and routers, you are ready to configure the default gateway address. The IP address of the router interface is the default gateway address for every computer within its network. For example, the workstation with IP address 172.20.0.10 has a default gateway IP address of 172.20.0.1.

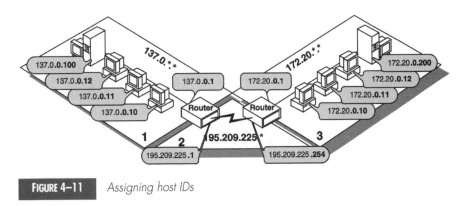

FIGURE 4–11   *Assigning host IDs*

Valid and Invalid Host IDs and Network IDs

Some of the network and host IDs are reserved for special use and should not be assigned to real hosts. Follow these guidelines when assigning host and network IDs:

- The network ID can not be 127. This ID is called the loopback address and is not for general use. For example, the IP address of 127.0.15.32 is invalid for use on the network.

- Neither the network ID nor the host ID may be all 0s. If all bits in either are set to zero, it is interpreted as "this network only." For example, the IP addresses 0.15.6.8 (Network ID is all 0s), 10.0.0.0 (Host ID is all 0s), and 195.209.225.0 (Host ID is all 0s) are invalid.
- The network ID and the host ID cannot be all 1s. If all bits within the network ID or host ID are set to 1, the address is interpreted as a broadcast message. For example, the IP addresses 255.255.255.255 (Network ID is all 1s), 10.255.255.255 (Host ID is all 1s), 172.20.255.255 (Host ID is all 1s), and 195.209.225.255 (Host ID is all 1s) are invalid.

SUGGESTIONS FOR ASSIGNING HOST IDS

Earlier, we mentioned that there are no rules for assigning valid IP addresses to hosts. You can assign IP addresses to hosts consecutively, or number hosts by their type. For example, workstations get low host IDs, servers get high host IDs. Numbering hosts this way helps identify your computers. You can also give particular host IDs to routers so that you could easily designate them by IP address.

Configuring Microsoft TCP/IP to Support Multiple Network Adapters

We just mentioned that every TCP/IP enabled host must have a valid IP address. What if your Windows 2000 computer has multiple network adapters? How would you configure TCP/IP in this case? When your Windows 2000 computer has multiple network adapters you must assign each network adapter an IP address for the network segment to which it is physically attached. (Of course we assume that network adapters are not on the same physical network segment.)

Note   Although Windows 2000 allows you to configure more than one network adapter on the same physical network, this is not a recommended configuration. In this book we will consider that if the system has multiple network adapters they are connected to physically different networks.

Consider, for a moment, the case when a Windows 2000 computer connects two networks with network IDs 137.0 and 172.20. In this situation, you must assign IP addresses to the network adapters as shown in Figure 4-12.

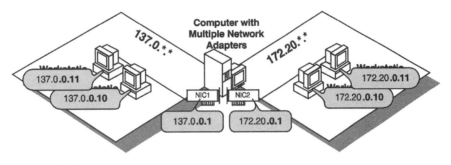

FIGURE 4–12 *Assigning IP addresses on a computer with multiple network adapters*

Practical Application

If you have a computer with multiple network adapters and have access to more than one physical network segment, try the following exercise. If you have only a single network adapter and physical segment, you can still accomplish the optional portion that has you assign multiple IP addresses to the same card.

To configure TCP/IP on a Windows 2000 computer with multiple network adapters, launch `Network and Dial-up Connections` in the `Control Panel`. For every network adapter Windows 2000 automatically creates a separate local area network (LAN) connection when a network adapter is installed. When you click on a local area connection icon, you will see its network adapter in the Network and Dial-up Connections window status bar (see Figure 4-13). Right-click the LAN connection you wish to configure and select Internet Protocol (TCP/IP). Click Properties.

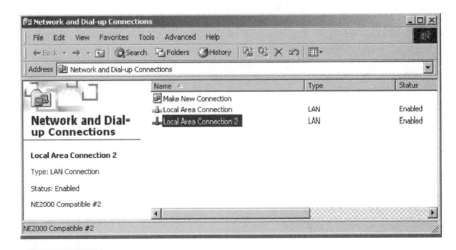

FIGURE 4–13 *Configuring TCP/IP on Windows 2000 with multiple network adapters*

Here you can assign an IP address. Remember that it must have the network ID portion that corresponds to the network segment to which the adapter is attached. You must also specify a subnet mask and, optionally, a default gateway and DNS server addresses. Accomplish the same settings for each network adapter on this computer.

Optionally you can configure a network adapter to use multiple IP addresses. You can do this by clicking `Advanced` in the Internet Protocol `(TCP/IP) Properties` dialog box. Use `Add` to add additional IP addresses to a selected network adapter (see Figure 4-14.) This capability is useful for a system that needs to use multiple IP addresses. (A single adapter card with multiple IP addresses from different subnets can act as a router between different subnets on the same wire. While placing multiple subnets on the same physical wire may not have much practical value it provides a good training experience and may be useful when you are forced to subnet to get enough IP addresses for all the machines on a single physical network.)

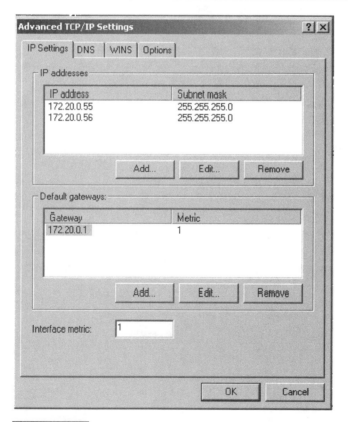

FIGURE 4-14   *Configuring a network adapter with multiple IP addresses*

In Chapter 5 we will see how a Windows 2000 computer with multiple network adapters can be configured to act as an IP router.

Practical Application

Which of the following IP addresses are invalid for host assignment? Explain why they are invalid.

172.0.0.1   _____

200.200.200.200   _____

123.350.2.18   _____

195.209.225.255   _____

172.18.2.255   _____

255.255.255.255   _____

127.12.3.4   _____

190.56.3.0   _____

Defining Subnet Masks

We already know how to determine the network ID and the host ID with the help of the IP address class. Based on this information, we can ascertain whether two computers are located in the same or different network segments. When you set TCP/IP on your computer, however, you have no ability to explicitly specify the IP address class. Instead of the IP address class you specify the *subnet mask*.

The subnet mask is also a 32-bit value but, unlike the IP address, the subnet mask doesn't identify any host in the network. It is used for blocking out a portion of the IP address to distinguish the network ID from the host ID (see Figure 4-15). In other words, the subnet mask specifies where the border between network ID and host ID lies.

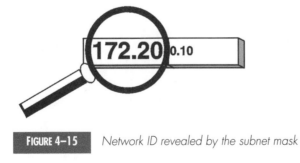

FIGURE 4–15   *Network ID revealed by the subnet mask*

The basic subnet mask is generated in the following way: bits that correspond to the network ID in the IP address are set to 1 in the subnet mask; all others are set to 0 (see Figure 4-16). Like IP addresses, subnet masks are often written in dotted decimal notation.

Note

In this chapter, we'll discuss subnet masking using only 255 and 0; in the next chapter we'll learn about subnet masks using different numbers.

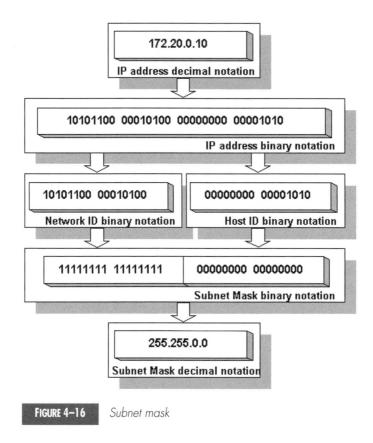

FIGURE 4-16   *Subnet mask*

When you configure TCP/IP on your computer, you have to specify the subnet mask, even if you have a single segment network. The subnet mask can be either a default subnet mask, when your network is not divided into subnets, or a custom subnet mask when your network is subnetted.

Default Subnet Masks

If you have assigned your network a network ID, and your network is not divided into segments by routers, you can use the default subnet mask. The default subnet mask depends on the address class, because different address classes have different numbers of bits dedicated for network and host IDs. Figure 4-17 shows the default subnet masks for Class A, Class B and Class C subnets.

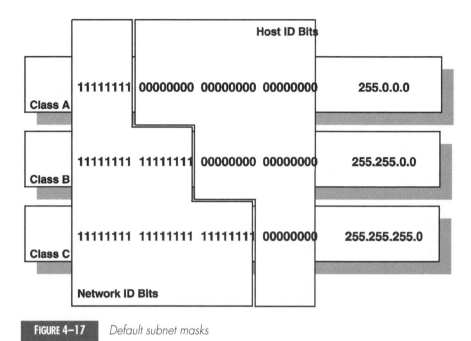

FIGURE 4-17   *Default subnet masks*

Using the Subnet Mask

When the computer sends a packet to another computer, it determines if the destination host is located in the same or a remote network. If the destination computer is in the same network, a broadcast Address Resolution Protocol (ARP) request is sent to obtain the hardware (MAC) address. If the destination computer is located on a remote network, a broadcast ARP request will not work, because broadcast messages will not pass through the router to the remote network. When the destination host is not on the local network the packet is sent to the IP address of the router, and the router takes care of delivery.

The subnet mask is used to determine whether the destination computer is local (in the same network segment) or remote (in another network segment). When TCP/IP is initialized, the computer ANDs its IP address with the configured subnet mask. Table 4.3 shows the rules of the AND operation.

TABLE 4.3   *AND Operation*

Operation	Result
1 AND 1	1
1 AND 0	0
0 AND 1	0
0 AND 0	0

ANDing extracts the network ID from the local computer IP address (see Figure 4-18).

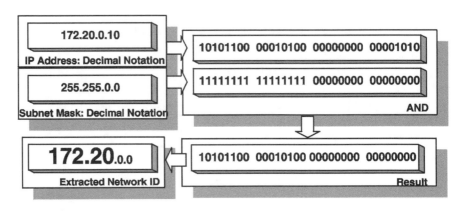

FIGURE 4–18   *Using the subnet mask to extract the network ID*

Before the packet is sent, the IP address of the destination computer is ANDed with the same subnet mask and compared to the network ID extracted earlier. If both results match, the destination computer has the same network ID and thus is located in the same network segment.

Let's look at the example on Figure 4-19. Workstation 1 is configured with the IP address, subnet mask, and default gateway shown on the picture. When Host 1 initializes, it ANDs its IP address (137.0.0.10) with its subnet mask (255.255.0.0). The result (137.0.0.0) is the network ID of Host 1. When Host 1 sends a packet to Server 1, Host 1 ANDs the IP address of Server 1 (137.0.0.100) with its subnet mask (255.255.0.0). The result is 137.0.0.0. Then Host 1 compares this result with its network ID and, since they are the same, Host 1 knows that the destination host is located in the same network segment. In this case, Host 1 broadcasts the ARP request and then sends the packet directly to Server 1.

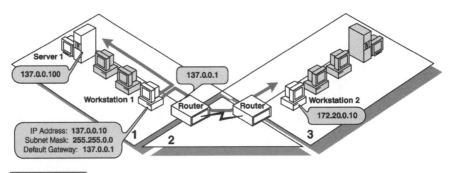

FIGURE 4–19   *Determining the destination of a packet*

If Host 1 sends a packet to Host 2, the same set of actions is performed. The IP address of Host 2 (172.20.0.10) is ANDed with the subnet mask of Host 1 (255.255.0.0). The result is 172.20.0.0. This is not equal to the network ID (137.0.0.0) of Host 1. Because of this, Host 1 knows that Host 2 is located on the remote subnet and thus sends the packet to its default gateway (137.0.0.1). The packet reaches the router interface (137.0.0.1) and the delivery of the packet becomes the responsibility of the router.

Practical Application

What is the default subnet mask for the following IP addresses?
131.107.3.4
200.20.20.1
191.56.2.9
192.7.34.6
10.6.0.0

Summary

In this chapter we looked at IP addressing. You learned what an IP address is and how to convert it from binary to dotted decimal notation. We discussed the two parts of the IP address: network ID and host ID and saw how to define these parts depending on the IP address class. We covered three main IP address classes and looked at their differences. We also studied how to assign network IDs depending on how many separate segments your network has. We examined a complex routed environment and considered the guidelines for assigning host IDs. Finally, we took a look at the subnet mask and how the computer uses it.

Test Yourself

1. When can two computers have the same host ID?
2. The first octet of a Class A IP address must be between:
    A. 1 and 126
    B. 1 and 127
    C. 191 and 223
    D. 128 and 191

3. Why won't an IP address with 127 in the first octet function properly in the network?

4. The IP addresses 141.128.0.2 and 141.128.5.1 are in the same network.
   A. True
   B. False

5. IP address 22.254.255.255 is an INVALID IP address.
   A. True
   B. False

Subnetting

This chapter explains fundamental subnetting concepts and procedures. You will be able to determine when subnetting is necessary and what is required to implement it. We will discuss how and when to use a default subnet mask and when to define a custom subnet mask. You will learn how to estimate the possible number of subnets and the number of hosts per subnet. At the end of this chapter we will review a real world example of subnetting.

Defining Subnets

Today most modern networks consist of several network segments. In many cases companies segment their networks to improve performance and maintainability or to enhance network capabilities. There are several reasons why an organization might want to use more that one segment of cable. Some of them are:

- Different technologies (for example, Ethernet and FDDI) can be mixed in a consolidated network. This not uncommon in a research environment where different topologies and network types are often combined.
- Limitations of current technologies, such as maximum segment length or maximum number of hosts per network, can be overcome.
- Smaller network segments are easier to support and troubleshoot.
- Sometimes the company's territory is split into two or more locations too far apart to connect using a particular local area network (LAN)

technology. In this case, high-speed point-to-point links between subnets can solve the problem.

● Redirecting traffic and localizing broadcasts within one physical network segment reduces network congestion.

Splitting networks into multiple segments has certain drawbacks when an administrator uses only the methods discussed in Chapter 3. Let's look at the following example: The Horns&Hoofs Corporation network is split into three segments with routers. The company plans to connect to the Internet (see Figure 5-1).

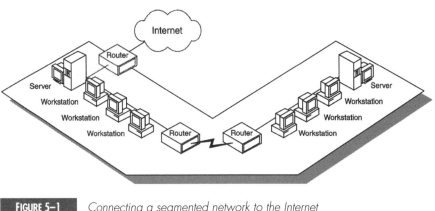

| **FIGURE 5-1** | *Connecting a segmented network to the Internet* |

Earlier, we said that each physical network segment must have a unique ID in order to communicate with other segments and the Internet. The question is, how many network IDs has Horns&Hoofs obtained from the InterNIC? With what we've learned so far, we would say the minimum number of network IDs is three (not counting the link to the Internet itself). Since each segment contains only a few computers, a Class C network is clearly in order—using a Class A or B network would result in a considerable number of wasted host addresses (see Figure 5-2). Even using three Class C networks, however, will consume 3x256 addresses from the global Internet Protocol (IP) addressing space—far too extravagant for fewer than a dozen computers. If every company with a few computers in a subnet requests several Class C networks, it will rapidly lead to the exhaustion of the Internet's IP address space. Someday, Horns & Hoofs may require another network segment. If the company needs to use another complete Class C network for just a few computers, the local administrator will need to obtain an additional network number (ID) from the InterNIC before the new network can be installed.

The address shortage problem is aggravated by the fact that portions of the IP address space have not been efficiently allocated. The problem is not that network administrators request more IP addresses than they need but that

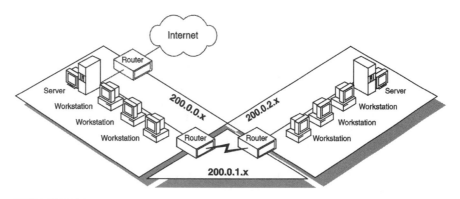

FIGURE 5-2   *An example of an inefficient allocation of IP address space*

the traditional model of classful addressing doesn't allow the address space to be used to its maximum potential.

Adding another level of hierarchy to the IP addressing structure will help to solve this problem. In the classful model we have a two-level hierarchy: network ID and host ID. Using *subnetting* we can add a third level. Let's look how it works.

Typically, an organization acquires only one network ID from the Inter-NIC, regardless of the number of separate physical network segments the organization will use. Since each segment should have a unique ID, a unique *subnet ID* is created for each of the segments by partitioning the bits in the host ID into two parts (see Figure 5-3). One part is used to identify the segment as a unique sub-network within the company's network, and the other part is used to identify hosts.

Note   The network ID together with the subnet ID is often referred to as *Extended Network Prefix*.

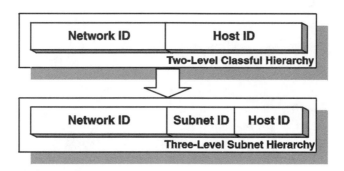

FIGURE 5-3   *Subnetting brings a third level to the hierarchy*

Note that it is the responsibility of the local administrator to plan and implement subnetting based on the needs of the company. Neither the Inter-NIC nor an Internet Service Provider (ISP) will do this for you.

Subnetting provides the following benefits:

- The administrator has the flexibility to deploy additional subnets without obtaining additional network IDs from the InterNIC.
- Changes within the corporate network do not affect Internet routing tables because all the subnets appear to the Internet as a united network.
- The Internet IP address space can be more economically employed.

Planning Considerations

When you implement subnetting, the basic task is to define the border between the subnet ID and the host ID. In other words, you need to identify how many bits are devoted to the subnet ID and how many to the host ID (see Figure 5-4). These values correspond to the number of segments your network has and the number of hosts per segment.

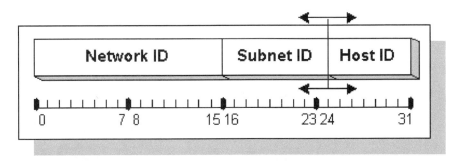

| FIGURE 5–4 | *Defining the border between the subnet ID and the host ID* |

As the figure illustrates, the more bits used for the subnet ID the more subnets are available, but fewer hosts are available per subnet. If you reserve more bits than needed for the subnet ID, it will permit you to easily add more network segments, but will limit the growth of each individual segment. On the other hand, using fewer bits than needed allows increasing the number of hosts per subnet, but limits the number of available subnets. Figure 5-5 shows the possible division of the Class A network.

Note   The more subnets you have the fewer hosts per subnet are allowed.

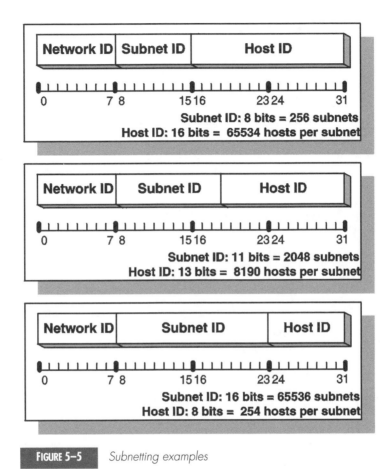

FIGURE 5–5   *Subnetting examples*

You can visualize the border between the subnet ID and host ID as a sliding bar. The main goal of subnet planning is to fix the bar's position to create the appropriate number of hosts and subnets.

Practical Application

Suppose you have a Class C network 195.209.225.0. You decide to subnet it so that the length of the subnet ID is 4 bits. What is the length of the host ID in this case? _____

Using the above division you want to implement 10 hosts in each subnet. Is that possible? _____

What is the maximum number of hosts per subnet in this example? _____

Design Considerations

The deployment of a Transport Control Protocol/Internet Protocol (TCP/IP) network requires careful thought on the part of the network administrator. Before you implement subnetting, you need to determine the current needs of your organization as well as plan for future requirements. There are several key questions that must be answered:

- How many physical network segments are there in your network? (Only segments connected with routers are counted. Do not count network segments that are connected with bridges or repeaters.)
- How many subnets (network segments) will your company need in the future?
- How many hosts are there in the company's largest subnet?
- How many hosts will there be in the company's largest subnet in the future?

Note   When determining the required number of hosts in each physical network segment, keep in mind that all computers, router interfaces, and other TCP/IP devices should be counted.

You should always estimate future network growth. After deployment, it is very time-consuming to rebuild the network when it fails to satisfy expanded needs. Based on the answers to the questions you should draft a subnetting plan that includes:

- Number of bits that should be allocated for the subnet ID to satisfy your needs
- One custom subnet mask for your all physical segments in your network
- Numerical descriptions for each network segment (subnet ID)
- A range of hosts for each network segment

Tip   You may want to make sure that the company's address allocation provides enough bits to deploy the required number of subnets and hosts per subnet. For instance, a single Class C network (256 IP addresses) does not provide the ability to deploy 16 subnets with 64 hosts in each. If your company's current network class does not permit you to fulfill your plan, you may want to acquire additional network IDs from InterNIC.

Changing Custom Subnet Mask Defaults

We discussed subnet masks in Chapter 4. As you remember, a subnet mask is essential for a host to distinguish local computers (located in the same network segment) from remote ones (located in different network segments). When we segment our network with routers we must recalculate the default subnet mask and define a *custom subnet mask*. Why should we define a custom subnet mask? Why won't the old subnet mask work? Figure 5-6 answers these questions. When the network is not subnetted, Computer 1 uses the default subnet mask to determine that Computer 2 is local. When we install a router and place Computer 2 on another network segment, we need to recalculate the old subnet mask. If we don't change the mask, Computer 1 will not notice the change and will still try to communicate with Computer 2 directly—the connection will be unsuccessful.

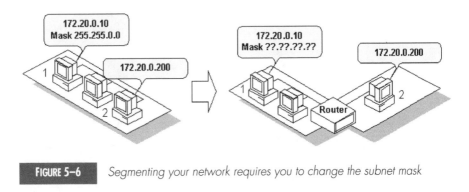

| FIGURE 5–6 | *Segmenting your network requires you to change the subnet mask* |

Now that we've answered the question why do we need a custom subnet mask, the next logical question is how do we calculate it?

CALCULATING THE NUMBER OF BITS FOR THE SUBNET ID

First, you must decide how many bits to allocate to the subnet ID to provide the required number of subnets. In other words, you must count the number of bits required to represent the number of network segments you need. For example, if your company needs 10 subnets, 3 bits for each subnet ID are not enough, since this provides only $2^3 = 8$ different subnet numbers. You will need to allocate 4 bits for the subnet ID. This provides $2^4 = 16$ different subnet numbers, which satisfies the company's current needs and allows some room for future growth.

One method to determine the required number of bits for the subnet ID is the following: You should convert the number of physical segments in your network to binary format and count the number of bits required to represent this number. For example, what if you need 6 subnets? Since 6 is represented as 110 in binary format, you need to devote 3 bits for the subnet ID.

When the number of required subnets gets larger, Table 5.1 may be helpful.

TABLE 5.1	*Determining the Number of Bits Required for Subnetting*
Number of Bits for the Subnet ID	**Number of Subnets**
1	2
2	4
3	8
4	16
5	32
6	64
7	128
8	256
9	512
10	1024
11	2048
12	4096

For example, if your company needs 70 subnets, you will need to allocate a minimum of 7 bits for the subnet ID, since 6 bits do not provide enough subnets.

CALCULATING THE SUBNET MASK

Once you've determined the number of bits for the subnet ID, you are ready to calculate the custom subnet mask. As you already know, the bits that correspond to the network ID (and now the subnet ID) should be set to 1. The bits that match the host ID should be set to 0.

Let's look at how a Class A network can be subnetted into 512 segments. According to Table 5.1, in order to provide 512 separate network segments, nine bits must be taken from the host ID portion (see Figure 5-7).

Next, you mask the network and subnet portions with 1s and convert the result into dotted decimal notation. The result is your custom subnet mask (see Figure 5-8).

When we look at the subnet mask "255.255.128.0" we can determine that the border between the extended network prefix (network ID plus subnet ID) and the host ID lies exactly between the 16th and the 17th bits.

Important   Since the network address can only be subnetted along binary boundaries, subnets must be created in blocks of powers of 2. Thus, it is impossible to define an IP address block that contains exactly 5 subnets.

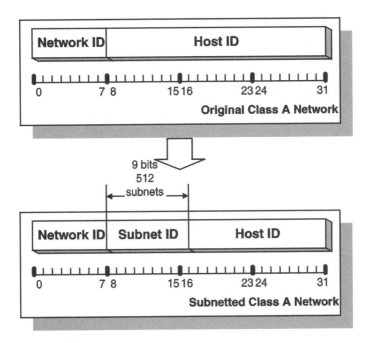

FIGURE 5-7   *In order to provide 512 subnets you must use 9 bits of the host ID*

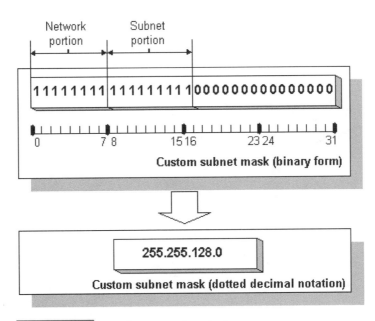

FIGURE 5-8   *Masking network and subnet bits*

1. What subnet mask is suitable for the following situations?
   * Class A network with 6 subnets
   * Class B network with 13 subnets
   * Class B network with 120 subnets
   * Class C network with 19 subnets

2. Suppose you are an administrator of a company that has been assigned a Class C network from the InterNIC. Now your network consists of 9 separate segments connected with routers. Two more segments will be added in the near future. What is the minimum number of bits required for the subnet ID? _____

   What is the number of hosts per subnet? _____

   What is the subnet mask?_____

3. Your network has been assigned a Class B network address. Currently there are 30 subnets that will grow to 60 within the next year. There will never be more than 500 hosts per subnet. What are the possible subnet masks for this scenario?
   How much growth (in terms of the maximum number of subnets and the maximum number of hosts per subnet) will these subnet masks provide?

SUBNET MASK CONSIDERATIONS

Since the bits that identify the subnet are specified by the bitmask, there is nothing to prevent a network administrator from using low-order or nonadjacent bits for the subnet ID. When subnetting was initially defined in RFC 950, it was *recommended* that the subnet bits were contiguous and located as the most significant (high-order) bits of an IP address. Today you should use the contiguous, high-order bits for the subnet ID, since most of the modern operating systems prevent you from doing otherwise.

Defining the Subnet Numbers

Once you have calculated the custom subnet mask, the next step is to number the subnets within your network. In order to do this, you must go through all of the bit combinations in the subnet ID portion. All possible subnet ID bit combinations are then evaluated and converted to a decimal format.

Let's look at the following example. The Class C network 192.168.18.0 needs to be subnetted into 8 subnets, numbered 0 through 7. We are required to describe each subnet in terms of the IP addresses and subnet masks. What we already can do is calculate the length of the subnet ID portion and the subnet mask. In this example we need to derive 3 bits from the original Class C host portion to get 8 subnets (see Figure 5-9).

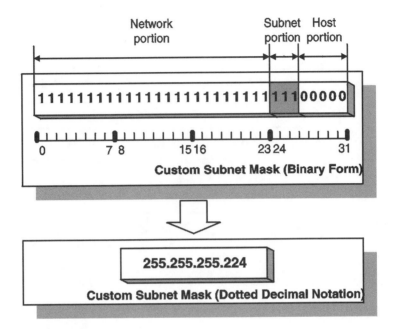

FIGURE 5–9 *Three bits in the subnet portion provide the necessary 8 subnets*

Now we must define each subnet. In general, to define subnet N, place the binary representation of *N* into the subnet field. To define Subnet #0, place binary 000 in the subnet field. To get Subnet #0 in dotted decimal notation, convert each octet to decimal form. (See Figure 5-10.)

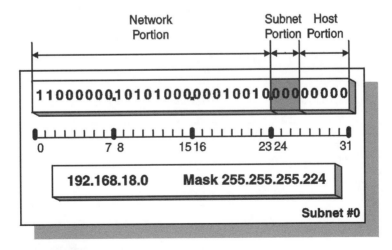

FIGURE 5–10 *Subnetting 192.168.18.0. Subnet #0 of 8*

To determine Subnet #1, place binary 001 into the subnet field. (See Figure 5-11.)

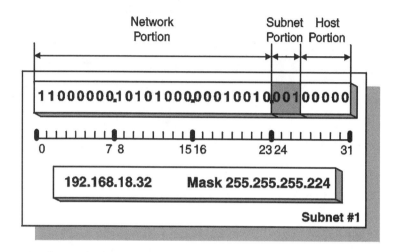

FIGURE 5-11   *Subnetting 192.168.18.0. Subnet #1 of 8*

Subnets 2 through 8 are calculated in a similar way.

Table 5.2 presents the subnetting results. The bold portion of each address indicates the subnet-number field.

TABLE 5.2   *Subnetting Class C Network 192.128.18.0 into 8 Subnets*

	Binary	**Decimal**	**Subnet mask**
Base	11000000.10101000.00010010.00000000	192.168.18.0	255.255.255.0
Subnet #0	11000000.10101000.00010010.00000000	192.168.18.0	255.255.255.224
Subnet #1	11000000.10101000.00010010.00100000	192.168.18.32	255.255.255.224
Subnet #2	11000000.10101000.00010010.01000000	192.168.18.64	255.255.255.224
Subnet #3	11000000.10101000.00010010.01100000	192.168.18.96	255.255.255.224
Subnet #4	11000000.10101000.00010010.10000000	192.168.18.128	255.255.255.224
Subnet #5	11000000.10101000.00010010.10100000	192.168.18.160	255.255.255.224
Subnet #6	11000000.10101000.00010010.11000000	192.168.18.192	255.255.255.224
Subnet #7	11000000.10101000.00010010.11100000	192.168.18.224	255.255.255.224

Note   The whole Class C network differs from the Subnet #0 only by the subnet mask. If you omit the subnet mask, there is no way to tell a particular network from its Subnet #0.

You can check if your calculations are correct, by ensuring that subnets are multiples of Subnet #1. In this example all subnets are multiples of 32 (see Table 5.3).

TABLE 5.3	*Subnet #N should be a multiple of Subnet #1*			
	Binary	**Decimal**	**Subnet mask**	
Base	11000000.10101000.00010010.00000000	192.168.18.0	255.255.255.0	
Subnet #0	11000000.10101000.00010010.00000000	192.168.18.**0**	255.255.255.224	
Subnet #1	11000000.10101000.00010010.00100000	192.168.18.**32**	255.255.255.224	
Subnet #2	11000000.10101000.00010010.01000000	192.168.18.**64**	255.255.255.224	
Subnet #3	11000000.10101000.00010010.01100000	192.168.18.**96**	255.255.255.224	
Subnet #4	11000000.10101000.00010010.10000000	192.168.18.**128**	255.255.255.224	
Subnet #5	11000000.10101000.00010010.10100000	192.168.18.**160**	255.255.255.224	
Subnet #6	11000000.10101000.00010010.11000000	192.168.18.**192**	255.255.255.224	
Subnet #7	11000000.10101000.00010010.11100000	192.168.18.**224**	255.255.255.224	

Tip   When you use more than 3 bits for subnetting, it's more practical to define only Subnet #1 using the above procedure. Since other subnets are multiples of Subnet #1, you can calculate them simply by multiplying by the value of Subnet #1.

SPECIAL CONSIDERATIONS FOR SUBNETS WITH ALL-1S OR ALL-0S

When subnetting was first defined in RFC 950 the use of subnets with all-0s or all-1s was prohibited. This is because the Routing Information Protocol (RIP-1), which is used to designate the networks and the paths to them, does not carry subnet masks as part of its routing table update messages. Earlier, we said that to differentiate between the entire network and its all-0s subnet (Subnet #0) we need to examine the subnet mask. (Refer to Table 5.2.) If the subnet mask is not transferred in network messages, the router can't create a true picture of the network. The routing advertisements for subnet 192.168.18.0, mask 255.255.255.224 and network 192.168.18.0, mask 255.255.255.0 are identical: 192.168.18.0.

The same applies to an all-1s subnet. Routers require a subnet mask to determine if the broadcast should be send only to the all-1s subnet or to the entire network.

You can use the all-0s and all-1s subnets only if all routers and hardware in your network support them. If you are unsure, it is safer not to use these subnet IDs. If you decide not to use all-0s and all-1s subnets, remember the following limitations:

- The number of valid subnets is decreased by 2.
- Splitting your network into only two subnets is not allowed (see Figure 5-12).

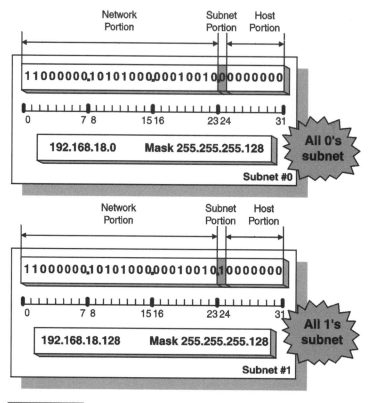

FIGURE 5-12 *All-0s and all-1s subnets*

Practical Application

Your company has been assigned a single Class C network 195.209.225.0. Currently there are only two subnets, but three more will be added in the near future. Each subnet must support the maximum possible number of hosts. You are required to implement a subnetting scheme. (Assume that routers do not support all 0s and all 1s subnets.)

1. How many bits would you allocate for the subnet ID? _____

2. What is the subnet mask? _____

3. Using the above calculations fill in the following table:
   ```
   base         195.209.225. [00000000] = 195.209.225.0
   subnet #0    195.209.225.[_____] = 195.209.225.__
   subnet #1    195.209.225.[_____] = 195.209.225.__
   subnet #2    195.209.225.[_____] = 195.209.225.__
   subnet #3    195.209.225.[_____] = 195.209.225.__
   subnet #4    195.209.225.[_____] = 195.209.225.__
   subnet #5    195.209.225.[_____] = 195.209.225.__
   ......
   ```

4. Can you use Subnet #0 in this example? _____

Alternative Designation of Subnet Masks

We've already gotten used to the fact that subnet masks are expressed in dotted decimal notation. With the assumption that subnet IDs are contiguous and derived from high-order bits, we can simply define the number of bits that are allocated for the extended network prefix (network ID plus subnet ID) to uniquely identify the position where the host number begins. For example, there is an agreement to refer to Class A networks as "/8s" (pronounced "slash eight" or just "eights") since they have the 8-bit network ID. Accordingly, Class B networks are called "/16s" and Class C are called "/24s." Windows 2000 uses the slash designation in many of its configuration options.

Let's look at the previous subnetting example with the slash designations. Let's look at the example with Class C network 192.168.18.0 and 8 subnets, numbered 0 through 7. Again we are required to express the subnet mask but now let's use "slashes."

A Class C network has a network prefix of "/24." To provide 8 subnets we need 3 bits, so the new extended network prefix should be /24 + 3 = /27. Looking at the custom subnet mask, /27, we see there are 32 - 27 = 5 bits for the host ID in each subnet. This tells us there are $2^5 = 32$ hosts per subnet. To calculate each subnet, you need to follow the same guidelines we described earlier. To define Subnet #N you need to put the binary representation of N into the subnet ID portion and convert the result into decimal form. The /27 can be easily converted to the more conventional dotted decimal notation 255.255.255.224.

Defining Host Addresses for Each Subnet

Once you have calculated the subnets, you can proceed to defining host addresses for each subnet. Remember, according to Internet practice, the host-number field of an IP address cannot be all-0s or all-1s. In Chapter 3, we mentioned that an IP address with all 0s in the host portion symbolizes "this network" and an address with all-1s in the host portion indicates a broadcast. Each subnet, therefore, comprises an address space block of 2^N-2 hosts, where N is the number of bits reserved for the host ID. For example, subnetting the Class C network 192.168.18.0 with the subnet mask 255.255.255.224 provides you with 30 host addresses in each subnet. (See Figure 5-13.) Note that the all-0s and all-1s subnets are dimmed to indicate you'd better not use them because of the limitations just discussed.

To determine the valid host numbers for a particular subnet, you need only look over all possible combinations in the host ID field, except all-0s and all-1s. Table 5.4 shows the possible host addresses for Subnet #5. The host portion of each IP address is displayed in bold print.

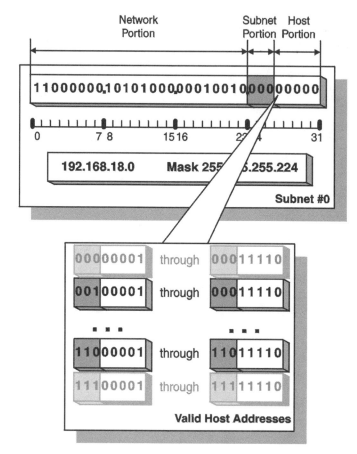

FIGURE 5–13 *Defining host addresses for each subnet*

TABLE 5.4 *Determining Valid Host Addresses for a Given Subnet*

	Binary	**Decimal**	**Subnet mask**
Subnet #5	11000000.10101000.00010010.10100000	192.168.18.160	255.255.255.0
Host #1	11000000.10101000.00010010.10100001	192.168.18.161	255.255.255.224
Host #2	11000000.10101000.00010010.10100010	192.168.18.162	255.255.255.224
.			
.			
.			
Host #14	11000000.10101000.00010010.10101110	192.168.18.174	255.255.255.224
Host #15	11000000.10101000.00010010.10101111	192.168.18.175	255.255.255.224
.			
.			
.			
Host #29	11000000.10101000.00010010.10111101	192.168.18.189	255.255.255.224
Host #30	11000000.10101000.00010010.10111110	192.168.18.190	255.255.255.224

Sometimes you need to determine the broadcast address for a particular subnet. Remember the broadcast address that has all 1s in the host ID portion. For example, the broadcast address for Subnet #5 (See Table 5.3) is 192.168.18.191. Note that the broadcast address for Subnet #N is exactly one less that the base address for Subnet #(N + 1).

You may have noticed that we lose IP addresses when we implement subnetting. In the previous example, a nonsubnetted Class C network 192.168.18.0 provided 254 valid host IDs. After subnetting, some of the host IDs became invalid (see Table 5.5.[1]). IP addresses that became invalid after subnetting are marked in bold print.

TABLE 5.5	IP Address Loss During Subnetting	
IP address	**Subnet Mask**	**Comment**
192.168.18.0	255.255.255.224	Symbolizes Subnet #0—not valid for host ID
192.168.18.1	255.255.255.224	Valid host IP address. Host #1 in Subnet #0
.		
192.168.18.30	255.255.255.224	Valid host IP address. Host #30 in Subnet #0
192.168.18.31	255.255.255.224	Broadcast address for Subnet #0
192.168.18.32	255.255.255.224	Symbolizes Subnet #1—not valid host ID
192.168.18.33	255.255.255.224	Valid host IP address. Host #1 in Subnet #1
.		
192.168.18.62	255.255.255.224	Valid host IP address. Host #30 in Subnet #1
192.168.18.63	255.255.255.224	Broadcast address for Subnet #1
192.168.18.64	255.255.255.224	Symbolizes Subnet #2—not valid host ID
192.168.18.65	255.255.255.224	Valid host IP address. Host #1 in Subnet #2
.		
192.168.18.254	255.255.255.224	Valid host IP address. Host #30 in Subnet #7
192.168.18.255	255.255.255.224	Broadcast address for Subnet #7

---

1. In this example we assumed that all equipment supports all-0s and all-1s subnets.

Practical Application

You have chosen a Class B network address of 172.31.0.0 for your company's network and you need to subnet it into 8 subnets using subnet mask 255.255.224.0. What are the valid host IP addresses for each subnet?

subnet #0	172.31.0.0	172.31.___.___	172.31.___.___
subnet #1	172.31.32.0	172.31.___.___	172.31.___.___
subnet #2	172.31.64.0	172.31.___.___	172.31.___.___
subnet #3	172.31.96.0	172.31.___.___	172.31.___.___
subnet #4	172.31.128.0	172.31.___.___	172.31.___.___
subnet #5	172.31.160.0	172.31.___.___	172.31.___.___
subnet #6	172.31.192.0	172.31.___.___	172.31.___.___
subnet #7	172.31.224.0	172.31.___.___	172.31.___.___

Supernetting

Let's consider an organization with 800 hosts. The network administrator can acquire a Class B network that provides 65,534 host addresses. Obviously, that is much more than needed. Rather than allocating the whole Class B network, an administrator may consider obtaining several Class C networks. In our example four Class C networks are enough. Since they allocate more than 1,024 hosts, they easily satisfy the requirement while providing future growth potential. Let's assume the organization is assigned the following Class C networks:

```
210.18.8.0 mask 255.255.255.0

210.18.9.0 mask 255.255.255.0

210.18.10.0 mask 255.255.255.0

210.18.11.0 mask 255.255.255.0
```

This technique helps to conserve Class A and B networks but creates a problem. To advertise the organization's network on the Internet, we must issue three additional entries. This can congest Internet routers and may cause delays in packet delivery.

By 1992, the exponential growth of the Internet was beginning to raise serious concerns about the ability of the Internet's routing system to scale and support future growth. These problems were related to the near-term exhaustion of the Class B network address space and the rapid growth in the size of the global Internet's routing tables. To solve these problems the concept of Supernetting or classless interdomain routing (CIDR) was developed. It is described in RFCs 1517, 1518, 1519, and 1520.

The main idea of CIDR is that it supports route aggregation where a single routing table entry can represent the address space of perhaps thousands of traditional classful routes. In contrast to subnetting, supernetting borrows bits from the network ID and masks them as the host ID.

Let's return to our example with the four Class C networks. Note, in Figure 5-14, that all four networks have identical parts in the network ID portion up to the grayed area. When we consolidate the IP address range allocated by each of these Class C networks, we get the range 210.18.9.1–210.18.11.254. On the other hand, the same block of IP addresses can be expressed with the single designation 210.18.9.0, mask 255.255.252.0. As you can see in Figure 5-14, the blocks of IP addresses described with both methods are identical. Supernetting, however, helps control the amount of routing information in the Internet's backbone routers, reduces route flapping (rapid changes in route availability), and eases the local administrative burden of updating external routing information.

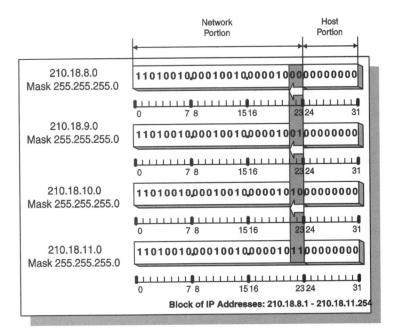

FIGURE 5-14   *Concept of supernetting*

Subnetting in Action

Now we are ready to perform a typical planning task. Suppose you are an administrator of an organization whose network plan is illustrated in Figure 5-15. Currently there are only five network segments, but six more will be required during the coming year. The number of computers in each segment is different but no segment has more that 2,000 hosts. Routers separate each segment. You are required to plan a subnetting scheme that will meet today's needs while allowing for future growth.

Since your company has no plans to connect to the Internet, you choose an IP address block from the private address space—172.16.0.0.

Important   In the *real world*, one should carefully consider the idea that they will never connect to the Internet. Are there really any successful organizations with an IT base that will *never* connect to the Internet? Unless the company will access the Internet through a proxy or firewall, which will mask its actual IP addresses, it is wise to plan your IP addressing with ultimate Internet connectivity in mind.

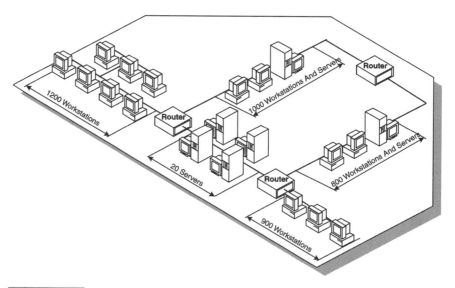

FIGURE 5–15   *Subnetting example*

To complete this task, you must:

- Determine the number of required subnets
- Calculate the number of bits required to support these subnets
- Verify that the chosen network ID is enough for deployment of the desired number of subnets with the given number of hosts per subnet
- Determine a custom subnet mask
- Assign each host an IP address from the corresponding subnet

The number of required subnets corresponds to the number of physical network segments. In our current example, we have five network segments and expect six in the coming year. Therefore, we need to plan for a minimum of eleven subnets.

The next step is to determine the number of bits that provide the required number of subnets. According to Table 5.2, three bits for the subnet ID portion will give us $2^3 = 8$ subnets, but since we don't know whether all our hardware supports all-0s or all-1s subnets we need to subtract two. So with three bits allocated for the subnet portion, we have only six valid subnets, which is not enough. The next step is to try allocating four bits to the subnet ID portion. Four bits provide $2^4 = 16$ subnets, but again, we need to subtract two to avoid problems with all-0s and all-1s subnets. Since we have chosen a Class B network ID, we have 16 bits in the host portion. Borrowing 4 bits for the subnet ID leaves 12 bits for hosts in each subnet. Twelve bits in the host ID field are enough for $2^{12} - 2 = 4094$ valid host IDs. We subtracted two to account for all 1s (broadcast address) and all 0s (this subnet) in the host portion. The capability to support more than 4.000 hosts per subnet satisfies the current requirement and allows future growth. You could also try allocating five or six bits to the subnet ID. Subnetting options are illustrated in Table 5.6. Bold lines indicate configurations that satisfy current requirements.

TABLE 5.6	*Variants of Subnetting*		
Bits for Subnet ID	**Bits for Host ID**	**Number of Subnets**	**Hosts per Subnet**
3	13	8(6)	8190
4	**12**	**16(14)**	**4094**
5	**11**	**32(30)**	**2046**
6	10	64(62)	1022

Let's choose 4 bits for the subnet ID and 12 bits for the host ID.

Now we should calculate the custom subnet mask. Recall we can get the custom subnet mask by setting all network ID and subnet ID bits to binary 1 and converting to dotted decimal form (see Figure 5-16).

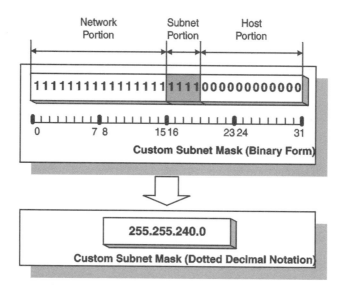

FIGURE 5-16   *Calculating a custom subnet mask*

The custom subnet mask becomes 255.255.240.0. Note that this subnet mask is used for every subnet within the network. With this subnet mask the network is divided into 16 subnets. Each subnet may have the same number of hosts: $2^{16} - 2 = 4094$.

Let's number the subnet as shown in Figure 5-17 and then calculate the range of the host IDs for each subnet.

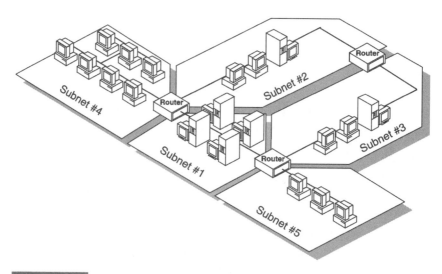

FIGURE 5-17   *Subnetting example. Number of subnets*

The next step is to express each subnet in dotted decimal notation. In order to do this, we must put the binary representation of the subnet number into the subnet portion and convert to decimal notation. Table 5.7 shows these steps. Binary values are written in square brackets. Bold values correspond to subnet IDs.

TABLE 5.7	Calculating the Subnet Numbers		
	Third Octet in Binary Form	**Decimal**	**Subnet Mask**
Base	172.16.0.0	172.16.0.0	255.255.255.0
Subnet #1	172.16.**[0001]**[0000].0	172.16.16.0	255.255.240.0
Subnet #2	172.16.**[0010]**[0000].0	172.16.32.0	255.255.240.0
Subnet #3	172.16.**[0011]**[0000].0	172.16.48.0	255.255.240.0
Subnet #4	172.16.**[0100]**[0000].0	172.16.64.0	255.255.240.0
Subnet #5	172.16.**[0101]**[0000].0	172.16.80.0	255.255.240.0

Table 5.5 shows only five subnets. Subnets 6 through 15 are not needed now, but we can calculate them using the shortcut method—multiplying by Subnet #1.

The next step is to determine the host IP addresses for each subnet. Remember, in order to define the IP address for Host #N within a particular subnet, you must place the binary representation of N in the host ID portion and then convert the result into dotted decimal form. In this example, however, for all subnets except Subnet #1, we will calculate the range of IP addresses instead of specifying them individually. Table 5.8 shows the calculations for Subnet #1. Again, binary values are written in square brackets. Bold symbols indicate the host portion.

TABLE 5.8	Calculating Host IP Addresses for Subnet #1		
	Third Octet in Binary Form	**Decimal**	**Subnet Mask**
Subnet #1	172.16.[0001][0000].**[00000000]**	172.16.16.0	255.255.240.0
Host #1	172.16.[0001][0000].**[00000001]**	172.16.16.1	255.255.240.0
Host #2	172.16.[0001][0000].**[00000010]**	172.16.16.2	255.255.240.0
.			
.			
.			
Host # 4094	172.16.[0001]**[1111]**.**[11111110]**	172.16.31.254	255.255.240.0
Broadcast	172.16.[0001]**[1111]**.**[11111111]**	172.16.31.255	255.255.240.0

Note that the first valid host IP address is one greater than the base address for Subnet #1. The last valid IP address is two less that the base address for the next subnet. Table 5.9 shows the host IP address ranges for other subnets.

TABLE 5.9   *Host IP Address Ranges*

	Subnet	Start IP Address	End IP Address	Subnet Mask
Subnet #1	172.16.16.0	172.16.16.1	172.16.31.254	255.255.240.0
Subnet #2	172.16.32.0	172.16.32.1	172.16.47.254	255.255.240.0
Subnet #3	172.16.48.0	172.16.48.1	172.16.63.254	255.255.240.0
Subnet #4	172.16.64.0	172.16.64.1	172.16.79.254	255.255.240.0
Subnet #5	172.16.80.0	172.16.80.1	172.16.95.254	255.255.240.0

Next, we should assign hosts and routers the IP addresses from the corresponding range (see Figure 5-18). The last step is to provide these values during TCP/IP setup.

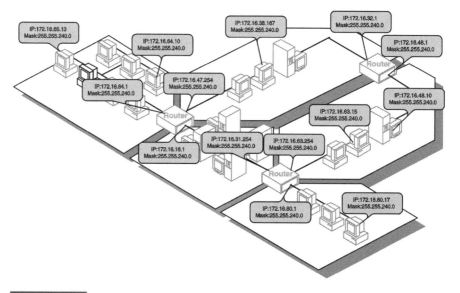

FIGURE 5–18   *Subnetting example. Assignment of IP addresses*

Summary

In this chapter we looked at the ins and outs of subnetting. You learned the benefits of subnetting as well as its drawbacks. We introduced a third level of hierarchy—the subnet ID—and discussed how to calculate it. You are now familiar with the process of determining custom subnet masks and evaluating the number of hosts they provide. Finally, we spent quite a bit of time with a subnetting example, which prepared you to effectively plan a real TCP/IP network.

Test Yourself

1. Which of the following are NOT questions to be asked when subnetting your network?
   - **A.** How many physical network segments are there in your network?
   - **B.** How many subnets (network segments) will your company need in the future?
   - **C.** How many hosts can share IP addresses with each other?
   - **D.** How many hosts are there in the company's largest subnet?
   - **E.** How many hosts will there be in the company's largest subnet in the future?

2. If your Class A network needs 40 subnets, your host IDs may have a maximum of _____ bits.

3. If your network needs 7 subnets, your subnet ID should have _____ bits.

4. Using the alternative subnet mask designation a Class B subnet would be designated:
   - **A.** /2
   - **B.** /4
   - **C.** /8
   - **D.** /16

5. A subnet mask of 255.255.255.192 will provide your network with _____ usable networks.
   - **A.** 2
   - **B.** 3
   - **C.** 4
   - **D.** 5

IP Routing

*N*ow that you are familiar with subnetting concepts, you might be wondering how all the packets get through the internetwork to the destination computer? Read on and you'll see how Internet Protocol (IP) routing works and how IP packets find their paths through routers. We'll discuss the differences between direct and indirect routing and learn how to build a router on a Windows 2000 computer. We'll also look at the concepts of dynamic routing and develop some guidelines on how to combine static and dynamic routers in one network. Finally, we will learn to use the TRACERT utility to trace and troubleshoot IP networks.

Routing Basics

While introducing subnetting in Chapter 5 we simply assumed that when a packet is destined for the remote network, it is forwarded to the host's default gateway and then delivered to the destination node. We said that it was the responsibility of the router to deliver the packet to the recipient computer. The process of transferring data across an internetwork from a source host to a destination host is called *routing*. Routing also implies choosing the best path over which to send packets. Routing can be understood in terms of two processes: *host routing* and *router routing*.

Host Routing

The simplest case of routing—*host routing*—occurs when a computer sends an IP packet and decides whether the destination is local or remote. You might remember that the computer does this by comparing the network ID of the destination host with its own network ID. If these two values match, the host can send the packet directly to the destination computer by querying the destination media access control (MAC) address. When a host can deliver the packet directly, this is referred to as a *direct delivery*. Host routing doesn't require any additional devices to participate in packet delivery (see Figure 6-1).

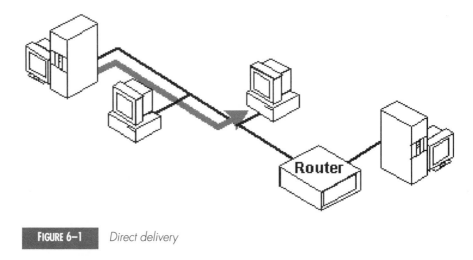

FIGURE 6–1   *Direct delivery*

If the destination host is located on the remote subnet, the computer forwards the packet to its configured default gateway. This is considered as an *indirect delivery*. If you intend to connect to remote subnets, you must configure your computer with the default gateway address. The default gateway IP address corresponds to the IP address of the router's interface to which your computer must send packets destined for other networks. Since routers are not transparent devices (in other words computers do not automatically become aware of routers), you must manually configure each Transmission Control Protocol/Internet Protocol (TCP/IP) host with the router IP address (default gateway address).

To configure a Windows 2000 computer with a default gateway address:

1. Launch **Control Panel**, double-click **Network** and **Dial-up Connections** from the **File** menu.
2. Double-click **Local Area Connection** and click **Properties**.
3. Select **Internet Protocol (TCP/IP)** and click **Properties** and enter the default gateway information in the appropriate field (see Figure 6-2).

Practical Application

You can configure your Windows 2000 computer with multiple default gateways. In order to do this,click Advanced on the Internet Protocol (TCP/IP) Properties dialog window and input additional default gateways in the TCP/IP Gateway Address dialog box. You can add up to five default gateways in this dialog box. As we'll see a bit later in this chapter, multiple default gateways are handy because when one fails, we can use one of the others.

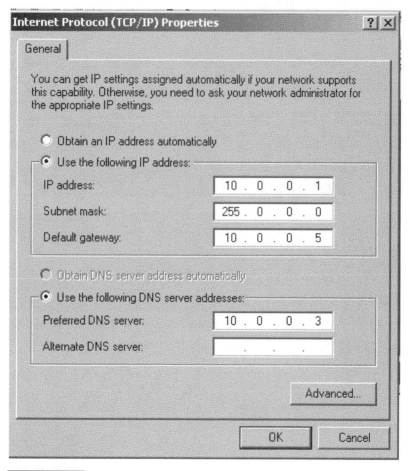

FIGURE 6–2 *Default gateway address configuration*

It's obvious that if a computer cannot deliver the packet directly, it forwards the packet to its default gateway. But what if there are several possible paths? In other words, what if there are several alternative routers to which an IP packet can be forwarded (see Figure 6-3)? In this case the computer has to decide in what direction a particular packet must go.

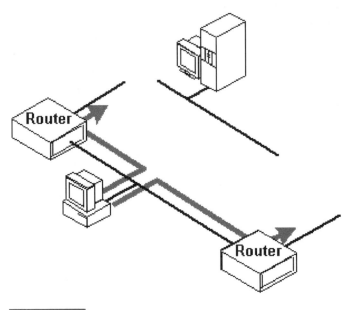

FIGURE 6–3   *The computer might have several ways to send the packet*

To make these decisions, the IP module of the host consults its *routing table*, which stores the preferable paths to remote subnets.

Routing Table

In TCP/IP networks, routing tables do not exist only on routers—every TCP/IP host has a routing table. The routing table consists of several entries, each of which symbolizes a path to a particular network or host. Figure 6-4 presents the structure of the routing table entry.

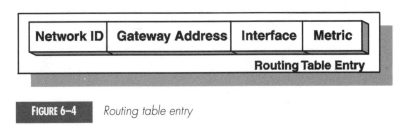

FIGURE 6–4   *Routing table entry*

NETWORK ID

The network ID field is the key point of the routing table entry. When a host consults its routing table for a path to the destination network, it compares the network ID with the destination IP address of the arrived packet header.

The network ID field is often represented by the IP address and subnet mask pair. For example the network ID of 172.20.0 will be represented by 172.20.0.0, mask 255.255.255.0.

GATEWAY ADDRESS

The gateway address field contains the address to which the packet destined to the given network is to be forwarded.

INTERFACE

The interface field represents the IP address of the host's interface (network adapter card) through which the packet will be forwarded. An important thing to check when ensuring that a routing table entry is correct is that the gateway address and the interface address have the same network ID.

METRIC

The metric field indicates the route cost. This field is useful when there are multiple routes to a given network. When several routes exist in the routing table, the route with the lowest metric will be chosen.

Metrics can be calculated using different preferences. For example, a most common metric type indicates the *hop count* or, in other words, the number of routers or networks that must be passed to reach the target network (see Figure 6-5).

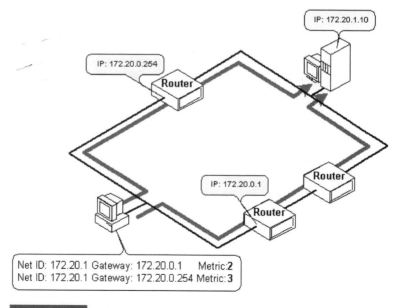

| Net ID: 172.20.1 Gateway: 172.20.0.1   Metric:2 |
| Net ID: 172.20.1 Gateway: 172.20.0.254 Metric:3 |

FIGURE 6–5   *The metric field in the routing table can indicate the number of hops to the given network*

The metric field can also express a delay, or a measure of time that is required for the packet to reach the destination network. In this case slow wide area network (WAN) links or congested networks will result in higher metrics and, therefore, will less likely be chosen by routers. Another good criterion for a metric value is the route's throughput.

The routing table entry also has a lifetime field to indicate the amount of time the route is considered valid. When the route entry's lifetime expires, the route is removed from the routing table. This provides a way for routers to conform to network changes.

Here is an example of a routing table:

```
Network Address Netmask          Gateway Address Interface     Metric
127.0.0.0       255.0.0.0        127.0.0.1       127.0.0.1     1
172.20.0.0      255.255.255.0    172.20.0.10     172.20.0.10   1
172.20.0.10     255.255.255.255  127.0.0.1       127.0.0.1     1
172.20.1.0      255.255.255.0    172.20.0.1      172.20.0.10   2
172.20.1.0      255.255.255.0    172.20.0.254    172.20.0.10   3
224.0.0.0       224.0.0.0        172.20.0.10     172.20.0.10   1
255.255.255.255 255.255.255.255  172.20.0.10     172.20.0.10   1
```

Note   The routing table lifetime field is typically not shown in routing table listings.

When you configure a Windows 2000 computer with a default gateway IP address, the new routing table entry for network ID 0.0.0.0 is added automatically. This is referred to as a *default route*. An example of a default route is:

```
0.0.0.0         0.0.0.0          172.20.0.1      172.20.0.10 1
```

Practical Application

To see your host routing table, type `route print` at the command prompt.

Does your routing table have default routes? Does the gateway address of the default route correspond with your computer's default gateway?

When a host wants to send an IP packet, it examines its routing table for the destination network ID. If a match is found, the host picks up the gateway's IP address and the IP address of the interface and sends the packet along the detected path. If no explicit route has been found, the host uses the default route to deliver the packet.

Let's trace the host's activity when it wants to send an IP packet to a remote host (see Figure 6-6).

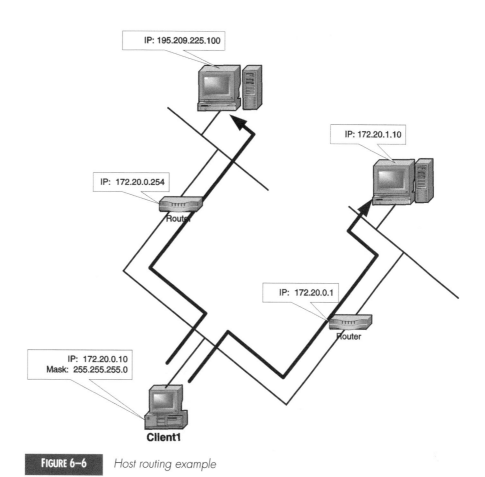

IP: 195.209.225.100

IP: 172.20.1.10

IP: 172.20.0.254

Router

IP: 172.20.0.1

Router

IP: 172.20.0.10
Mask: 255.255.255.0

Client1

FIGURE 6–6   *Host routing example*

Let's assume the routing table of the host contains the following entries:

```
Network Address Netmask         Gateway Address Interface    Metric
0.0.0.0         0.0.0.0         172.20.0.1      172.20.0.10 1
195.209.225.0   255.255.255.0   172.20.0.254    172.20.0.10 2
```

When computer CLIENT1 wants to send an IP packet to the computer with IP address 195.209.225.100, CLIENT1 checks its routing table. The second line of the routing table gives the path to the appropriate subnet. (Although route 0.0.0.0 is listed first, it will be used *only* if no explicit route for the target network is found.) The packet is forwarded to router 172.20.0.254 through interface 172.20.0.10. Later we will discuss how routers handle incoming packets.

When computer CLIENT1 wants to send an IP packet to 172.20.1.10, there is no explicit route in the routing table. In this case, the default route is used and the IP packet is forwarded to router 172.20.0.1.

TCP/IP Dead Gateway Detection

A Windows 2000 computer can be configured with multiple default gateways. Each default gateway is assigned an Interface Metric, and Windows 2000 selects the default gateway with the lowest metric. When the gateway with the lowest metric has failed, the TCP module makes the necessary adjustments to the routing table to use another default gateway. This is referred to as *dead gateway detection*.

Let's discuss how it works in Windows 2000. Suppose the TCP connection attempts to send a TCP packet through the first configured default gateway but receives no response because of router failure. After the TCP timeout value, subsequent connections will be attempted until the total number of attempts reaches one-half of the Registry value TCPMaxDataRetransmissions. (This value is a REG_DWORD entry and is found in HKEY_LOCAL_MACHINE\SYSTEM\CurrentControlSet\Services\Tcpip\Parameters\; the default is 5.) If no response has been received, the dead gateway detection algorithm switches to the next gateway in the list. If the original gateway comes up again, the algorithm does not use it. There are some implementations of dead gateway detection algorithms that are more cautious about advising the IP to switch gateways. With these algorithms, only the IP address that detects the unresponsive gateway is switched to the new gateway. Once 25 percent of the TCP connections have been moved to the next default gateway, the algorithm advises the IP to change the default gateway for the whole computer.

Default gateway detection is enabled by default on computers that have multiple default gateways configured. The Registry parameter that enables dead gateway detection can be found in HKEY_LOCAL_MACHINE\SYSTEM\CurrentControlSet\Services\Tcpip\Parameters\EnableDeadGWDetect.

Router's Decisions

When an IP packet arrives at the router's interface, the router first checks whether the packet is destined to the router itself. It does this by examining the destination IP address in the packet's header. If the destination IP address matches the router's IP address, the packet is passed to the next upper layer, TCP, for further processing.

In most cases, the packet is not destined for the router since routers do not normally provide high-level services. In this case the router must either deliver it to the destination host or forward the packet to another router.

If the destination network matches the network to which the router is attached this is considered a direct delivery. (When we say the router is attached to the network, we mean the router has at least one interface with an IP address from the network.) The router obtains the hardware address of the destination host through an ARP request, and forwards the IP packet to the destination host's physical address (see Figure 6-7).

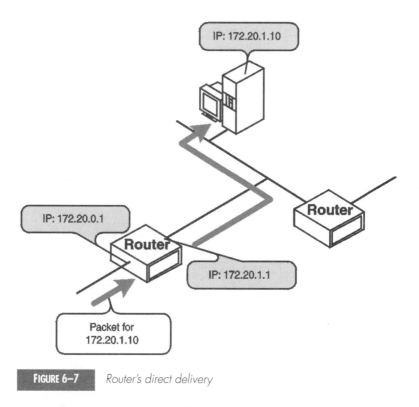

IP: 172.20.1.10

IP: 172.20.0.1

Router

Router

IP: 172.20.1.1

Packet for
172.20.1.10

FIGURE 6–7   *Router's direct delivery*

If the destination network is not directly attached, the router forwards
the IP packet to the next intermediate router. To do this the MAC address of
the intermediate router is obtained and the packet is sent to the intermediate
router's physical address—this is referred to as an indirect delivery of the IP
packet. (Before forwarding the packet to the intermediate router, the routing
table is consulted to find the best path to the target network (see Figure 6-8).)

Types of Routing

Now that we have discussed the basics of routing, you know that, before forwarding an IP packet, each TCP/IP device consults its routing table. Note that
all routing decisions are made based on the information in a local routing
table that physically resides on the system making the routing decision. That
means there is no single view of the internetwork. Each router and end host
makes its *own* routing decisions. This can cause the path taken from the
source to the destination to differ from the path taken from the destination
back to source.

For routing between networks to work correctly, routers and hosts must
have knowledge of other network IDs and preferred paths to those IDs or

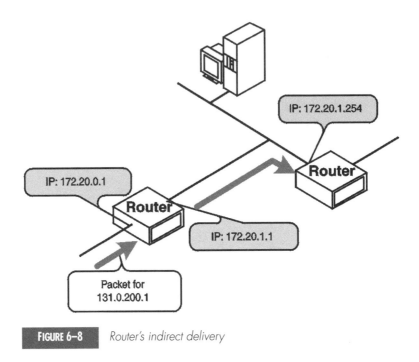

IP: 172.20.1.254

Router

IP: 172.20.0.1

Router

IP: 172.20.1.1

Packet for
131.0.200.1

FIGURE 6–8   *Router's indirect delivery*

they must be configured with a default route. On large enterprise networks, the routing tables must be configured such that network traffic travels along optimal paths. If a new network is added, it must be reflected in all routing tables, so every computer can reach it. There must be, therefore, a mechanism to permit routers and hosts to exchange routing information. Without such a mechanism, network administrators will have to modify the routing tables manually to reflect network topology changes, such as the addition of a new network segment.

Static Routing

A router that does not exchange routing table information with other routers is known as a *static* router. The routing table of a static router is constructed manually. A network administrator, based on his/her knowledge of the internetwork topology, manually builds and updates the routing table by explicitly defining all routes or using default route entries.

By default, a static router can communicate only with networks to which it has a configured interface. For example, in Figure 6-9 static Router A can send IP packets only to its adjoining networks. Shaded areas are unreachable for Router A and thus Computer 1 cannot communicate with Computer 2 with the current network configuration.

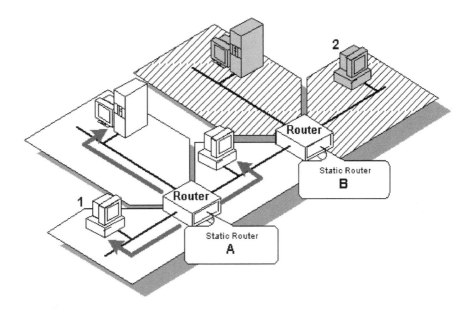

FIGURE 6–9 *Static router behavior*

To route packets to other networks, each static router must be manually configured with a route for each network in the internetwork. Manual configuration of every routing table entry can be very time-consuming. You can alternatively configure a static router with a default route. This can be illustrated by the following example. We'll configure static routes in one direction and a default route in the other direction. (Either solution will work, of course, for either direction.)

To route IP packets to network 172.20.5.0 (See Figure 6-10.) a static routing table entry must be created on Router A:

```
Network Address Netmask          Gateway Address Interface   Metric
172.20.5.0      255.255.255.0    172.20.3.254    172.20.3.1  2
```

This routing table entry specifies that in order to reach network 127.20.5.0, mask 255.255.255.0 the packet must be sent to 172.20.3.254 through interface 172.20.3.1. When Router B receives packets destined to network 172.20.5.0, it can deliver it directly since it has a configured interface in that network.

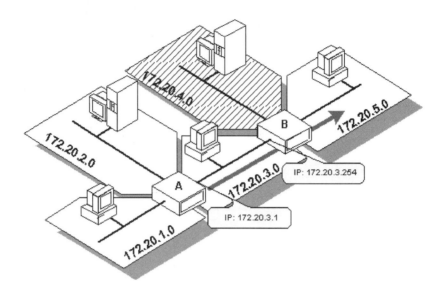

To reach the remote network a static route must be created (1)

To reach network 172.20.4.0 (see Figure 6-11), the second static routing table entry must be added on Router A:

Network Address	Netmask	Gateway Address	Interface	Metric
172.20.4.0	255.255.255.0	172.20.3.254	172.20.3.1	2

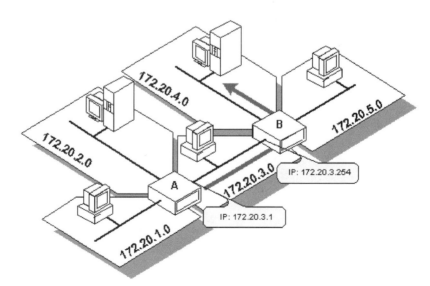

To reach the remote network a static route must be created (2)

The next step is to configure Router B so that it can route packets to networks 172.20.1.0 and 172.20.2.0. To demonstrate another approach, let's configure a default route on Router B. (Of course we could have created two static routes to networks 172.20.1.0 and 172.20.2.0 instead of specifying the default route.)

```
Network Address Netmask        Gateway Address Interface    Metric
0.0.0.0         0.0.0.0        172.20.3.1      172.20.3.254 1
```

In this example, for hosts to communicate with other hosts on the internetwork, their default gateway address must be configured to match the IP address of the nearest router interface.

Configuring a Windows 2000 Server Computer to Function as a Static IP Router

Windows 2000 has the built-in ability to function as a static IP router. The static IP router can be enabled by creating a multihomed system and enabling IP forwarding in the registry.

Note

The preferred method for creating a Windows 2000 router is through Routing and Remote Access Services (RRAS), which we will explore in Chapter 14. The procedure described below, however, is a simple, one-step procedure to enable a Windows 2000 computer to provide a basic static routing capability.

Multihoming

There are two kinds of multihoming: Multiple Network Interface Cards (NICs) and multiple IP addresses per NIC. Additional IP addresses can be added through the **Advanced** button of the TCP/IP properties sheet.

Practical Application

To configure a Windows 2000 computer to function as a static router you must:

1. Install multiple network adapter cards and appropriate drivers or configure multiple IP addresses on a single card.

2. Configure each adapter with a valid IP address and subnet mask in the TCP/IP Properties dialog box.

3. Open **Registry Editor** (type **regedt32** in the command prompt) and navigate to the following registry key:

HKEY_LOCAL_MACHINE\SYSTEM\CurrentControlSet\ Services\Tcpip \Parameters

4. Select the following entry:

IPEnableRouter: REG_DWORD: 0x0

Double-click and assign a value of **1**. This will enable IP forwarding for all network connections installed and used by this computer (see Figure 6-12).

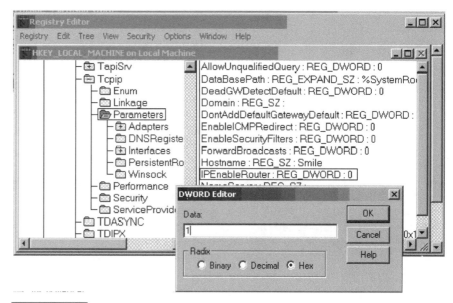

FIGURE 6–12   *Enable IP routing*

After doing this, you will need to add static routes or a default route to remote networks using the ROUTE add command (which we will cover shortly) in order to communicate with remote networks. One method of configuring a static route without manually adding routes to a routing table is to configure a multihomed computer's default gateway address as the local interface of the next router (see Figure 6-13).

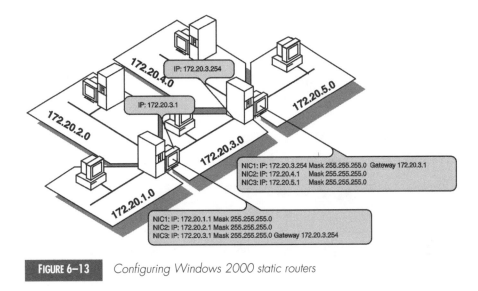

FIGURE 6–13   *Configuring Windows 2000 static routers*

Note that in the TCP/IP configuration, you can add a default route for each network card. This will create a 0.0.0.0 route for each. Only one default route, however, will actually be used.

Modifying the Routing Table

So far, we've discussed how the routing table should look, but haven't discussed how to create or change one. In Windows 2000 the ROUTE command is used to add, delete, and modify static entries in the routing table. Table 6.1 shows the ROUTE command syntax:

TABLE 6.1   *ROUTE Command*

Syntax	Description
ROUTE add [network] MASK [netmask] [gateway]	Adds a route to the routing table
ROUTE -p add [network] MASK [netmask] [gateway]	Adds a persistent route
ROUTE delete [network] [gateway]	Deletes a route from the routing table
ROUTE change [network] [gateway]	Modifies a route
ROUTE print	Displays the routing table
ROUTE -f	Clears all routes

For example, to configure static Routers A and B from our recent discussion (refer to Figures 6-10 and 6-11), you can use the following sequence of commands:

```
Router A:
route add 172.20.5.0 MASK 255.255.255.0 172.20.3.254
route add 172.20.4.0 MASK 255.255.255.0 172.20.3.254

Router B:
route add 0.0.0.0 MASK 0.0.0.0 172.20.3.1
```

Persistent Routes

Static routes are stored in memory and are deleted when the computer is restarted. To preserve routes use the –p parameter. Persistent routes are stored in the Windows 2000 registry. If you want to always route to a particular machine for a given network, you'll need to make your routing entry persistent. On the other hand, you may wish to purge your routing information if you've changed some routes in your local network and wish to repopulate the route entries on your computer.

Practical Application

1. To view your computer's routing table, launch the command prompt and type `route print`. Do you have default routes? If yes, record the default gateway address.

   _____

2. Type `route add 10.0.0.0 MASK 255.255.0.0` *your_default_gateway.*
3. Type `route print`. Do you have a route to network 10.0?
4. To change a route, type `route change 10.0.0.0` *another_host_from_your_network.*
5. Type `route print` to view the routing table. Which gateway does the route to 10.0 have?
6. To delete an unneeded route, type `route delete 10.0.0.0`.
7. Type `route print` and verify that the route has been deleted.

Dynamic Routing

Although static routers can work well on small networks, static networks are not suited to large, dynamic environments. Static routers are not fault tolerant—if a network link goes down, a static router cannot automatically update its routing table and provide an alternative path for IP packets. It's time to look at *dynamic routers.*

A router with dynamically configured routing tables is known as a dynamic router. Dynamic routers have their routing tables built and maintained automatically by communicating with other dynamic routers. Dynamic routers automatically exchange update messages with routes to known networks. If Routers A and B in Figure 6-11 were dynamic routers, no additional configuration would be needed for all subnets to communicate.

Dynamic routers are fault tolerant. The dynamic routing table entries learned from other routers have a finite lifetime and must be constantly updated to be valid. If a network link goes down, update messages stop coming and the associated routing table entries expire. When the routing table entry expires, the router does not send IP packets along the failed path. These changes are propagated to other dynamic routers. Using these procedures, dynamic routers sense the internetwork topology through the discovery and expiration of learned routes.

Dynamic routing relies on special routing protocols such as Routing Information Protocol (RIP) or Open Shortest Path First (OSPF).

Routing Internet Protocol

RIP for IP is used by dynamic routers to exchange routing information on an IP internetwork. RIP relies on the User Datagram Protocol (UDP) to forward route announcements. All RIP messages are sent over UDP port 520. A RIP-enabled router sends broadcast messages containing network IDs of the networks it—the router—can reach and the distance (hop count) to these networks. Each time a RIP router receives a network ID announcement, it increases the hop count value, updates its routing table, and advertises the learned router to any intermediate routers. The maximum hop count for RIP is 15—networks requiring a greater number of hops are considered unreachable.

Note   Not all RIP-enabled routers send out RIP packets. A RIP router that receives RIP broadcasts but does not propagate any RIP messages is known as a *silent RIP* router.

Figure 6-14 shows the Network Monitor capture of RIP packets. Note that each RIP packet can carry several network ID announcements.

Although RIP can work well in small- and medium-size networks with a small number of routers, it is not suitable for large enterprises. The following features of RIP make it a less desirable solution for large networks:

- The maximum RIP packet size is 512 bytes—large routing tables have to be sent as multiple RIP packets.

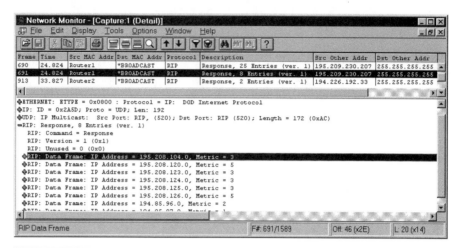

FIGURE 6–14   *RIP broadcasts*

- A RIP-enabled router sends RIP packets every 30 seconds through all attached interfaces. Since RIP uses MAC-level broadcasts, large routing tables can create a significant impact on network throughput. This is especially problematic on slow WAN links (for example, dial-up connections) where RIP packets can take large portions of bandwidth.

- Each routing table entry learned through RIP is given a three-minute timeout. If no update message is received, the entry is removed from the routing table after that period has elapsed. When a link problem develops, it can take several minutes before the router discovers the problem and even longer before the topology change is propagated to the rest of network. This feature is often referred to as a *slow convergence.*

- RIP networks cannot be farther than 15 hops from each other. Since RIP packets have 15 as the maximum hop count, networks that require a greater number of hops are considered unreachable.

To overcome these limitations other routing protocols can be used. For example, Windows 2000 Server includes support for routing protocol OSPF.

Open Shortest Path First

OSPF is an Internet Engineering Task Force (IETF) standard link-state routing protocol used for IP routing. OSPF is a more sophisticated routing protocol than RIP. Developed in response to the inability of RIP to serve large, heterogeneous internetworks, OSPF is a link-state protocol based on the Shortest Path First (SPF) algorithm, which sometimes is referred to as the Dijkstra algorithm. This algorithm computes the shortest path between one source node and the other nodes in the network.

OSPF calls for the sending of *link-state advertisements* (LSAs) to all other routers within the same hierarchical area. Information on attached interfaces, metrics used, and other variables are included in OSPF LSAs. As OSPF routers accumulate link-state information, they use the SPF algorithm to calculate the shortest path to each node.

As a link-state routing protocol, OSPF contrasts with RIP and Interior Gateway Routing Protocol (IGRP), which are distance-*vector* routing protocols. Routers running the distance-vector algorithm send all or a portion of their routing tables in routing-update messages to their neighbors.

Unlike RIP, OSPF can operate within a hierarchy. The largest entity within the hierarchy is the *autonomous system* (AS), which is a collection of networks under a common administration that share a common routing strategy. OSPF is an intra-AS routing protocol. OSPF is capable, however, of receiving routes from and sending routes to other ASs.

Additional OSPF features include equal-cost, *multipath routing,* and routing based on upper-layer *type-of-service* (TOS) requests. TOS-based routing supports those upper-layer protocols that can specify particular types of service. An application, for example, might specify that certain data is urgent. If OSPF has high-priority links at its disposal, these can be used to transport the urgent datagram.

OSPF supports one or more metrics. If only one metric is used, it is considered to be arbitrary, and TOS is not supported. If more than one metric is used, TOS is optionally supported through the use of a separate metric (and, therefore, a separate routing table) for each of the eight combinations created by the three IP TOS bits (*delay, throughput,* and *reliability*). If, for example, the IP TOS bits specify low delay, low throughput, and high reliability, OSPF calculates routes to all destinations based on this TOS designation.

IP subnet masks are included with each advertised destination, enabling *variable-length subnet masks.* With variable-length subnet masks, an IP network can be broken into many subnets of various sizes. This provides network administrators with extra network-configuration flexibility.

Windows 2000 Computer as a Dynamic Router

A computer running Windows 2000 can be configured as a dynamic router by installing the OSPF or the RIP for IP service. We will cover the actual installation of these services in Chapter 14, "Routing and Remote Access Service."

Static and Dynamic Routers in the Same Network

A static router does not exchange routing information with dynamic routers. This can cause potential problems in environments where static and dynamic routers are used together. To solve the problem, you must add static routes to the routing tables of both the static and dynamic routes (see Figure 6-15). The procedure for configuring static routes on a RIP router will vary with each type of RIP router. Figure 6-15 assumes the RIP router is Windows 2000-based and can be configured using the ROUTE command.

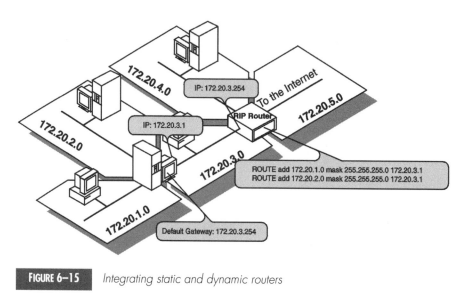

| FIGURE 6–15 | *Integrating static and dynamic routers* |

Important   Some RIP implementations do not propagate static routes. For the network in Figure 6-15 to be visible from the Internet, you may need to configure static routes on remote routers as well.

Using the TRACERT Utility to Verify IP Routes

The TRACERT command is a route-tracing utility used to determine the path that an IP packet has taken to reach a destination. The TRACERT utility is useful for determining route problems such as routing table errors, slow routers, and router malfunction. TRACERT has the functionality of the PING utility but goes further to display the path taken by the packet to the destination computer. The TRACERT command can be used to determine where a packet stopped on the network. Following is an example of the TRACERT output:

```
C:\WINDOWS>tracert www.ru

Tracing route to www.ru [194.87.12.23]
over a maximum of 30 hops:

1    40 ms     80 ms     <10 ms   gw.csa.ru [194.226.192.33]
2    <10 ms    10 ms     10 ms    2048K.RUN.NET [194.85.165.169]
3    10 ms     <10 ms    10 ms    bbn-spb-gw.runnet.ru [194.85.36.30]
4    10 ms     10 ms     20 ms    Moscow-M9-IX-T0.RUN.NET [193.232.80.246]
```

```
5   41 ms   20 ms   20 ms   M9-IX-100M.demos.NET [193.232.244.35]
6   194.87.0.1 reports: Destination net unreachable.
Trace complete.
```

The output's first column is the Time To Live (TTL) value set by TRAC-ERT (as we'll soon see, this is actually a hop count). The next three columns show round-trip times in milliseconds for three attempts to reach the destination with the set TTL. An asterisk (*) means that the attempt timed out. The fifth column is the host name (if it was resolved) and IP address of the resource that replied to the TRACERT packet.

Note   TRACERT is a standard TCP/IP utility for route checking. In some operating systems it is known as TRACEROUTE.

The TRACERT utility determines the route taken to the destination host by sending ICMP messages with varying TTL values. As you may remember, each router must decrease the value in the TTL field by at least 1 and, when the new TTL reaches 0, the router discards the packet and sends the ICMP Time Exceeded message. In practice, the TTL is the hop count a packet can go before it is discarded. The TRACERT command utilizes this feature and starts by sending an ICMP packet with TTL = 1. The first router to receive this packet decreases the TTL value and (since the new TTL now equals 0) discards the packet and returns an ICMP Time Exceeded message. The TRACERT utility receives the ICMP Time Exceeded message and displays the first router in the trace list. The TRACERT increments the TTL by 1 on each subsequent transmission until the target responds or the maximum TTL (hop count) is reached.

Note   Some routers do not send ICMP Time Exceeded messages but drop IP packets with the zero TTLs silently. Such routers are invisible to the TRACERT utility.

Practical Application

To check the route to your default gateway type `tracert your_default_gateway.`

How many hops are there between your computer and your default gateway?

To check the route to www.alidatrain.com type `tracert www.alidatrain.com.`

How far is www.microsoft.com?

Summary

This chapter introduced some important routing concepts. You learned that routing functions are not only performed by routers but also by host computers. When a host makes routing decisions we refer to it as host routing. We saw that direct delivery occurs when a TCP/IP host or a router can deliver the packet itself. We compared direct delivery to indirect delivery, which occurs when a packet must be forwarded to an intermediate router. Hosts and routers make forwarding decisions based on their local routing tables. We studied routing table entries and learned the purpose of the network ID, gateway, and metric fields. We discussed the concept of the default gateway and how it is used by the routing table. You may remember that configuring a computer with a default gateway address adds the special default route (0.0.0.0) to the host's routing table. When multiple default gateways have been configured on a particular Windows 2000 computer, the host can take advantage of the TCP dead gateway detection algorithm and automatically switch to the next gateway when the primary one is unavailable. We mentioned that a computer running Windows 2000 can be configured as a static router by installing multiple network adapter cards and enabling IP forwarding. It was pointed out that static routes must be added in order to communicate with remote networks. We also saw that a Windows 2000 computer can act as a dynamic router. To implement dynamic routing on a Windows 2000 machine, OSPF or RIP for Internet Protocol Service must be installed. We reviewed the primary features of the RIP and saw that RIP wasn't a desirable solution in large dynamic networks because of its broadcast nature and nontrivial impact on network performance. Finally, we learned how to modify a Windows 2000 routing table and demonstrated the use of the TRACERT utility.

Test Yourself

1. What is the purpose of a default gateway?
2. What command is used to view a machine's routing table?
   A. route view
   B. route print
   C. show route
   D. routing table
3. Installing dynamic routing on one router will update all static routers in your network and permit them to participate in dynamic routing.
   A. True
   B. False

4. The metric field in a routing table is used to:
   A. Compute the actual cost of transmission for each route
   B. Determine the best route to use when multiple routes are available
   C. Ensure consistent routing in the United States and Europe
   D. Track the amount of time the entry will remain valid (before it is deleted from the table)

5. The Routing Information Protocol is widely used by Internet routers.
   A. True
   B. False

Automatic Private IP Addressing and DHCP

*W**hile configuring a few machines with Internet Protocol (IP) addresses can be a moderately tedious task, the management of configuring a large number of client and server computers properly can quickly become a nightmare. Even minor errors in IP addresses and subnet masks can cause a machine to become unavailable to the network. Duplicate IP addresses can bring down every machine with the duplicate address or possibly the entire network. In addition to duplicate IP addresses problems, the physical movement of computers can cause other inconsistencies. Simply connecting a computer to a new wire can place it on a subnet it's not configured for—once again causing its network functions to cease.*

Note

Microsoft Transport Control Protocol/Internet Protocol (TCP/IP) mitigates the duplicate address problem by sending an *Address Resolution Protocol* (ARP) broadcast prior to initializing the TCP/IP stack. If another machine responds (indicating the address is already in use), the address is not initialized on the new machine. Additionally, each machine receives a duplicate IP address warning.

When configuring a computer to use TCP/IP we also need to configure a number of other features. Incorrect settings for *Windows Internet Naming Service* (WINS), *Domain Name System* (DNS), and *default gateway* can occur through machine movement or reconfiguration and can result in disastrous network consequences. Keeping track of all these factors on a large number of computers could quickly take all the network administrator's time. Even a relatively minor network change (such as the introduction of a new WINS server) could require the reconfiguration of a large number of workstations with the attendant possibility of misconfiguration and network paralysis.

Before you head for the Internet to find another line of work, take heart! Windows 2000 features *Automatic Private IP Addressing* (APIPA) and the *dynamic host configuration protocol* (DHCP). Although it won't provide information on default gateways, DNS servers, or other network services, APIPA permits a Windows 2000 machine to automatically select a unique IP address and subnet mask without the assistance of other network resources. The DHCP can be installed on one or more machines in your network to permit the automatic and centralized administration and configuration of a number of critical TCP/IP factors (including all those mentioned previously). DHCP was developed as a cooperative effort between vendors and the *Internet Engineering Task Force*. It is covered under the following *Requests for Comment* (RFCs): 1533, 1534, 1541, 1542, 2131, and 2132. DHCP works by "leasing" an IP address to a client for a specified period of time. When the client "signs" the lease, the DHCP server can throw in a number of options, such as WINS and DNS addresses and default gateways, at no additional charge!

Automatic Private IP Addressing

APIPA works by using blocks of IP addresses reserved by the Internet for use by private networks. This allows computers on IP version 4 networks to have unique addresses automatically assigned to them with no effort on the part of a user or administrator. You can plug computers and peripherals such as printers and scanners into a device such as an Ethernet hub. Each node is given a unique IP address, while you can separately assign the device a simple friendly name.

APIPA uses an algorithm to guarantee that each address used is unique to a single host on the private network. Although the IP addresses use a block of address space that can't be accessed across the Internet, APIPA-addressed hosts can be connected to the Internet through the use of a Network Address Translator (NAT), or an Internet proxy server such as Microsoft Proxy Server.

The APIPA Process

If a TCP/IP client host is installed and set to obtain TCP/IP protocol configuration information automatically, the machine's DHCP client service is engaged each time the computer is restarted. The DHCP client service uses a two-step process to configure the client with an IP address and other configuration information.

When the client host is installed, it attempts to locate a DHCP server and obtain configuration from it. If the attempt to locate a DHCP server fails, the Windows 2000 DHCP client autoconfigures with a selected IP address from the IANA-reserved Class B network 169.254.0.0 with a subnet mask 255.255.0.0. Then, using a gratuitous Address Resolution Protocol (ARP), the DHCP client tests to make sure that the IP address that it has chosen is not in use. If it is in use, it selects another IP address and does this for up to 10 addresses until a unique address in obtained.

Note

IP autoconfiguration can be disabled using the *IPAutoconfigurationEnabled* registry key. The subnet and subnet mask used can be controlled using the *IPAutoconfigurationSubnet* and *IPAutoconfigurationMask* registry keys

A "gratuitous" ARP broadcast refers to a broadcast by a computer to request a media access control (MAC) address mapping for its own IP address. If it receives a response, it knows it's attempting to employ an IP address already in use by another machine.

Once the DHCP client has selected an address that is verifiably not in use, it configures the interface with this address. It continues to check for a DHCP server in the background every five minutes. If a DHCP server is found, the APIPA autoconfiguration information is abandoned, and the configuration offered by the DHCP server is used instead.

The DHCP Process

The choreography between a DHCP client and a DHCP server is a four-step process that permits the allocation and confirmation of important TCP/IP configuration information:

1. During the start-up process, the client computer initializes with a NULL IP address and broadcasts a DHCPDISCOVER message containing its, hardware address and computer name, to request an IP address from any DHCP server. (At this point the machine knows no valid TCP/IP parameters so it uses 0.0.0.0 as the source address and 255.255.255.255 as the destination address of the DHCPDISCOVER message.)

2. Any DHCP server that receives the DHCPDISCOVER broadcast and that has available valid configuration information for the client will respond with a DHCPOFFER message. Since the client still doesn't have an IP address at this point, the DHCPOFFER is sent via broadcast. The message contains the client's hardware address, an IP address offer, an appropriate subnet mask, the IP address of the server making the offer, and the

lease duration. When the offer is made, the DHCP server marks the offered IP address as unavailable to prevent it from being offered to another client pending the original client's decision to take the lease.

3. The client selects one of the DHCP offers (normally the first one it receives) and responds with a DHCPREQUEST message. This message contains the IP address of the selected DHCP server as well as a request for additional configuration information (e.g., WINS server address, DNS server address, etc). Because the client's TCP/IP protocol is still not fully initialized, this message is also sent via broadcast. Since the DHCPRE-QUEST broadcast is received by all the DHCP servers who originally responded to the DHCPDISCOVER broadcast, the unselected servers are able to determine that their offers were rejected (by examining the message for the IP address of the *selected* server). Rejected servers then mark the IP addresses they offered as available.

4. The selected DHCP server responds with a DHCPACK (acknowledgement) message containing a lease for the accepted IP address and any other configuration parameters that might be available. This message is also sent via broadcast but, once it is received, the TCP/IP initialization is completed on the client. With initialization complete, the client machine is considered a *Bound DHCP Client,* which will be able to use TCP/IP for network communications.

If a Windows 2000-based DHCP client is unable to locate a DHCP server at boot-up, it will configure itself using APIPA unless it already has an unexpired DHCP lease. When in possession of an unexpired lease, the client attempts to ping the default gateway previously obtained in the lease. If the ping fails, the machine assumes it has been moved to a network that has no available DHCP services and configures through APIPA. Once configured, the machine continues to try to find a DHCP server every five minutes. If APIPA has been disabled, the client will continue to use an existing lease if it has one. If there is no current lease or if the lease expires before a DHCP server can be located, TCP/IP communication ceases and the client attempts to find a DHCP server every five minutes until a new lease is obtained.

Tip

Although the steps outlined above may seem fairly complex, they can be reduced to four short lines:
— IP Lease Request
— IP Lease Offer
— IP Lease Selection
— IP Lease Acknowledgement

DHCP Lease Duration

DHCP leases may be assigned for a duration as short as one minute; as long as 999 days, 23 hours, and 59 minutes; or may be assigned for an unlimited duration. When half of the client's lease period has elapsed, the client will attempt to renew the lease with the original DHCP server. If the server responds with a DHCPACK message, the lease is renewed and the client continues to use the originally assigned parameters. If the server responds with a DHCPNACK (negative acknowledgement) message, the client is forced to send a DHCPDISCOVER broadcast and seek a new lease. If the original server doesn't respond, the client will continue to attempt to contact that machine until its lease is 7/8 (87.5%) complete. Once past the 7/8 point, the client will broadcast to any DHCP server in an attempt to renew its current lease. Any server can respond with a DHCPACK to renew or a DHCPNACK to force negotiation of a new lease. If the client fails to renew or renegotiate a lease prior to the expiration time of its current lease it will lose its capability to use TCP/IP until it can obtain a new lease.

Note   When a lease expires, the server granting the lease actually keeps the lease marked as leased and unavailable for an additional 24 hours from the expiration time. This delay protects the lease if the client is in a time zone different from the DHCP server and the two computers' clocks are not synchronized. It also allows for the situation where the lease expired when the client was off the network.

When a DHCP client is shut down it retains its lease.[2] When the machine is restarted it attempts to renew the lease. If it receives a DHCPACK, the lease is renewed. A DHCPNACK will force the negotiation of a new lease. If the client gets neither a DHCPACK nor a DHCPNACK it will revert to APIPA or continue to use the existing lease as detailed in the previous section.

Installing DHCP on a Windows 2000 Server

All this discussion of DHCP won't do anyone any good unless a DHCP server is actually installed, configured, and available on the network. To that end, let's take some time and install one. Any Windows 2000 Server can be configured as a DHCP server. The machine MUST have a static IP Address and sub-

---

2. The lease information is retained in the registry for Windows 2000/NT/Windows9x and in DHCP.BIN for Windows for Workgroups or DOS clients.

net mask. Additionally, if DHCP is running on a network with no DHCP relay agents and with routers that do not support RFC 1542, a DHCP server is required on each subnet. (RFC 1542 and DHCP Relay Agents will be discussed later in this chapter.)

The installation of a DHCP server is done through the Windows Component Wizard:

- Open Control Panel, double-click **Add/Remove Programs**, and then click **Add/Remove Windows Components.**
- Click **Components**, then scroll to and select **Networking Services** (see Figure 7-1).

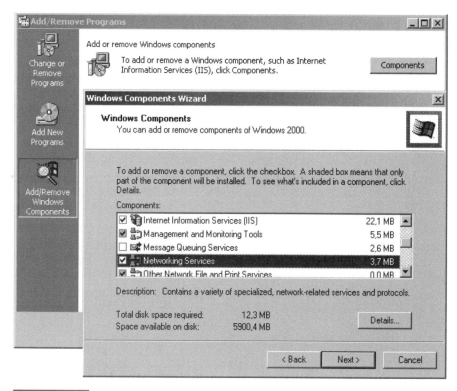

FIGURE 7-1 *Windows Components Wizard*

- Click **Details**.
  - Under **Subcomponents of Networking Services**, click **Dynamic Host Configuration Protocol (DHCP)**, and then click **OK** (see Figure 7-2.)

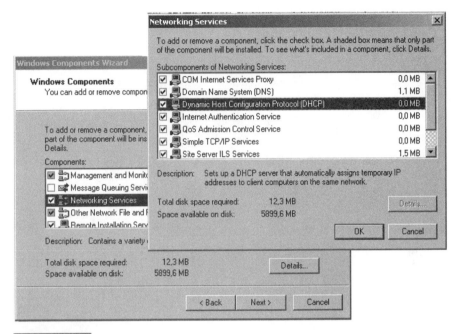

Selecting Dynamic Host Configuration Protocol

- If prompted, type the full path to the Windows 2000 distribution files and click **Continue**.

In this case, required files will be copied to your hard disk. You can start using server software after restarting the system.

Configuring DHCP Scopes and Options

Once we have installed DHCP, we still need to configure a *scope* and options for it to do us any good. DHCP server configuration is accomplished through the *DHCP* console program, accessible through *Administrative Tools* in the **Start** menu.

Adding a Scope

A *scope* is simply a range (or pool) of IP addresses and a subnet mask that the DHCP server can lease to its clients. The scope also includes the lease duration and an optional name and comment. Each DHCP server must have at least one scope. Each scope on the server can represent a pool of IP

addresses for one and only one subnet (although the server may be configured with scopes for several different subnets).

To add a scope, open the *DHCP* console through the *Administrative
Tools* menu option. By default, DHCP console gets aligned with your local
server and automatically detects your IP address (see Figure 7-3).

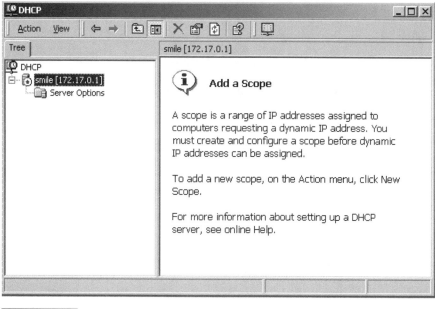

| **FIGURE 7–3** | *DHCP console* |

Next, click on the **Action** menu and select **New Scope** to reveal the
New Scope Wizard dialog box (see Figure 7-4). Enter the scope's name and
description and click *Next*.

Under *IP Address Range*, enter the starting and ending IP addresses you
wish to place in your scope as well as the appropriate subnet mask for the
scope's subnet (see Figure 7-5). Click *Next*.

If you have some IP addresses within the scope that are not to be given
out to DHCP clients[3], you can enter the starting and ending addresses of the
excluded range in the *Add Exclusions* window and click **Add** to enter the
range in the *Excluded address range* box. You may enter several ranges of
excluded addresses if required (this is not a mandatory entry) (see Figure 7-
6). Click *Next*.

---

3. This may be because the scope contains IP addresses that have already been assigned to non-
   DHCP clients as static addresses.

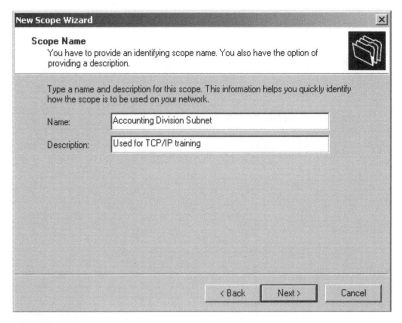

New scope wizard. Providing a new scope name.

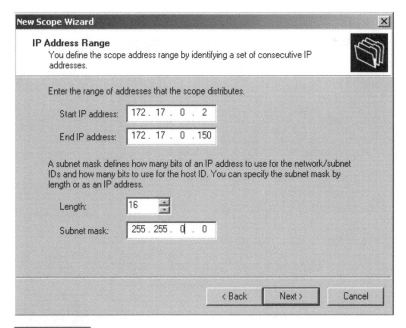

Defining scope IP address range

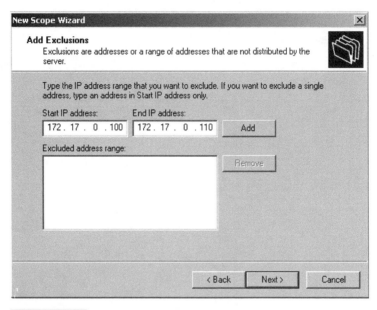

FIGURE 7-6   *Adding scope exclusions range*

In the *Lease Duration* window, enter the desired values for **Day(s)**, **Hour(s)**, and **Minute(s)** before the lease must be renewed (see Figure 7-7). Click *Next*.

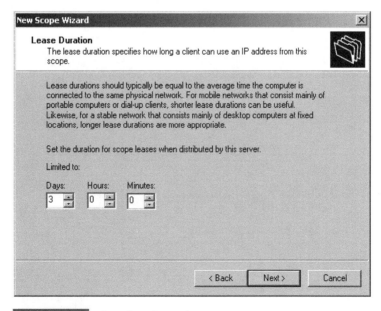

FIGURE 7-7   *Specifying lease duration*

The new scope is now visible in the DHCP manager screen as shown in Figure 7-8. As currently configured, the server will be available, when started, to provide IP addresses and subnet masks to any DHCP client that asks for an IP address on the subnet covered by the scope we just created. Although DHCP servers would be quite useful if they provided only IP addresses, their capability to provide additional TCP/IP information further reduces the burden of TCP/IP administration. To configure this additional information, we must set DHCP options.

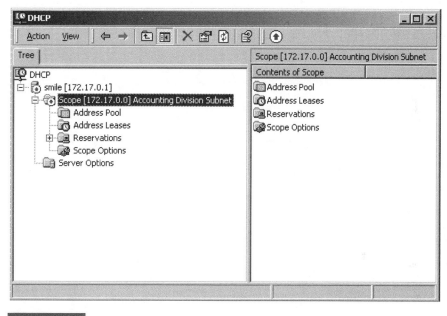

FIGURE 7–8   *New scope is created*

Note   DHCP also allows you to define a *multicast scope*. Ordinarily, you use DHCP scopes to provide client configurations by allocating ranges of IP addresses from the standard address classes (Class A, B, or C). By using DHCP scopes, you can assign IP addresses from the ranges provided by these addresses for your DHCP clients to be configured to use unicast (or point-to-point) directed communication between other TCP/IP networked computers. The multicast address range uses an additional address class, Class D, that includes IP addresses that range from 224.0.0.0 to 239.255.255.255 for use in IP multicasting. Addresses in this class are used for multicasting only and not for regular DHCP scopes.

Configuring DHCP Options

Now that you have set the IP address and subnet mask information for your clients, you'll want to take advantage of DHCP to provide other TCP/IP configuration settings. You can configure options through the *DHCP* console **Action** → **Configure Options** menu. Windows 2000 allows you to manage DHCP options at several levels:

- **Server options.** Here you can assign values for options that should apply by default to or be inherited by *all* scopes and clients of the DHCP server, unless otherwise overridden (See Figure 7-9).

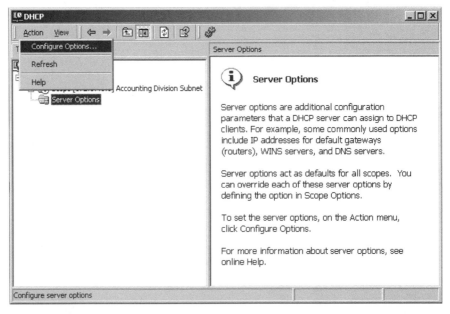

FIGURE 7–9   *Configuring server options*

- **Scope options.** Here you can assign values (using the **General** tab) for options that should apply only to clients of an applicable scope selected in the DHCP console tree (see Figure 7-10).
- **Client options.** You may assign values for options that apply only to a specific *reserved* DHCP client. To use this level of assignment, you must first add a reservation for the applicable client (as explained shortly).
- **Class options.** When using any of the option configuration dialog boxes (**Server Options** or **Scope Options**), you can click the **Advanced** tab of the applicable dialog box to configure and enable options for assignment to identifying member clients of a specified user or vendor class.

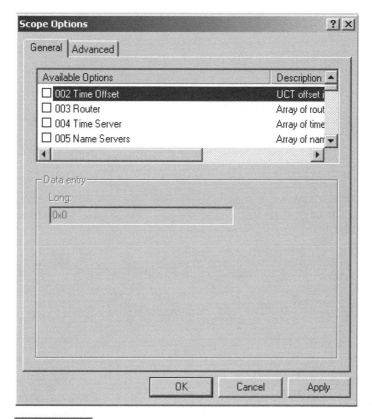

FIGURE 7–10   *Scope options configuration window*

Depending on the context, only those DHCP clients that identify themselves according to the selected class are given data you have configured for that class.

COMMON DHCP OPTIONS

Although DHCP permits the configuration of a myriad of options, we'll limit our discussion to the following common options:

- **Routers.** The use of this option is required to provide clients with one or more default gateways. (Only one will be used; lower priority gateways will be accessed if the primary gateway is unavailable.)
- **DNS servers.** IP addresses for DNS name servers that DHCP clients can contact and use to resolve a domain host name query.
- **WINS node type.** A preferred NetBIOS name resolution method for the DHCP client to use (such as B-node for broadcast only or H-node for a hybrid of point-to-point and broadcast methods).
- **WINS server.** IP addresses of primary and secondary WINS servers for the DHCP client to use.

ROUTER

A *router* (default gateway) can permit the client to seek contact with machines not on its subnet. Since the address of a router is subnet specific, we will add the router as a scope option.

In the *DHCP* console tree select **Scope Options**, then go to the **Action → Configure Options** menu. In the list of **Available Options**, select the check box for **003 Router** and type the router's IP address under **Data entry** (as shown in Figure 7-11).

Click **Add** to add this option to the list and click **OK** to exit the *Scope Options* dialog window and the router option is complete. Additional routers may be specified. The one at the top of the list will be the primary Default Gateway; the others will be used if the primary one is unavailable. To adjust their priority of use, move them up or down the list with the **Up** and **Down** buttons.

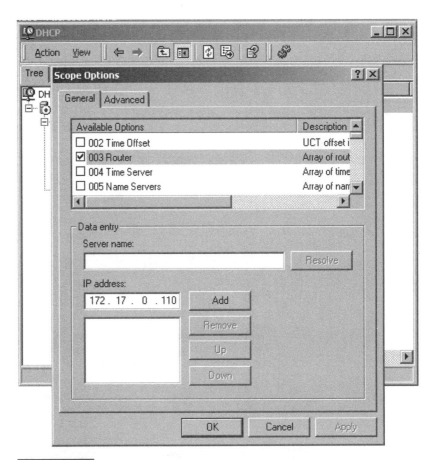

FIGURE 7–11   *Adding a router*

DNS SERVER

Installation of the DNS server option is very similar to adding a router. Since the address of our DNS server will be applicable to all subnets we will install it as a *Server Option*. In the *DHCP* console tree, select **Server Options**, then go to the **Action → Configure Options** menu to open the *Server Options* window and select option **006 DNS Servers.** Enter the IP address of the DNS server. Next, click **Add** and then **OK** to apply the setting. The DNS server appears now in both the *Scope Options* and *Server Options* windows.

WINS SERVER

Setting options for a WINS server is a bit more involved than adding a DNS server or router. We will need to set both the IP address of the WINS server and the method for NetBIOS name resolution. Since these items are not specific to a particular subnet, we will add our WINS server as a *Server Option*.

Select **Server Options** from the **Action** menu, choose **Configure Options,** and select option **044 WINS/NBNS Servers**. Enter the IP address of the WINS server in the same manner we used for the router and DNS server and click **Add.** Now we should also add the **046 WINS/NBT Node Type** option. Select it from the *Available Options* box. By default, no node type is selected (0x0) (see Figure 7-12).

This screen gives you the option to select a *B-node (0x1)*, a *P-node (0x2), an M-node (0x4)*, or an *H-node (0x8)*—all of which appears very interesting but somewhat meaningless without a brief explanation.

A *B-node* is a *broadcast* node. If configured to use a B-node, the client will attempt NetBIOS name resolution through broadcast only and will never call on the WINS server. A *P-node* is a *Point-to-Point* node. When using a P-node, the client will attempt name resolution through the WINS server only. (Computers configured to use P-node will neither use a broadcast message for name resolution nor respond to a name resolution broadcast made by another machine on the network.) An *M-node* is a *mixed* node. Using this scheme, broadcast resolution is attempted first. If that method fails, the client will contact the WINS server. Finally, an *H-node* is a *hybrid* node. With a hybrid node, the client first contacts the WINS server. If the WINS server cannot provide resolution, the client resorts to a broadcast. Since the H-node provides primary use of WINS with a broadcast backup, select this node type by entering *0x8* in the edit box.

Click **OK** to close *the Server Options* dialog box and you have completed your DHCP configuration.

As shown in Figure 7-13, your DHCP server is now capable of providing clients with an IP address and subnet mask as well as a router and the addresses for WINS and DNS servers. This has sharply reduced the client TCP/IP configuration load. Furthermore, in order to change the address of one of the servers or the node type, the administrator needs only to alter

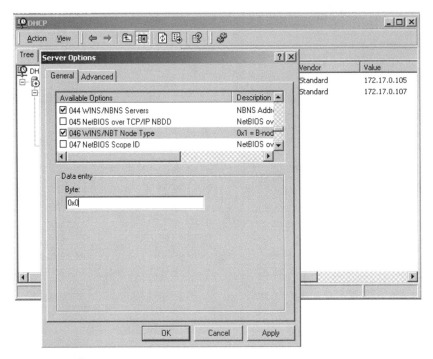

FIGURE 7-12   *Edit node type*

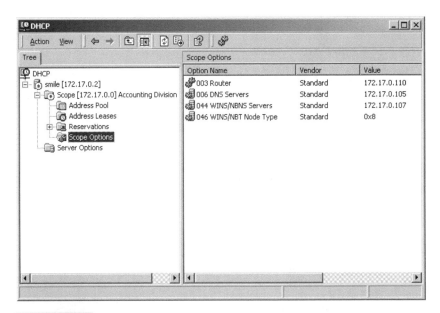

FIGURE 7-13   *DHCP scope options*

those values at the DHCP server rather than visiting every workstation in the network!

Authorizing DHCP in Active Directory

To provide a useful administrative service within a Windows 2000 domain, DHCP servers must be not only configured correctly, but also authorized in Active Directory for use on a network. This is needed to avoid most of the accidental damage caused by running DHCP servers with incorrect configurations or correct configurations on the wrong network.

When a misconfigured or unauthorized DHCP server is introduced into a network, it can cause problems. For example, if an unauthorized DHCP server starts, it might begin either leasing incorrect IP addresses to clients or negatively acknowledging DHCP clients attempting to renew current address leases. Either of these situations can produce further problems for DHCP-enabled clients. For example, clients that obtain a configuration lease from the unauthorized server can fail to locate valid domain controllers, preventing clients from successfully logging onto the network. To avoid these problems in Windows 2000, servers are verified as legal (authorized) in the network before they can service clients.

The authorization process for DHCP server computers in Active Directory depends on the role of the server within your network. A Windows2000 Server can be employed in three basic server roles:

- **Domain controller.** The computer keeps and maintains a copy of the Active Directory service database and provides secure account management for domain member users and computers.
- **Member server.** The computer is not operating as a domain controller but has joined a domain in which it has a membership account in the Active Directory service database.
- **Stand-alone server.** The computer is not operating as a domain controller or a member server in a domain. Instead, the server computer is made known to the network through a specified workgroup name, which can be shared by other computers, but is used only for browsing purposes and not to provide secured logon access to shared domain resources.

If we deploy Active Directory, all computers operating as DHCP servers must be either domain controllers or domain member servers before they can be authorized in the directory service and provide DHCP services to clients.

The following steps may be employed to authorize a DHCP server:

- Log onto the network with administrative privileges. In most cases, it is simplest to log onto the network from the computer where you want to authorize the new DHCP server. This ensures that another

TCP/IP configuration of the authorized computer has been set up correctly prior to authorization.

● Start the **DHCP** console and in the console tree click **DHCP**.

● On the **Action** menu, click **Manage authorized servers**. The **Manage Authorized Servers** dialog box appears.

● Click **Authorize**. When prompted, type the name or IP address of the DHCP server to be authorized, and then click **OK** (see Figure 7-14).

When a DHCP server is authorized, the server computer is added to the list of authorized DHCP servers maintained in the directory service database. If a stand-alone server is currently providing DHCP services outside an active directory domain, it will need to be authorized after joining the domain as either a member server or domain controller. While DHCP authorization provides an excellent safety feature, it applies only to Windows 2000 servers. If a Windows NT or third-party DHCP server is introduced into the domain, it will be capable of providing configuration information without authorization. That is to say, a non-Windows 2000 DHCP server will freely operate in the environment and will supply (possibly bogus) information to any client that is able to contact it to request a DHCP lease.

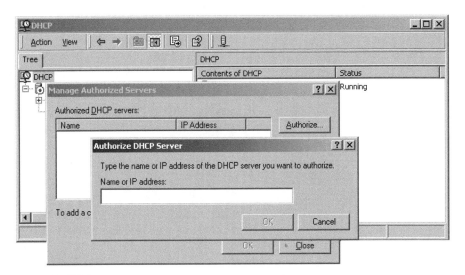

FIGURE 7-14   *Authorizing DHCP in Active Directory*

DHCP Relay Agent

Now that your DHCP server is up and running with a single scope, what if you wanted to add another scope? You could give out IP addresses for machines on other subnets but, since they must use non-routable broadcast traffic to reach your DHCP server, how will they communicate with the DHCP server? The answer is the *DHCP Relay Agent!* A router that conforms to RFC 1542 will perform as a DHCP Relay Agent.[4] When an IP request packet reaches a DHCP Relay Agent, the relay agent will forward the request to the next network but will tag the packet with the requestor's home network to ensure the DHCP server will return an address for the appropriate subnet.

Configuring a Windows 2000 Server as a DHCP Relay Agent

A multihomed Windows 2000 Server configured as a router can be additionally configured as a DHCP Relay Agent, making it an RFC 1542 compliant router. You may also install the DHCP Relay Agent on a Windows 2000 Server that is NOT configured as a router. A nonrouter DHCP Relay Agent will accept the IP Lease Request and forward it through the appropriate router to a DHCP server on a remote network.

Note

A *multihomed* server is one equipped with more than one network interface card and which can operate on more than one subnet. It may be configured with multiple IP addresses and with *IP Forwarding* enabled in the registry or with Routing and Remote Access Services configured to provide routing.

Install the DHCP Relay Agent service through the **Routing and Remote Access** (**Start** → **Programs** → **Administrative Tools**). In the console tree go to **<server name>** → **IP Routing** → **General**. Right-click **General**, and then click **New Routing Protocol**. In the **Select Routing Protocol** dialog box, click **DHCP Relay Agent**, and then click **OK** (see Figure 7-15).

---

4. DHCP is partially based on an earlier RFC called the Bootstrap Protocol. Because of this, DHCP Relay Agents are sometimes referred to as *BOOTP Relay Agents.*

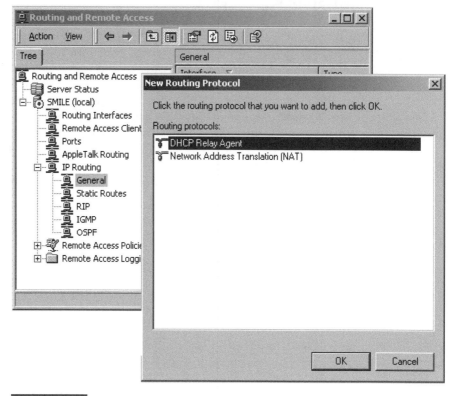

FIGURE 7-15   *DHCP Relay*

Once the service is installed, you must link it to an interface and configure it. Right-click **DHCP Relay Agent** and select **New Interface** (see Figure 7-16).

Next, click on the interface you wish to have the DHCP Relay Agent operate on. This will normally be the interface listed as **Local Area Connection** (unless you have renamed it) (see Figure 7-17).

After you click **OK**, you are asked to configure the interface (see Figure 7-18). Ensure the **Relay DHCP packets** check box is checked. (If this is cleared, the DHCP Relay Agent function of the interface is turned off.) *Boot Threshold (seconds)* and *Hop Count threshold* may be left at their default values. *Boot Threshold* represents the amount of time the IP request packet will be limited to the local subnet before the relay agent will forward it. *Hop Count threshold* sets the maximum number of times the IP request packet will be routed before it is discarded.

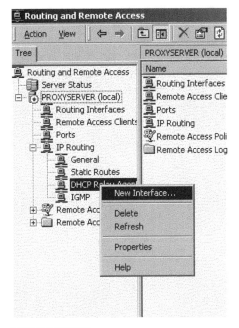

FIGURE 7–16 *Add new interface*

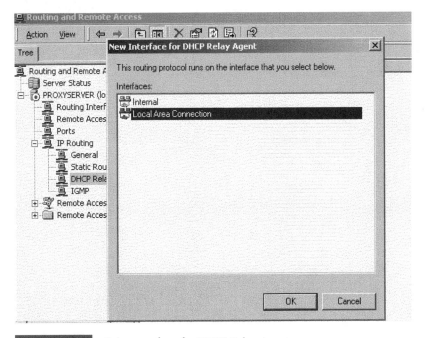

FIGURE 7–17 *Select interface for DHCP Relay Agent*

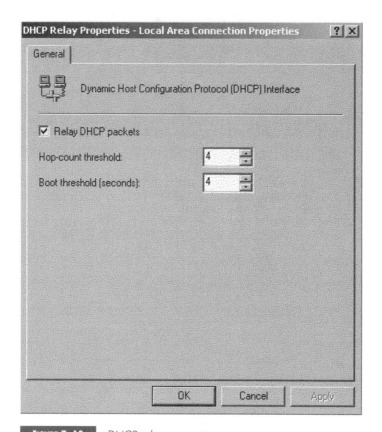

FIGURE 7–18 *DHCP relay properties*

To complete the installation, you should add an IP address for a DHCP server. In the **Routing and Remote Access** window right-click **DHCP Relay Agent,** select **Properties**, and enter the IP addresses of all the DHCP servers to which you want your relay agent to forward IP request packets (see Figure 7-19).

With the DHCP Relay Agent functioning, your DHCP server can provide IP addresses to DHCP clients on subnets beyond its home network (provided it possesses valid IP address information for them). This will permit you, for instance, to maintain DHCP servers on a single subnet that can provide DHCP information to clients on neighboring subnets. It also allows you to give each DHCP server addresses for neighboring subnets. Each DHCP server can then give out appropriate addresses (through the relay agent) in the event the DHCP server that usually services the subnet has gone down.

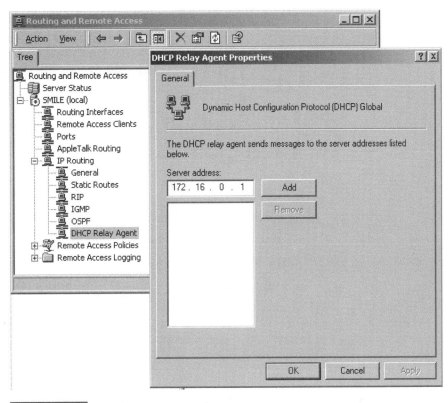

FIGURE 7-19   *Configuring DHCP Relay Agent properties*

DHCP Planning Considerations

Now that we have seen how to set up and configure a DHCP server and DHCP capable routers, let's spend a little time looking at how to plan and optimize DHCP services on the network.

Clients

Will all your machines become DHCP clients? If not, you'll need to ensure the non-DHCP clients have static addresses that don't conflict with any of your DHCP address pools. Does a DHCP client require a specific IP address? If so, you'll need to reserve the address using DHCP console. Under **Scope** right-click **Reservations** to open the **New Reservation** dialog box (see Figure 7-20).

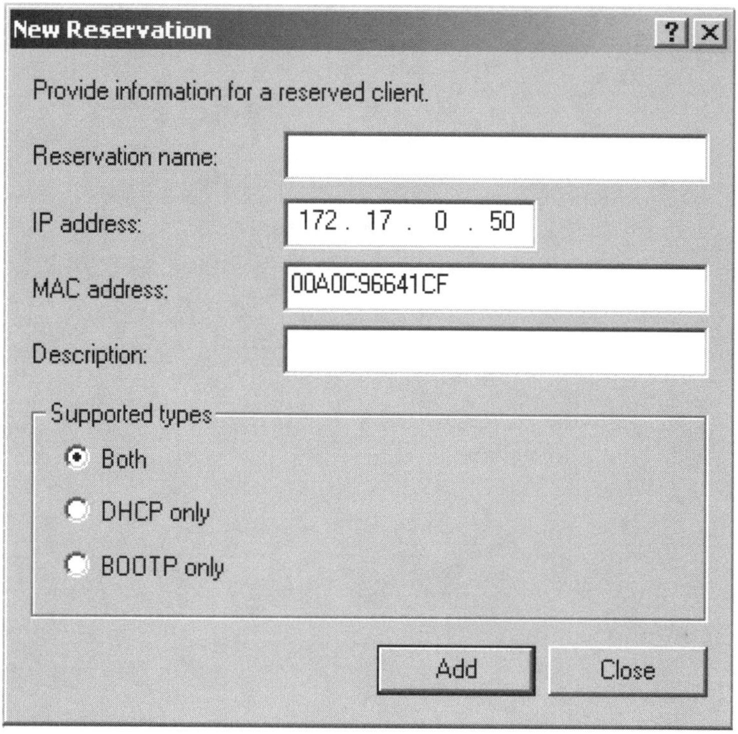

FIGURE 7–20   *Adding reserved clients*

Enter the machine name (reservation name), the IP address you wish to reserve, and the machine's MAC address[5]. You may also enter a *Description* for better identification. DHCP clients can be configured on computers running Windows 2000, Windows NT, Windows 95/98, Windows for Workgroups 3.11 (running TCP/IP-32), Microsoft Network Client 3.0 for Microsoft-DOS (with the real-mode TCP/IP driver), or LAN Manager 2.2c.

Subnets

Will your server provide IP addresses for multiple subnets? If so, ensure you've installed DHCP Relay Agent unless all your routers are RFC 1542 compliant.

---

5. Note that the MAC address is entered here without the hyphens we normally see when looking at it using *ipconfig* (discussed in the next section) and other utilities.

Servers

Remember that DHCP servers must operate on a Windows 2000 Server using a static IP address. How many servers are required? If your network has multiple subnets and you don't have RFC 1542 compliant routers or DHCP relay agents, you'll need a DHCP server on each subnet. There should always be at least two DHCP servers available to DHCP clients to ensure clients can get addresses when a server goes down. When servers are used across multiple subnets, Microsoft recommends that each server should have scopes that comprise 70-80 percent of the available IP addresses on its local subnet and 20-30 percent of the available addresses of a remote subnet. Remember that DHCP servers don't talk to each other; it is critical, therefore, to ensure each server has a pool of IP addresses that aren't contained in any other server's address list.

Options

Determine what options your DHCP server will use. Will you configure your server to supply a router address, DNS server address, WINS server address, or any additional options?

Client Configuration

All this excitement about DHCP won't do us much good unless we configure some machines to act as DHCP clients. DHCP cannot force its information on any machine. The machine must first be configured to ask for the information. To configure a Windows 2000 computer to act as a DHCP client, simply go to the **Network and Dial-up Connections** dialog and select **Local Area Connection | Properties | Internet Protocol (TCP/IP) | Properties**. Click the **Obtain an IP address automatically** radio button (see Figure 7-21). If the system previously had static *IP Address*, *Subnet Mask*, and *Default Gateway* values they will be lost when you click **OK.** If you wish to allow DHCP to set DNS Server information, ensure the **Obtain DNS server address automatically** is set. Note that if any settings (e.g., DNS and WINS server addresses) are set on the tabs accessed by clicking the **Advanced** button, they will override settings provided by the DHCP server.

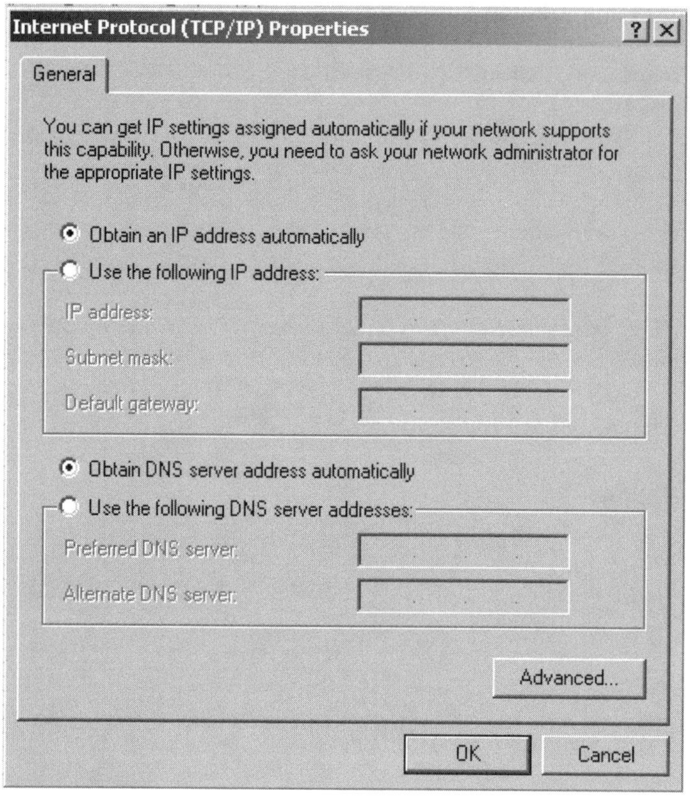

FIGURE 7–21   *DHCP client configuration*

IPCONFIG and IP Parameters

The **IPCONFIG** utility permits the viewing of client configuration information as well as the release and renewal of IP address leases. **IPCONFIG** is executed from the Windows 2000 command line with the following syntax: **Ipconfig [/? | /all | /release [adapter] | /renew [adapter]]**.

By typing **IPCONFIG** you can view the machine's IP address, subnet mask, and default gateway. If the IP address is shown as 0.0.0.0 or is from the APIPA reserved address space, you can conclude that the client was unable to obtain an IP address from the DHCP server (if, of course, the machine is a DHCP client). You can use **IPCONFIG /RENEW** to force an IP address renewal for the adapter specified or **IPCONFIG /RELEASE** to force the release of a DHCP supplied address for a particular adapter. If no adapter names are supplied, the release or renew will be for all adapters bound to

TCP/IP on the machine. By typing **IPCONFIG /ALL** you can view the detailed parameter list displayed in Figure 7-22. In addition to the basic information provided by **IPCONFIG**, the **/ALL** option provides other important information such as WINS and DNS server addresses, the default gateway address, and the computer's MAC address (physical address). If any DHCP supplied data is shown as zeros or is not available, suspect a problem with the DHCP lease.

```
C:\>ipconfig /all

Windows 2000 IP Configuration

        Host Name . . . . . . . . . . . . : FilSvr3
        Primary DNS Suffix  . . . . . . . :
        Node Type . . . . . . . . . . . . : Hybrid
        IP Routing Enabled. . . . . . . . : No
        WINS Proxy Enabled. . . . . . . . : No

Ethernet adapter Local Area Connection:

        Connection-specific DNS Suffix  . :
        Description . . . . . . . . . . . : 3Com 3C90x Ethernet Adapter
        Physical Address. . . . . . . . . : 00-40-05-E3-88-D5
        DHCP Enabled. . . . . . . . . . . : Yes
        IP Address. . . . . . . . . . . . : 172.16.0.20
        Subnet Mask . . . . . . . . . . . : 255.255.0.0
        Default Gateway . . . . . . . . . : 172.16.0.9
        DNS Servers . . . . . . . . . . . : 172.17.0.105
```

FIGURE 7-22   *Results of IPCONFIG /ALL*

Managing the DHCP Database

As you might have guessed, since DHCP must handle a large amount of data (IP addresses, subnet masks, lease durations, WINS/DNS addresses, etc.), it must maintain a database. Fortunately, DHCP uses the Microsoft Jet database engine (the same engine that runs Microsoft Access), which has proven to be a robust and reliable product requiring very little user intervention.

Database Backup and Restoration

The database is automatically backed up every hour and written to the ***systemroot**\SYSTEM32\DHCP\BACKUP\JET directory. In the event of corruption, the database is automatically restored when the DHCP server service is started (or restarted) but manual restoration may be accomplished using two methods:

1. Copy the contents of the ***systemroot**\SYSTEM32\DHCP\BACKUP\JET directory to the ***systemroot**\SYSTEM32\DHCP directory and restart the DHCP Server service.

2. Set the HKEY_LOCAL_MACHINE\SYSTEM\CurrentControlSet\Services\ DHCPServer\Parameters\RestoreFlag value to 1 and restart the service. This will force the server to accomplish an automatic restore. Once the restore is complete, the RestoreFlag value will be automatically reset to 0.

Compacting the Database

Windows 2000 Server will automatically compact the DHCP database. Earlier Windows versions did not offer this convenience, however. Whenever the database approaches 30 MB on a Windows NT 3.51, or earlier, system you should take action to compact the database. To compact the database, first stop the DHCP Server service. Next, go to the *systemroot*\SYSTEM32 directory and run the JETPACK utility. To run JETPACK, type **jetpack dhcp.mdb temp.mdb**. This action causes the dhcp.mdb to be compacted into temp.mdb. When the compact is complete, temp.mdb is copied back to dhcp.mdb and temp.mdb is deleted. Once you have compacted the database, restart the DHCP Server service.

Files Used by the DHCP Database

The files listed below are used by the DHCP database. They are located in the ***systemroot**\SYSTEM32\DHCP and should be neither deleted nor modified (see Table 7.1).

TABLE 7.1   DHCP Database Files

File Name	Description
DHCP MDB	DHCP Database
DHCP.TMP	DHCP.TMP
J50.LOG	Database transaction log—used by DHCP for automatic data recovery

Analyzing the Impact of DHCP Traffic on the Network

The DHCP is designed to place minimal impact on the network. While you won't typically need to spend a lot of time trying to optimize DHCP network traffic, a good working knowledge of the DHCP network signature will permit you to isolate difficulties arising from DHCP configuration problems, such as short lease durations or forwarding of DHCP messages from subnets for which the server has no scope. There are two main types of DHCP network communications: *IP Address Lease Acquisition* and *IP Address Lease Renewal*.

IP Address Lease Acquisition

As we mentioned at the start of this chapter, the IP Address Lease Acquisition process consists of four steps: *Discover*, *Offer*, *Request*, and *Acknowledgement*. Each step uses a frame of 342-590 bytes, depending on the client and selected configuration options. The total process is depicted in Figure 7-23. The four steps are typically accomplished in a quarter second and place 1,368 bytes on the network. You'll remember we said that all the initial lease acquisition traffic is accomplished through broadcast—this is verified by the Network Monitor depiction. All four frames have essentially the same structure, so we'll look at the features of the Discover frame to help us understand what is going on in the process.

Looking, first, at the frame's Ethernet header (shown in Figure 7-24), we can see a destination address of all Fs, indicating a media access control broadcast. We can also verify a 342-byte frame length. A look at the IP header (shown by Figure 7-25) shows a source address of 0.0.0.0 and a destination address of 255.255.255.255. The zeros indicate this client still needs an IP address. The 255s signify a network broadcast—if the network has BOOTP compliant routers, this addressing will permit forwarding these packets to other subnets.

Frame	Time	Src MAC Addr	Dst MAC Addr	Protocol	Description
7	92.676	Client1	*BROADCAST	DHCP	Discover
8	92.702	DHCPSVR	*BROADCAST	DHCP	Offer
9	92.703	Client1	*BROADCAST	DHCP	Request
10	92.764	DHCPSVR	*BROADCAST	DHCP	ACK

FIGURE 7-23   *Lease acquisition steps as shown in network monitor*

```
⊟ETHERNET: ETYPE = 0x0800 : Protocol = IP:  DOD Internet Protocol
 ⊞ETHERNET: Destination address : FFFFFFFFFFFF
 ⊞ETHERNET: Source address : 00600820A286
  ETHERNET: Frame Length : 342 (0x0156)
  ETHERNET: Ethernet Type : 0x0800 (IP:  DOD Internet Protocol)
  ETHERNET: Ethernet Data: Number of data bytes remaining = 328 (0x0148)
```

FIGURE 7-24   *Ethernet header*

```
IP: ID = 0x0; Proto = UDP; Len: 328
  IP: Version = 4 (0x4)
  IP: Header Length = 20 (0x14)
  IP: Service Type = 0 (0x0)
  IP: Total Length = 328 (0x148)
  IP: Identification = 0 (0x0)
  IP: Flags Summary = 0 (0x0)
  IP: Fragment Offset = 0 (0x0) bytes
  IP: Time to Live = 128 (0x80)
  IP: Protocol = UDP - User Datagram
  IP: Checksum = 0x39A6
  IP: Source Address = 0.0.0.0
  IP: Destination Address = 255.255.255.255
  IP: Data: Number of data bytes remaining = 308 (0x0134)
```

FIGURE 7–25   *IP header*

```
UDP: IP Multicast:   Src Port: BOOTP Client, (68); Dst Port: BOOTP Server (67)
  UDP: Source Port = BOOTP Client
  UDP: Destination Port = BOOTP Server
  UDP: Total length = 308 (0x134) bytes
  UDP: UDP Checksum = 0xE14F
  UDP: Data: Number of data bytes remaining = 300 (0x012C)
```

FIGURE 7–26   *UDP header*

The *User Datagram Protocol* (UDP) header shows a source port (BOOTP Client) of 68 and a destination port (BOOTP Server) of 67 (see Figure 7-26). If your routers support these ports, they are BOOTP (RFC 1542) compliant and will be able to forward your IP requests to other subnets. As you might expect, all of the DHCP work is done under the DHCP header. Looking at the request header, we can see all the IP addresses are set to 0 in the Discover message (see Figure 7-27). This, obviously, is because no DHCP lease has been consummated at this point. The only identification here is the client's MAC address. By the time we get to the Acknowledgement message (see Figure 7-28), the client can find its leased IP address in the *Your IP Address* field and the other provided network options under the *Option* field.

Note   The discerning reader will notice the lease length is set to four minutes. Although such a short lease duration is hardly recommended, it did facilitate a quick lease renewal for the purpose of generating renewal frames to depict in this book!

```
DHCP: Discover              (xid=4D4621AF)
  DHCP: Op Code              (op)     = 1 (0x1)
  DHCP: Hardware Type        (htype)  = 1 (0x1) 10Mb Ethernet
  DHCP: Hardware Address Length (hlen) = 6 (0x6)
  DHCP: Hops                 (hops)   = 0 (0x0)
  DHCP: Transaction ID       (xid)    = 1296441775 (0x4D4621AF)
  DHCP: Seconds              (secs)   = 0 (0x0)
  DHCP: Flags                (flags)  = 0 (0x0)
  DHCP: Client IP Address (ciaddr) = 0.0.0.0
  DHCP: Your   IP Address (yiaddr) = 0.0.0.0
  DHCP: Server IP Address (siaddr) = 0.0.0.0
  DHCP: Relay  IP Address (giaddr) = 0.0.0.0
  DHCP: Client Ethernet Address (chaddr) = 00600820A286
  DHCP: Server Host Name  (sname)  = <Blank>
  DHCP: Boot File Name    (file)   = <Blank>
  DHCP: Magic Cookie = [OK]
  DHCP: Option Field         (options)
```

FIGURE 7–27   *DHCP Discover header*

```
DHCP: ACK                   (xid=5F84263B)
  DHCP: Op Code              (op)     = 2 (0x2)
  DHCP: Hardware Type        (htype)  = 1 (0x1) 10Mb Ethernet
  DHCP: Hardware Address Length (hlen) = 6 (0x6)
  DHCP: Hops                 (hops)   = 0 (0x0)
  DHCP: Transaction ID       (xid)    = 1602496059 (0x5F84263B)
  DHCP: Seconds              (secs)   = 0 (0x0)
  DHCP: Flags                (flags)  = 0 (0x0)
  DHCP: Client IP Address (ciaddr) = 0.0.0.0
  DHCP: Your   IP Address (yiaddr) = 172.16.0.1
  DHCP: Server IP Address (siaddr) = 0.0.0.0
  DHCP: Relay  IP Address (giaddr) = 0.0.0.0
  DHCP: Client Ethernet Address (chaddr) = 00600820A286
  DHCP: Server Host Name  (sname)  = <Blank>
  DHCP: Boot File Name    (file)   = <Blank>
  DHCP: Magic Cookie = [OK]
  DHCP: Option Field       (options)
    DHCP: DHCP Message Type       = DHCP ACK
    DHCP: Renewal Time Value (T1) =  0:02:00
    DHCP: Rebinding Time Value (T2) =  0:03:30
    DHCP: IP Address Lease Time   =  0:04:00
    DHCP: Server Identifier       = 172.16.0.10
    DHCP: Subnet Mask             = 255.255.0.0
    DHCP: Router                  = 172.16.0.9
    DHCP: NetBIOS Name Service    = 172.17.0.107
    DHCP: NetBIOS Node Type       = (Length: 1) 08
    DHCP: Domain Name Server      = 172.17.0.105
    DHCP: End of this option field
```

FIGURE 7–28   *DHCP Acknowledge header*

Address Lease Renewal

The lease renewal process is quite similar to the acquisition process except that we can go directly to the *request* phase and, since the DHCP client has a valid IP address when making the renewal request, communications need not be carried out at the broadcast level. Were you to examine the frames shown in Figure 7-29, you would find their contents very similar to those of the *IP Address Acquisition Process*. As with acquisition frames, these are typically 342 bytes in length and the entire renewal process takes about 100 milliseconds.

Frame	Time	Src MAC Addr	Dst MAC Addr	Protocol	Description
1183	212.858	Client1	DHCPSVR	DHCP	Request
1184	212.889	DHCPSVR	Client1	DHCP	ACK

FIGURE 7-29   *IP address renewal*

DHCP Traffic Optimization

As we've already stated, DHCP has only a minor impact on the network. There are, in fact, only two areas where optimization can prove fruitful:

LEASE DURATION

Obviously, the longer the lease duration, the less DHCP renewal traffic will be required on the network. Why, then, don't we simply make all our leases good forever? If you have a very large address pool and a static environment, this would be a great idea. Most of us need to make changes from time to time, however. If, for instance, your DHCP clients never need to ask to renew their leases, they run the risk of missing changes and additions you make to WINS servers, DNS servers, and other DHCP-supplied information. If this were the case, your only choice would be to cancel each DHCP lease and force all your clients to renegotiate their leases. Additionally, if your address pool is close to the number of DHCP clients in your environment, you run the risk of running out of addresses when machines go down or are moved to different subnets. To optimize the lease duration, take a look at address pool size and the stability of your network. As the pool size and stability grow, you can consider increasing the lease duration beyond the default eight days. Conversely, if you have a particularly small pool or dynamic environment, you may need to shorten the lease duration.

DHCP THRESHOLD

If you're using DHCP Relay Agents to accomplish DHCP leases across multiple networks, you may be forwarding DHCP packets when you don't need to, contributing to unnecessary cross-network traffic. This occurs when the local DHCP server is slow to respond to DHCP requests and the relay agents forward the requests to other servers. This may occur if the local server is tasked with other operations in addition to DHCP or if it is busy handling DHCP requests. If you discover that too many of your DHCP requests are going to other networks, you may want to lighten the load of the DHCP server or create another local DHCP server and split your address pool between the two local servers. If you can't make either of those modifications, you may be able to configure the relay agent to wait longer before forwarding the DHCP request. If you are using the Windows 2000 Server DHCP relay agent, this property can be configured using the DHCP Relay tab of the TCP/IP properties dialog (see Figure 7-18). The Boot Threshold (seconds) value determines how long the relay agent will wait for a client to get a DHCP offer before forwarding the request to another network. The default value is 4. If your DHCP requests consistently forward to other networks, try increasing this value to 10. This should permit two complete local DHCP requests before they are forwarded across the network.

Note

You'll remember, from our discussion of the *DHCP process*, that clients do not wait forever for a DHCP response. Be careful when adjusting the Boot Threshold that you don't make it longer than the client is willing to wait.

Summary

In this chapter we discovered that APIPA and the DHCP permit us to dynamically assign IP addresses and other pertinent TCP/IP parameters. APIPA permits machines to autonomously configure IP address and subnet mask information while DHCP makes use of a server to supply this and other TCP/IP configuration information. We saw the DHCP process was a simple four-step process consisting of *Lease Request, Lease Offer, Lease Selection*, and *Lease Acknowledgement*. We saw that DHCP clients obtain a lease for a specified duration and attempt renewal prior to the lease's expiration. We installed a DHCP server, configured a scope, and set scope and global options for a default gateway and WINS and DNS servers. We found that a DHCP relay agent is required to forward DHCP requests to other networks and saw how to install and configure one. We saw how to test the DHCP implementation using *ipconfig /all* and looked at some ways to maintain the DHCP database itself. Finally, we spent some time with Network Monitor to see how the DHCP packet traffic actually looks on the network.

Test Yourself

1. Which of these messages will cause a host to seek a new lease?
   A. DHCPACK
   B. DHCPNACK
   C. DHCPPACK
   D. DHCPSNACK

2. To configure a host to obtain its IP configuration automatically, you must supply the IP address of at least one DHCP server.
   A. True
   B. False

3. Non-APIPA hosts unable to receive an IP address from the DHCP server will set their IP address to:
   A. 0.0.0.0
   B. 127.0.0.1
   C. 255.255.255.255
   D. 169.255.0.0

4. A client may obtain an IP address from a DHCP server on an external network:
   A. If the DHCP server has a valid IP address for the client.
   B. If the DHCP server's IP address is entered in the client's DHCP properties dialog.
   C. With the help of a DHCP Relay Agent.
   D. A and C

5. If an APIPA capable client cannot obtain a lease from a DHCP server it can automatically configure its (select all that apply):
   A. Subnet mask
   B. IP address
   C. Default gateway
   D. DNS server address

NetBIOS Over TCP/IP

*R*unning in its native mode, Windows 2000 can function with-out the Network Basic Input/Output System or NetBIOS. This is the first Windows operating system that can work without a Net-BIOS component. Having said that, there is still a plethora of applications and operating systems that expect to communicate via NetBIOS. The Windows 2000 Transport Control Protocol/Inter-net Protocol (TCP/IP) suite, therefore, offers full NetBIOS support. In the TCP/IP arena, NetBIOS is transmitted over the network by TCP/IP as a protocol within a protocol.

Sytek Corporation developed NetBIOS in the early 1980s for IBM to permit applications to communicate over a network. NetBIOS is essentially a session level interface and a session management and data transport protocol.

NetBIOS operates at the application level and the session/trans-port level. At the application level, it is a standard application pro-gramming interface (API) that permits user applications to communicate with network protocol software. Any protocol (such as TCP/IP) that supports the NetBIOS interface will support pro-grams using the NetBIOS API. At the session/transport level, Net-BIOS functions through underlying protocol software—such as the NetBIOS Frames Protocol (NBFP), NetBIOS Extended User Interface (NetBEUI), or NetBIOS Over TCP/IP (NetBT)—to accom-plish the network input/output (I/O) required for the NetBIOS API to function on the network.

NetBIOS supports the following network services:

- *Network name registration and verification*
- *Session establishment and termination*
- *Connection-oriented session data transfer*
- *Connectionless datagram data transfer*
- *Support protocol (driver) and adapter monitoring and management*

Of all the services provided by NetBIOS, the one we have most control over is its network-naming feature. Because of this, we'll spend the rest of the chapter learning about NetBIOS names and how we can find a particular computer (host) through the use of those names and the NetBIOS services.

NetBIOS Names

NetBIOS names are simply those we give computers and other NetBIOS resources within a network. These names make it easy for us to identify a resource (it is far easier to remember the name Server1, for instance, than try to remember an IP address or a media access channel (MAC) address). NetBIOS names allow us to identify particular resources (such as an Exchange Server or an SQL Server) without regard to a particular transport protocol. An Exchange Server could, for instance, function on multiple protocols using the NetBIOS name as long as there was a way to associate that name with a particular address (much more on this later).

A NetBIOS name is a unique 16-byte address. NetBIOS names may be unique (to identify a single resource) or group (to communicate with several computers simultaneously). As we'll see, unique names are used not merely to communicate with a single computer but with a single process running on that computer. NetBIOS names consist of a 15-character computer name plus a 16th character that identifies the particular process. Table 8.1 shows the 16th character associated with some common processes. Every Windows 2000 network service registers a NetBIOS name and each Windows 2000 network command uses these services through their NetBIOS names.

TABLE 8.1	*Common NetBIOS Names*
Registered Name	**Description**
\\computer_name[00h]	Name registered for Workstation Service
\\computer_name[03h]	Name registered for Messenger Service

TABLE 8.1	*Common NetBIOS Names (continued)*
Registered Name	**Description**
\\computer_name[20h]	Name registered for Server Service
\\username[03h]	Name of current user. This name is registered by the messenger service. This permits the user to receive messages sent through net send. If the user is logged onto several computers, the first computer the user logs onto receives the message.
\\domain_name[1Bh]	The domain name registered by the PDC emulator that is also the domain master browser. If a WINS server is queried for this name, it resolves it to the IP address of the computer that registered the name.

NetBIOS Name Registration, Discovery, and Release

NetBIOS names are only useful if they are recognized by the machines on a network. To make this happen, the names must be registered, machines must be able to determine what name corresponds to a particular machine, and when the machine owning the name leaves the network, the name should be removed from the list of valid names.

Name Registration

When a computer boots up and initializes its services, it registers its NetBIOS name with a NetBIOS *name registration request*. The request is made either through a direct message to a NetBIOS name server or through a broadcast. If the name was previously registered by another host, a *negative name registration response* is returned. If registration was attempted through broadcast, the negative response comes from the computer that previously registered the name. If a message to a name server was used, the response comes from the name server. If a negative name registration response is received, the computer suffers an initialization error; otherwise, the machine continues its initialization with the knowledge that it has successfully registered its name with the network.

Name Discovery

When a machine on a local network wishes to find a machine by a NetBIOS name, it either uses a broadcast or queries the local NetBIOS name server. If the designated name is found on the network, a *positive name query response* is sent by the name server or (if a broadcast was used) by the host possessing the name.

Name Release

When a NetBIOS application or service stops, the host sends a *name release* message to the name server (if a name server was used) or simply stops sending negative name resolution responses when another machine attempts to register the same name (if a broadcast was used). This releases the NetBIOS name and makes it available to other hosts.

NetBIOS Name Scopes

The NetBIOS name space can be segmented by appending a scope ID to the NetBIOS name. In Figure 8-1 WORKSTN1.ENG and WORKSTN2.ENG can communicate with SERVER1.ENG but not SERVER1.ACTG, and WORKSTN1.ACTG and WORKSTN2.ACTG can communicate with SERVER1.ACTG but not SERVER1.ENG.

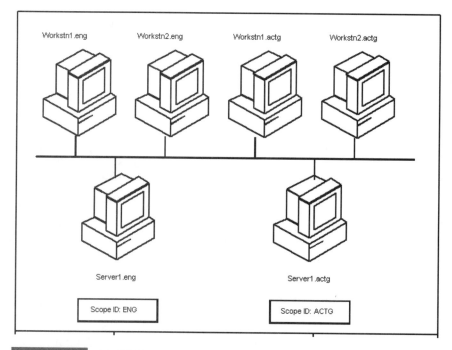

FIGURE 8–1   *NetBIOS scopes*

When scope IDs are not used, NetBIOS names must be unique throughout the entire network; with scope IDs, names must be unique only within the scope. NetBIOS resources within the scope, however, are not able to communicate with resources outside their own scope using NetBIOS over TCP/IP. The NetBIOS scope becomes part of the NetBIOS name resulting in a unique NetBIOS name. In Figure 8-1, even though the two servers have the same NetBIOS name, the different scope IDs make them unique. To configure the NetBIOS scope ID, set the following registry value to the name of the scope ID that you want to use:

```
HKEY_LOCAL_MACHINE\SYSTEM\CurrentControlSet\Services\NetBT\
Parameters\ScopeID
```

Previous versions of Windows NT permitted scope ID configuration through a tabbed dialog box. Windows 2000 has de-emphasized name scopes by removing the graphical user interface (GUI) based configuration capability. While Windows 2000 fully supports name scopes, this was intended primarily for backward compatibility. Name scopes, when improperly used, can result in a great deal of network confusion. This option should be employed only with great caution and only when absolutely necessary.

NetBIOS Name Resolution

TCP/IP does NOT use NetBIOS names. However, NetBIOS names permit us to identify resources in a protocol-independent fashion. They also make it easier for humans to remember and identify resources. How then do we resolve the issue of using NetBIOS names with TCP/IP? The key to this question is name *resolution*. In order for TCP/IP to function when presented with a NetBIOS name, it must have a way to determine the IP address that goes with the name. This determination is called mapping or resolution. There are several methods to accomplish this name resolution.

Standard Name Resolution Methods

The following methods are standard throughout TCP/IP networks:

NETBIOS NAME CACHE

Every time a machine resolves a name, it places it into its local name cache. When it needs to find the IP address for a NetBIOS resource, it checks its own cache first.

NETBIOS NAME SERVER

A NetBIOS Name Server (NBNS) is any server implemented under RFC 1001/ 1002 to provide NetBIOS name resolution. A computer trying to locate a Net-BIOS resource can query the NBNS for a name/IP address mapping. Microsoft's implementation is called the *Windows Internet Name Service* and is the subject of the next chapter.

LOCAL BROADCAST

If a computer can't find a mapping in its cache or from a name server, it can send a broadcast over the local network. If the target computer receives the broadcast, it will respond with its IP address to permit full TCP/IP communication.

Microsoft Name Resolution Methods

In addition to the standard resolution methods, Microsoft has developed additional ways to map NetBIOS names and IP addresses:

LMHOSTS FILE

An LMHOSTS file is a text file on the local computer that contains both the NetBIOS name and IP address of Windows networking computers on remote networks. As we will see later in this chapter, an LMHOSTS file requires manual entry and maintenance.

HOSTS FILE

Like the LMHOSTS file, the HOSTS file is a text file on the local computer that requires manual entry and maintenance. Unlike the LMHOSTS file, the HOSTS file maps IP addresses to host names or fully qualified domain names (e.g., SERVER1.MYNET.COM) rather than NetBIOS names. HOSTS files use the same format as the 4.3 Berkeley Software Distribution UNIX\etc\hosts file.

For this reason, HOSTS files may be used to resolve IP addresses for both Windows and non-Windows networks. This file is frequently used in name resolution for TCP/IP utilities. (HOSTS files are fully covered in Chapter 11.)

DOMAIN NAME SYSTEM

The Domain Name System (DNS) is a server that maintains a database of IP addresses and fully qualified domain names. Like the HOSTS file, DNS requires manual entry and maintenance and can be used for resolution in Windows and non-Windows networks. When a client needs an IP address mapping, it can query the DNS server in much the same way as it would query a NetBIOS name server. (DNS is fully covered in Chapters 12 and 13.)

Broadcast Name Resolution

Broadcast resolution is the most basic form of name resolution. When a computer (source computer) needs to establish a TCP/IP session with another machine (target computer), it first checks its NetBIOS name cache. If the target computer's name was resolved recently by the source computer, the IP address mapping will be found in the source computer's cache and no further action will be required. If, on the other hand, the cache does not contain a mapping for the target computer, the source computer will broadcast a *name query request* on the local network. The request contains the *target computer's* NetBIOS name and the *source computer's* IP address.

Every computer on the network, upon receiving the broadcast, checks its NetBIOS name table to determine if it owns the name being sought. The computer that owns the name uses the *Address Resolution Protocol* and the source computer's IP address to determine the source computer's MAC address. Using the MAC address, the target computer sends the IP address resolution message (*name query response*) to the source computer and a network session is established.

The problem with broadcast name resolution is that it usually works only on the local network. This is because most routers are incapable of forwarding broadcast traffic. Routers that can forward broadcasts typically have the capability turned off to prevent excessive network traffic. In order to reliably obtain name resolution across multiple networks, we will need to develop additional name resolution capabilities.

Using a NetBIOS Name Server to Resolve Names

Using an NBNS will reduce broadcast traffic on the local network and can permit the resolution of NetBIOS names for hosts on other networks. The typical NetBIOS name server collects IP address mappings from its client computers when they initialize on the network. (The NBNS used in Windows environments is WINS, which will be fully explored in the next chapter.) When an NBNS client needs to contact another computer and can't find the appropriate IP address mapping in its cache, it contacts the NBNS for the information. If the NBNS cannot be found or doesn't have the required mapping information, the client may resort to a broadcast or other methods depending on how it's configured.

NBNS clients typically find the name server by using the server's IP address. This means they can route to a designated server on another network if required. It also means they can obtain name resolution without adding to the local network's broadcast traffic.

Name Resolution Nodes

How does a computer know when to broadcast and when to query a Net-BIOS name server? The answer is through use of NetBIOS over TCP/IP Resolution Nodes. These nodes are simply Windows 2000 registry values that tell the computer how to go about name resolution. (Name Resolution Nodes are defined in RFCs 1001 and 1002.) You'll remember, in the last chapter we saw how DHCP can automatically set the node for you. If you're not using DHCP, you can change the node type manually by entering the appropriate hexadecimal value in:

```
HKEY_LOCAL_MACHINE\SYSTEM\CurrentControlSet\Services\Netbt\
Parameters\DhcpNode Type.
```

Let's take a look at the nodes we can use:

B-node

The B-node is represented by a value of 0x1. This is a *Broadcast* node and it tells the system to use broadcast (actually a UDP datagram) resolution. If broadcast resolution fails, the computer will not attempt to find a NetBIOS name server.

Microsoft systems use the *Microsoft Enhanced B-node*. With the enhanced B-node (also designated by 0x1), computers search the LMHOSTS file at TCP/IP initialization for entries designated by "#PRE." Those entries are loaded into the machine's NetBIOS name cache, which, as we've seen, is the first name resolution method used by a computer. (LMHOSTS will be covered more thoroughly later in this chapter.)

Microsoft systems default to the Enhanced B-node unless they are configured to use a WINS server.

Note   Remember that broadcast name resolution typically works only within the local network and can increase the network load because of the attendant increase in broadcast message traffic.

P-node

Designated by 0x2, the P-node is called a *Peer-to-Peer* node. Computers using the P-node will accomplish name resolution through use of a NetBIOS name server. If the name server is down or if the name server cannot provide the appropriate mapping, the P-node computer will NOT resort to broadcast name resolution. While this can curtail local broadcast traffic, when the name server goes down it will bring communications, even on the local network, to a halt.

M-node

The M-node is a *Mixed* node and is represented by 0x4. M-node systems use B-node resolution first and resort to P-node resolution if the B-node attempt fails. While this is the most complete resolution plan we've seen so far, it does little to limit network broadcast traffic.

H-node

A value of 0x8 indicates an H-node or *Hybrid* node. Under an H-node, a system first attempts P-node resolution. Should that fail, the system seeks resolution through B-node broadcasts. The H-node not only provides a comprehensive resolution plan, it limits network traffic by ensuring broadcasts are used only as a last resort. Microsoft systems configured to use at least one WINS server are configured to use the H-node by default.

DNS Name Resolution

When broadcast and NetBIOS name server resolution fail, the system still has a few tricks up its sleeve. One of these tricks is the DNS server. If the computer is configured to obtain information from a DNS server, it can use the server much like it would use a NetBIOS name server. The DNS server doesn't resolve a NetBIOS name, however; it resolves a fully qualified domain name (e.g., SERVER1.MYNET.COM). If the fully qualified domain name exists and represents the NetBIOS name being sought, an IP address mapping will be returned. DNS can provide name resolution for both Windows and non-Windows clients.

The LMHOSTS File

Another name resolution method is the LMHOSTS file. This is a static text file that is stored on the local machine. The LMHOSTS file is named *LMHOSTS* (with no extension) and it resides in the **\systemroot\system32\drivers\etc** directory. In this context, **\systemroot** refers to the directory containing the Windows 2000 system files. This directory is \WINNT by default in Windows 2000.

The file contains NetBIOS names and IP address mappings for computers on the remote network. You can create an LMHOSTS file with any text editor or you can use the sample LMHOSTS file (LMHOSTS.SAM) found in *\systemroot*system32\drivers\etc as a template. Figure 8-2 shows a sample LMHOSTS file.

```
205.10.12.10    Wkstn1
205.10.12.11    Wkstn2
200.18.22.10    Server1    #PRE        # SQL Server
200.18.22.12    Server2    #PRE        # Print Server
210.22.18.10    Server3    #PRE        # Exchange Server
```

FIGURE 8-2   *Sample LMHOSTS file*

Use the following guidelines when creating an LMHOSTS file:

- Entries are not case sensitive.
- Place each entry on a separate line.
- Enter the IP address in the first column, and type its corresponding computer name immediately after it.
- Separate the address and the computer name by at least one space or tab.
- The **#** character usually marks the start of a comment. It is also used to designate special keywords, as described in the following section.

LMHOSTS Keywords

LMHOSTS files use a number of predefined keywords to make the list more useful and easier to create and maintain. Some of the more useful keywords are detailed in Table 8.2, while Figure 8-3 provides an example of how to employ them.

TABLE 8.2   *LMHOSTS Keywords*

Keyword	Meaning
#PRE	Causes an entry to be preloaded into the NetBIOS name cache. #PRE entries in LMHOSTS are looked up and cached prior to WINS lookup.
#DOM:*domain_name*	Associates an entry with the domain specified by domain. This affects how the Browser and Logon services behave in routed TCP/IP environments. It ensures datagram requests are forwarded to remote subnets and will permit machines to obtain logon validation by browsing domain controllers (for their domains) located in other subnets.

TABLE 8.2	LMHOSTS Keywords (continued)

Keyword	Meaning
#INCLUDE *filename*	Causes the system to seek the LMHOSTS formatted file called *filename* and parse it as if it were local. If you use a universal naming convention (UNC) *filename,* you can use a centralized LMHOSTS file on a server. You must place an IP address mapping in your LMHOSTS file for the server and identify it with the #PRE keyword before the #INCLUDE section (otherwise, the #INCLUDE will be ignored).
#BEGIN_ALTERNATE	Groups multiple #INCLUDE statements. The success of any #INCLUDE statement causes the group to succeed.
#END_ALTERNATE	Marks the end of an #INCLUDE grouping.
#NOFNR	Prevents the use of NetBIOS directed name queries on LAN Manager UNIX systems.
#MH	Permits multiple entries for multihomed computers.
\0x*nn*	Allows the entry of nonprinting characters in NetBIOS names. Enclose the NetBIOS name in quotation marks and use \0xnn hexadecimal notation to specify a hexadecimal value for the character.

Note

Keywords listed in this section can be used in LMHOSTS files using Microsoft TCP/IP. LAN Manager 2.*x*, however, will treat these keywords as comments.

Of all the LMHOSTS keywords, the one used most frequently is **#PRE**. When using this entry, it's important to remember that the NetBIOS name cache and LMHOSTS file are read sequentially. To increase efficiency, it is best to put the computers you access most frequently at the top of the list and entries tagged with **#PRE** at the bottom. Since **#PRE** tagged entries are cached at TCP/IP initialization, they'll be read from the list only once (at initialization).

Important

LMHOSTS files are static and must be maintained on each computer (except for those portions that are #INCLUDEd from another server). Make sure you update all LMHOSTS files each time a computer is added, removed, or renamed in your networking environment.

```
205.10.12.10 Wkstn1
205.10.12.11 Wkstn2
200.18.22.20 "sfile        \0x14"                        # Special file server
210.22.18.12 Server4          #PRE
210.22.18.14 Server5          #PRE   #DOM:Resource1      # Resource group's PDC
200.18.22.10 Server1          #PRE                       # SQL Server
200.18.22.12 Server2          #PRE                       # Print Server
210.22.18.10 Server3          #PRE                       # Exchange Server
#BEGIN_ALTERNATE
#INCLUDE \\Server4\public\lmhosts                        # adds LMHOSTS from server4
#INCLUDE \\Server5\public\lmhosts                        # adds LMHOSTS from server5
#END_ALTERNATE
```

- The server named **"sfile   \0x14"** contains a special character after the 15 characters in its name (including blanks), so its name is enclosed in quotation marks.
- Server4 and Server5 are preloaded so they can be used later in an #INCLUDE statement as centrally maintained LMHOSTS files.
- Server1, Server2 and Server3 are preloaded, based on the #PRE keyword.

FIGURE 8–3   *LMHOSTS file showing keyword use*

Enabling LMHOSTS Lookup and Importing LMHOSTS Files

LMHOSTS lookup is enabled on the **WINS** tab of the **Advanced TCP/IP Settings** dialog box as shown in Figure 8-4. By default, the LMHOSTS name resolution method is enabled when TCP/IP is installed on a computer. Figure 8-4 also reveals the **Import LMHOSTS** button. Depressing this button permits you to import LMHOSTS from another text file. (The file can be in another directory, a network share, or on a floppy disk. As long as the text in the file meets the LMHOSTS format, the file can have any valid file name.) When the file is selected through this option, the contents are imported into the **\system-root\system32\drivers\etc** directory and given the name LMHOSTS. The new file will replace any existing LMHOSTS file currently in that directory.

LMHOSTS Name Resolution Problems

LMHOSTS name resolution is a simple and reliable process. Unfortunately, as with any manual system, we frequently induce our own problems. Here are the most common LMHOSTS name resolution problems:

An entry for a remote host doesn't exist in the LMHOSTS file. It is likely a machine was added or renamed within your networking environment and a corresponding LMHOSTS entry wasn't made. This could be a problem in the local LMHOSTS file or an oversight in a file that is #INCLUDEd in the local LMHOSTS file.

The NetBIOS name in the LMHOSTS file is misspelled. A misspelled entry is as good as no entry at all. We frequently look at the file, see the

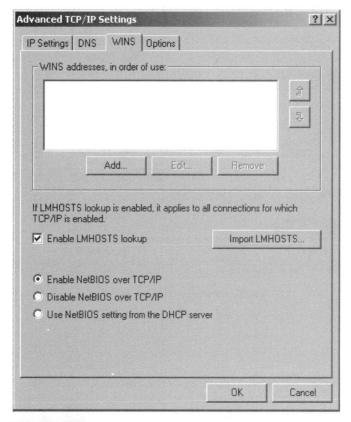

FIGURE 8–4   *Enable LMHOSTS lookup*

name, and decide the problem must lie somewhere else. Attention to detail in LMHOSTS files is of critical importance.

The IP address is invalid for the NetBIOS name. Getting the numbers right is as important as good spelling. Other possible problems here could be that the machine was given a new IP address, became a DHCP client, or has a conflicting mapping on a DNS server.

There are multiple entries for the same NetBIOS name. Carefully check your LMHOSTS file to ensure each entry is unique. When duplicate names are listed in the file, only the first name is used. If the first entry is incorrect, the mapping will not work. You may be looking at a good entry in the file while your problems are being caused by a bogus entry above.

Tip

Try to use each entry in the LMHOSTS file after you enter it to verify that it is correct. You can use an entry by using the **net** command or by **ping**ing the resource using its NetBIOS name.

Using NBTSTAT

The NBTSTAT command line utility enables us to check the state of current NetBIOS over TCP/IP connections. It also allows you to determine your registered name and scope ID and permits you to update the LMHOSTS cache. NBTSTAT is particularly useful for troubleshooting the NetBIOS name cache. NBTSTAT features are described in Table 7.3.

NBTSTAT SYNTAX

`nbtstat` [`-a` *RemoteName*] [`-A` *IP_address*] [`-c`] [`-n`] [`-R`] [`-r`]
[`-S`] [`-s`] [-RR] [*interval*]

TABLE 8.3	NBTSTAT Parameters

Parameter	Description
-a	Returns the remote computer's name table given its host name.
-A	Lists the remote computer's name table given its IP address.
-c	Displays the NetBIOS name cache.
-n	Lists the NetBIOS names registered by the client, either by B-node broadcast or by a WINS server.
-R	Manually purges and reloads the NetBIOS name cache using LMHOSTS entries tagged with #PRE. Ensure you use this after changing entries tagged by #PRE to update their new values in the current cache.
-r	Lists name resolution statistics for Windows networking.
-S	Displays workstation and server sessions, listing the remote hosts by IP address only.
-s	Displays workstation and server sessions. It attempts to convert the remote host IP address to a name using the HOSTS file.
-RR	Sends Name Release packets to WINs followed by a Refresh.
Interval	Redisplays selected statistics, pausing *interval* seconds between each display. Press Ctrl+C to stop redisplaying statistics. If this parameter is omitted, **nbtstat** prints the current configuration information once.

Microsoft Methods of Resolving NetBIOS Names

Windows 2000 has a wide repertoire of techniques for NetBIOS name resolution as shown in Figure 8-5 and described here.

- **Name Cache**: The first step in name resolution always is to check the local name cache.

- **NetBIOS Name Server**: If the cache does not yield the appropriate information, three attempts are made to contact a NetBIOS name server. For this to happen, the machine must be configured to go to a name server. This step is normally accomplished before resorting to broadcast but may be attempted after broadcast depending on the setting of the *Name Resolution Node*.
- **Broadcast**: If the NetBIOS name server doesn't resolve the name, the computer will generate three broadcasts on the local network.
- **LMHOSTS**: If broadcast doesn't yield the necessary information, the local LMHOSTS file is parsed.
- **HOSTS**: At this point, NetBIOS resolution has failed and the system attempts host name resolution. This is resolution through a host name or fully qualified domain name, which corresponds to a NetBIOS name. To proceed to this step, the computer must be configured to use a DNS server. The first step in host name resolution is to check the HOSTS file on the local computer for an IP address mapping. (We'll thoroughly discuss the HOSTS file in Chapter 10.)
- **DNS**: If a mapping was not found in the HOSTS file, the computer sends a resolution request to its configured DNS server.

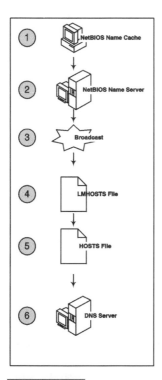

FIGURE 8–5   *Microsoft NetBIOS name resolution steps*

If none of the name resolution techniques is successful, the Windows 2000 command that prompted the resolution attempt fails and returns an error.

Disabling NetBIOS

As we mentioned at the start of the chapter, a Windows 2000 network operating in Native Mode can fully function without the use of NetBIOS. To disable NetBIOS, go to the **WINS** tab of the **Advanced TCP/IP Settings** dialog box as shown in Figure 8-6. NetBIOS over TCP/IP is enabled by default but you may disable it or set it to be automatically configured by DHCP. Although Windows 2000 can function properly without NetBIOS, you should exercise great caution when disabling it. Without NetBIOS, many other network operating systems (to include previous versions of Windows and Windows NT) will be unable to fully communicate with your Windows 2000 installation. Additionally, a great number of legacy applications depend on NetBIOS connectivity. The good news is that the Windows 2000 implementation of NetBIOS over TCP/IP is very robust and performs very efficiently on your Windows 2000 network!

Summary

In this chapter we saw that NetBIOS was a native language for network application communication and that NetBIOS could be carried by a transport protocol over the network. NetBIOS over TCP/IP is really, therefore, a protocol within a protocol.

We saw that NetBIOS provided a number of important networking functions to include session establishment, and connection-oriented and connectionless data transfer. The function we spent most of our time with, however, was NetBIOS name registration and resolution. We saw that, before a TCP/IP connection can be established, NetBIOS names must be resolved to an IP address (and then to a MAC address), and we learned a number of ways name resolution could be accomplished.

When a computer first initializes under TCP/IP, it attempts to register its NetBIOS name with a name server or (by broadcast) with the machines on the local network. If the name hasn't already been registered by another machine, the name is registered on the network and becomes that machine's identity.

When a computer needs to establish a session with another computer it first checks its own NetBIOS name cache to resolve the target computer's name to an IP address. If the cache doesn't yield an IP address mapping, the computer queries a NetBIOS name server, then tries a name resolution broadcast, checks the LMHOSTS file, then the HOSTS file, and finally queries its DNS server. If none of these methods yield an IP address mapping, the TCP/IP session will not be established. We discovered that we can set a *name resolution node* to control the order in which the computer uses name server and broadcast resolution and saw that the NBTSTAT utility provides a way to monitor and control a number of NetBIOS over TCP/IP functions.

We also learned how to create an LMHOSTS file and saw that it was simply a text file that contains IP addresses and NetBIOS names. We reviewed a number of keywords that permitted us to preload selected LMHOSTS entries into the NetBIOS name cache and include other LMHOSTS entries into the local machine's LMHOSTS file. We found that, although the LMHOSTS file is a simple text file, it requires constant manual maintenance to ensure it contains the NetBIOS names and IP addresses of network resources the local computer needs to communicate with.

Test Yourself

1. NetBIOS operates at the _____ layer.
   A. Datalink
   B. Application
   C. Presentation
   D. Network

2. What is the first step a computer takes when it needs to find the IP address for a NetBIOS resource?
   A. Broadcasts for a response
   B. Checks Local cache
   C. Queries the local NetBIOS name server
   D. Depends on the NetBIOS Name Resolution Node

3. The LMHOSTS table can provide quick NetBIOS name resolution. What is NOT a potential problem in creating LMHOSTS tables?
   A. Multiple entries for the same host
   B. Case sensitivity
   C. Table out of date
   D. Entry misspelled

4. A NetBIOS client can obtain NetBIOS name resolution through a DNS server.

A. True

B. False

5. Machines on the local network may have identical NetBIOS names:

A. If they have different host names

B. If everyone knows they'll not be able to differentiate between them

C. As long as they use different name scopes

D. Never

Implementing Windows Internet Name Service

*B*y now, you should have determined that NetBIOS name resolution may be critical to the operation of your network and its applications. You should also have decided that NetBIOS name resolution broadcasts don't enhance network operation and that the maintenance of an LMHOSTS file is a real pain! Before you start looking for another protocol to meet your needs, read on. The Windows Internet Name Service (WINS) will automatically track NetBIOS names for your network and make sure all your machines can match names and IP addresses with ease. This chapter will tell you how to put a WINS server on the job, how to tell other machines in the network about it, how to get it to work with other WINS servers, and how to maintain and monitor it.

The WINS Process

In order for WINS to operate, each machine that will use it for name resolution must know the WINS server's IP address. This includes machines that register their names with WINS as well as machines that interrogate WINS for a name/IP address match. Machines configured with the WINS server's IP address are known as *WINS clients*. Since WINS clients must always know where to find the WINS server, WINS servers *must* have static IP addresses.

The basic WINS process consists of three simple steps:

- When a WINS client starts up, it registers with the designated WINS server, providing its NetBIOS name and IP address.

- When a WINS client wishes to contact another machine, it queries the designated WINS server for an IP address to match the NetBIOS name of the computer it's looking for.
- If the WINS server finds a NetBIOS name/IP address mapping for the desired machine in its database, it returns the information to the client.

As you can see, the WINS database is dynamically updated (each time a client starts up). Because of this, the WINS database is always up to date.

Now that we know the basic WINS process, let's dig a bit deeper. WINS concerns itself with four basic processes: *Name Registration*, *Name Renewal*, *Name Release*, and *Name Query and Response*. WINS is based on RFC 1001 and RFC 1002 and uses standard methods for name registration, discovery, and release. The WINS Name Renewal procedures are peculiar to NetBIOS name servers.

Name Registration

When the WINS client starts, it sends a name registration request directly to the designated WINS server. The name registration actually occurs when the client's services (such as Workstation and Server) start. When it receives the registration request, the WINS server checks its database to determine if this name is already registered by another machine. If the client's NetBIOS name is unique, the server returns a message indicating successful registration and the amount of time the registration will be valid. (This registration duration is known as *Time to Live* or TTL.) If the WINS server finds a duplicate NetBIOS name in its database, it sends a name query request to the currently registered owner. The request is sent three times at half-second intervals. (If the computer has more than one network interface card, three requests are sent to each card). If the currently registered computer answers one of the queries, the new client receives a negative registration response from the WINS server. If the currently registered machine fails to respond, a successful registration message is returned to the new client. If the WINS client isn't able to contact the designated WINS server at startup, it makes two additional attempts (by default at 15-second intervals). If after the three attempts it still can't find the designated WINS server, it will attempt to contact a secondary WINS server (provided it has been configured with the IP address of additional servers). If the client is unable to reach a WINS server, it may broadcast its NetBIOS name to the network to ensure another machine isn't currently using that name. Additionally, the client will continue to attempt contact with a WINS server every 10 minutes until one responds.

Name Renewal

As we have seen, a successful name registration is good only for a specified duration. After one-eighth of the TTL has elapsed, the client will attempt to refresh its name registration. If the WINS server doesn't respond, the client continues to seek a refresh every 10 minutes for an hour. If unsuccessful, the client continues to cycle through alternate WINS servers in the same manner (if it gets to the end, it will cycle back through the primary server) until it gets a response or until its TTL has expired. If no response is received by TTL expiration, the client releases its WINS registration. The WINS server's name refresh response contains a new TTL, effectively extending the client's name registration. After the client successfully refreshes its initial name registration, future refresh requests are sent when 50 percent of the new TTL has elapsed.

Name Release

Since we don't wish to fill the WINS database with any unnecessary data, a well-behaved WINS client will release its name at shutdown. When a WINS client undergoes a normal shutdown, it sends a name release request to the server for each of its registered names. The request contains the NetBIOS names to be removed and their associated IP addresses. When the server receives the request, it checks its name database. If its database shows the NetBIOS name associated with a different IP address or if it discovers a database error, it will send a negative response to the client. Otherwise, the WINS server marks the client's name as released and sends a positive response containing the released name with a TTL of 0. (More on the subject later in the chapter.)

Name Query/Response

The default configuration for a WINS client uses the Hybrid node (H-node) for NetBIOS over TCP/IP. Under the H-node, a client first queries a WINS server and, if unable to find a NetBIOS name/IP address mapping, resorts to a broadcast. The process consists of only three basic steps:

- When the client executes a network command, it first checks its own NetBIOS name cache of an IP address/NetBIOS name mapping for the machine it's trying to reach.
- If the desired information isn't found in cache, the client queries its primary WINS server. If the primary server fails to respond, the client makes two additional attempts before trying a secondary WINS server (if one is designated). The client will continue to cycle through designated WINS servers (making three attempts each) until it makes contact or exhausts the list.
- If WINS servers are available but they cannot resolve the name request, the WINS client receives a "Requested name does not exist" message. If the client receives such a message or if it receives no WINS server response, it will resort to a broadcast. (The client will actually make three B-node broadcasts.) If the client still cannot find

a NetBIOS name/IP address match, it may be able to obtain name resolution through the LMHOSTS or HOSTS files or by querying a DNS server.

WINS Planning Considerations

Now that you're sold on WINS, let's look at some planning considerations prior to actually installing and configuring a WINS server.

What are the requirements for a WINS server? A WINS server must be a Windows 2000 server (does not need to be a domain controller) with a static IP address, subnet mask, default gateway, and other TCP/IP parameters as required.

How many WINS servers do I need to install? Since name resolution requests are directed datagrams that route between subnets, one WINS server can service an entire internetwork. The addition of at least one more WINS server is a good idea, however, since it provides a measure of fault tolerance.

How many clients can a WINS server handle? The average WINS server can handle 10,000 clients.

What are the requirements to be a WINS client? Any computer running Windows 2000, Windows NT, Windows 95, Windows 98, Windows for Workgroups 3.11, Microsoft Network Client 3.0 for MS-DOS, or LAN Manager 2.2c for MS-DOS can become a WINS client. To become a WINS client, the computer must be provided with the IP address of a primary WINS server and (optionally) the IP address of one or more secondary WINS servers.

WINS Implementation

To implement WINS on our network, we'll first install WINS on a Windows 2000 server. Once the server is installed, we'll need to configure static mappings for non-WINS clients and will configure a WINS proxy agent to extend WINS name resolution to non-WINS clients. Finally, we'll configure our client machines to participate in WINS. We've already seen how to use the Dynamic Host Configuration Protocol (DCHP) to configure a WINS client; here we'll use a static configuration to accomplish the same thing.

WINS Installation

To install WINS go to the **Control Panel → Add/Remove Programs** dialog window, click **Add/Remove Windows Components**, and then the **Components** button to open **Windows Components Wizard**. Select **Networking Services** and click **Details** (see Figure 9-1). Select **Windows Internet Name Service (WINS)** and click **OK** (see Figure 9-2). Click **Next** to let Windows install and configure the necessary components.

Tip

If WINS is installed on a multihomed server, it will accept name registrations and queries on each IP address.

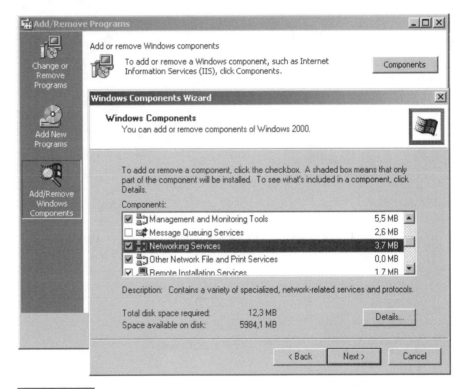

FIGURE 9–1   *Installing WINS through Windows components wizard*

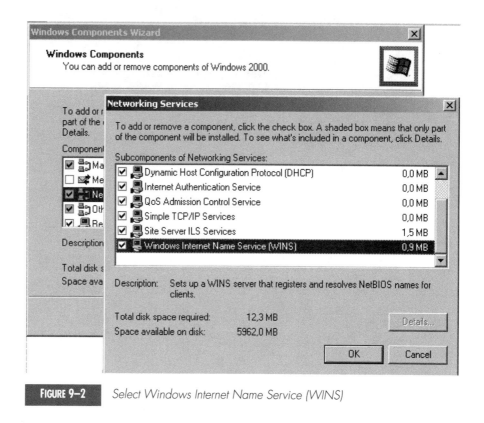

FIGURE 9–2 *Select Windows Internet Name Service (WINS)*

Configuring Static Entries and Proxy Agents

Although your newly installed WINS is now fully functional and ready to handle the requests of any DHCP client, a bit of configuration will enable it to service non-DHCP clients too.

Static Entries

By adding static IP/address/NetBIOS name mappings for non-WINS clients, we can use the WINS server to provide this information to our WINS clients. To configure a static mapping, go to **Start | Programs**, select **Administrative Tools**, and launch the **WINS** console snap-in, which was installed on your system when you installed the WINS server (see Figure 9-3).

In the console tree select your WINS server and click **Active Registrations**. Then, on the **Action** menu click **New Static Mapping** to open the

New Static Mapping dialog box (see Figure 9-4). There you can enter the following information to complete the static mapping:

- In **Computer name**, type the NetBIOS name of the computer.
- In **NetBIOS scope (optional)**, you can type a NetBIOS scope identifier, if one is used for the computer. Otherwise, leave this field blank.
- In **Type**, click one of the supported types to indicate whether this entry is a **Unique**, **Group**, **Domain Name**, **Internet**, or **Multi-homed** type entry (Table 9.1 details the meaning of each type).
- In **IP address**, type the address for the computer.
- Click **Apply** to add the static mapping entry to the database.
- Click on the **Mappings** menu and select **Static Mappings**.
- When the **Static Mappings** dialog box opens, click **Add Mappings**.
- You now see the **Add Static Mappings** dialog box. Type the name and IP address of the non-WINS client in the appropriate fields and select the appropriate type in the Type box (Table 9.1 details the meaning of each type).
- Next click on **Add** and the mapping is added to the database. If you wish to add more static mappings, repeat the above process for each and click **OK** when you're done.
- If you have an LMHOSTS file that already contains static mappings, you may import the mappings from the file by choosing the **Import LMHOSTS File** option from the **Action** menu and providing the path to the LMHOSTS file you wish to import.

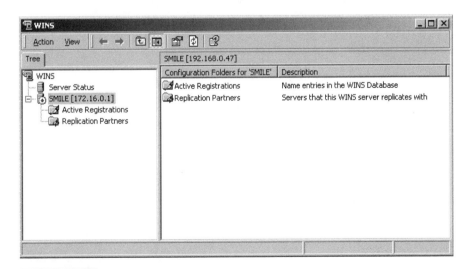

FIGURE 9–3   *WINS console*

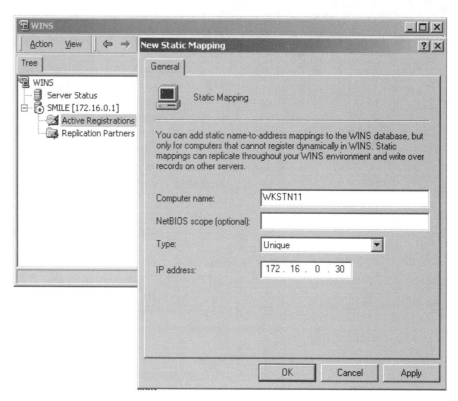

FIGURE 9–4   *WINS static mappings*

TABLE 9.1   *Static Mapping Types*

Option	Description
Unique	Allows you to specify a unique name in the database, with one address per name.
Group	Allows you to specify a normal group, where addresses of individual members are not stored in the WINS database and there is no limit to the number of members that can be added to the group. The client broadcasts name packets to communicate with normal groups.
Domain Name	Allows you to specify a group with NetBIOS names that have 0x1C as the 16th byte. A domain name group stores up to 25 addresses for members. For registrations after the 25th address, WINS overwrites a replica address or, if none is present, it overwrites the oldest registration. If you choose this option, additional controls appear so that you can add multiple addresses to the list.

TABLE 9.1	*Static Mapping Types (continued)*

Option	Description
Internet Group	Internet groups are user-defined special groups that store up to 25 addresses for members. Click this option to specify your own group of NetBIOS names and IP addresses. By default, a space character (0x20) is appended to the name as the 16th byte. You can override this by placing a new character in brackets at the end of the Internet group name. WINS will pad the name with spaces up to the 15th character and use the new character (the one in brackets) as the 16th character.
	This option will permit you to group resources, such as printers, RAS Servers, and Network Monitor Agents, for easy browsing. If you choose this option, additional controls appear so that you can add multiple addresses to the list.
Multihomed	Allows you to specify a unique name that can have more than one address (multihomed computers). The maximum number of addresses is 25. For registrations after the 25th address, WINS overwrites a replica address or, if none is present, it overwrites the oldest registration. If you choose this option, additional controls appear so that you can add multiple addresses to the list

WINS Proxy Agents

Now that our WINS clients can get addresses of non-WINS clients through static mappings, it is only fair that we provide non-WINS clients an opportunity to obtain name resolution from our WINS server. To do this, we can employ WINS proxy agents which simply listen for a NetBIOS name resolution broadcast and forward it as a request to a designated WINS server.

When a non-WINS client broadcasts a name registration message, the proxy agent forwards the request to the WINS server to ensure a duplicate name isn't already registered. In this capacity, the WINS server provides a validity check only; the non-WINS client's NetBIOS name is not registered in the WINS server's database.

On the other hand, when a non-WINS client makes a name resolution request, the proxy agent comes to its aid! First, the proxy agent checks its own NetBIOS name cache. If it can make the name resolution from the cache, it returns the information to the client and the WINS server is never bothered. If the proxy agent can't provide the requested information, it forwards the request to the WINS server. When the WINS server responds with the address match, the proxy agent adds the information to its cache and passes it onto the client.

It is a good idea to place a WINS proxy agent on each subnet that has non-WINS clients. Even if the subnet has routers configured to forward broadcasts, placing a WINS proxy agent on each subnet will reduce broadcast traffic and is encouraged. No more than one WINS proxy agent should be placed on any subnet (multiple proxy agents on the same subnet will result in multiple resolution messages to the WINS server for the same client and will impact smooth network operation), and each proxy agent must be a WINS client (proxy agents cannot be WINS servers). Any computer running Winows 2000, Windows NT, Windows 95, Windows 98, or Windows for Workgroups 3.11 can be configured as a WINS proxy agent.

CONFIGURING A WINDOWS 2000 COMPUTER AS A WINS PROXY AGENT

Creating a proxy agent requires only a simple registry edit. Launch the Registry Editor (Regedit or Regedt32) and open HKEY_LOCAL_MACHINE\System\CurrentControlSet\Services\ NetBT\Parameters and set EnableProxy (REG_DWORD) to 1. Once this value is changed, simply restart the machine and you have a WINS proxy agent (ensure this machine is configured as a WINS client).

WINS Client Configuration

Now that our WINS server and proxy agents are functioning, we still need to configure some computers to be WINS clients. Actually, Windows 2000 clients are configured by default to use a DHCP server to obtain an IP address. In this case, no further client-side configuration is needed provided the DHCP server is set to provide WINS configuration information.

Let's see how we can do it manually as well. This step turns out to be the easiest of all. Go to the **Network and Dial-up Connections** dialog box, open the **Internet Protocol (TCP/IP) Properties** window, and then **Advanced TCP/IP Settings**. Select the **WINS** tab and use **Add** to add WINS server(s), as shown in Figure 9-5.

Primary/Secondary WINS Servers

What happens if we add more than one WINS server? Let's see how WINS servers are used by clients. Usually, a client makes use of a WINS server in one of two ways: as a primary or secondary WINS server. (Windows 2000 permits up to 11 secondary servers. While it might be more appropriate to term these "alternate" servers, "secondary" is used to relate to earlier Windows implementations that allowed only one primary and one secondary server.) The difference between primary and secondary WINS servers is only in the way the client looks at them. Normally, the client uses only the primary WINS server for its NetBIOS name service functions (name registration, renewal,

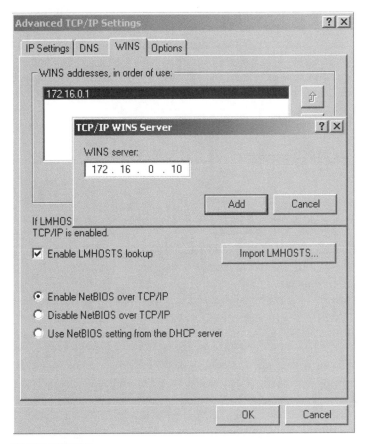

FIGURE 9–5 *WINS addresses*

query, and resolution). Secondary WINS servers are queried only when the primary WINS server is not available on the network or when it is unable to resolve a name for the client. (This latter issue is a recent enhancement to WINS. In earlier WINS implementations, a secondary WINS server was contacted only when the primary was unavailable. When the primary was unable to provide a mapping, the client would resort to non-WINS resolution methods without querying the secondary server.) When the client resorts to a secondary server because the primary is unavailable, it—the client—periodically tries to switch back to its primary WINS server for future service requests.

Although Windows 2000 and Windows 98 WINS clients permit a list of up to 12 secondary WINS servers, configuring more than one or two secondary servers may be counterproductive. Since a properly configured WINS server system should employ replication (which we'll discuss shortly), all WINS servers should contain the same information most of the time (there may be some inconsistencies arising from normal replication delays but this should be rare). Since a client will cycle through the list of secondary servers when it is unable to get name resolution from the primary server, it will likely make an unsuccessful query to every server on the list. This will delay the client's decision to resort to non-WINS methods and may result in a longer time to connect to the target computer.

Database Replication Between WINS Servers

So far we've had fun configuring WINS servers and WINS proxy agents but what if we want to operate a WINS service on multiple subnets or between subnets? What if we want to ensure a client can get a WINS name resolution on another subnet quickly and efficiently, and what if we want to minimize the amount of traffic routed between subnets? The solution to all of this is as simple as configuring our WINS server to replicate its database with a WINS server on another subnet (see Figure 9-6). Properly configured, WINS servers can get the name resolution information for another subnet directly from that subnet's WINS server. This permits the server to fully service all of its clients and eliminates the requirement for multiple routed client requests to a WINS server on the other subnet. Since replication between servers is accomplished only when a particular entry changes, internetwork WINS communication is sharply reduced.

WINS servers configured to replicate their databases are known as *push partners*, *pull partners*, or *push-pull partners*.

- A push partner sends a message to its pull partners that its database has changed. The pull partners then respond with a replication request, which causes the push partner to send a copy of the new entries. Change messages are transmitted based on an arbitrary number of WINS updates, as configured by the WINS administrator or initiated by the WINS administrator immediately by using WINS snap-in. A push partner may also be configured to send a push message at system start up.
- A pull partner requests WINS entries having a higher version number than that received during its last replication. The version number comparison ensures the pull partner always receives the most up-to-date information without requiring the transmission of redundant information. Pull partners request changes at system start up, based on a message from their push partner, an arbitrary time interval, as configured by the WINS administrator, or immediate replication, initiated by the WINS administrator by using the WINS snap-in.

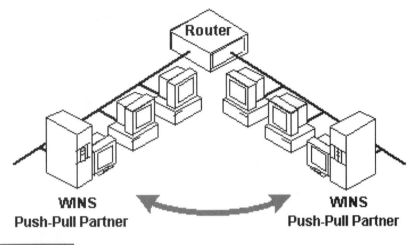

FIGURE 9–6   *Push-Pull partners on multiple subnets*

Typically, WINS servers are configured as both push and pull partners to ensure complete database replication. Primary and secondary WINS server pairs *must* be push-pull partners to ensure complete database replication. You may want to configure a machine as just a pull partner if it will replicate between sites and over a slow link, since you can configure replication to occur at specific intervals. When a fast network link is available, push partners (or push-pull partners) provide the best response since replication will occur after a predetermined number of changes have occurred to the database.

Configuring WINS Database Replication

Configuring your own push and pull partners couldn't be easier. First, launch the **WINS snap-in** from the **Administrative Tools** program group. From the console tree select **Replication Partners**; right-click and choose **New Replication Partner** to reveal the dialog box (see Figure 9-7).

Enter the **IP address** of the WINS server you want to partner with and click **OK**. Now the server can be seen in the **Replication Partners** box of the WINS console. Right-click the newly added replication partner in the details pane, select **Properties**, and click the **Advanced** tab to configure properties (see Figure 9-8). You may select *Push*, *Pull*, or *Push/Pull* replication partner types. (Push/Pull is the default and permits you to configure properties for both replication types.)

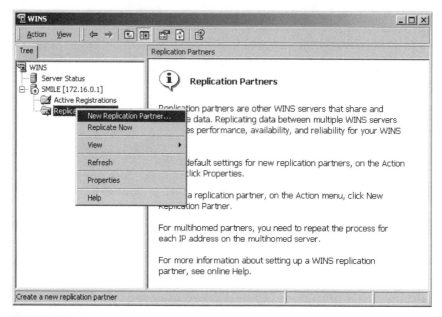

FIGURE 9–7   *Adding a new replication partner*

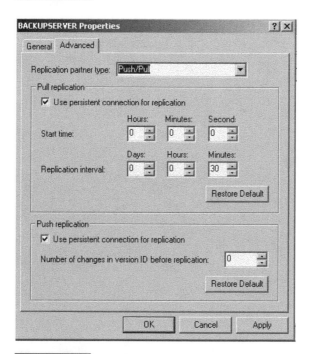

FIGURE 9–8   *Configuring replication*

Important When configuring WINS servers running on multihomed computers for replication, all of their IP addresses must be entered as replication partners.

Once your replication partners are installed, you can spend a few moments configuring your server to support them. To view replication partner properties right-click the **Replication Partners** folder and select **Properties** to reveal the dialog box shown in Figure 9-9.

By default, this server will replicate only with partners you've added. If you clear the *Replicate only with partners* check box, it will replicate with any WINS server on the network. Typically, unique and multihomed records entered as static mappings are not removed from the database when a conflict is discovered. By checking *Overwrite unique static mappings at this server (migrate on)*, you can make your server treat these records as dynamic entries when a conflict is detected.

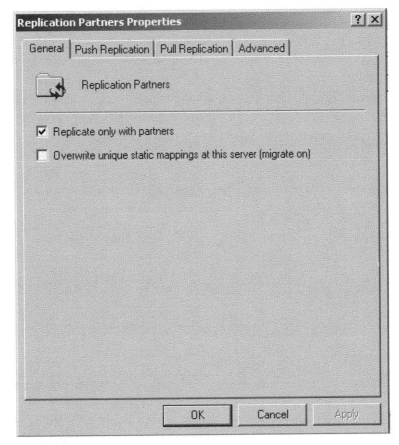

FIGURE 9-9   *Replication partners properties—General tab*

The **Push Replication** tab (Figure 9-10) permits you to configure the start characteristics and replication criteria. You may force a push when the service starts (you'll notice that this is unchecked by default). You may also force a push when an address mapping changes. You should enter the number of changes that will be required to force a replication; entering 0 prevents push replication from occurring. (This parameter is a default; it becomes part of the individual partner properties when a new partner is added. To configure existing partners, right-click the partner, select **Properties**, select the **Advanced** tab, and click **Restore Default** under **Push replication**.) By selecting persistent connections, you can ensure WINS servers maintain constant session connections with their partners. If all machines are connected by high-speed links (e.g., a LAN), it is a good idea to keep them connected to reduce the overhead of continually connecting and disconnecting (this is a *default* setting and is propagated to individual partner properties as described earlier).

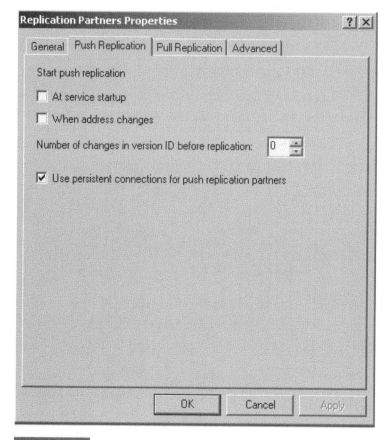

FIGURE 9–10 *Replication partners properties—Push Replication tab*

Figure 9-11 shows the **Pull Replication** tab. Here you may configure the time replication is to begin and the time between pull replications. If **Start time** is set to all 0s, no pull replication will be undertaken. The **Number of retries** option sets the number of times the system will attempt to connect to a partner (if the partner fails to respond the first time). When the number of retries is used up, pull replication will be attempted again once the **Replication interval** has elapsed. You may configure pull replication to start when the service starts (unlike push replication this feature is on by default). You may also configure persistent connections in the same manner as with push replication. The **Start time**, **Replication interval**, and **Persistent connections** features are defaults and are propagated to individual partner properties as described in the previous paragraph.

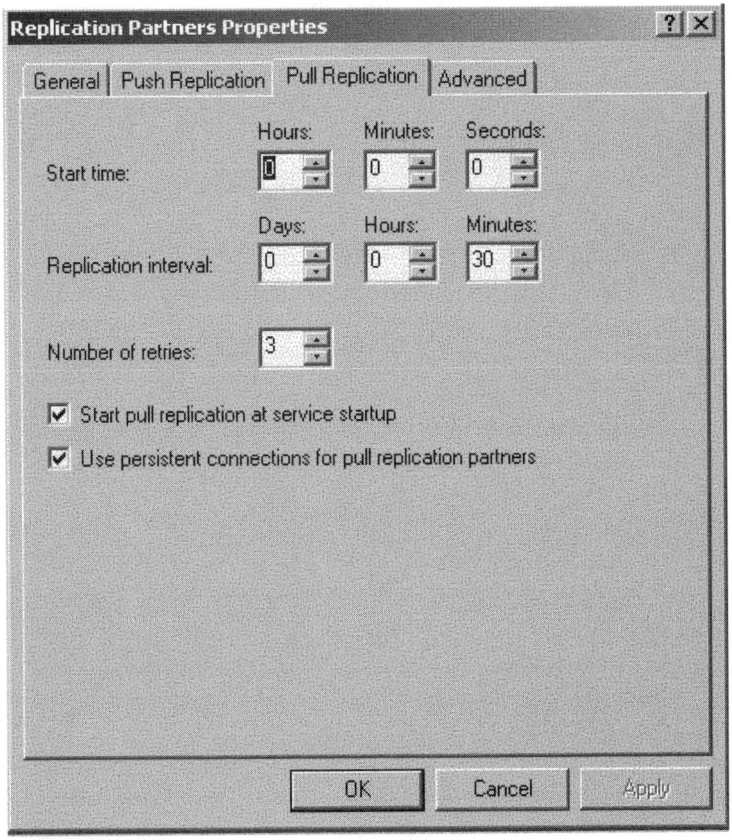

FIGURE 9–11   *Replication partners properties—Pull Replication tab*

The **Advanced** tab is shown in Figure 9-12. You can add addresses for WINS servers that have become inactive under *Block records from these owners*. This will filter replicated databases and take out records that belong to a server that is no longer active and, therefore, can no longer update or delete them. You may also enable automatic replication as described in the next section. (This feature is not enabled by default.) You may also set the multicast interval and TTL, also described in the next section.

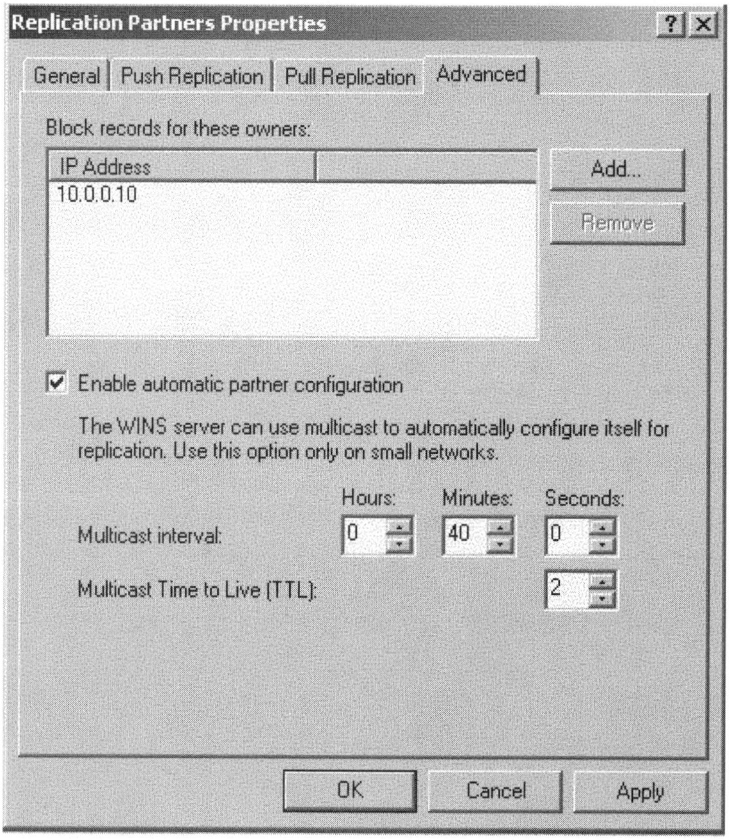

FIGURE 9–12   *Replication partners proprieties—Advanced tab*

Automatic Replication Partners

Replication may be configured to occur automatically on your network. If your network is capable of multicasting, the WINS server will automatically find other WINS servers. This is done by multicasting to 224.0.1.24 every 40 minutes (By default, the multicast datagram has a TTL of only two seconds to minimize its impact on other network traffic.) If it finds a WINS server, it automatically configures it as a push and pull partner with pull replication set for every 2 hours. Automatically created partnership data is also maintained automatically. When a WINS server is discovered through multicast, it is automatically removed as a replication partner at shutdown. This option should be used only on small networks with three or fewer WINS servers because of the network overhead created by the multicast announcements. (If the network doesn't support multicasting, automatic replication will occur only for WINS servers found on the local subnet.)

WINS Server Configuration

Although WINS servers generally take care of themselves quite well, we can take a few configuration steps to make our network more efficient. The most important WINS configuration consideration is to ensure that the WINS database is periodically purged of entries that are no longer valid. These may be entries that were previously released or those registered by another WINS server but never removed. This can be done manually by using the **Scavenge Database** option from the WINS console **Action** menu (see Figure 9-13) or it may be accomplished by setting the appropriate options in the **Server Configuration** dialog box. To set configuration options, select the desired server from the console tree, right-click, and select **Properties** to open the corresponding window. The options in this window will drive the server to perform cleanup activities at specified intervals.

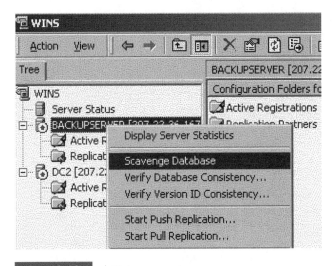

FIGURE 9–13   *Initiate scavenging*

More configuration options are available by right-clicking the server in the WINS console and selecting **Properties**. This will reveal the dialog box shown in Figure 9-14.

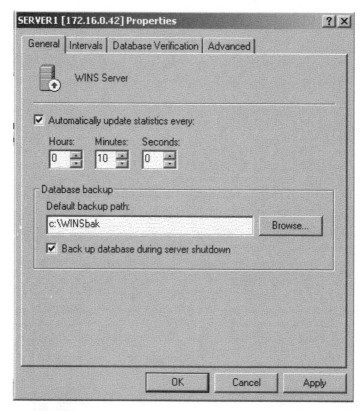

FIGURE 9–14   *WINS server properties—General tab*

You may view server statistics by right-clicking the server and selecting statistics, which, by default, are updated every 10 minutes. You may disable statistics generation or alter the time interval on the **General** tab of the server properties. The **General** tab is also where you configure a backup path for the WINS database. We'll discuss database backups in the next section but no backup action will transpire if you don't first enter a path here (one is not entered by default). You may also control whether the database is automatically backed up when the WINS service shuts down.

The **Intervals** tab in Figure 9-15 controls how long WINS records will remain in the database. The *Renew Interval* sets the time interval at which a client *must* renew its name on the server; WINS clients begin attempting to refresh their name registrations after one half of this interval has elapsed. The

Extinction Interval is the interval between the time a database entry is marked as *released* and the time it's marked *extinct*, and the *Extinction Timeout* is the length of time before an extinct entry is scavenged from the WINS database. The default time for Renew Interval is 6 days. The Extinction Interval defaults to 4 days; it must be at least the Renew Interval or 4 days, whichever is smaller. The Extinction Timeout defaults to 6 days; it must be at least 1 day and equal to or greater than the Renew Interval. As you can see, by default, a released entry will remain in the database for 10 days (4 to become extinct and 6 more to be removed). An entry from a machine that leaves the network without releasing its information can remain in the database for 16 days.

Verification Interval specifies the time after which the WINS server checks to ensure names it received from other servers are still active. This option is set to 24 days, which is the minimum allowable value.

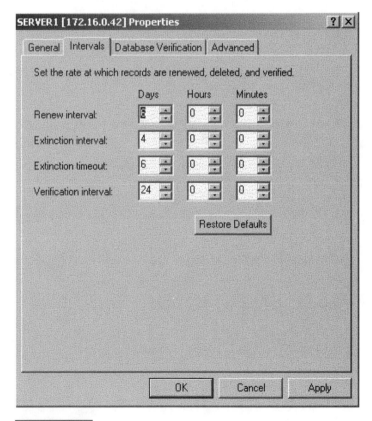

FIGURE 9–15   *WINS server properties—Intervals tab*

The **Database Verification** tab (see Figure 9-16) permits you to enable database consistency checking (disabled by default). Enabling consistency checking ensures integrity among WINS servers in a large network. The server doing consistency checking retrieves records from the other servers' databases and compares them with its own records. If the records are identical, the local server updates its record's time stamp. If the records differ and if the remote record has a higher version number, the remote record is added to the local database and the original record is marked for deletion.

The default check interval is 24 hours but can be modified in the dialog box. Verification is scheduled to start at 2:00 A.M., but this may be altered using the *Begin verifying at* edit windows. The default verification checks up to 30,000 records but this, too, may be customized. Finally, you can choose to verify against only the servers that own the records (the default) against other WINS servers selected on a random basis.

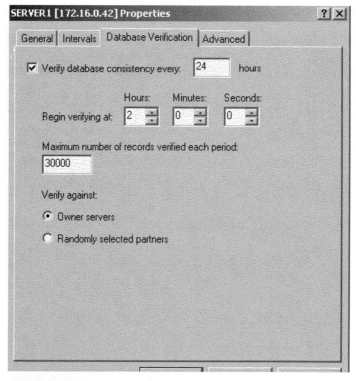

FIGURE 9-16   *WINS server properties—Database Verification tab*

Clicking the **Advanced** tab will reveal several "advanced options:"

- *Log detailed events to Windows event log* permits verbose event logging (leave off to enhance performance).

- *Enable burst handling* sets the number of requests that the server can handle at one time before clients have to retry registration or renewal.
- *Database path* shows the current path to the database and permits you to change it to a new location. Changing the path is a nontrivial issue. As a minimum, the WINS service will restart. You'll also need to copy the files from the old path to the new path or force immediate replication to rebuild the database.
- *Starting version ID* sets the highest version ID number for the database. Use this to specify a new version when the database becomes corrupt and requires a fresh start.
- By default, computer names are expected to use the LAN Manager naming convention, which limits names to 15 characters with the 16th byte representing the name type. The check box at the bottom of the dialog box enforces those conventions. Leave this checked unless your network accepts NetBIOS names from sources that don't comply with the convention.

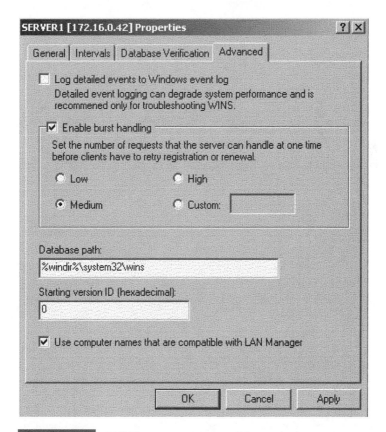

FIGURE 9–17   *WINS server properties—Advanced tab*

Burst Handling

The WINS *burst handling* feature enables WINS servers to cope with peak loads arising from a large number of clients attempting to register names at the same time. This can occur because of a power failure or because users report to work and power their machines up at the same time. When a preset number of simultaneous registration attempts (default is 500) is detected, the server shifts to burst mode. In burst mode, clients are immediately given a positive response without a check of the WINS database. The accompanying TTL, however, is random and relatively short (5 to 50 minutes). The assumption is that the random short TTLs will force the clients to reregister after the peak load has abated, when the server can perform a full check of the data.

The number of simultaneous registrations that cause the server to switch to burst mode can be configured on the erver properties **Advanced** tab (see Figure 9-17). *Low* sets the number to 300, *Medium*—the default—sets the threshold to 500, and *High* places the number at 1,000. If none of these values suit you, select **Custom** and enter your own threshold value.

The WINS Database

You're probably tired of reading about the WINS database without actually getting to see it. We can fix that right now! In the WINS console tree, click **Active Registrations** of the applicable WINS server. On the **Action** menu, click **Find by Owner** to reveal the corresponding dialog window. Under **Display records for**, click **This owner**, and then click a selected owner from the list.

After you click **Find Now**, the filtered WINS database appears in the details pane, showing only those records that are registered to the selected owner (see Figure 9-18.)

You may display the database sorted by any of the headers shown simply by clicking on the header. Each time you click, the sort order changes from ascending to descending. Note that the type of record is spelled out (along with the NetBIOS 16th character identifier name) in the **Type** column. The figure shows active, tombstoned, and released records. Records with an 'x' in the **Static** column are statically mapped records. Numbers in the **Version** column are unique hexadecimal numbers used by the server's pull-partner to determine if this is a new record. The **Expiration** column shows the date and time when the entry will need to be renewed.

If you select a record and right-click it, you are given the option to delete it from the database (see Figure 9-19). If you select *Delete the record only from this server,* the record is immediately deleted from the local machine. If it has replicated to other servers, however, it will remain in their databases and **may**, ultimately, replicate back to this machine. By selecting

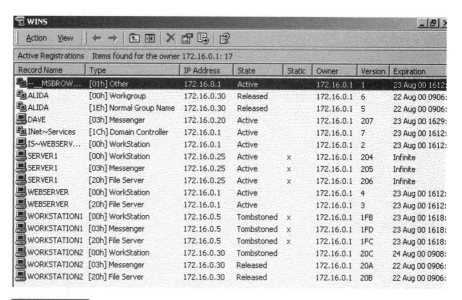

FIGURE 9-18   *WINS database*

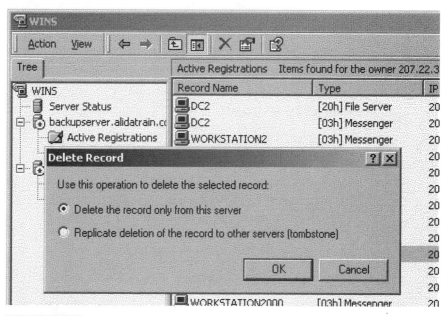

FIGURE 9-19   *Delete record*

Replicate deletion of the record to other servers (tombstone), you force your server to take ownership of the record and change the record's status to *tombstoned.* Although the record isn't immediately deleted, the tombstoning process will ultimately purge the record from the entire network.

The *Delete Owner* option from the **Action** menu permits you to delete a WINS server and all its entries from the current database. Ensure the desired WINS server is selected in the WINS console tree window and click **Delete Owner**.

WINS Database Maintenance

Like DHCP, WINS uses the Microsoft Jet database engine, a reliable database product that requires very little user intervention.

DATABASE BACKUP AND RESTORATION

The database is automatically backed up every 3 hours after you specify the backup directory in the WINS Manager. You may also force an immediate backup using the **Backup** option on the **Mappings** menu. In the event of corruption you can restore the database using one of the following methods:

1. Stop and restart the WINS server service. The WINS server service will automatically restore the database if it detects corruption.
2. Stop the WINS server service, go to the WINS console **Action** menu, and click **Restore Database**. You can specify the directory containing the backup copy and the restore will be initiated. At the completion of the restore, the service starts automatically.

COMPACTING THE DATABASE

Windows 2000 will automatically compact the WINS database. Earlier Windows versions did not offer this convenience. To manually compact the database, first stop the WINS server service. Next, go to the *\systemroot*SYSTEM32\WINS directory and run the **JETPACK** utility. To run **JETPACK**, type **jetpack wins.mdb temp.mdb**. This action causes the wins.mdb to be compacted into temp.mdb. When the compact is complete, temp.mdb is copied back to wins.mdb and temp.mdb is deleted. Once you have compacted the database, restart the WINS server service.

FILES USED BY THE WINS DATABASE

The files listed in Table 9.2 are used by the WINS database. They are located in the *\systemroot*SYSTEM32\WINS and should be neither deleted nor modified.

TABLE 9.2	*WINS Database Files*

File Name	**Description**
WINS.MDB	WINS database
WINSTMP.MDB	Temporary database file
J50.LOG	Database transaction logs—used by WINS for automatic data recovery
J50.CHK	A WINS checkpoint file

Summary

This chapter has shown us that the use of WINS permits the quick resolution of a NetBIOS name with its IP address. Because WINS maintains a database of NetBIOS name and IP address mappings the resolution can be done quickly, efficiently, and without broadcast traffic. The WINS process is automatic and covers both database construction and employment. When a WINS client starts, it provides the WINS server with its NetBIOS name and IP address. When a WINS client requires a NetBIOS name resolution, it queries the WINS server, which replies with the mapping if it is available. If a client can't obtain a mapping from the WINS server, it may resort to a broadcast. Any Windows 2000 server can become a WINS server. Although only one server is required per subnet, adding a second server provides backup capability. Most Microsoft operating systems can be configured as WINS clients. WINS clients may be configured statically or through the DHRP. In addition to the automatically created WINS database entries, we may configure static mappings in the database to cover computers that cannot be configured as WINS clients. WINS proxy agents can be installed to permit non-WINS clients to receive WINS name resolution information. WINS servers can be configured to replicate database information as pull, push, or push-pull partners. WINS database replication allows WINS servers on different subnets to provide WINS resolution while minimizing internetwork traffic. Replication also permits primary and backup WINS servers to maintain identical databases. The WINS server can be configured to properly clean up expired entries at optimal time intervals. Database entries can be viewed through the WINS console. Although the WINS database is based on the relatively self-maintaining Jet database engine, capabilities exist to manually backup, restore, and compact the data.

Test Yourself

1. WINS servers must have static IP addresses.
   - **A.** True
   - **B.** False

2. Can WINS clients resolve NetBIOS names of non-WINS clients through a WINS server?
   - **A.** No
   - **B.** Yes—Using a WINS proxy agent
   - **C.** Yes—Using a WINS static entry
   - **D.** Yes—By accessing the non-WINS client's LMHOSTS table

3. Non-WINS clients can obtain WINS resolution.
   - **A.** Never
   - **B.** If they're on the same network segment as the WINS server
   - **C.** Through a WINS proxy agent
   - **D.** Through WINS static mappings

4. WINS database replication isn't important when WINS servers are operating on the same network segment.
   - **A.** True
   - **B.** False

5. WINS burst handling
   - **A.** Was removed in Windows 2000
   - **B.** Provides quick recovery when the WINS database is found to be corrupted
   - **C.** Replicates to several WINS servers simultaneously
   - **D.** Is used during peak load periods on the WINS server

IP Internetwork Browsing and Domain Functions

*B*y now you are already familiar with Network Basic Input/Output System (NetBIOS) name resolution and Windows Internet Name Service. It's time now to put your knowledge to use. Remember how often you open network neighborhood and see an incorrect or incomplete list of servers and workstations? You may remember situations where a computer has been shut down but the network neighborhood application still shows it active. Sometimes you are surprised that you can connect to a server but cannot see it in the browse list. Now it's time to shed some light on issues such as these. This chapter explains how browsing for NetBIOS resources and domain functions works in a TCP/IP environment. You will be presented the ins and outs of the browser service. You will learn how to configure and use the LMHOSTS file to support domain activity. We will also discuss how implementing WINS can solve internetwork browsing problems.

Browsing Overview

In large organizations it may be very tedious to locate a desired resource, such as a shared folder or a network printer. To share resources efficiently, users must be able to view what servers and workstations are available in the network and what shared resources they can access. Users on a Windows 2000 network often need to know what computers are accessible from their workstations. For example, when you double-click the My Network Places

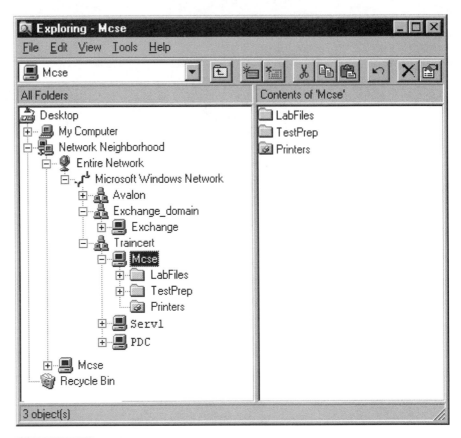

Browsing network resources with Windows Explorer

icon or launch Windows Explorer, it's convenient to see the graphical representation of all available network resources in your workgroup or domain (and perhaps in other domains as well) (see Figure 10-1.) The list of network resources is often referred to as the *browse list*.

The browse list of the network resources is maintained by the Windows 2000 *computer browser service.* Viewing the list of available network resources is called *browsing.*

The computer browser service was first introduced in Microsoft Windows for Workgroups. The main purpose of the browser service is to collect and distribute the list of network computers that are sharing file, print, and other resources. The browser service was initially designed for computers located on a single network segment and, originally, did not support wide area network (WAN) environments. Since then, browser features have been significantly enhanced. The current browser service has WAN capabilities that permit Windows 2000 computers to browse resources located on both local and remote network segments.

Note

Note The ability to browse should not be confused with the ability to *connect* to a computer (e.g., through the **net use** command). In many cases you may be able to successfully connect to a remote computer even if you can't see it in the browse list.

Browser Roles

Technically, the computer browser service is simply a series of lists of available network resources. These lists are distributed to specifically assigned computers that perform browser services on behalf of other computers. Windows 2000 assigns browser tasks to specific computers. Computers work together to provide a centralized list of shared resources. Thanks to the browser service, not every computer on the network has to maintain its own browser list. This fact reduces the amount of network traffic required to build and support a list of available network resources, which saves CPU time and memory resources.

There are several browser types: *domain master browser, master browser, backup browser, potential browser,* and *browser client* (nonbrowser). Table 10.1 presents the main functions of each browser type. We will cover each of them in greater detail a bit later.

TABLE 10.1   *Browser Roles*

Role	Description
Browser Client	Browser Client (often referred to as nonbrowser) does not maintain a browse list. When a list of network resources is needed, the browser client queries backup browsers for one.
Master Browser	Master Browser (MBR) is responsible for collecting browse information to create and maintain a browse list. If a domain spans more that one subnetwork, the master browser maintains the browse list for the portion of the domain on its subnetwork. The master browser then distributes the browse list to the backup browsers.
Backup Browser	Backup Browser (BBR) receives a copy of the network resource browse list from the master browser and distributes the list upon request to computers in the domain or workgroup.

TABLE 10.1	*Browser Roles (continued)*
Role	**Description**
Potential Browser	Potential Browser (PBR) is not a browser server. It is capable of maintaining a network resource browse list, however, and can be elected as a master browser. A potential browser can also act as a backup browser, if instructed to do so by the existing master browser.
Domain Master Browser	Domain Master Browser (DMBR) is responsible for collecting announcements for the entire domain including remote subnets. The domain master browser then provides the synchronized list of all domain resources to master browsers in other subnets. The domain master browser is always the primary domain controller of the domain. (Since Windows 2000 does not actually use a primary domain controller, this role falls to the Windows 2000 domain controller designated as the *PDC Emulator.*)

Note
A single computer can play multiple browser roles. For example, the master browser computer may also be a backup browser. You can identify the computer's current browse role using the **browmon** and **browstat** utilities from the Microsoft Windows 2000 Resource Kit.

Browsing in One IP Subnet

Browsing within one subnet is a little different from browsing across a wide area network (WAN). We'll start our discussion with common browsing concepts using local browsing as an example. We will then discuss how browsing works across routes. We will also look at potential browsing problems and discuss some recommended solutions.

How Does the Computer Get into the Browse List?

Computers that have server components installed (such as Windows 95/98 computers with File and Print Services for Microsoft Networks, Windows NT, or Windows 2000 computers) should be presented in the browse list to permit users to locate them easily. When a computer with a server component starts, it announces itself to the network to advertise its ability to service clients' requests.

The browser host announcement packet in Transport Control Protocol/Internet Protocol (TCP/IP) networks is a broadcast frame destined for the NetBIOS name *domain <1Db>*, where *domain* is the domain name to which the announcing computer belongs.

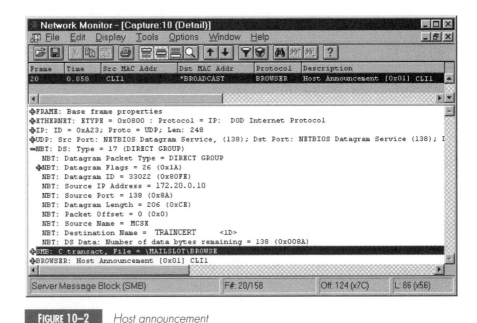

FIGURE 10–2   *Host announcement*

Figure 10-2 depicts the host announcement for computer named CLI1 which is a member of TRAINCERT domain.

Once a nonbrowser computer has started, it announces itself every 12 minutes.

Note

You can change the browser announcement time in the registry. To do this, go to the HKEY_LOCAL_MACHINE\System\CurrentControlSet\Services\lanmanserver\ **parameters** and add an **Announce** key with a type of **REG_DWORD**. Set its value to the number of seconds that the browser should wait between announcements.

Master Browser

Now we know that computers announce their presence to the network with a special broadcast packet, but who catches these announcement packets? The answer is the *"master browser."* The MBR is responsible for creating the primary copy of the browse list. The master browser picks up the computer announcements destined to the *domain <1Dh>* NetBIOS name. When the MBR receives such an announcement from a computer, it adds that computer to its browse list. This is often referred to as a *collection process* (see Figure 10-3). Initially the network has only one computer online—the one named **PDC**.

In Figure 10-3, computers **CLI1** and **Serv1** are powered down (shown as dimmed). The powered-down machines do not appear in the browse list. At boot time each computer sends a broadcast announcement, which causes it to appear in the browse list.

Note   Remember, in Windows 2000 all domain controllers (DCs) are equal and are referred to as DC. The machine named *PDC* is actually the DC that serves as the *PDC Emulator.*

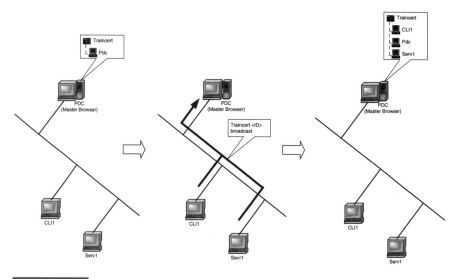

FIGURE 10–3   *Browsing collection process*

If your domain consists of several subnets separated by routers, each subnet has its own MBR.

Being an MBR, the computer has one more function. It broadcasts a *DomainAnnouncement* datagram once every 15 minutes. A *DomainAnnouncement* datagram contains the name of the domain, the name of the master browser for that domain, and additional information. When another master browser receives such a datagram, it adds the new domain to its browse list.

Backup Browser

The backup browser receives a copy of the browse list from the MBR. Later in this chapter, we'll see that the backup browser also services client requests by sending them a copy of the browse list. Backup browsers contact the master browser every 12 minutes to get the updated copy of the browse list (see Figure 10-4). The process of pulling the browse list from the master browser to the backup browser is referred to as the *distribution process.*

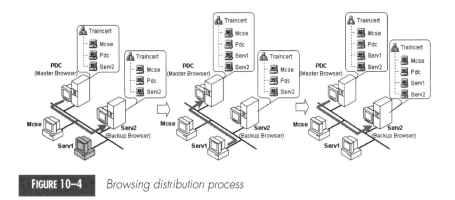

FIGURE 10-4 *Browsing distribution process*

If a backup browser cannot contact the master browser, a new master browser is elected. This is called a *browser election* and will be discussed in detail later in this chapter.

All Windows 2000 domain controllers are automatically configured to become backup browsers if needed. Normally there is one backup browser for every 32 computers.

What Happens When a Computer Needs to Browse?

When a nonbrowser computer (one that does not maintain its own copy of a browse list) needs to browse, it obtains the current browse list from a backup browser. But before this, the browser client needs to determine the IP addresses of the backup browsers. To get the addresses of the backup browsers, the computer sends a so-called *GetBackupListReq* request to the NetBIOS name *domain<1Db>*. (In TCP/IP networks, the *GetBackupListReq* request for *domain <1Db>* is encapsulated in a broadcast IP datagram.) Additionally, if the browser client is configured with a WINS server address, the request for a Domain Master Browser (*domain <1Bh>*) is sent to the WINS server.

When the master browser gets the *GetBackupListReq* it will respond with a list of backup browsers for the given subnet. This is accomplished with a *GetBackupListResponse* packet. The response includes a list of all the backup browsers for the domain/workgroup on the local subnet (see Figure 10-5).

Once the client has received a list of backup browsers from the master browser, it selects three servers from this list and caches them. Using backup browsers for future client requests reduces load on the master browser. Later, when a computer needs to browse, it selects one of the three cached names, and:

- Establishes a TCP session with the chosen backup browser.
- Establishes a NetBIOS session with the chosen backup browser.
- Establishes a null session to IPC$.

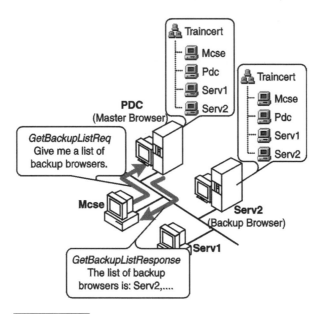

Browser client retrieves a list of backup browsers

The client then issues a remote procedure call (RPC) to the backup browser requesting a browse list, which the backup browser returns (see Figure 10-6.)

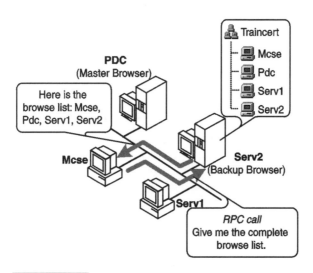

Browser client retrieves the browse list from a backup browser

The full conversation of the browser client with master and backup browsers is illustrated in Figure 10-7. Once the browser client gets the browse list, it can display it in My Network Places or Windows 2000 Explorer. If the user double-clicks a particular server in the browse list, the client contacts this server and acquires a list of the server's available shared resources.

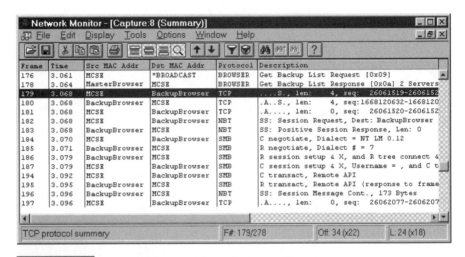

FIGURE 10–7   *Browser client requesting the browse list*

Note

In Windows versions prior to Windows NT 4.0, as well as in Windows 95 and Windows for Workgroups, the data limit for the list of servers is set to 64K. Because of this, the browse list for a single workgroup or domain is limited to approximately 3,000 computers under these operating systems.

When Does the Computer Disappear from the Browse List?

Have you noticed that a computer can be turned off but it will remain in the browse list for awhile? Under what conditions does the computer disappear from the browse list? Unfortunately, the computer browser service does not have a special announcement to indicate the computer is about to be turned off. Instead, computers are deleted from the browse list silently. If the master browser has not heard from the nonbrowser for three consecutive announcement periods, the master browser will remove the nonbrowser from its browse list. Thus, a nonbrowser computer will be in the master browser's browse list for three 12-minute announcement cycles after it—the nonbrowser—has been shut down. Because it can take up to 15 minutes for a backup browser to receive an updated browse list, it is possible that a computer will appear in the browse list as long as 51 minutes after it is no longer available to the network. This behavior is by design.

Browser Elections

What happens if the master browser goes down unexpectedly? Who will maintain the browse list then? Fortunately, the computer browser service is designed to handle such situations. For example, when a computer fails to locate the master browser, it forces the designation of a new master browser by sending an *ElectionForce* datagram. This process of determining the new master browser is called *browser election*.

When an election is being forced, one of the master browser candidates initiates the election by sending a special datagram called the *election datagram*. When other master browser candidates receive this election datagram they examine the *election criteria* inside it. If a particular browser has better election criteria than the computer that sent the election datagram, it will issue its own election datagram. The election criterion for the browser is based on the operating system type, the browser's current role, and its current state. For example, a Windows 2000 server will win a browser election over a Windows 2000 client. (Machines are elected in the following order: Windows 2000 server, Windows 2000 client, Windows NT server, Windows NT workstation, and Windows for Workgroups/Windows 9x. In the event of a tie, the system resorts to using criteria such as the way the computers' names alpha-sort and the amount of time the computers have been running.)

The election process ensures there will always be only one master browser in a given subnet.

Configuring Browsers

You may ask, how can I control whether or not a computer becomes a browser? Unfortunately, Windows 2000 does not provide a convenient way to configure the browser service. You must edit the registry.

Using the registry editor, you can configure your Windows 2000 computer:

- To be a browser (which means the computer will become a browser).
- Never to be a browser (which means that the computer will not participate in browser elections and never becomes a browser, neither master nor backup).
- To be a potential browser (which means that the computer will become a browser depending on the number of currently active browsers).

To set up the browser configuration, use the registry path `HKEY_LOCAL_MACHINE\System\CurrentControlSet\Services\Browser\Parameters\MaintainServerList`.

The allowable values for the MaintainServerList parameter are:

No   The computer will never participate as a browser.

Configuring Browsers (continued)

Yes   The computer will become a browser. Upon startup the computer attempts to locate the master browser and, if it fails to do so, will force an election. This computer will always become a browser, either master or backup. (This is the default value for domain controllers.)

Auto This computer will possibly become a browser, depending on the number of currently active browsers. It is referred to as a potential browser. (This is the default value for Windows 2000 clients and Windows 2000 member servers.)

Another parameter in registry helps to determine which servers become master browsers and backup browsers. The registry path for it is: `HKEY_LOCAL_MACHINE\System\CurrentControlSet\Services\Browser\Parameters\IsDomainMaster`.

Setting this parameter to True or Yes makes a computer a preferred master browser. When a preferred master browser starts, it forces an election. A preferred master browser has priority in browser elections. That means, if nothing prevents it, the preferred master browser will always win.

Unless the computer is configured as a preferred master browser, this parameter will always be False or No.

Browsing Across Subnets

Browsing is usually no problem in a single network segment. When your domain spans more that one subnetwork, however, each subnetwork acts as an independent browsing entity. Every subnet has its own master browser and backup browsers. You may already have noticed that browser information transmission relies on broadcast traffic. Since browser packets do not cross routers, browsing across IP networks can create certain problems. Because of this, computers on your network segment are often unable to browse remote members of the domain (see Figure 10-8).

To browse across subnets, either routers must be configured to forward broadcasts or there must be a special computer able to gather information from all network segments. Let's discuss these two solutions.

The IP Router Solution

When computers in different subnets cannot see each other's browse lists, IP routers can be configured to forward broadcast packets between the subnets. All NetBIOS over TCP/IP (NetBT) broadcasts are sent to UDP port 137, which is defined as a NetBT name service. If the router is configured to forward NetBIOS broadcasts, browsing works just as if all computers were on the same network segment. While the IP router solution solves the incomplete browse list problem, it has the following drawbacks:

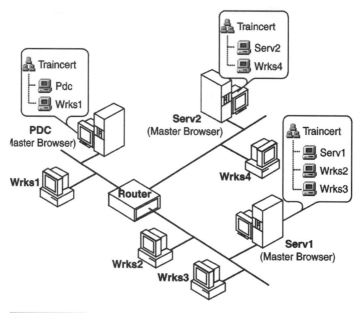

| FIGURE 10–8 | *In a subnetted network each segment acts as an independent browsing entity* |

- Propagates all NetBIOS over TCP/IP broadcast traffic across an internetwork
- Requires additional router configuration
- Can lead to browser election conflicts and error reports in the event log

As you can see, router reconfiguration is, perhaps, not the best solution. To make browsing work across routers you can configure a computer to gather information from all network segments. This is a job for the domain master browser and is the next area we'll examine.

Domain Master Browser

Let's now discuss how WAN browsing can be implemented with the domain master browser. As we saw in Table 10.1, the domain master browser is always the domain controller performing the PDC Emulator role. The domain master browser is responsible for collecting computer-name information for the entire domain, including remote network segments. Based on this information, the domain master browser builds the domain browse list.

The master browsers on each network segment announce themselves to the domain master browser by using a directed datagram[6] called a *Master-*

---

6. A *directed* datagram, you'll recall, resolves to an IP address and, therefore, *will* travel across a router.

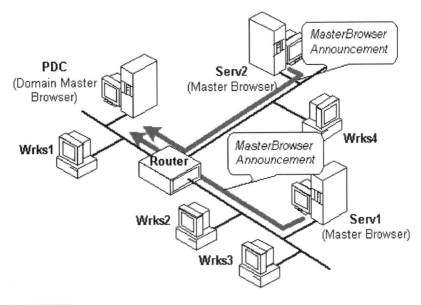

Master browser announcement

BrowserAnnouncement datagram (see Figure 10-9). Later in this chapter, we will see how the subnet master browser finds the domain master browser.

Once it receives the *MasterBrowserAnnouncement* datagram, the domain master browser knows there are master browsers in the same domain. The domain master browser then sends the *NetServerEnum* call to the master browser of the particular network segment to obtain a copy of that master browser's browse list (see Figure 10-10).

The domain master browser next *merges* its own browse list with the browse list from the master browsers. Now the domain master browser has an updated browse list with computers from other subnets (see Figure 10-11).

The described process repeats every 15 minutes and guaranties the domain master browser has a complete browse list of all computers in the domain.

Note

Since a workgroup does not have a domain controller, it has neither a PDC emulator nor a domain master browser. This imposes some limitations to workgroup browsing, particularly if the network spans more that one subnet. A workgroup can't span subnets. If a workgroup is found on two subnets, it actually functions as two workgroups with identical names. Since there is no domain master browser to unite the two workgroups, browsing between them cannot occur.

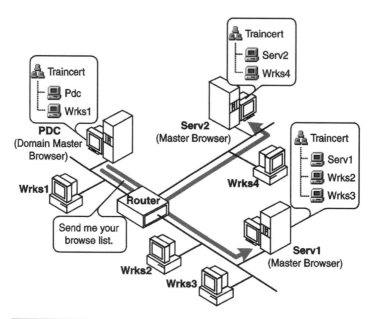

FIGURE 10–10   *Domain master browser requests the master browser's browse list*

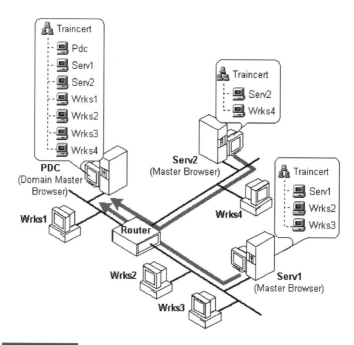

FIGURE 10–11   *Domain master browser updates its browse list*

So we seem to have found a solution. If your domain spans several subnets, the PDC Emulator, acting as a domain master browser, takes care of synchronizing your subnet browser lists. But stop! There is one question that is still unanswered. We mentioned that subnet master browsers contact the domain master browser with a directed datagram, but how do the master browsers know where their domain master browser is? Fortunately, there are three methods to solve this problem:

- LMHOSTS file
- WINS
- DNS

LMHOSTS File Solution

To implement direct communication between master browsers from remote subnets and the domain master browser, NetBIOS name resolution must function correctly. You might remember that configuring an LMHOSTS file can permit your system to resolve NetBIOS names for machines on remote subnets.

To ensure that each master browser can directly communicate with the domain master browser, a special LMHOSTS file entry must be added. This entry must include the IP address of the domain master browser (the IP address of the PDC), #DOM, and #PRE options. For example:

```
172.20.0.100    PDC  #PRE  #DOM:TRAINCERT
```

You must include this entry in every master browser's LMHOSTS file. Additionally, the domain master browser must have an LMHOSTS file with mappings for every master browser for each network segment.

An example of an LMHOSTS file implementation is illustrated in Figure 10-12.

Note   Optionally, you can use #PRE #DOM switches for master browser entries. When multiple entries exist for the same domain, the master browser will try them all, but only the domain master browser will respond.

Note   When dealing with multiple domains and multiple subnets, the most reliable way to ensure all machines can browse all other machines is to include entries for each domain controller in the local domain and at least an entry for each PDC emulator in each remote domain.

If you're thinking the LMHOSTS solution sounds a bit complicated and fraught with potential errors, you're correct. Fortunately, we're about to discuss two automated methods which are available to you. Use of the LMHOSTS file is not the recommended solution for Windows 2000 domains

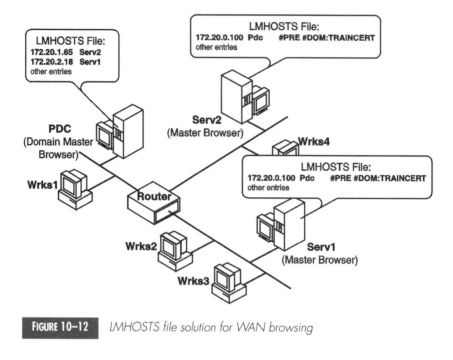

FIGURE 10-12 *LMHOSTS file solution for WAN browsing*

because the other methods are far more reliable. The coverage was presented here for completeness and in case someone, someday, asks you a question about it on an examination.

WINS Solution

WINS also solves NetBIOS broadcast problems. As we learned earlier, WINS does this by dynamically registering a computer's NetBIOS name and IP address. The domain master browser registers a special NetBIOS name *domain<1Bh>*. Master browsers periodically query the WINS server and thus know the domain master browser's IP address. Additionally, the domain master browser will periodically request the list of *other* domains that are registered in the WINS database. The domain master browser does this by issuing a wild card query ending with *<1Bh>*. The WINS server responds with a list of all domains that have their domain master browsers registered in the WINS database. The domain master browser, then, does a reverse query for each individual *domain<1Bh>* name to learn the location of domain master browsers for that domain.

WINS has certain enhancements that make it superior to the LMHOSTS file. For example, WINS is far more flexible with remote domain browsing, it is easily monitored, and WINS problems can be quickly diagnosed.

DNS Solution

Before Windows 2000, the WINS solution was the recommended method for domain browsing. While WINS is a robust solution that provides many network services, the Domain Name System (DNS) (which we'll start covering in Chapter 12), is a key part of the Active Directory and is the recommended solution for cross-network browsing. The Windows 2000 DNS supports Service Resource (SRV) records. A DNS server supporting the Windows 2000 domain will contain SRV records for each domain controller as well as an SRV record for the PDC emulator. Active Directory DNS clients, therefore, can get immediate access to the domain master browser through SRV records. Although the DNS solution is the preferred domain browsing solution, if your network contains Windows machines that need NetBIOS name resolution, the inclusion of a WINS server (along with the DNS server) is a good idea.

Domain Functions in the TCP/IP Environment

Browsing is not the only domain function that relies on broadcasts. Activities such as logging on to a domain, changing passwords, and replication among domain controllers also prompt broadcasts. Since, as we've seen, IP routers do not normally forward broadcasts, a form of directed traffic must be used to accomplish such tasks across subnetworks. Once again, we can rely on the LMHOSTS file, the WINS server, and the DNS server to help us.

LMHOSTS Solution

To log on to the domain, the client broadcasts the message directly to the domain and also looks for any #DOM:*domain* entries in the LMHOSTS file. If such an entry exists, the client sends the message directly to the computer listed in this entry. You should ensure each domain controller in the client's LMHOSTS file is identified with the **#DOM** tag. If the domain controller on the local subnet is offline, the client will be able to find a domain controller on a remote subnet and log onto the domain.

Note If there are no domain controllers in the client's subnet, a #DOM entry is required if the user wants to log on.

To permit domain user account database synchronization, the primary domain controller must have #DOM entries for all backup domain controllers and vice versa. Additionally, each backup domain controller should have a

#DOM entry for the domain's other backup domain controllers. This will allow domain controller promotions and demotions to occur seamlessly.

WINS Solution

If WINS is implemented, the client will contact the WINS server and ask for a list of domain controllers within the particular domain. The query is issued for the *domain <1Ch>* group entry, where *domain* is the name of the domain the client wishes to log onto. The WINS server replies with a list of up to 25 domain controllers. The client can then send messages directly to the domain controller.

DNS Solution

The client queries the DNS server servicing the domain's Active Directory and obtains a list of domain controllers. The client first attempts to obtain a list from the local site (local network segment) and then looks to other sites within the domain (if they exist). The client attempts contact with the domain controllers on the list in a random order (to provide load balancing) and uses the first one to respond to its query.

Summary

This chapter provided a detailed description of the Windows 2000 computer browser service. We discovered the browser service is used to build a list of available network servers and their shared resources. We learned that not every computer has to maintain a browse list, but that browse lists are distributed to specifically assigned computers that perform browser services on behalf of other computers. We saw that browsers have specific roles, such as master browser, backup browser, and nonbrowser. It is also important to remember that the domain controller acting as the PDC emulator is assigned a specific role as domain master browser.

We have seen that browsing in a single network segment is usually a straightforward process with no attendant difficulty. WAN browsing, however, was shown to be a bit more complex, since routers do not typically forward broadcasts. We described three methods that make WAN browsing possible: LMHOSTS files, WINS, and DNS. Finally, we extended the browser discussion to other domain functions that rely on broadcasts and saw that they also require an LMHOSTS file or a WINS or DNS server to be able to function across subnetworks.

Test Yourself

1. A domain announcement datagram:
   A. Contains the domain name and master browser's name.
   B. Is issued by the master browser every 15 minutes.
   C. Is used to update other master browsers.
   D. All of the above

2. After being shut down, a computer can remain on the browse list for:
   A. 6 hours
   B. Over 50 minutes
   C. Over 30 minutes
   D. Over 30 seconds
   E. No time at all; it is immediately removed from browse lists.

3. When the master browser goes down:
   A. There is a browser coup.
   B. There is a browser election.
   C. The vice-master browser is inaugurated.
   D. The next browser in the queue takes over until the master is backed up.

4. It is possible to browse across subnets because of:
   A. BootP routers
   B. Domain master browsers
   C. WINS servers
   D. LMHosts files

5. The domain master browser can be located through:
   A. LMHosts
   B. WINS
   C. DNS
   D. All of the above

Host Name Resolution

So far we've looked chiefly at Transport Control Protocol/Internet Protocol (TCP/IP) and its interaction with Windows-based machines. Most of our study has centered on how to communicate with computers possessing Network Basic Input/Output System (NetBIOS) names and much of our concern has been on how to resolve a NetBIOS name to an IP address and, ultimately, to a media access channel (MAC) address. We will now broaden our horizon a bit and discuss a computer naming system that can be used with any computer running TCP/IP. While we will still concentrate on how to network with Windows 2000 computers, we will see that in the TCP/IP world, you can communicate if you know only the IP address. (You ultimately need a MAC address for communication but TCP/IP will help you get that as long as you have an IP address.) As we've seen, using just an IP address can get tiresome for us humans. Unfortunately, NetBIOS names are available only in the Windows environment (or on other systems that have third-party NetBIOS helper programs) and are being de-emphasized in the Windows 2000 world. The good news is that before there were NetBIOS names there were host names—a host name that can be related to an IP address just like a NetBIOS name. Windows computers have and work with host names just as every other computer running TCP/IP. Because they are universal in the TCP/IP world, host names are a very robust method of computer naming.

TCP/IP Naming Schemes

As we've already determined, network communication ultimately requires a MAC address. On TCP/IP networks, an IP address is a necessary piece of information to acquire a MAC address. Using IP addresses for everything in large environments can be tedious for humans, and applications rarely use IP addresses. Because of this, friendly computer names are used almost exclusively. We must have, therefore, some method or methods to resolve friendly names to IP addresses and vice versa.

In the Windows world, we can use NetBIOS names which permit us to identify IP addresses in a format that is easier to work with and remember. NetBIOS names have the added advantage of providing some degree of protocol independence within Windows networks. If, for instance, I identify a machine with a NetBIOS name (e.g., "MyComputer") that corresponds to a particular IP address, the IP address will have no meaning if I access the machine using the IPX/SPX protocol but the machine will *still* be known as "MyComputer." While most network communications in a Windows environment can be accomplished by using a NetBIOS name *or* an IP address, some applications are written specifically for named communication (e.g., connecting to a Microsoft SQL Server or Exchange Server). Connectivity in these cases *must* be accomplished through use of a NetBIOS (or host) name.

In the UNIX environment, all network communication can be accomplished through the use of an IP address (which, of course, is translated to a MAC address). To relieve the tedium of always using IP addresses, however, you may also use a host name or *fully qualified domain name (FQDN)*. (An FQDN is a combination of the host and domain name. FQDNs are fully explored in the next chapter.) Windows systems can also communicate through host names and FQDNs.

Note

Originally, Windows computers using Microsoft network commands, such as **net use**, could use only NetBIOS names in those commands. Current Windows operating systems permit the use of IP addresses, host names, and FQDNs in most network commands. Windows 2000 can operate using only host names but some third-party legacy applications may still require NetBIOS name support to function.

Defining Host Names

A *host name* is any alias that can be assigned to a computer to identify a TCP/IP host. By default, in a Windows environment, the host name and the NetBIOS name are the same. This, however, is not required—a host name can be any 256-character string. A single computer can even have multiple host names.

Like the NetBIOS name, a host name can be used in place of an IP address in TCP/IP utilities. The host name will always correspond to an IP address stored in the machine's HOSTS file or in a Domain Name System (DNS) database. If the host name is the same as the NetBIOS name, it will also correspond to an IP address stored on a NetBIOS name server or LMHOSTS file.

Unlike NetBIOS names, host names are created when they are placed in a HOSTS file or loaded on a DNS server. To assign a computer name to a Windows 2000 computer, right-click the **My Computer** icon on your desktop and select **Properties** to open the **System Properties** window. Select the **Network Identification** tab and click **Properties**. Now you can set the name, as shown in Figure 11-1. In the figure, the computer's name is **MyComputer** and the FQDN is **MyComputer.mydomain.com**. Typing **HOSTNAME** at the command prompt will reveal the hostname of the local computer.

The computer will always assume its host and NetBIOS names are the same. Remember, however, we said earlier that the host name is created when it is placed in a HOSTS file or DNS server. Unlike a NetBIOS name, the computer doesn't use its own host name to reply to a name resolution broadcast. The machine uses its host name only when sending updates to the dynamic DNS (which we'll cover in Chapter 13), and in determining if it is sending a message to itself. The actual host name resolution for a machine comes from a source outside the machine in question.

Host Name Resolution

Just as with NetBIOS names, a host name doesn't do much good if we can't resolve it to an IP address. The methods of name resolution listed below should look familiar since they're essentially the same methods we discussed for NetBIOS name resolution. The perceptive student will notice, however, that they're listed in a different order.

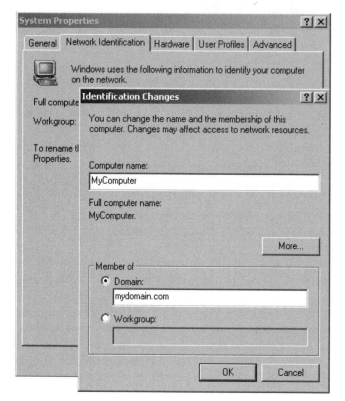

Setting the host name of a Windows 2000 computer

Standard Name Resolution Methods

The following methods are standard throughout TCP/IP networks:

LOCAL HOST NAME

The first step in host name resolution occurs when the local machine checks its own host name. If it discovers the destination host name is the same as its configured host name, it doesn't need to perform any further resolution.

HOSTS FILE

The HOSTS file is a text file on the local computer that requires manual entry and maintenance. Checking this file is *always* the second host name resolution step (after checking the local host name). The HOSTS file maps IP addresses to host names or FQDNs. HOSTS files use the same format as the 4.3 Berkeley Software Distribution UNIX\etc\hosts file. We will look at HOSTS files in some detail later in this chapter.

DOMAIN NAME SYSTEM

DNS is a server that maintains a database of IP addresses and FQDNs. Like the HOSTS file, conventional DNS requires manual entry and maintenance. As we'll soon see, however, the Windows 2000 dynamic DNS will accept updates from Windows 2000 clients or dynamic host configuration protocol (DHCP) servers. (DNS is fully covered in the next two chapters.)

Microsoft Name Resolution Methods

In addition to the standard resolution methods, if the host name and the Net-BIOS name are the same, some Microsoft methods can be used to map host names to IP addresses on Windows systems:

NETBIOS NAME SERVER

A NetBIOS Name Server (NBNS) is any server implemented under RFC 1001/1002 to provide NetBIOS name resolution. A computer trying to contact a machine with a particular host name can query the NBNS for a name/IP address mapping. If the host name is equivalent to a NetBIOS name found in the NBNS database, the NBNS will return the IP address mapped to the NetBIOS name. (As we've seen, the Microsoft implementation of an NBNS is WINS.)

LOCAL BROADCAST

If a computer can't find a mapping from a name server, it can send a broadcast over the local network. If the target computer receives the broadcast and recognizes the host name as its NetBIOS name, it will respond with its IP address to permit full TCP/IP communication.

LMHOSTS FILE

An LMHOSTS file is a text file on the local computer that contains both the NetBIOS name and IP address of Windows networking computers on remote networks. If the host name is equivalent to a NetBIOS name found in the LMHOSTS file, the computer will use the IP address mapped to the NetBIOS name.

Name Resolution Using a HOSTS File

If you remember what you learned about name resolution using the LMHOSTS file, you already have a good idea about the function of the HOSTS file. Like the LMHOSTS file, the HOSTS file resides on the local machine and requires manual update and maintenance. Unlike the LMHOSTS file, which is used to find only remote machines, the HOSTS file contains mappings for both local and remote hosts.

When a computer needs to resolve a host name, it first checks to see if the host name is the same as the local host name (in other words, it checks to see if the name it's looking for is its own). If the host name being sought is not the local host name, the computer checks its HOSTS file for an appropriate mapping. If the HOSTS file doesn't contain the required information, the computer will attempt name resolution using the alternate methods described in the previous section (DNS, NBNS, etc.). If none of the host name resolution methods yield an IP address mapping, the network communication fails and the user receives an error message.

Once an IP address mapping is obtained (through the HOSTS file or other name resolution method), the computer will use the Address Resolution Protocol (ARP) to resolve the host name to a hardware address. If the host is on the local network, ARP will return the host's hardware address. (ARP first checks its cache to see if it has already obtained a mapping; if none is found, it uses a broadcast to resolve the IP address to a MAC address.) If the host is on a remote network, ARP returns the hardware address of a router that can lead to the destination host and the communication is *routed* to it. (In Windows 2000, the *router* is typically the *default gateway.*)

Name Resolution Using a DNS Server

Like the HOSTS file, a DNS server maintains IP address mappings in a manually maintained and updated list (DNS is fully explored in the next two chapters). As you might expect, however, the DNS does not need to reside on the local computer. Another distinction between the HOSTS file and a DNS server is, while a HOSTS file can contain host names and FQDNs, the DNS server contains only FQDNs. (Host name resolution using FQDNs is no problem since the host name is found within the FQDN.)

DNS name resolution is very similar to resolution using the HOSTS file. Assuming the calling computer is configured to use DNS name resolution, when it is unable to locate a mapping in its HOSTS file, it queries the configured DNS server. If the DNS server has a mapping, it returns the information and the computer will use ARP to resolve the host name to a hardware address. If the host is on the local network, ARP will return the host's hardware address. If the host is on a remote network, ARP returns the hardware address of a router that can lead to the destination host and the communication is routed to it.

If the server does not respond, the client makes several additional attempts at varying intervals. If the server fails to respond after the additional attempts or if it responds but has no mapping for the desired target host, the client tries other methods. If the client isn't configured to use additional resolution methods, or if they fail, communication cannot be established with the target host and an error message is returned.

The Microsoft Host Name Resolution Process

Windows 2000 computers can be configured to use several host name resolution methods. The name resolution sequence is depicted in Figure 11-2. If one of the methods fails, the Windows 2000 computer continues to the next method until it obtains a mapping or until all methods have failed. In order for all methods to function properly, the Windows 2000 computer must be configured to use them. In order for the NetBIOS based methods to properly operate, the host name being sought must be equivalent to the target computer's NetBIOS name.

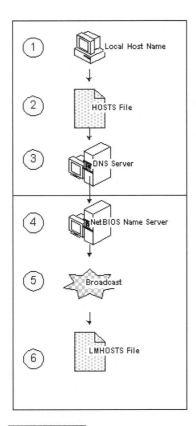

FIGURE 11-2   *Microsoft host name resolution process*

- **Local host name**: The first step in host name resolution is to check to see if the host name being sought is the same as the local host name. If they are the same, the name is resolved and the communication is accomplished without actual network activity.
- **HOSTS**: If the host name being sought is different from the local host name, the computer checks its HOSTS file. If a mapping is found, the host name is resolved.
- **DNS**: If a mapping was not found in the HOSTS file, the computer sends a resolution request to its configured DNS server. If the DNS server doesn't initially respond, the computer will make additional attempts at 1, 3, 5, 9, and 17 seconds (actually it's a bit more complex than this but we'll save the rest of the discussion for the next two chapters).
- **NetBIOS name server**: If DNS cannot resolve the host name, the client computer makes an assumption that the host name it seeks is on a computer whose NetBIOS name is the same as its host name. (If this is a bad assumption, this and the remaining steps will yield an incorrect—or no—result.) The client first checks its NetBIOS name cache to see if it has recently resolved a NetBIOS name that is the same as the host name. If the cache does not yield the appropriate information, three attempts are made to contact a NetBIOS name server. For this to happen, the machine must be configured to go to a name server. This step is normally accomplished before resorting to broadcast but may be attempted after broadcast depending on the setting of the *Name Resolution Node*. (The Name Resolution Node was fully explained in Chapter 8.)
- **Broadcast**: If the NetBIOS name server doesn't resolve the name, the computer will broadcast on the local network.
- **LMHOSTS**: If broadcast doesn't yield the necessary information, the local LMHOSTS file is parsed.

If none of these methods yields an IP address mapping, the client computer will be able to communicate with the host it is seeking only through use of the IP address.

Configuring the HOSTS File

As we've already learned, a HOSTS file is simply a text file found on the local machine with IP address mappings that correspond to host names (or FQDNs) for machines with which the local computer is likely to want to communicate. If you fully understand the construction of the LMHOSTS file, discussed in Chapter 8, you already know a great deal about the HOSTS file.

```
127.0.0.1        Localhost          #loopback
205.10.12.10     Wkstn1
205.10.12.11     Wkstn2

205.10.12.24     gateway            #Default Gateway2

200.18.22.10     Server1            # SQL Server
200.18.22.12     Server2            # Print Server
210.22.18.10     Server3            # Exchange Server

102.54.94.97     rhino.microsoft.com

131.107.2.100    unixhost
131.107.2.100    UNIXHOST

131.107.3.1      unixhost2.udomain.com
131.107.3.1      UNIXHOST2.UDOMAIN.COM
```

FIGURE 11-3   *Sample HOSTS file*

HOSTS files contain only IP addresses, host names or FQDNs, and comments, making them a bit easier to construct than LMHOSTS files. An example HOSTS file is depicted in Figure 11-3.

In constructing a HOSTS file, simply enter the IP address followed by at least one space or tab character. Next, type the host name or FQDN. Finally, if you wish to include a comment, type a pound sign (#) followed by your comment. Each line is limited to 255 characters. The localhost entry is found in HOSTS files by default.

Host name resolution by and for Windows computers is **not** case sensitive. UNIX computers are case-sensitive when referring to host names. An easy way to ensure your HOST file will work regardless of the system is to enter both an upper case and lower case entry for the same host name (as shown in Figure 11-3 for **unixhost** and **unixhost2**).

Just as with the LMHOSTS file, the HOSTS file resides in the **\system-root\system32\drivers\etc** directory. (In this context, **\systemroot** refers to the directory containing the Windows 2000 system files. This directory is \WINNT by default in Windows 2000.) The HOSTS file is simply named **hosts**, with no file extension. All TCP/IP configured Windows 2000 computers have a default HOSTS file. The default file contains a few example mappings (commented out) as well as a mapping for the loopback address.

Summary

In this chapter we looked at host names and how they're resolved to IP addresses and, ultimately, to MAC addresses. We saw that a host name is simply a way of referring to a computer without actually using the machine's IP address. We learned the host name could be the same as or different from the NetBIOS name (although the default in Windows systems is for both names to be the same). While a NetBIOS name is the computer's name because it is stored on the computer itself, a host name refers to a computer because it is stored in a HOSTS file or DNS server. The host name stored on the local computer permits it to determine if it's trying to communicate with itself and is also used in dynamic DNS and DHCP updates. A computer can have multiple host names. We say a host name is, essentially, any name that can be mapped to a machine's IP address.

We discovered that host name resolution begins when the computer checks to see if the host name it's seeking is its own. If the host name differs from the local computer's name, we saw that the calling host checks its local HOSTS file and then a DNS server (if so configured). We also saw that Microsoft computers can resort to the NetBIOS methods of using a NetBIOS name server, broadcast, or LMHOSTS file if the standard host name resolution methods fail. We learned that the NetBIOS methods work only when the host name and NetBIOS name is the same (which is usually the case).

Finally we learned how to construct a HOSTS file. We discovered that HOSTS files contain IP addresses and host names or FQDNs. We also learned that, although Windows systems are not concerned about capitalization when using the HOSTS file, other systems (such as UNIX) are. We should, therefore, make our entries case accurate or use both upper and lower case entries when creating HOSTS files that will be used with non-Windows systems.

Test Yourself

1. In TCP/IP utilities, the use of host names is:
   A. Useless because the utilities have no way of resolving.
   B. Interchangeable because the utilities can obtain host name resolution.
   C. More efficient than passing IP addresses.
   D. B and C

2. Once an IP address mapping is obtained, the computer will use the ARP to resolve the host name to an IP address.
   A. True
   B. False

3. The HOSTS file is:
   A. A file that reconfigures routing tables.
   B. An executable file that binds host names to IP addresses.
   C. A text file containing host names and IP addresses.
   D. A series of network diagrams for quick user reference.

4. _____ hosts are case sensitive when resolving host names.
   A. Windows 2000
   B. Windows NT
   C. UNIX
   D. All of the above

5. The first step in name resolution is to:
   A. Check the HOSTS file
   B. Query DNS
   C. Check the name cache
   D. Determine if the host name being sought is that of the local computer

Domain Name System

Are you tired of name resolution yet? As we've seen, name reso-lution is, arguably, the most critical piece in the network commu-nication puzzle. We've become proficient in a number of name resolution methods but, so far, they've all been useful only within our local network or in networks close to it. To date, our name resolution methods have been able to handle only a relatively small list of Network Basic Input/Output System (NetBIOS) or host names. In this chapter, we'll learn how to resolve names for the entire Internet . . . and beyond.

This chapter presents the general theory and background of domain name space and the Domain Name System (DNS). We will discuss the basic installation and configuration of the Win-dows 2000 DNS server. Chapter 13 will cover the DNS Windows 2000 DNS and how it works to support the Active Directory.

The Need for a Domain Name System

In its infancy, the ARPANET consisted of only a few hundred machines. As you might imagine, name resolution could have been accomplished with a simple HOSTS file. In fact, the ARPANET originally did use such a file! It was located on a server at the Stanford Research Institute's Network Information Center (SRI-NIC) and was called Hosts.txt. The ARPANET naming system was a flat name structure or *flat name space*. This rather impressive sounding term simply means that the system merely consisted of a list of unique names.

Names did not fit into any kind of hierarchy. In other words, in a flat name space, hosts were like people with only first names. We could have only one each of Bill, Bob, Mary, and Lisa, but since we could think of more first names than we had computers, this wasn't a problem.

In those early days, we rarely changed or added computer names, so the Hosts.txt file needed to be updated only a couple of times a week. With a small number of hosts, there was little difficulty in getting to the file even though it was maintained on only a single server at one location.

If the ARPANET had remained a network of a few hundred computers, there is little chance you'd be reading this book. We all know the Internet has grown exponentially since those good old days. Can you imagine trying to come up with a first name for your computer that is unique across the entire Internet? How long do you think it would take to access the Hosts.txt file today? How large a hard drive would be required for the Hosts.txt file and how long would it take to search through it? How would you like to add or subtract entries in Hosts.txt every time a machine joins or leaves the Internet?

Clearly some changes were required! The first step was to go from the flat name space to a *hierarchical name space*. Now Bill, Bob, Mary, and Lisa can have last names to differentiate them from other Bills, Bobs, Marys, and Lisas. Bill might become *Bill Microsoft* while Mary might be *Mary Senate*. With the new name space came a new system of servers to maintain it. Now, instead of a single text file on a single machine, we have DNS servers scattered throughout the Internet (as well as on countless private networks). Each server can maintain its own list of names and can contact other DNS servers if it needs to find names it doesn't maintain.

The Domain Name System

The DNS is simply a client/server-based distributed database management system that maintains records for computers in *domain name space*. Described in RFCs 1034 and 1035, DNS operates at the application layer and uses the User Datagram Protocol (UDP) and the Transmission Control Protocol (TCP). (The client will always attempt to use UDP for increased performance. If the returned information is too long for a UDP broadcast message it will return in a truncated form. In this case, the client will resort to TCP.) You can think of DNS as an automated telephone book. If you wanted to call Mary Senate, you would look for *Mary* by checking all the *Senates* in the book's *S* section. When you find Mary's entry, you would write down her telephone number and give her a call. In a similar manner, using DNS, we work our way through the hierarchy of the Domain Name Space until we find the appropriate host and determine its IP address.

Resolvers

The client side of the DNS process is called the *resolver*. Resolver can refer to the computer that is attempting to obtain a name resolution or to the piece of software running on that computer that will make the actual name request. Resolvers can be built into applications or can be library routines designed for just this purpose.

Name Servers

As you may have deduced, the *name server* is the server side of the DNS process. Just as with resolver, this term may be used to refer to a machine or a piece of software. The name server attempts to provide a computer or domain name to IP address mapping. If it cannot, it may forward a request to another name server that can. Name servers are grouped into levels known as *domains*.

Domain Name Space

Domain name space provides a hierarchical way of naming hosts. It is analogous to the layout of a phone book where we first located the book for the appropriate locale, then found the *S* section, looked for the *Senates*, and finally found *Mary Senate*. Domain name space is divided into a number of domains at different levels, as shown in Figure 12-1.

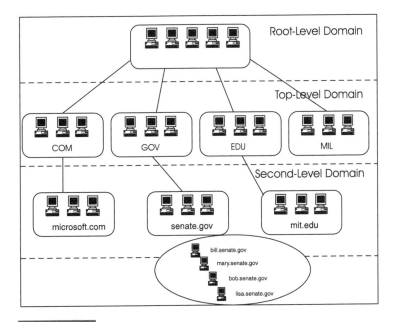

| **FIGURE 12-1** | *Domain name space* |

ROOT-LEVEL DOMAIN

The top domain name space level is called the *root* domain. This is simply the starting reference from which all lower domains are located. The root domain has no label or, more accurately, has a null label. It is depicted by a single dot (.) in a domain name. The root-level domain is simply "understood" in domain names. Using a final dot is strictly optional.

TOP-LEVEL DOMAINS

Top-level domains represent the major divisions of domain name space. These domains contain *second-level* domains and hosts. Table 12.1 shows some of the current top-level domains.

TABLE 12.1	Top-Level Domains
Domain Name	**Definition**
com	Commercial organizations
edu	Educational institutions
org	Not-for-profit organizations
net	Internet related networks
gov	Nonmilitary government organizations
mil	Military government organizations
num	Phone numbers
arpa	Reverse DNS
xx	Two-letter country code

SECOND-LEVEL DOMAINS

Second-level domains are directly subordinate to the top-level domains. These domains contain host names as well as lower-level domains (*subdomains*). Typically, second-level domains represent major organizations such as a company, college, governmental branch, or military service. The Senate domain, for instance, could contain computers such as ftp.senate.gov, and subdomains like finance.senate.gov. The finance subdomain might contain a computer called chmn.finance.senate.gov.

HOST NAMES

Host names represent individual computers within domains or subdomains. When the host name is appended to the domain name, we call the resulting concatenation a *fully qualified domain name* (FQDN). The FQDN for the host *Mary*, shown in Figure 12-1, would be *mary.senate.gov*.

Zones of Authority

A *zone of authority* delineates the portion of the domain name space that belongs to a particular name server. The name server is responsible for storing address mappings for everything within its zone of authority. A zone of authority contains at least one domain (or subdomain) and may contain some or all of the subdomains in the zone's root domain.

Note The zone's root domain shouldn't be confused with the root-level domain. A zone's root domain is simply the highest level domain contained in the zone. The zone's root domain may or may not contain subdomains.

In Figure 12-2, Zone 1 encompasses the senate domain (*senate.gov*) as well as the subdomain for the rules committee (*rules.senate.gov*). Zone 2 contains *finance.senate.gov*, while Zone 3 controls *ethics.senate.gov*. The advantage found in separating a domain into different zones may be found in better workload distribution for the name servers or for more efficient data replication. While a single domain can be split into multiple zones of authority, a single name server can be assigned more than one zone.

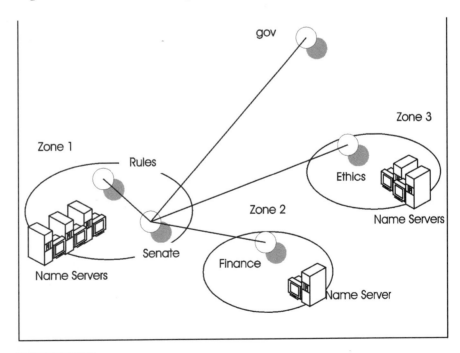

FIGURE 12-2   *Zones of authority*

Roles for Name Servers

DNS servers can be configured to operate in a variety of roles. Beyond simply maintaining their zone databases, servers can function as a team to manage zone data across the entire network.

Primary Name Servers

The primary name server is what you have likely envisioned during the discussion thus far. A primary server maintains zone data in local files. When you make changes to zone data (add, delete, or alter domains or hosts), you do it at the primary server level.

Secondary Name Servers

In its *secondary server* role, the DNS server obtains zone information from another server in the network—one with authority for the particular zone. When a secondary server acquires such information, the operation is known as a *zone transfer*.

Using secondary servers provides a number of enhancements to the DNS environment. A secondary name server provides a backup for the primary. Once it has completed a zone transfer, it will be capable of supporting clients for a period while the primary is off-line. A secondary server can provide faster data access. If your network is separated by a wide area network (WAN) link, maintaining a primary server on one side of the link and a secondary server on the other side will permit clients to access DNS zone information without the attendant delay in crossing the slow link. In a busy DNS environment, a secondary server can also reduce the load on the primary name server.

Since information for each zone is stored in a separate file, a secondary server for one zone can be a primary server for another. This dual role capability permits a more efficient way of managing DNS servers.

Master Name Servers

A *master name server* is a primary or secondary name server from which a secondary server obtains zone information in a zone transfer. When you define a secondary zone on a name server, you must also designate a *master name server* for that zone. This designation is known to the server, upon which you've defined the secondary zone only.

When the secondary server starts up it conducts a zone transfer with the designated master server. A secondary server cares only that it can get the zone information and pays no attention to the master server's status as primary or secondary for that zone.

Caching-Only Servers

As we'll soon see, all DNS servers cache name queries they have resolved. A *caching-only server*, however, does nothing else. These machines are not authoritative for any zones and conduct no zone transfers. They keep no zone data in their local databases. Every time a caching-only server takes part in a name resolution, it stores the information in its cache.

Caching-only servers can help in reducing the load on a primary or secondary server where the same names are frequently resolved. They can relieve traffic across a slow link much as a secondary server can. When employing a caching-only server, remember that it will have no information at all when it starts but must "learn" everything it knows in the course of its business. (We'll start to cover that information in the next section.) This can actually increase efficiency across a slow link since the caching-only server can give out frequently requested information on its side of the link without effecting a zone transfer that would increase overall link traffic.

Forwarders

When a DNS name server must communicate with other DNS name servers on the public Internet to resolve a name request, it does so through a *forwarder*. Servers designated as forwarders are the only computers allowed to carry out the WAN communications across the Internet. Any other DNS name server within the local network would be configured to use a forwarder and supplied with IP addresses for the DNS name servers designated as forwarders. A server configured to use forwarders receives a DNS request that it can't resolve through its own files and passes the request to a forwarder. The forwarder takes action to resolve the request and returns the result to the requesting server, which provides the information to the original requester. If the forwarder is unable to satisfy the request, the original name server will take other action to attempt to locate the desired information.

Slaves

DNS servers that have been configured to use forwarders exclusively are known as *slaves*. These machines are configured to return a failure message if the forwarder is unable to resolve the request and do not attempt to contact other name servers if the forwarder fails to satisfy the request.

DNS Name Resolution

Now that we understand some of the basics of DNS, let's take a look at the query process. When looking for information, the resolver (client) can make three different kinds of queries: *recursive*, *iterative*, or *inverse*.

Recursive Query

If a resolver sends a *recursive query* to a name server, that name server must return the requested information. It cannot simply return a message referring the resolver to a different name server. If the name server receiving the recursive query is unable to locate the requested information, it may query other name servers but it *must* respond to the resolver with either the information request or an error message stating the name or domain does not exist. This is the type of request typically made by a resolver to a name server or by a name server to a forwarder.

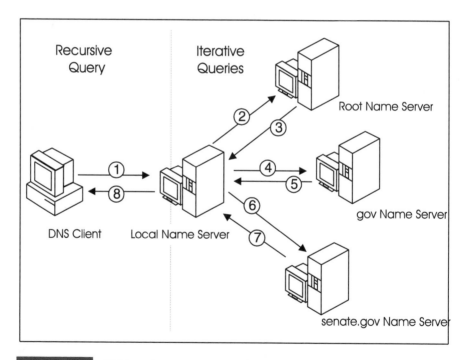

FIGURE 12–3   *DNS resolution: recursive and iterative queries*

Iterative Query

An *iterative query* is typically made by a DNS server to other DNS servers in response to a recursive query from a resolver which it—the original server—cannot answer. Under an iterative query, the queried server responds with the best answer it currently has.

Figure 12-3 illustrates an iterative query that begins as a recursive query. The local client (resolver) needs to contact the machine known as **mary.senate.gov**. The resolution process is as follows:

1. The resolver, using a recursive query, asks the local name server for a mapping to **mary.senate.gov**.
2. Unable to find the requested domain name (**senate.gov**) in its local zone files but required to provide an answer to the resolver, the local server sends an iterative query to a *root name server* to obtain a mapping for **mary.senate.gov**.
3. The root name server responds with the IP address of a name server for the **gov** top-level domain.
4. The local name server sends an iterative query for **mary.senate.gov** to the **gov** server.
5. The **gov** server responds with the IP address of a name server for the **senate.gov** domain.
6. The local server then sends an iterative query to the **senate.gov** server.
7. The **senate.gov** server returns the IP address mapping for **mary.senate.gov**.
8. The local name server returns the mapping to the resolver.

Inverse Query

Sometimes we know an IP address but need to know the host name. Unfortunately, DNS name space is constructed to provide IP addresses when host names are known and not the other way around. Originally, the only way to find this information was by performing an exhaustive search of every domain in existence!

Since the number of hosts and domains in the world is increasing at a rapid rate, searching the entire Internet each time a host name is required would result in a lot of network traffic, consume many resources and much time, and wouldn't be any fun. Fortunately, the creation of a special domain called **in-addr.arpa** solves this problem. This domain contains reverse lookup information in nodes named after the dotted decimal numbers that make up IP addresses.

As you've noticed, IP addresses get more specific from left to right while domain names get more specific from right to left. To resolve this discontinuity, the octets are reversed in the **in-addr.arpa** domain. When organizations are assigned their Class A, B, or C IP addresses, they are also assigned administration of the appropriate lower limbs of the **in-addr.arpa** domain.

The **in-addr.arpa** domain contains special resource records known as *pointer* (PTR) records that associate the IP address with the appropriate host name. To find the host name associated with **200.22.18.36**, for instance, you'd query the DNS server for the PTR for **36.18.22.200.in-addr.arpa**. The PTR would contain both the host name and its associated IP address.

Ensuring the creation of pointer records is an extremely important part of DNS administration.

Caching and Time to Live

Each time a name server receives information it caches it for later use. As you might imagine, in the process of servicing a recursive query, a name server will likely accumulate a great deal of information. Retaining this information for an extended period of time creates two problems. Since DNS data can change over time, the data can become inaccurate. Even if data accuracy could be assured, retaining every bit of data received by a name server for every one-time request it serviced over the course of its lifetime would require a great deal of storage space.

The *Time to Live* (TTL) value alleviates both problems by limiting the time the name server will cache a particular piece of data. When entering information into the name server, the administrator sets a TTL for each record. A small TTL guards against inaccurate and inconsistent data while a larger TTL reduces the load on name servers by permitting more cached data. When selecting a TTL, it is important to balance these two factors.

As soon as a name server caches a piece of data, it begins to decrement the TTL. When the TTL reaches zero, the data is flushed from the cache. If a name server receives a request that can be filled from its cache, it will forward the information with the *decremented* TTL. This is analogous to buying a bottle of milk at the supermarket. Let's say you buy a bottle with a freshness date that expires in seven days. You bring it home, put it in your refrigerator for three days, and then give it to your neighbor. Your neighbor will be able to safely use the milk for only four (not seven) days. When the resolver receives DNS data, it will also cache it for further use. The TTL is honored on resolvers just as it is on name servers.

DNS Files

Typically, DNS systems are configured by editing text files. Windows 2000, however, provides a user-friendly interface, which makes administration of local and remote Microsoft DNS servers much more pleasant. With the understanding that your administrative tasks can be carried out easily under a Windows graphical user interface (GUI), we will turn to the actual text files to help us build a better understanding of what really goes on inside a DNS server.

Under RFCs 1034 and 1035, several text files define the DNS system configuration and database. These files include the *database, cache, reverse lookup*, and *127 reverse lookup* files and can include a *boot* file. Even though we rarely look at the raw files when using the Windows 2000 DNS GUI, they are critical to the operation of the DNS server and are explained in detail in this section.

Database File

The DNS database file is a text file that represents most of the name servers' knowledge base for a particular zone. By default, the database file uses the zone name with .dns appended to it. If your zone is **senate.gov**, the database file would be called **senate.gov.dns**. Windows 2000 provides a sample DNS database file called **place.dns**. (Look for the file in the **WNNT\System32\DNS\Samples** directory). You can rename this file using the aforementioned naming convention and add records to it for your DNS zone (assuming you didn't wish to use the GUI provided by Windows).

The database file is the file that is replicated, ultimately, between DNS *master name servers* and *secondary name servers*. The information contained in the database file is found in a series of line entries called resource records. The SOA, A, NS, PTR, CNAME, MX, and HINFO record types are defined in RFC 1034 (we'll discuss the PTR record in the next section) and the SRV record is defined in RFC 2782. Additionally, Microsoft has created the Microsoft-specific record types WINS and WINS-R. Even if you never plan to create a record outside the GUI, understanding how the records are put together will help you when configuring your DNS server.

START OF AUTHORITY RECORD

The first record in a DNS database file must be the Start of Authority (SOA) record. This record contains the general parameters that control the DNS zone using the format:

```
IN SOA <source host> <contact e-mail> <serial number>
<refresh time> <retry time> <expiration time> <Time to
Live>
```

- **Source host**: Host name of computer on which the DNS server is running.
- **Contact email**: Internet email address of the DNS server's administrator.

- **Serial number**: This is the version number of the database file. Expect this number to increase each time the database file changes.
- **Refresh time**: The interval (in seconds) a secondary server uses to check with its master server to determine if the database file has changed and to request a zone transfer.
- **Retry time**: The amount of time (in seconds) that a secondary server will wait before reattempting a zone transfer after a communications failure with the master server.
- **Expiration time**: The amount of time (in seconds) that a secondary server will keep trying to download a zone. If the secondary server is unable to obtain the new zone information after this period, it will discard the old zone information.
- **Time to live**: The amount of time (in seconds) another DNS server is allowed to cache resource records from this database file. If an individual resource record does not contain an overriding TTL value, it is this parameter that determines the record's TTL.

Figure 12-4 shows a sample SOA record. Note that the at sign (@) indicates this computer and IN identifies this as an Internet record. The senate.gov host name is terminated by a period. This is because any host name not so terminated will automatically have the root domain appended to it. The normal at sign (@) found in the administrator's email address has been replaced with a period (that is, **administrator@senate.gov** has become **administrator.senate.gov**). Note the use of semicolons to indicate comments and the use of parentheses to enclose line breaks that span more than one line.

```
@  IN SOA  mary.senate.gov. administrator.senate.gov. (
   1        ; serial number
   10800    ; refresh [3 hours]
   3600     ; retry [1hour]
   604800   ; expire [7 days]
   86400 )  ; time to live [1 day]
```

FIGURE 12-4   *SOA record*

NAME SERVER RECORD

The name server (NS) record contains a reference to each name server that can be used to look up hosts in the domain. A zone may have several NS records if several name servers are applicable to that zone. The record uses the format:

```
<domain> IN NS <nameserver host >
```

Look at the following NS record:

```
@ IN NS lisa.senate.gov
```

In this case the at sign (@) means this domain, IN identifies this as an Internet record, and **lisa.senate.gov** is identified as an additional name server that can service the domain.

HOST RECORD

The Host Record (**A** record) maps a host name to an IP address. Host records make up the bulk of the database file and look like the following:

```
mary          IN A 202.22.18.32
lisa          IN A 202.22.18.34
localhost     IN A 127.0.0.1
```

CNAME RECORD

The CNAME record is a canonical name record. This entry permits you to associate more than one host name with the same IP address. Also referred to as aliasing, this record permits you to identify a single machine with several functions. This is particularly useful when configuring a particular machine for Internet roles. The following records identify the machine **lisa.senate.gov** as a generic file server called SenateFiles as well as the Internet related www and ftp servers:

```
SenateFiles     CNAME lisa
www             CNAME lisa
ftp             CNAME lisa
```

Communication for **SenateFiles.senate.gov**, **www.senate.gov**, and **ftp.senate.gov** will all be referred to the machine called **lisa**.

MAIL EXCHANGE RECORD

The mail exchange (MX) record identifies the host that processes mail for this domain. If there is more than one MX record, the resolver will attempt contact with mail servers starting with the lowest preference value (which indicates the highest priority). The MX record format is:

```
<domain> IN MX <preference> <mailserver host >
```

The following records would ensure that mail addressed to **sensmith@senate.gov** would be delivered first to **sensmith@bill.senate.gov** if the **bill** server is available, and then to **sensmith@bob.senate.gov** if the **bill** server is unavailable:

```
@ IN MX 1 Bill
@ IN MX 2 Bob
```

Proper entry of the MX record is one of the most critical steps to setting up any email service and cannot be overemphasized.

Warning

A mail server identified with an MX record also requires an A record. Failure to employ both records is one of the most common causes of email failure!

HOST INFORMATION RECORD

The host information (HINFO) record contains information about a host's hardware type and operating system. Originally, this record was intended to permit services like FTP sites to determine how to work with the host. Machine and system types used in the record should come from those listed in RFC 1340. In practice, however, the use of this record is rarely implemented and most people use it only to track hardware information within their network. Entries from the RFC are usually replaced by information meaningful to the local administrator but completely meaningless to the Internet. If you choose to use the HINFO record, consider that you are, essentially, telegraphing your machine types and operating systems to the world—easing, considerably, the job of any would-be hacker. The proper format for the HINFO record is:

```
<host name> IN HINFO <machine_type> <operating_system>
```

SERVICE RESOURCE RECORD

A service (SRV) resource record permits the system to locate a server with a specific service, protocol, and DNS domain (e.g., a domain controller or a web server). The proper format for the SRV record is:

```
_<service>._<proto>.<name> IN SRV <priority> <weight>
<port> <host>
```

- `<service>` indicates the name of the service (e.g. http); Services not defined in standards may be user defined.
- `<proto>` specifies the protocol (e.g. TCP or UDP)
- `<name>` represents the domain name to which the resource record refers.
- `<priority>` indicates the host's precedence. Clients attempt to connect to the host with the lowest priority.
- `<weight>` is used for load balancing. When the priorities are equal for two or more records in the same domain, clients should attempt contact to records with higher weights more often.
- `<port>` refers to the port the service will use on the host.
- `<host>` contains the FQDN for the computer providing the service indicated.

The Windows 2000 DNS will automatically create the necessary SRV records to find domain controllers and other critical domain services. You can create SRV records for web servers and other network resources. A web server record would look like the following:

```
_http._tcp.senate.gov. IN SRV 0 0 80 web1.senate.gov.
```

A domain controller would require several SRV records to advertise its services. The following example shows the SRV record that allows clients to locate the domain controller dc1 within the senate.gov domain:

```
_ldap._tcp.dc._msdcs.senate.gov. IN SRV0 0 389
dc1.senate.gov.
```

WINS RECORD

The WINS record is defined as part of the zone database file. Specific to Windows 2000, it may be attached only to the zone root domain. The record provides the DNS server the IP address of an appropriate WINS server. This permits the DNS server to use the WINS lookup for any requests for hosts in the zone root not found in its database. The WINS record uses the following format:

```
<domain> IN WINS <IP address of WINS server>
```

WINS-R RECORD

The WINS-R record provides reverse lookup capability for hosts identified through a DNS/WINS tie. The WINS-R permits the DNS server to use a NetBIOS name lookup for any reverse lookup requests for IP addresses in the zone root that are not statically defined with PTR records. The WINS-R record uses the following format:

```
<domain> IN WINS-R <domain to append to returned NetBIOS
names>
```

Example:

```
@ IN WINS-R senate.gov.
```

Reverse Lookup File

The reverse lookup file contains the pointer (PTR) records to permit a resolver to find a host name when an IP address is known. The reverse lookup file is named like a zone file according to the in-addr.arpa zone for which it contains PTR records. The format for the zone file name is **z.y.x.w.in-addr.arpa** where *w, x, y*, and *z* represent the octets of the IP address. In the case of the Class B network 152.60.22.0, the file name would become **60.152.in-addr.arpa**. In addition to PTR records, the reverse lookup file contains SOA and NS records.

A number of applications implement security based on names of connecting hosts. If a client attempts to access a particular resource under this security method, the server controlling the resource would contact the DNS server to determine the client's host name. If the host name didn't match the list of approved hosts on the resource server or if the DNS was unable to find the host name, access to the resource would be denied.

THE POINTER RECORD

Central to the reverse lookup file is the PTR. The pointer record contains a static mapping of IP addresses to host names within a reverse-lookup zone. The IP numbers are entered with their octets in reverse order and in-addr.arpa. is appended to the end to create the record. The address, 200.22.18.30, for instance would be represented by 30.18.22.200.in-addr.arpa. The pointer record uses the following format:

```
<ip reverse domain name> IN PTR <host name>
```

Example:

```
10.18.22.200.in-addr.arpa. IN PTR filsvr.senate.gov.
```

127-Reverse Lookup File

Known as the Arpa-127.rev File, this is the database for the 127.in-addr.arpa. domain. It is used for reverse-lookups of IP numbers in the 127 network, such as localhost.

Cache File

Known as cache.dns, the cache file contains host information needed to resolve names beyond the DNS server's authoritative domains. In Windows 2000, you'll find this file in *<systemroot>*\system32\dns. It is automatically loaded.

It contains names and addresses of Internet root name servers. Microsoft provides a default file (see Figure 12-5) for users on the Internet that provides the DNS server with the root domains. The cache.dns file is depicted on the *Root Hints* tab of the DNS server properties dialog (more on this later). If you will *not* connect to the Internet, replace the default cache file with a file that contains the name servers authoritative for the root of your private network. You can find a current Internet cache file at:

```
FTP://rs.internic.net/domain/named.cache
```

```
.                           3600000  IN  NS  A.ROOT-SERVERS.NET.
A.ROOT-SERVERS.NET.         3600000      A   198.41.0.4
;
; formerly NS1.ISI.EDU
;
.                           3600000      NS  B.ROOT-SERVERS.NET.
B.ROOT-SERVERS.NET.         3600000      A   128.9.0.107
;
; formerly C.PSI.NET
.
.
H.ROOT-SERVERS.NET.         3600000      A   128.63.2.53
;
; formerly NIC.NORDU.NET
;
.                           3600000      NS  I.ROOT-SERVERS.NET.
I.ROOT-SERVERS.NET.         3600000      A   192.36.148.17
```

FIGURE 12–5	*Excerpt from Microsoft default cache.dns file*

Note   Are you confused by the "3600000" entries in the record fields? When the cache file was originally constructed the field was used for a cache TTL for these values (1,000 hours in this case). Current name servers do not, in fact, discard root server data so this field is actually DNS folklore now, and has no actual function.

Boot File

The boot file is not actually defined in any RFC but is part of the Berkeley Internet Name Domain (BIND) implementation of DNS. If you are going to administer your DNS through changes to the text files instead of using the GUI, you should configure your server to use a boot file. By default, the Windows 2000 DNS server uses information from the registry. You can use the DNS GUI to configure it to use a boot file (we'll further explore this later in the chapter). The boot file is named boot and controls the startup behavior of the DNS server. Boot file commands must start at the beginning of a line. The following commands are used in the boot file:

DIRECTORY COMMAND

This specifies the directory containing the other files referred to in the boot file. It uses the format: **directory <directory>**.

```
Example: directory c:\windows\system32\dns
```

CACHE COMMAND

The cache command identifies the cache file. This command is a mandatory entry and the cache file it refers to MUST be present on the disk. The command uses the following format: **cache . <filename>**.

Example: cache . cache

PRIMARY COMMAND

The primary command identifies this name server as authoritative for a particular domain and specifies a zone file which contains the resource records for that domain. The boot file can contain more than one primary command record. The command uses the following format: **primary <domain> <filename>**.

Example: primary senate.gov senate.dns
            primary ethics.senate.gov ethics.dns

SECONDARY COMMAND

The secondary command specifies a domain for which this name server is authoritative in a secondary role. It includes a list of master server IP addresses from which the zone information may be downloaded. It also specifies a local file for caching the zone. As with the primary command, the boot file can contain more than one secondary command record. The command uses the following format: **secondary <domain> <hostlist> <local filename>**.

Example: secondary rules.senate.gov 200.22.18.32 rules.dns

FORWARDERS COMMAND

The forwarders command identifies a DNS server designated as a forwarder. The command uses the following format: **forwarders <hostlist>**.

Example: forwarders 200.22.18.38 202.20.200.99

SLAVE COMMAND

The slave command indicates the use of the forwarders command as the only way to resolve queries. This command can only follow a forwarders command.

Example: forwarders 200.22.18.38 202.20.200.99
         slave

DNS Implementation Planning

With your newfound DNS knowledge, I'm sure you're eager to begin setting up DNS servers right away. Before we get down to installing the software, let's look at some planning factors. In this chapter we'll cover general DNS planning without regard to the dynamic DNS and support to the Active Directory. We'll look at how to position DNS servers to support a Windows 2000 domain in Chapter 13.

The overall configuration of a DNS environment depends on a number of considerations not the least of which are the size of your organization and its operating locations and the degree of fault tolerance you need in your network.

If your organization (or at least its network) is small, it may be more efficient to have your DNS clients work with DNS servers maintained by your Internet service provider (ISP). Your ISP will likely charge for the service but will be able to maintain entries for all the hosts you designate. Regardless of who actually maintains the DNS servers, any organization that plans to connect to the Internet must provide the InterNIC with its domain name and the IP address of at least two DNS servers that service that domain. (Depending on the arrangement with your ISP, all of these tasks may be accomplished by the ISP. If you aren't going to use the Internet, you will, of course, not need to coordinate with the InterNIC but will need to create your own DNS servers.)

Important   This discussion pertains only to providing general network IP address mappings. A Windows 2000 domain requires DNS servers to directly support the domain with SRV records. As we'll see in the next chapter, there is an alternative that permits you to use your ISP to provide network DNS services while using your own DNS servers to support your Windows 2000 domain.

If you're setting up your own DNS servers, it's a good idea to configure at least two per domain—a primary and a secondary. (Note that we haven't differentiated between an *Internet domain* and a *Windows 2000 domain* here. That is because a Windows 2000 domain is—or should be—congruent with an Internet domain.) This will provide sufficient redundancy to allow your network to continue to function if one goes down. When using two or more DNS servers, another consideration is the replication schedule (you'll recall that replication is governed by information entered in the SOA record). If your host name information is very dynamic, you'll need a relatively short replication interval. This will ensure your secondary server remains up-to-date but will increase the degree of network traffic. A good balance in this area is very important, as you might imagine.

Once your DNS servers are installed and running, you'll need to register with the DNS server that is immediately above you in the domain name space (see Figure 12-6). If your DNS servers are on the second level, you'll need to contact the InterNIC and provide information such as the names and addresses of your DNS servers, contact information for your domain administrator(s), and the date that the domain will become available on the network.

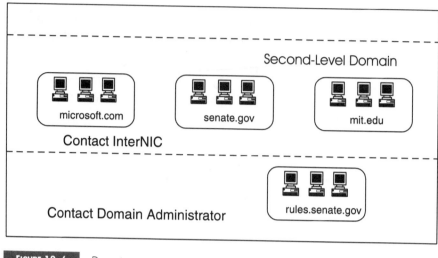

| FIGURE 12-6 | *Domain registration* |

If your domain is below the second level, you must contact the domain administrator for the domain immediately above you. You'll need to provide your DNS information as well as anything else he or she may require.

Note

If you need to register with the InterNIC, you can find online registration services at http://internic.net or can call the help line at (703) 742-4777.

DNS Installation and Configuration

Now that we understand how DNS works and have a good idea of the overarching planning considerations for DNS implementation, it's time to install a DNS server on a Windows 2000 server. In this chapter, we'll install a DNS server and configure it to operate with a standard DNS zone. In Chapter 13, we'll take on the Active Directory integrated zone and see how that fits with the Windows 2000 domain.

Before we actually install DNS, we need to ensure TCP/IP is properly configured on the machine that will run the DNS server. Obviously, the machine *must* have a static IP address. This means it should have an IP address set on the machine itself or should be a DHCP client with a client address reservation, as defined in Chapter 7. Additionally, you should check the **Network Identification** tab of the **System Properties** dialog box. Click **More** to ensure host and domain names are properly specified (see Figure 12-7).

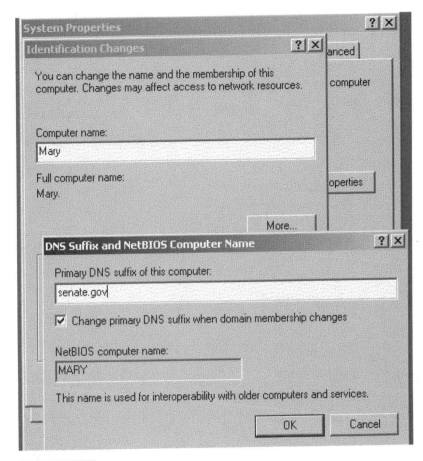

FIGURE 12–7   *Host and domain names*

Installing the Service

Once we're sure our TCP/IP data is correctly configured, we can proceed to the server installation. As you might have guessed, DNS installation is very similar to that of all the other TCP/IP services we've installed thus far. The first step is a visit to the **Add/Remove Programs** dialog window and select **Add/Remove Windows Components**. When the **Windows Components Wizard** opens, select **Networking Services,** click **Details**, and in the dialog box that appears, highlight and check **Domain Name System (DNS)** as shown in Figure 12-8. (The installation program will need to copy files from the installation CD-ROM.) Click **OK** to close the dialog box and click **Next**. Once the appropriate files are copied, you have the DNS service installed.

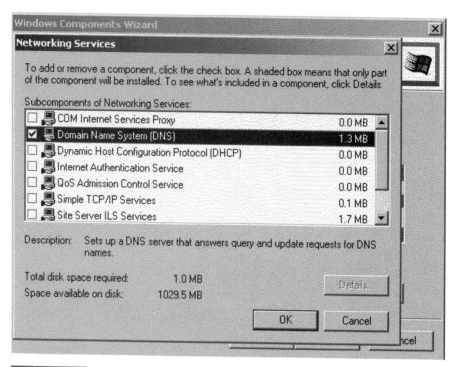

FIGURE 12–8   *Installing Microsoft DNS server*

Configuring the DNS Server

Now that your DNS server is installed and running it needs to be configured to do some work! Right now it is running as a caching-only Internet name server because it has only the Internet root information it has found in the default cache file and knows nothing about the network on which it operates. (Actually, even if the DNS server were completely configured, it wouldn't do a lot of good unless we configured some clients to use it. We'll see how to do that a bit later.) The first step in DNS configuration is to configure your server in the **DNS** console. You can launch the DNS console from the *Administrative Tools* program group.

Important   To make sure you see all available options and information, ensure *Advanced* is selected on the *View* menu.

Once you have the DNS console running, click the DNS server to expand it. Right-click the name of the server, and select **Configure the server** from the context menu, as shown in Figure 12-9. The Configure DNS Server wizard starts and guides you through the process of setting up DNS.

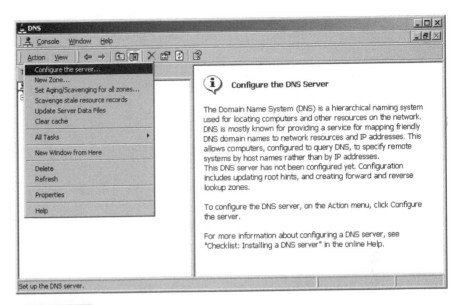

FIGURE 12–9   *Configuring a DNS server*

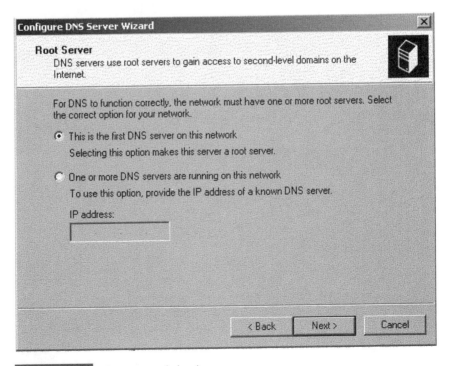

FIGURE 12–10   *Root server dialog box*

When you click **Next>**, the server analyzes the system and brings up the dialog box shown in Figure 12-10. Select the first option (This is the first DNS...) if this will be the first DNS server on your network to support the zone you'll create. This will make your server *authoritative* for the zone. If one or more DNS servers exist on the network and this server will receive part of its information from other DNS servers, select the second option (One or more DNS Servers are already running on this network). Click **Next>**.

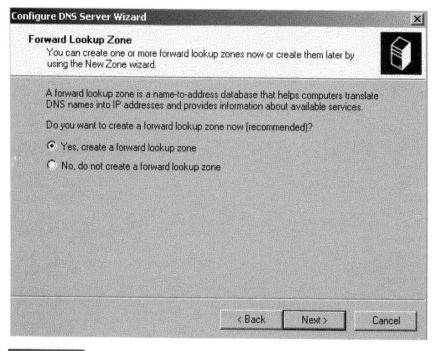

Forward lookup zone

The next dialog box (Figure 12-11) allows you to create a *forward lookup zone*. If you already know the information for the zone(s) this server will support click **Yes**, otherwise click **No**. If you select No, you'll be able to add the zone(s) later. We'll configure the *senate.gov* zone so we'll leave **Yes** selected and click **Next>**.

Figure 12-12 shows the **Zone Type** dialog box. Since our server is not a domain controller, the *Active Directory integrated* choice is unavailable (more on this in Chapter 13). The **Standard primary** zone (which we'll select) permits you to create a conventional (versus Active Directory) zone that will reside on your server. Selecting a standard secondary zone will allow your server to perform a zone transfer from an existing DNS server to obtain zone information from an existing zone. With **Standard primary** selected, click **Next>**.

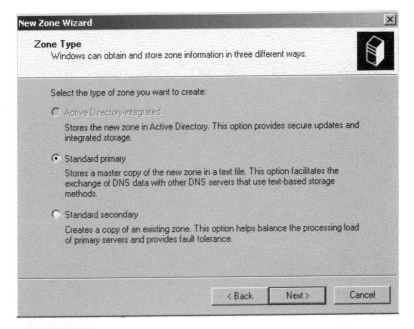

FIGURE 12–12   *Zone type*

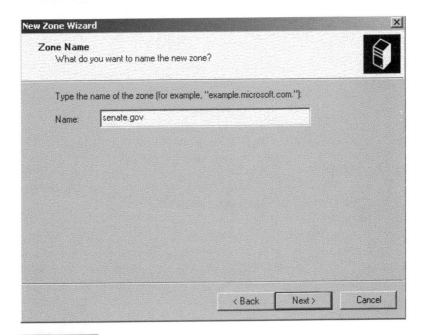

FIGURE 12–13   *Zone name dialog box*

When the Zone Name dialog box appears, enter the name your zone will use (see Figure 12-13) and click **Next>**.

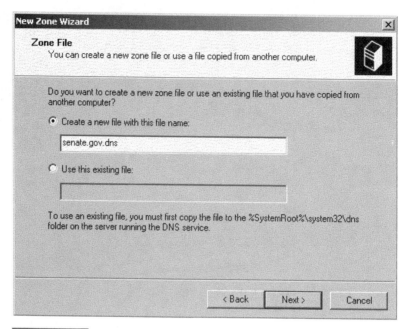

New Zone Wizard

Zone File
You can create a new zone file or use a file copied from another computer.

Do you want to create a new zone file or use an existing file that you have copied from another computer?

⦿ Create a new file with this file name:

senate.gov.dns

○ Use this existing file:

To use an existing file, you must first copy the file to the %SystemRoot%\system32\dns folder on the server running the DNS service.

< Back   Next >   Cancel

FIGURE 12–14   *Zone file dialog box*

The Zone File dialog box shown in Figure 12-14 permits you to enter/ change the name of the file that will contain the zone data. The default name is the zone name with a **.dns** extension. This is usually the best convention to use, so we'll leave the screen as is and click **Next>**.

Next, you're given an opportunity to create a reverse lookup zone (see Figure 12-15). The wizard makes an error-prone task much easier so if you'll require a reverse lookup zone, it's a good idea to create one now. Click **Next>**. The next dialog box is similar to that shown in Figure 12-12. You're asked to select the kind of zone for the reverse lookup. You should normally select the same zone type as you selected for the corresponding forward lookup zone. Click **Next>**.

The next dialog box (see Figure 12-16) asks for a *Network ID* or *Reverse lookup zone name*. If you enter the Network ID, the system will automatically create the zone name. Since we're using the Class B network 172.16.0.0, we'll enter 172.16 as a network ID. (Note that if we include the zeros in the address, the wizard will assume they are a valid part of the network ID.) Click **Next>**. The next dialog box is similar to Figure 12-14 and permits you to select a file name for the reverse lookup zone. Click **Next>**.

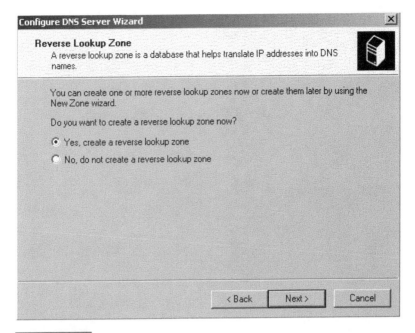

FIGURE 12–15   *Reverse lookup zone*

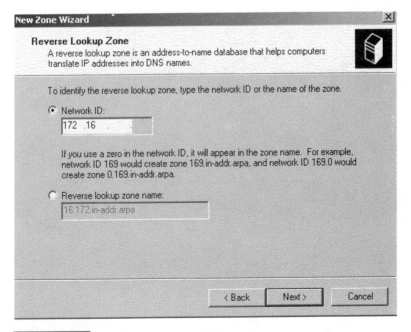

FIGURE 12–16   *Configure a reverse lookup zone*

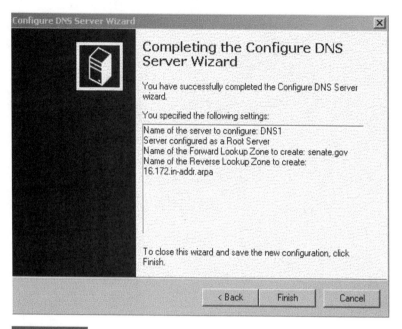

FIGURE 12–17 *Finish DNS configuration*

The final dialog box (see Figure 12-17) shows the options you've selected. After reviewing them, click **Finish**.

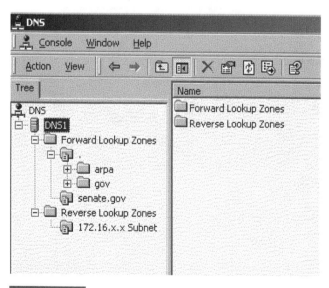

FIGURE 12–18 *Complete configuration*

At the conclusion of the configuration wizard, your DNS server should be configured, as shown in Figure 12-18. Note the dot (.) with the **arpa** and **gov** subzones in Figure 12-18. These were added because we made our server authoritative for the senate.gov zone. As configured, the server assumes that it knows all about the root-level domain and the top-level domain, **gov**. The problem here is, unless we provide the server with all the root- and top-level domain information, it's not as smart as it thinks. As configured, our server will never use its cache file to query other DNS servers for information it doesn't have.

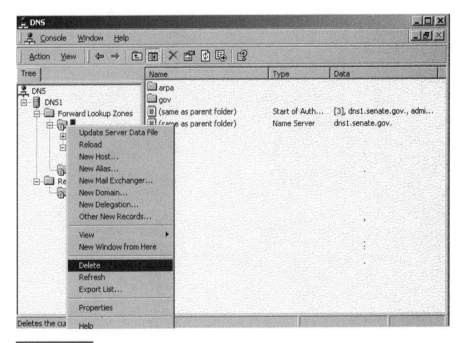

FIGURE 12–19   *Deleting the top-level zone*

The solution to this is to right-click the dot and select **Delete**, as shown in Figure 12-19. Your server will now be able to provide information for the senate.gov zone but will query other servers for information for other zones.

Now that our initial zones are set up, let's take a look at some of the other DNS server configuration options available to us.

Right-click your server and select **Properties** to reveal the properties dialog box shown in Figure 12-20. The **Interfaces** tab permits you to identify which network interface cards will participate in DNS on a multihomed computer. The default is to use all interfaces.

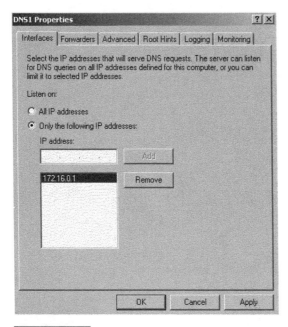

FIGURE 12–20 *Server properties: interfaces*

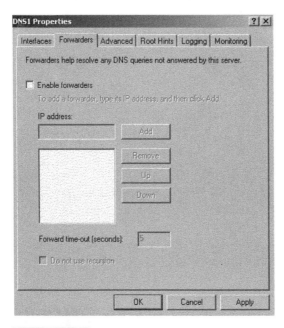

FIGURE 12–21 *Server properties: forwarders*

The **Forwarders** tab (see Figure 12-21) permits you to configure your server to use a forwarder and also enables you to make it a slave to the forwarder. To use one or more forwarders, check the **Enable forwarders** check box and enter the IP address(es) for the forwarder(s) below. To make this a slave server, check the **Do not use recursion** check box. The **Forward time-out** value controls how long the server will wait for a forwarder to respond before going to the next forwarder, going recursive, or returning an error message.

The **Advanced** tab (see Figure 12-22) lets you set specific server options. A definition of the selections in the **Server Options** window is listed in Table 12.2. The **Name checking** option allows you to select the character set to use for names contained on the server. The default (**Multibyte**) permits the use of Unicode data and is a Windows 2000 enhancement. If you are working with servers that can't support Unicode, you may wish to select **Strict RFC** from the drop-down box. The **Load zone data on startup** window allows you to select the server's boot method. The default (**From Active Directory and registry**) will load data from the Active Directory and the local machine's registry. Selecting **From registry** will load initialization data from the registry only (if the server doesn't operate in an Active Directory environment, both options are the same). Selecting **From file** causes the server to boot using data in a Boot.dns file (described earlier in this chapter). Do not select this option unless you have properly constructed a Boot.dns

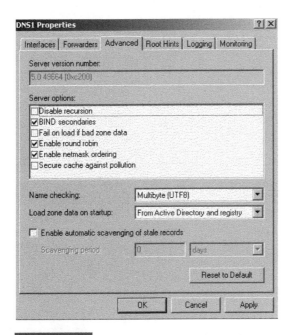

FIGURE 12–22   *Server properties: advanced*

file. By checking **Enable automatic scavenging of stale records** you can have the server check for records that haven't been refreshed during the Scavenging period and delete them. This option is intended for records that are dynamically updated (discussed in the next chapter) but will remove both dynamic and static records. Unless stale records are causing a significant problem on your server and you fully understand the consequences of deleting records that are seldom refreshed but important to your network, this option is not recommended.

TABLE 12.2	Advanced Server Options
Option	**Definition**
Disable recursion	Disables recursion on the DNS server. If so configured, the server will *not* seek information from other DNS servers if it does not have the information requested.
BIND secondaries	Causes the server to conduct zone transfers using compression and multiple records per TCP message. This is set by default. If your environment contains non-BIND compliant DNS servers that can't handle this method, clear the check box.
Fail on load if bad data	Causes the server to refuse to load a zone data file that contains errors. When this is unchecked (the default), the server logs the errors and ignores the erroneous data but loads the rest of the zone file.
Enable round robin	Causes the server to rotate and reorder a list of multiple host records if the requested host name is for a computer with multiple IP addresses. (This is set by default.)
Enable netmask ordering	Causes the server to reorder a list of multiple host records based on subnet priority if the queried host name is for a multihomed computer. If an IP address exists on the revolver's local network, that address will be returned first. (This is set by default.)
Secure cache against pollution	Causes the server to discard referral responses from the cache that aren't related to the domain name originally requested. (For example, if a request was made for www.alidatrain.com and a referral answer for alidaconnection.com was received, that response would not be cached.)

The **Root Hints** tab (see Figure 12-23) shows the contents of the cache.dns file that was loaded at startup. In this dialog box, you can add, edit, or delete information for root servers. If your network doesn't participate on the Internet but needs the addresses of route servers within your private orga-

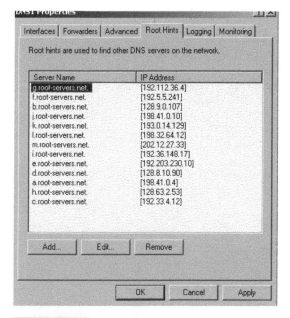

FIGURE 12–23   *Server properties: root hints*

nization, you can enter that information here. If this list is empty, it may be because your server is configured as *authoritative*. If you didn't want to have an authoritative server, check for and delete the dot (.) zone as described earlier. You may need to restart the Windows 2000 server to load the cache file after doing this.

The **Logging** tab (see Figure 12-24) permits you to select logging information to be saved to the log file (dns.log). These options provide a very useful debugging tool but you should select only the options you need since this places a nontrivial workload on the server.

The **Monitoring** tab (see Figure 12-25) permits you to perform manual or automatic testing of the server configuration. You can test a *simple query* where the server verifies it can find its own name mapping from the local DNS server or a *recursive query* where the server uses the route hints to find an authoritative server that will direct it back to itself to resolve, once again, its own name. You can initiate one or both tests with the **Test Now** button or schedule the tests to run on a recurring basis by checking the **Perform automatic testing at the following interval** check box. The status of either the automatic or manual test is shown in the **Test results** window. Additionally, a warning symbol is superimposed on the server icon when the most recent test was unsuccessful (see Figure 12-26).

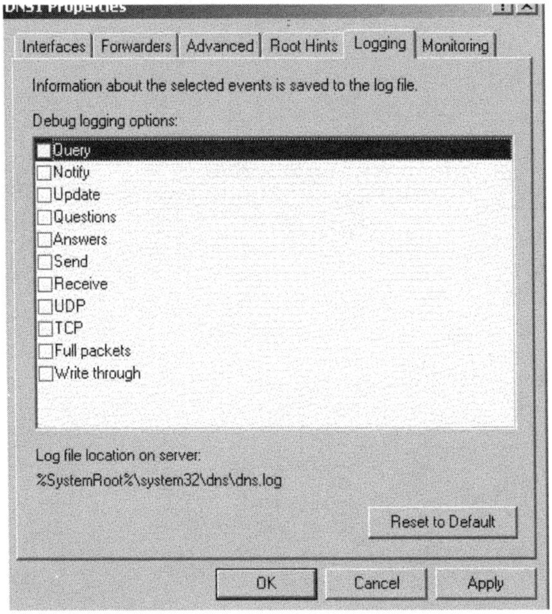

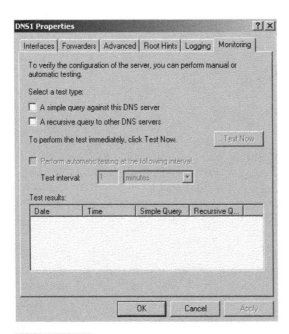

FIGURE 12-24 *Server properties: logging*

FIGURE 12-25 *Server properties: monitoring*

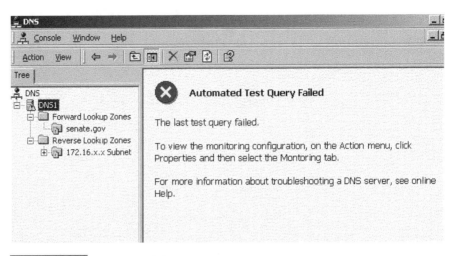

FIGURE 12–26   *Test query failure*

ADDING ZONES AND SUBDOMAINS

The configuration wizard we ran earlier permitted us to add a single zone to our server. We may want, however, to add additional primary or secondary zones. To add a zone, right-click **Forward Lookup Zones** and select **New Zone**, as shown in Figure 12-27. This starts the New Zone Wizard, which runs exactly like the Configuration Wizard.

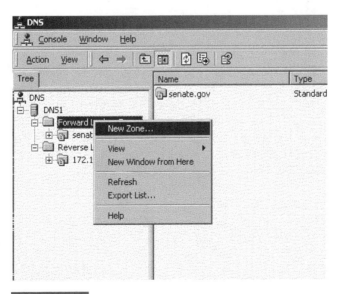

FIGURE 12–27   *New zone*

Click **Next>**, but this time select **Standard secondary** to create a secondary zone. Click **Next>** again and enter the name of the secondary zone you'd like to create (see Figure 12-28). (Note that you can also use the browse button to locate the zone if it's in your local network.)

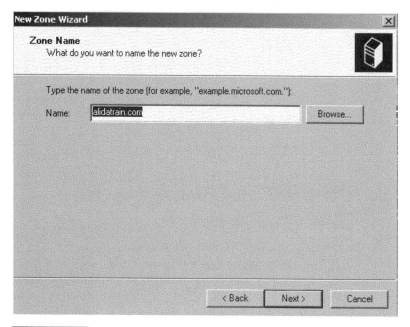

FIGURE 12-28   *Enter zone name*

Click **Next>**, enter the IP address of the DNS server from which you'll copy the zone data, and click **Add** (see Figure 12-29).

Click **Next>** and **Finish** and the DNS server transfers the zone from the master server and adds the new secondary zone (see Figure 12-30). Note that we added a secondary zone here to demonstrate the procedure for adding one. We could have used the same procedure to create a primary zone instead—the steps would be virtually identical to those we used during the initial configuration.

You can add a subdomain to your new zone by highlighting the zone selecting **New Domain** from the **Action** menu bar. This reveals the **New Domain** dialog box that permits you to add the name of the desired subdomain (see Figure 12-31).

Click **OK** and the subdomain is created (see Figure 12-32).

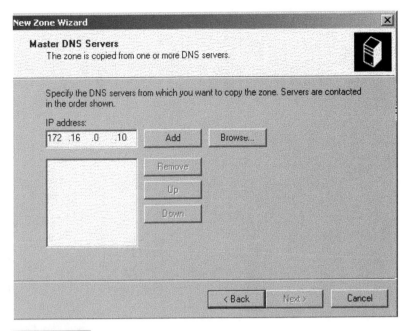

FIGURE 12–29 *Enter IP address for master DNS server*

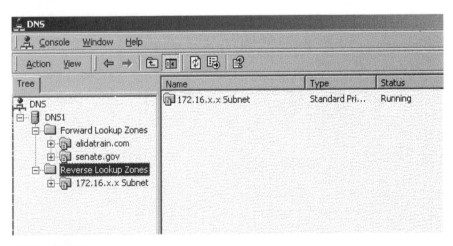

FIGURE 12–30 *New secondary zone: alidatrain.com*

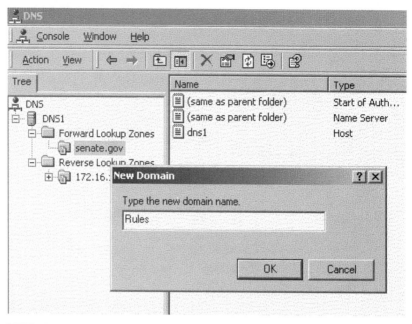

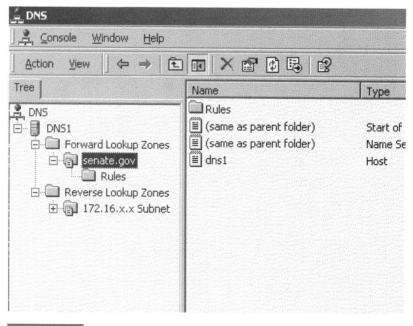

ZONE PROPERTIES

You can conFigure zone properties by highlighting the zone and selecting **Properties** from the **Action** menu. This reveals the zone **Properties** dialog box and its five tabs. The **General** tab (see Figure 12-33) permits you to pause or restart the zone, to change the zone file name, to set it as a primary or secondary zone, to allow or disallow dynamic updates (more on this in the next chapter), and to set aging/scavenging properties. To set aging/scavenging properties, click **Aging** to reveal the dialog box depicted in Figure 12-34.

To enable scavenging, check the **Scavenge stale resource records** check box. The function here is identical to that of setting scavenging for the entire database (explained earlier). Enabling scavenging here, however, applies only to the selected zone and not the entire database. The **No-refresh interval** may be altered here. This is the time interval for dynamic updates between refreshes. Shortening the value will result in more traffic and load on the system but will reduce the likelihood of stale records. Increasing

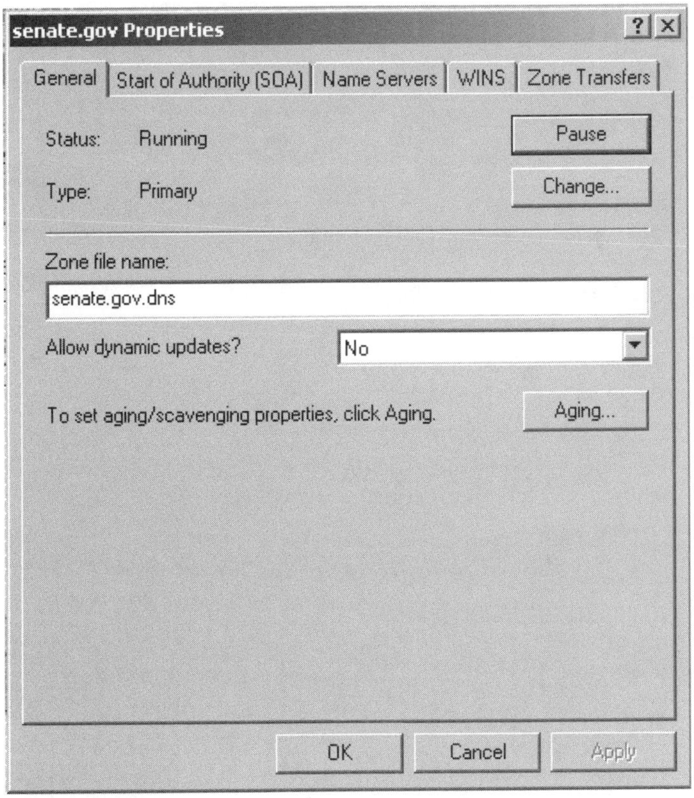

FIGURE 12-33   *Zone properties—General tab*

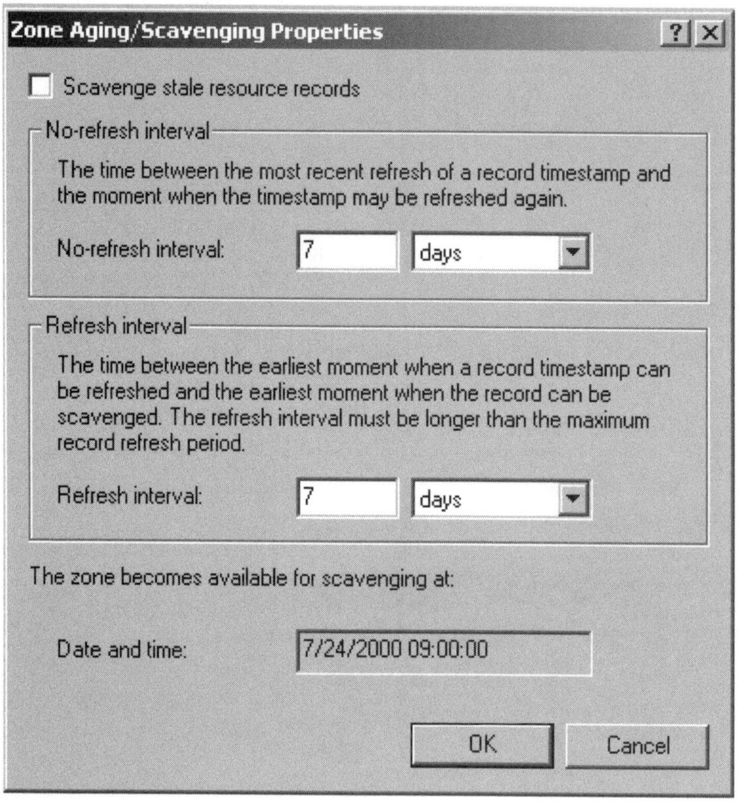

Zone Aging/Scavenging Properties   [?] [X]

☐ Scavenge stale resource records

┌─ No-refresh interval ──────────────────────────────────┐
The time between the most recent refresh of a record timestamp and
the moment when the timestamp may be refreshed again.

No-refresh interval: [7   ] [days   ▼]
└──┘

┌─ Refresh interval ─────────────────────────────────────┐
The time between the earliest moment when a record timestamp can
be refreshed and the earliest moment when the record can be
scavenged. The refresh interval must be longer than the maximum
record refresh period.

Refresh interval: [7   ] [days   ▼]
└──┘

The zone becomes available for scavenging at:

Date and time: [7/24/2000 09:00:00   ]

[OK   ]   [Cancel]

FIGURE 12–34   *Setting zone aging/scavenging properties*

the interval will increase the likelihood of stale records. You may also set the refresh interval. This is the amount time after the no-refresh interval expires before the record can be scavenged. This value shouldn't be less than the longest time you expect it to take for a resource record to be refreshed. In Windows 2000 this would normally correspond to the four-day DHCP renewal period.

The **Start of Authority (SOA)** tab (See Figure 12-35) permits you to configure all the zone configuration information stored in the SOA record.

The *Serial Number* field is automatically incremented each time any information in the zone changes. This is how servers know whether or not a zone transfer is required. To force a zone transfer, click **Increment**—this will increase the serial number and signal the requirement to perform a transfer. The *Primary server* field indicates which DNS server is expected to provide the information during zone transfers. You may change the information in the field by clicking **Browse**. The *Responsible person* field provides an email

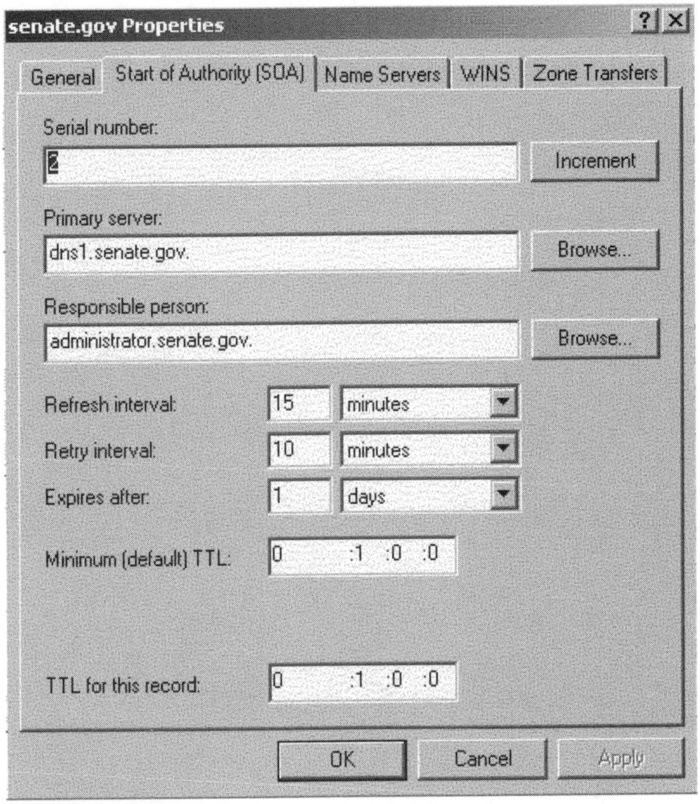

FIGURE 12-35   *Zone properties SOA tab*

address for the zone's contact point. By default, this is assumed to be the account named "Administrator" in the domain. Note that the at sign ('@') is replaced by a dot (i.e., administrator@senate.gov becomes administrator.senate.gov.). The *Refresh interval* field specifies how often a secondary server must check with the master name server to verify the accuracy of its database. *Retry interval* specifies how often a secondary server attempts a zone transfer when it cannot contact the master name server. *Minimum (default) TTL* is the shortest TTL (in days, hours, minutes, and seconds) provided by the server.

The **Name Servers** tab (see Figure 12-36) displays a list of name servers authoritative for the zone. This would include all secondary servers. While in this dialog box, you may add, modify, or delete the information for these servers. Any changes made here are manifested in the zone by the addition, deletion, or alteration of name server (NS) records.

The fourth tab configures *WINS lookup*, which we will discuss in the next section. The fifth tab—**Zone Transfers**—allows you to determine if the

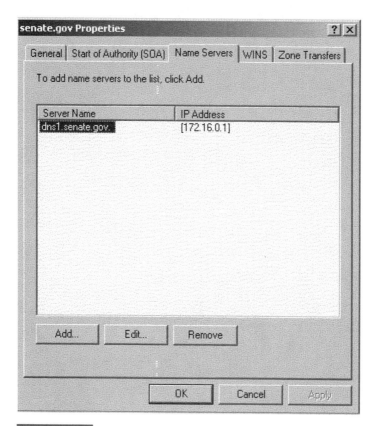

FIGURE 12–36 *Zone properties—Name Servers tab*

server will permit zone transfers for this zone. If it does allow transfers, you may permit it to transfer to any server, those listed as name servers, or only servers whose IP addresses you supply. This enhances the security of the zone information contained on the server (see Figure 12-37) Clicking the **Notify** button reveals the dialog box shown in Figure 12-38. When the *Automatically notify* check box is set (the default) secondary servers are notified when changes occur to the zone. You may send notifications to all the servers on the Name Servers tab or only servers which you specify by IP address.

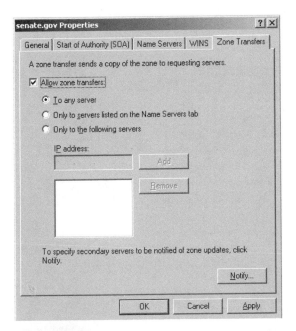

FIGURE 12-37   *Zone properties—Zone Transfers tab*

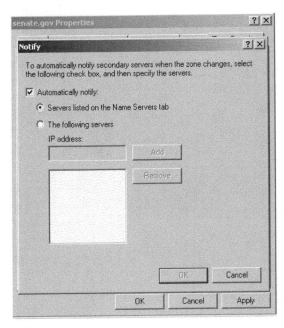

FIGURE 12-38   *Zone properties—Zone Transfers tab: Notify*

THE REVERSE LOOKUP ZONE

Just when you thought you had added and configured all the zones you would need, it is time to think about reverse lookup. As you remember, reverse lookup is accomplished through the use of PTR records. Where do you suppose the PTR records go? Right. We need to create a zone in which to place them. You need to create a reverse lookup zone for every network that you'll administer. In our case, we've used the **172.16.0.0** network and the reverse lookup zone was created automatically when we ran the configuration wizard. Let's assume the rules.senate.gov domain uses the **200.22.18.0** network. We'll need to create a reverse lookup zone for it. Remember, to create a reverse lookup zone you must reverse the octets and suffix **.in-addr.arpa**. For the **200.22.18.0** network, we'll need to create a zone called **18.22.200.in-addr.arpa**. The good news is that a reverse lookup zone is created in the same way you create any other zone. We can right-click the **Reverse Lookup Zone**'s folder and select **New Zone**. This will take us through the wizard and will create the zone for us! (See Figures 12-39 and 12-40.)

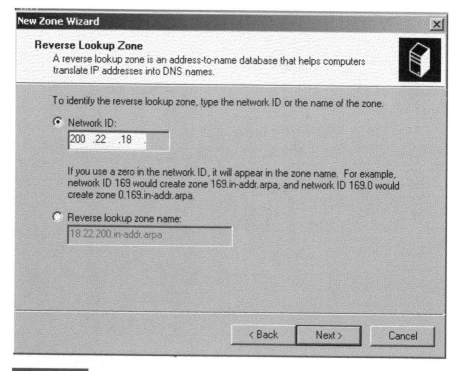

FIGURE 12–39   *Creating the reverse lookup zone*

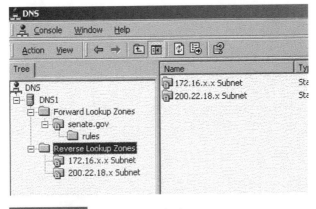

FIGURE 12-40   *New reverse lookup zone*

RESOURCE RECORDS

Now that we've configured a framework of zones and subdomains, we need to enter some resource records to make the system work. The most common record to add is a host record. To add a host record, highlight the desired zone and select **New Host** from the **Action** menu. This will reveal the New Host dialog box, as shown in Figure 12-41. Enter the host name and IP address. If you check the **Create associated pointer (PTR) record** check box the server will automatically create a PTR record in the reverse-lookup zone. Click **Add Host** and then click **Done** to close the dialog window, and the new record is entered (See Figures 12-42 and 12-43).

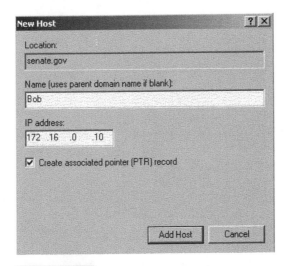

FIGURE 12-41   *New host record dialog box*

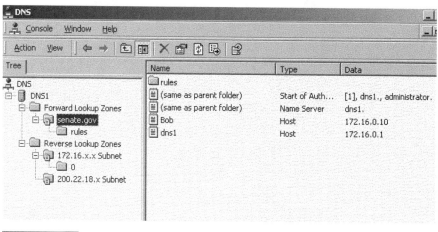

FIGURE 12-42 New host record

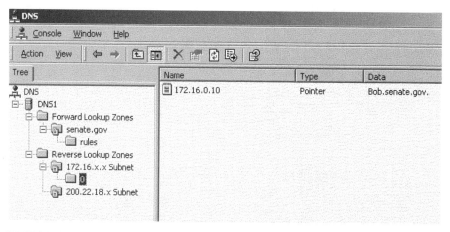

FIGURE 12-43 New PTR record

Other records may be created as easily as the host record. Ensure the appropriate zone is highlighted and select **Other New Records** from the **Action** Menu. This will bring up the **New Resource Record** wizard (see Figure 12-44). You can select the desired record type in the record type window, then click **Create record**, and enter the appropriate information in the dialog box. The TTL shown in the dialog box is the default set by the zone's SOA record. You may leave it as set or enter a different value. When you click **OK** and then **Done** to close the wizard, the record is added (see Figure 12-45). Although the information for particular record types differs, the procedure for adding records is the same in all cases. You may also add records by directly

editing the database files found in the **<*system root*>\system32\dns** directory (see Figure 12-46). You must stop and start the DNS service to get these
manually entered changes to appear in the server.

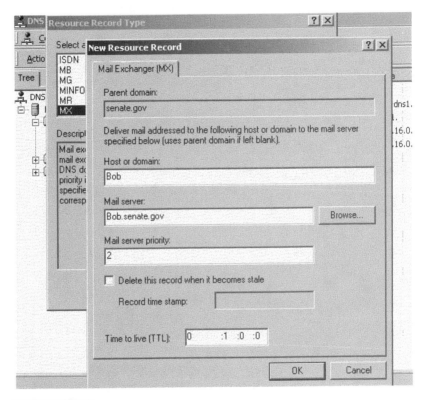

FIGURE 12–44 *New resource record*

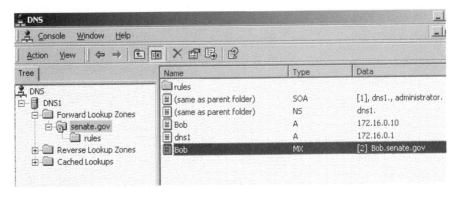

FIGURE 12–45 *New MX record*

```
;   Database file senate.gov.dns for senate.gov zone.
;       Zone version:  4
;

@                            IN   SOA dns1.  administrator. (
                                  4                 ; serial number
                                  900               ; refresh
                                  600               ; retry
                                  86400             ; expire
                                  3600         ) ; minimum TTL

;
;  Zone NS records
;

@                            NS        dns1.

;
;  Zone records
;

Bob                          A         172.16.0.10
                             MX        2         bob.senate.gov.
dns1                         A         172.16.0.1
```

FIGURE 12–46   *Senate.gov database file*

UPDATE SERVER DATA FILES

When you enter information into the DNS server it is not saved in the database file immediately. The database file is written when the service stops and is periodically flushed during the DNS server's normal operation. To ensure your files are written to the database file immediately, select **Update Server Data Files** from the **Action** menu (see Figure 12-47).

Practical Application

It's time to try your hand at installing and configuring a DNS server. If you are on an isolated network segment and not connected to the Internet, you can do just about anything you wish. If you're part of a larger network, however, consult with your administrator to ensure you have the correct domain name and other information. Ensure your Windows 2000 CD-ROM is in the drive so the system can copy the required files.

Install the Service

Make sure your TCP/IP data is correct, refer to this chapter's *Installing the Service* section, and follow the steps to create a DNS server on your machine. After you restart the computer, open the DNS console from the Administrative Tools program group and add your server, as detailed in the *Configuring the DNS Server* section. Do you see the cache and reverse lookup zones?

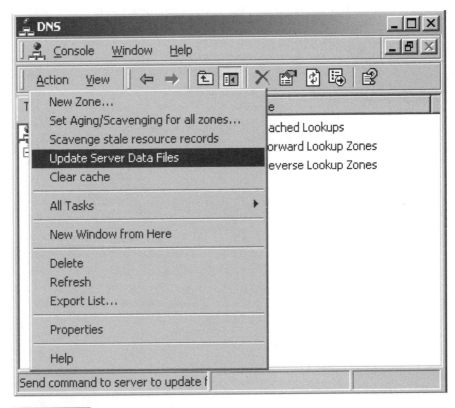

FIGURE 12-47   *Update server data files*

Adding a Zone

Now that your server is running and visible in the DNS console, refer to the *Adding Zones and Subdomains* subsection of the *Configuring the DNS Server* section and follow the steps to create a primary zone. If you're on an isolated network segment, you can create your own zone name (should be based on your domain name). If you're on a larger network, be sure to check with your administrator. Were SOA, NS, and *A* records automatically added for your server?

Integrating DNS with Other Name Servers

Integration is a prime concept for DNS. We've already looked at a great deal of DNS name server integration. Recall that a DNS server will make iterative queries to several other DNS servers to "piece together" a fully qualified domain name. We've also looked at primary and secondary servers where DNS servers work together to share the load from DNS client queries. We've seen how to integrate DNS servers through forwarders to reach out to other DNS servers across the WAN and we've seen how to slave DNS servers to forwarders to obtain name resolution.

Connecting DNS to a DNS Root Server

If the DNS server is to do its job in finding mappings outside its domain, it is absolutely critical that it be able to connect to a server that is authoritative for the domain that ultimately owns the host for which it seeks a mapping. Fortunately, this is a simple task for the administrator. You'll remember from our previous discussion that the information required to locate an InterNIC root server is located in the cache.dns file. If this file is made available to your server (as discussed earlier in the chapter), the server will be able to find a root server which will tell it where to locate the next lower level in the DNS hierarchy. If, for instance, we were attempting to locate **bob.senate.gov** from a machine in another domain, the root server would give us an address to a DNS server that is authoritative for the **.gov** domain. The **.gov** server would, in turn, help us to find the DNS server authoritative for **senate.gov**, which should give us a mapping to **bob.senate.gov**.

As you can see, without the root server information found in cache.dns, the DNS server would be unable to start its quest for outside information. When you install the DNS server, a cache.dns file with the required InterNIC root server data is installed. If you need to obtain a new Internet cache file you can obtain one at **FTP://rs.internic.net/domain/named.cache**. If you are using DNS on a network that is not part of the Internet, you'll need to create a cache.dns file using the same format illustrated in Figure 12-5, but with information on the name servers which are authoritative for your network.

Connecting DNS to a WINS Server

While integration between DNS servers is critical for DNS to do its job, Windows 2000 has an additional name server integration feature that can make the job of DNS administration *much* easier. Remember that, although the DNS server's database is static, requiring manual updating, a WINS server automatically updates its database from using input from its client machines. Unfortunately, WINS does not provide the robust host name resolution capability of

DNS. Combining these two systems, however, can allow us the best of both worlds: DNS in hierarchical domain name space and WINS in the flat NetBIOS name space.

Note

As we'll see in the next chapter, the Windows 2000 DNS can be dynamically updated. At this point, however, we're looking at the Windows 2000 DNS in its traditional DNS role. Using WINS resolution within DNS will also ensure dynamic updates for systems that do not support dynamic DNS updating.

As we saw earlier in this chapter, the Microsoft DNS server can use a WINS record to permit it to find an appropriate WINS server. A DNS server equipped with a WINS record will still attempt to obtain host name resolution in the conventional manner. If the DNS server is unable to find a mapping in its database for a host in a zone for which it is authoritative, it will convert the host portion of the FQDN to a NetBIOS name and query its mated WINS server. If the WINS server can resolve the NetBIOS name, it will return the IP address to the DNS, which, in turn, returns the mapping to its client.

DNS servers configured to integrate with WINS servers can provide mappings for DHCP clients whose IP addresses periodically change. WINS integration relieves the DNS administrator of the burden of entering data for every computer in the network into the DNS database—provided the network computers are WINS clients.

If a zone is to provide WINS resolution, every DNS server *authoritative* for that zone must be configured for WINS resolution. Note that this applies only to authoritative servers; secondary servers and caching-only servers need not be configured for WINS lookup.

Configuring a DNS Server for WINS Lookup

Now that we're convinced of the benefits of DNS/WINS integration, just how do we go about linking these resources together? To provide your zone with WINS lookup capability, select the appropriate zone in the **DNS** console, select the **Action** menu, and click **Properties** to reveal the zone **Properties** dialog box. From this dialog box, select the **WINS** tab (See Figure 12-48).

Check the **Use WINS forward lookup** check box, enter the IP address of the applicable WINS server(s) in the IP address edit box, and click **Add**. If multiple WINS servers are entered, the **Up** and **Down** buttons may be used to alter the order in which they're queried. If your DNS server has secondary servers that are not Microsoft DNS servers, check the **Do not replicate this record** check box to prevent copying WINS records to the non-Microsoft server(s).

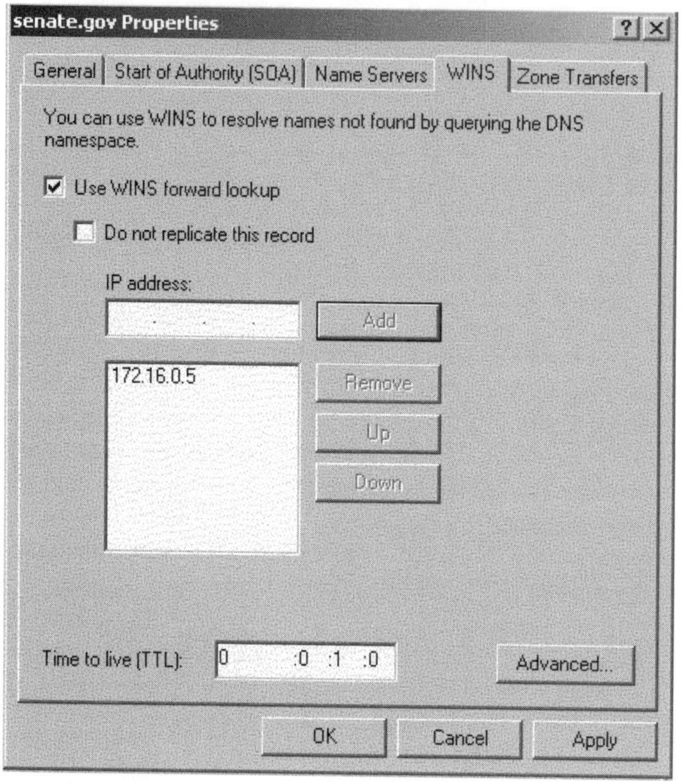

senate.gov Properties

General | Start of Authority (SOA) | Name Servers | WINS | Zone Transfers

You can use WINS to resolve names not found by querying the DNS namespace.

☑ Use WINS forward lookup

☐ Do not replicate this record

IP address:

[   ]   Add

172.16.0.5   Remove
              Up
              Down

Time to live (TTL): [0   :0 :1 :0]   Advanced...

OK   Cancel   Apply

FIGURE 12–48   *Zone properties dialog box—WINS tab*

WINS REVERSE LOOKUP

There is also a reverse lookup capability inherent in the DNS/WINS link-up. You'll remember we discussed a WINS-R record earlier. To enable the reverse lookup capability, select the appropriate reverse lookup (in-addr.arpa) zone in the **DNS** console, select the **Action** menu and click **Properties** to reveal the zone **Properties** dialog box. From this dialog box, select the **WINS-R** tab (see Figure 12-49).

Check the **Use WINS-R lookup** check box and enter the host domain name that will be appended to the NetBIOS name (during a reverse resolution) in the **Domain to append to returned name** edit box. As in the forward lookup case, check the **Do not replicate this record** check box if your DNS server uses non-Microsoft DNS servers.

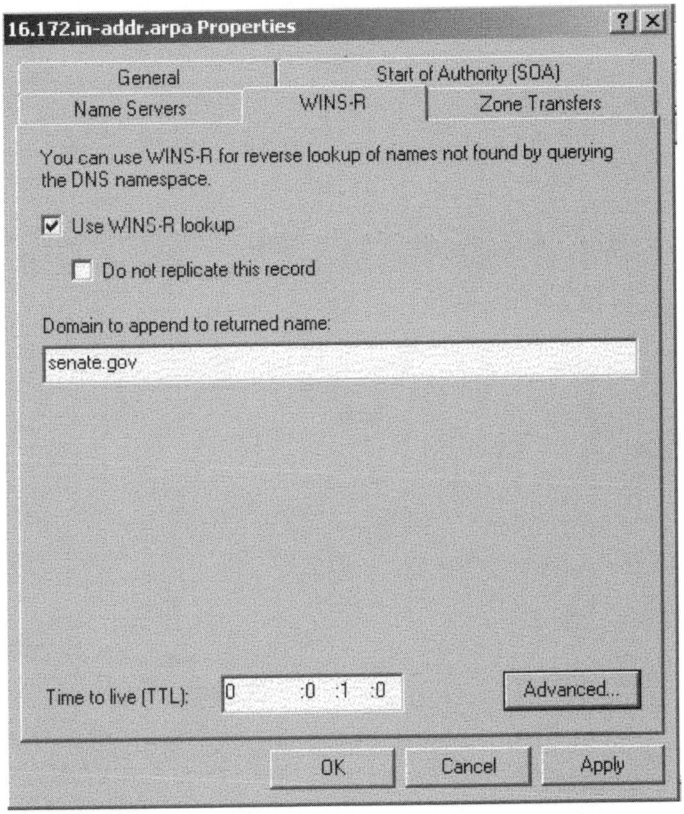

FIGURE 12–49   *Zone properties dialog box—WINS-R tab*

WINS TIME TO LIVE AND LOOKUP TIMEOUT

As with other DNS data, WINS supplied data is associated with a TTL. To adjust the TTL, click **Advanced** on the **WINS** or **WINS-R** tab of the **Zone Properties** dialog box (see Figures 12-50 and 12-51).

When a mapping is provided by a WINS server, it has a TTL as set in the **Cache time-out** value (15 minutes, by default). The **Lookup time-out** value sets the amount of time the DNS server will wait for the WINS server to respond. Once this value is exceeded, the DNS server will give up and return an error message to the requester.

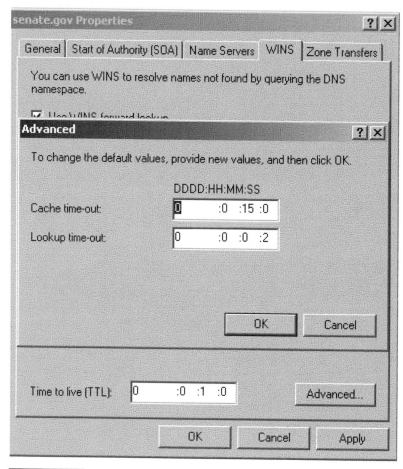

FIGURE 12–50   *WINS advanced properties*

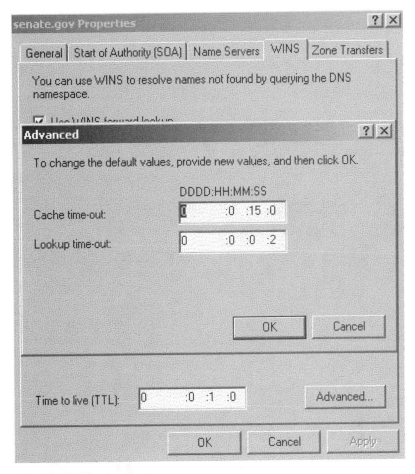

FIGURE 12-51   *WINS-R advanced properties*

Delegating Zones

As your domain grows, you may decide to create additional subdomains. You may also decide to place the new subdomains in new zones on their own servers. This is called *delegation* and can be a good initiative for concerns like load balancing and decentralized administration. Delegation may also be appropriate to place a particular zone on a DNS server that has capability for the zone. (As we'll see in the next chapter, not all DNS servers can support Active Directory integrated zones, and delegation can ensure that these zones exist on Windows 2000 DNS servers while the parent domain may be found, for example, on UNIX machines.) When you delegate a zone it is critical that the DNS server authoritative for the parent domain be able to find the DNS server for the delegated domain. This is because, as you'll recall, resolvers will start with the root domain and work their way through the parent domain to the delegated domain when performing an iterative query. The way to tell the parent domain DNS how to find the delegated zone is by placing an A record and an NS record for the delegated domain on it.

Let's say we wish to create a subdomain called ethics.senate.gov and that we want to host the domain on the server called DNS2 which is located in the new subdomain. We first install DNS2 and configure our new zone (ethics.senate.gov) on that machine. Next we return to DNS1 (the server authoritative for senate.gov) and select that zone. Right-clicking the zone, we select **New Delegation** from the context menu, as shown in Figure 12-52.

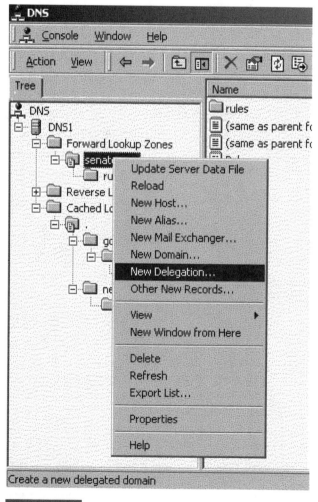

FIGURE 12–52   *New delegation*

This launches the New Delegation wizard. On the wizard's second screen, we enter the delegated domain name "Ethics," as shown in Figure 12-53.

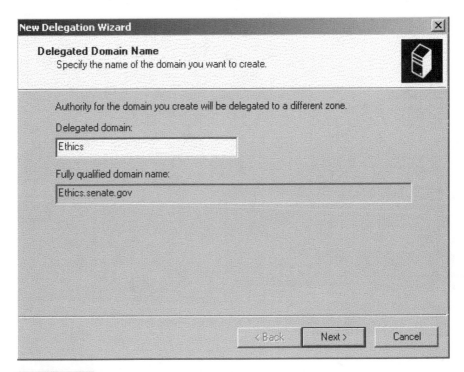

FIGURE 12-53   *Enter delegated domain name*

On the next screen, we select **Add** and enter the name and IP address of the server authoritative for the new zone, as shown in Figure 12-54. This creates both an NS and an A record for DNS2 on DNS1.

Going to the final screen and clicking **Finish** creates the delegated zone on DNS1, as depicted in Figure 12-55.

Although the DNS manager reveals only the NS record, a look at the actual database file (see Figure 12-56) reveals both an NS and an A record.

With this information, the DNS server DNS1 will be able to refer resolvers to DNS2 for requests against ethics.senate.gov.

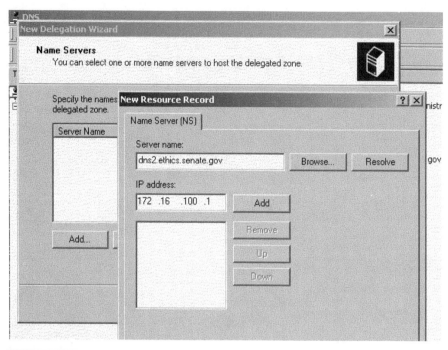

FIGURE 12-54 *Enter name server information*

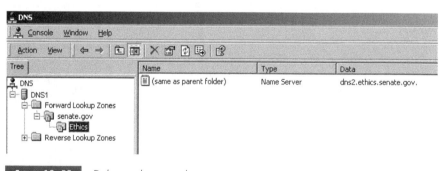

FIGURE 12-55 *Delegated zone: ethics*

```
;
@                              IN   SOA dns1.  administrator. (
                                    36              ; serial number
                                    900             ; refresh
                                    600             ; retry
                                    86400           ; expire
                                    3600          ) ; minimum TTL


;
;  Zone NS records
;

@                              NS        dns1.
dns1.                          A         172.16.0.1


;
;  Zone records
;

bob                            A         172.16.0.10
                               MX        2        bob.senate.gov.
dns1                           A         172.16.0.1

;
;  Delegated sub-zone:  ethics.senate.gov.
;
ethics                         NS        dns2.ethics.senate.gov.
dns2.ethics                    A         172.16.100.1
;  End delegation
```

FIGURE 12–56   *Database file showing information for delegated zone*

Practical Application

Let's take a few moments to see how our DNS server can integrate with the rest of cyberspace.

Cache.dns

Go to the *WINNT\System32\DNS\Samples* directory and, using **Notepad**, open the **Cache.dns** sample file. Look at the A and NS records contained in the file. With what you've learned, you should be able to create similar records for root servers in your network. (Remember that you shouldn't write your own cache.dns records if you'll operate on the Internet.)

WINS

Refer to this chapter's *Configuring a DNS Server for WINS Lookup* section and set your DNS server to use the WINS server you installed in Chapter 9. With this integration what host names will you need to manually add to your DNS database?

Configuring DNS Server Roles

Throughout this chapter we've discussed myriad DNS server roles. Let's review the roles to make sure we know how to configure each of them.

Primary Name Server

Your server becomes a *primary name server* when it is configured with a primary zone. Add a primary zone as we discussed in the section titled *Adding Zones and Subdomains*.

Secondary Name Server

Your server will function as a secondary name server when configured with a secondary zone. To add a secondary zone, follow the guidance in *Adding Zones and Subdomains*.

Master Name Server

You do not actually configure a DNS server to be a *master name server*. Instead, you configure a secondary server to *recognize* one or more name servers as a master name server. Enter this information at the *secondary* server, as illustrated in Figure 12-29.

Caching-Only Server

Since a *caching-only* server is authoritative for no zones, this is an easy configuration. To create a caching-only server, simply install the server and create no primary or secondary zones for it!

Forwarder

As with master name servers, forwarders are not actually configured. Instead, you decide which machines will act as forwarders and configure the rest of the DNS servers to use these designated machines. This configuration must be accomplished at each server. To configure a server to use forwarders, select the DNS **Properties** dialog in the **DNS** console and click the **Forwarders** tab. As shown in Figure 12-57, check the **Enable forwarders** check box and enter the IP address(es) of your designated forwarders. The **Forward time-out** value determines how long this server will attempt to contact a forwarder before moving on to the next one on the list.

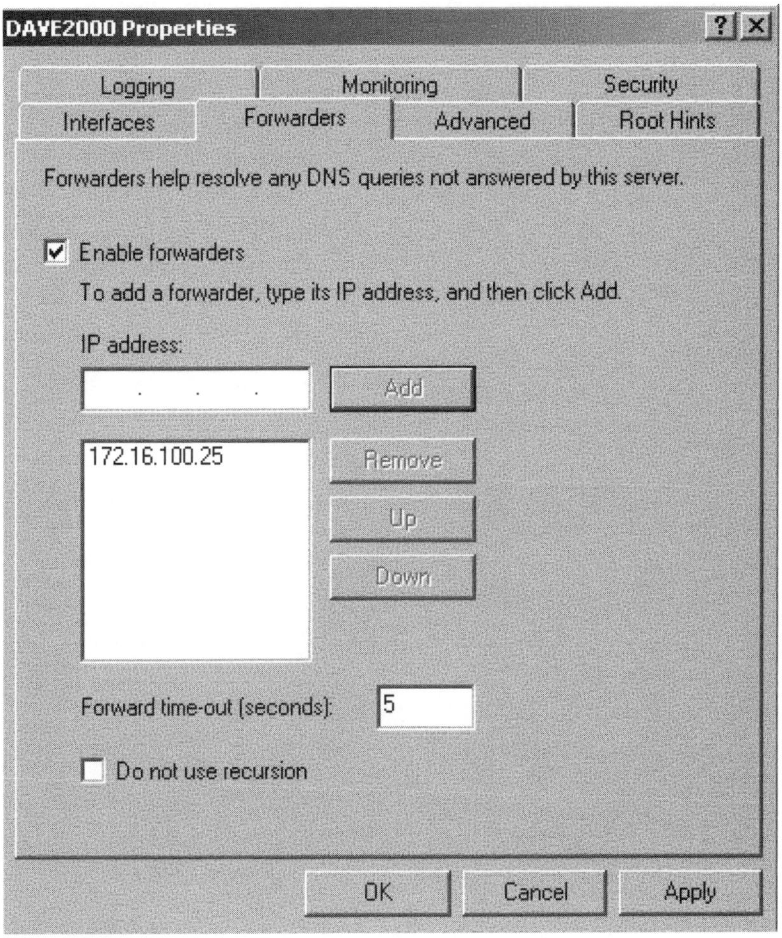

FIGURE 12–57   *Server properties dialog box—Forwarders tab*

Practical Application

Your DNS server is currently functioning as a primary name server. If there is another DNS server operating on your network, you can give it a secondary name server role too. Refer to the Adding a Secondary Zone subsection of this chapter's *Configuring the DNS Server* section to add a secondary zone. Wait a few minutes for the system to complete a zone transfer. Do you see records for the newly added zone?

Configuring a DNS Client

All this work in configuring DNS servers won't do us very much good if we don't configure some machines to act as DNS clients. Fortunately, this is an easy process. In Chapter 7, we learned how to configure clients using the DHCP. Now we'll take a few moments to learn about a static configuration.

There are two steps to accomplish DNS client configuration. First, you can configure the host name and domain, using the **Network Identification** tab of the **System Properties** dialog box, as shown in Figure 12-7. However, you must access the **DNS** tab of the **Advanced TCP/IP Settings** dialog box and add one or more DNS servers. Simply enter the IP address(es) of the applicable DNS servers in the **DNS server addresses, in order of use** edit box to designate the DNS servers your client will use (See Figure 12-58).

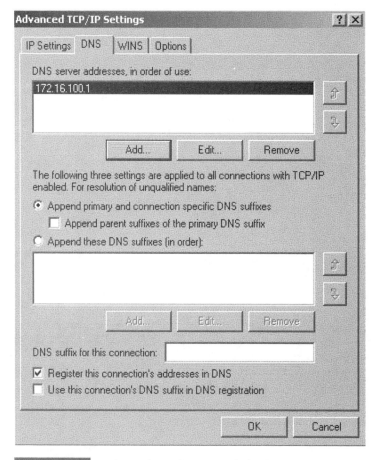

FIGURE 12–58   *Advanced TCP/IP settings dialog box—DNS tab*

The lower part of the dialog box tells the machine how to resolve names that are not fully qualified (i.e., a host name without a domain name). By default, the *Append primary and connection-specific DNS suffixes* radio button is selected. This means that when a host name is used by itself, the system will append your domain name (configured on the **Network Identification** tab) to the host name before resolving it. If that query yields no resolution and there is a connection-specific suffix designated in the *DNS suffix for this connection* edit box (at the bottom of the dialog box) the system will append the connection-specific suffix and try again. If the *Append parent suffixes of the primary DNS suffix* check box is checked (the default), queries are also made by appending the host name to parent suffixes up to the second level domain. In other words, if your domain is chmn.ethics.senate.gov and you type *ping Mary*, the system will try to resolve mary.chmn.ethics.senate.gov; if that fails it will try mary.ethics.senate.gov; and if that fails it will finally attempt mary.senate.gov.

If you select the *Append these DNS suffixes (in order)* radio button, you can enter suffixes for the system to use in resolving unqualified names. If you make this selection, neither the primary nor the connection-specific suffix will be used.

If the *Register this connection's addresses in DNS* check box is checked (the default), the Windows 2000 computer will attempt to register its mapping(s) with the dynamic DNS server(s) in its domain (more on this in Chapter 13). The *Use this connection's DNS suffix in DNS registration* check box tells the computer to attempt to register its connection-specific name with the DNS server(s). The connection-specific name is the computer's host name suffixed by the connection-specific suffix (designated in the *DNS suffix for this connection* edit box). This option is unchecked by default. If both boxes are checked, both the fully qualified computer name and the connection-specific name will be registered.

Using NSLOOKUP for DNS Troubleshooting

The NSLOOKUP utility is the primary DNS diagnostic tool. In its simplest form, NSLOOKUP permits you to quickly retrieve an IP address or host name from your default DNS server. NSLOOKUP has both an interactive and noninteractive mode. You would use the noninteractive mode when you need only a quick piece of data (e.g., the IP address of a particular host) and would use the interactive mode when several queries are required.

The NSLOOKUP syntax is:

```
nslookup [-option...] [computer-to-find | - [server]]
```

In this notation, *option* signifies one or more NSLOOKUP options; *computer-to-find* represents a host name, FQDN, or IP address to look up (if a hyphen is used here, nslookup switches to interactive mode); and *server* refers to the DNS server. If you simply type *nslookup*, you'll enter the interactive mode for the default name server. If you enter a *computer-to-find*, you'll seek that information in noninteractive mode using the default name server.

Figure 12-59 shows the result of a simple noninteractive query. The name server was the default server (in this case, mary.senate.gov). The non-authoritative answer simply indicates the mapping came from the name server's cache and not the server authoritative for the host's domain. This would indicate the default name server had recently resolved the mapping (TTL not expired).

```
C:\>nslookup www.house.gov
Server:  mary.senate.gov
Address:  200.22.18.36

Non-authoritative answer:
Name:    www.house.gov
Address:  143.231.86.196
```

FIGURE 12–59   *Simple use of NSLOOKUP*

To enter the interactive mode, simply type **NSLOOKUP** at the command line. You're presented with a prompt (>) from which you may enter repeated NSLOOKUP queries. For a detailed list of NSLOOKUP options, type **HELP** at the prompt. To exit the interactive mode, type **EXIT** at the prompt (see Figure 12-60).

```
C:\>nslookup
Default Server: mary.senate.gov
Address:  200.22.18.36

>
```

FIGURE 12–60   *NSLOOKUP interactive mode*

Some Useful NSLOOKUP Commands

You can learn a plethora of NSLOOKUP commands by typing **HELP** at the NSLOOKUP prompt. We'll point out two useful commands here, however:

DEBUG

You can turn debugging mode on or off by typing **SET DEBUG** or **SET NODEBUG**. Debugging is off by default. When debugging is turned on you receive much more information about the packet sent to the server and the resulting answer. If you wish to use **DEBUG** or **NODEBUG** for a noninteractive query, use them on the command line with a hyphen (e.g., **nslookup – debug mary.senate.gov**).

DOMAIN INFORMATION

You can retrieve domain information through use of the **ls** option and the domain (rather than host name). This will provide the output shown in Figure 12-61.

```
C:\>nslookup
Default Server: mary.senate.gov
Address:  200.22.18.36

> ls senate.gov
[mary.senate.gov]
  senate.gov.                 NS      server = mary.senate.gov
  mary                        A       200.22.18.36
  bill                        A       200.22.18.64
  bob                         A       200.22.18.44
  lisa                        A       200.22.18.46

>
```

FIGURE 12-61   *NSLOOKUP ls option*

Summary

In this chapter we saw that the rapid growth of the Internet dictated a system for the resolution of host names to IP addresses that was sufficiently robust to provide service to millions of users throughout the world. We found that the first step in such a system was the production of a hierarchical name space and the creation of DNS servers to manage the lists of hosts and IP addresses.

In DNS parlance, *resolvers* are clients while *name servers* are the DNS servers that provide name resolution to the resolvers. Name servers are responsible for a subset of the domain name space referred to as their *zone(s) of authority*. If a name server needs to resolve a name not in its zone of authority, it can contact other DNS servers to obtain the mapping. It starts with a root-level name server, which will give it the IP address of the next name server in the chain and so on until the name server authoritative for the desired zone is located. When a name server obtains IP address information, it retains it in its cache for a specified TTL. When the TTL expires, the data is flushed from the server's cache. When cached data is passed to another machine, a decremented TTL is passed with it.

Name servers can function in a number of roles. *Primary name servers* are authoritative for one or more zones. *Secondary name servers* provide zone information using the data maintained on a *master name server*. The process of obtaining zone information from a master name server is called a *zone transfer*. A server with no primary or secondary zone information is known as a *caching-only server*. A caching-only server maintains only data it has obtained in querying other servers. A server designated as a *forwarder* will forward requests from local name servers to name servers operating across the Internet. A name server configured as a *slave* can only request information through its designated forwarder(s).

When a resolver makes a *recursive* query to a name server, the name server must return the requested information or an error message indicating it cannot find the desired data—it cannot return a reference to another name server. The name server responding to the recursive query may need to perform an *iterative* query to obtain the requested data. In an iterative query, the server may have to contact a series of name servers—each one providing an address to the next one at successively lower levels in domain name space until the desired host mapping is located.

An *inverse query* will provide a host name when an IP address is known. Inverse queries are facilitated by records stored in the in-addr.arpa domain.

DNS servers utilize a number of files to operate and to maintain their data. The *Database File* is a text file that contains a series of records containing DNS mapping information. We discussed the *SOA, A, NS, PTR, SRV, CNAME, MX, HINFO, WINS,* and *WINS-R* records. The *Reverse Lookup File* is a database file that contains the pointer (PTR) records that permit DNS reverse lookups. The *Cache File* contains the host information that enables a name server to find root servers in the Internetwork allowing it to resolve names beyond its authoritative domains. Finally, the *Boot File* contains initialization data for the DNS server itself. Normally, a DNS server running on a Windows 2000 system will initialize using information in the system's registry but can be configured to use boot file information instead.

When planning for a DNS installation, you should first determine if your DNS services should be run within your organization or by your servicing ISP. (As we'll see in the next chapter, the Active Directory in an Windows 2000 domain may require that we run at least some DNS services locally within our domain.) If you will operate on the Internet, you'll need to register a domain name with the InterNIC and you will need to provide that agency with IP addresses of at least two DNS servers that service the domain (these services *may* be performed by your ISP). You should ensure you have at least a primary and secondary DNS server for each domain and you will need to register your servers with a DNS server immediately above them in the domain name space.

DNS is installed and configured much as any other Windows 2000 network service. The first installation step is to ensure that the server's TCP/IP parameters are properly configured. If all TCP/IP parameters are correct, the installation will automatically create SOA and NS records for your server. Once you have installed the service you can use the Windows 2000 *DNS console* to add primary, secondary, and reverse lookup zones. Resource records may also be entered using the DNS console.

In order for a DNS server to adequately function, it *must* be able to integrate with other name servers. Most basically, a DNS server must be able to locate the Internet root name server (or root servers on your local network if you aren't on the Internet). The root name servers provide the name server with IP addresses for other name servers that can provide information for the network's top-level domains. The name server can then contact servers at successively lower levels until it obtains the requested information. Addresses for the root name servers are contained in the cache.dns file. An Internet cache.dns file is automatically installed when DNS is installed. Alternatively, you may download an updated one from the Internet. If you will use DNS name resolution on a network other than the Internet, you must edit the cache.dns file (either by editing the text or by using the Root Hints tab of the DNS Properties dialog box) to reflect the root servers in *your* network. It is also possible to integrate a DNS server with a local WINS server. DNS servers so configured are able to obtain individual host mappings from the WINS server, obviating the necessity of entering a host record for each machine in the domain.

DNS client computers may be configured automatically by the DHCP or manually by supplying IP addresses for applicable DNS servers in the TCP/IP Properties dialog box.

The NSLOOKUP utility provides a command line capability to retrieve information from a selected DNS server. The utility has both interactive and non-interactive modes to allow for several queries or just a single request.

Test Yourself

1. DNS servers that have been configured to use forwarders exclusively are known as:
   A. Primary masters
   B. Secondary masters
   C. Forwarding masters
   D. Slaves

2. The NS record contains:
   A. A reference to each name server that can be used to look up hosts in the domain.
   B. A list of name servers used by a given resolver.
   C. A list of DNS servers for the given zone.
   D. A reference to each name server that is configured as a slave.

3. Once your DNS servers are installed and running, you'll need to:
   A. Register with the DNS server that is immediately above you in the domain name space.
   B. Register with your local hosts file.
   C. Register with the BIND server that is immediately above you in the domain name space.
   D. None of these.

4. You can improve a DNS server's resolution capability by configuring it to:
   A. Use a HOSTS file.
   B. Use WINS.
   C. Remove itself from the local network periodically.
   D. None of these.

5. The Reverse Lookup Zone:
   A. Permits you to "undo" a bad DNS configuration.
   B. Is used when a secondary server must update a master server after the master server has crashed.
   C. Permits you to find an IP address when an FQDN is known.
   D. Permits you to obtain a fully qualified domain name when an IP address is known.

DNS: Integration with Active Directory

Now that you understand the operation of a traditional Domain Name System (DNS) server and how traditional DNS functions are implemented in Windows 2000, it's time to look at how the Windows 2000 DNS integrates with the Active Directory and how the new features of the Windows 2000 DNS permit automatic updates. Since the Windows 2000 Active Directory depends on DNS, it will be a good idea to take a look at alternatives for employing your DNS resources both within the Windows 2000 domain and on the Internet.

Active Directory Service Integration

As we've mentioned several times, a Windows 2000 Active Directory domain depends on service (SRV) records for its operation. One of the first things the Active Directory installation program checks for is the availability of a DNS that can support the Active Directory's needs. If the installation wizard can't be absolutely sure there is a DNS to perform this task, you'll see the message box shown in Figure 13-1. (If a DNS server is already present in the domain and servicing the zone for which you're installing the Active Directory, DNS verification is made and the message box will not appear.)

The good news is the message in Figure 13-1 is accompanied by the dialog box shown in Figure 13-2. When a DNS server cannot be verified, Windows 2000 can automatically install and configure one to support the Active Directory zone.

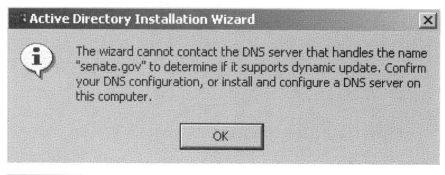

FIGURE 13-1   *Unable to contact DNS server*

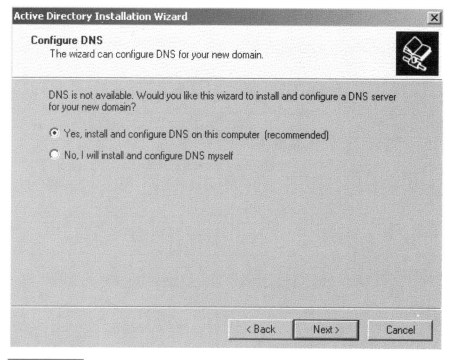

FIGURE 13-2   *Configure DNS*

Once Active Directory installation is complete, the new DNS server is installed on the domain controller and the Active Directory integrated zone is automatically configured, as shown in Figure 13-3. (You'll recall that installation of Active Directory transforms a Windows 2000 server into a Windows 2000 domain controller.)

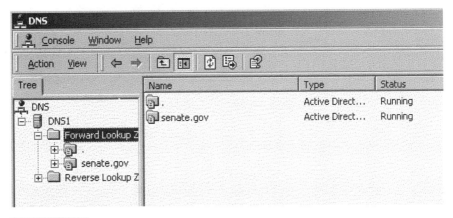

FIGURE 13-3   *Senate.gov zone*

You'll notice this DNS server thinks it's *authoritative* for the entire zone (from the presence of the dot (.) zone). If you were to check Root Hints, you would discover no cache file had been loaded. As configured, this machine will never forward a request to another DNS server. Just as in Chapter 12, the solution to this is to delete the dot (.) zone. You'll also need to go to the server's Action menu and select *Update Server Data Files* and then *Refresh* to populate the Root Hints.

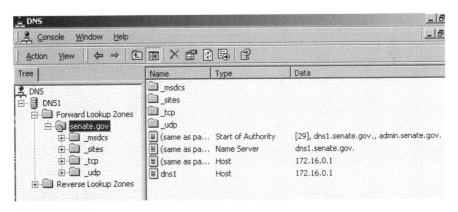

FIGURE 13-4   *Senate.gov resource records*

Expanding the zone reveals that resource records have been automatically created, as shown in Figure 13-4. You may also notice folders for the SRV records listed within the zone. Figure 13-5 shows one set of these automatically created resource records. Here we see the record for the Kerberos service and the Lightweight Directory Access Protocol (LDAP). Kerberos provides security services to the domain while LDAP permits us to find resources within the domain.

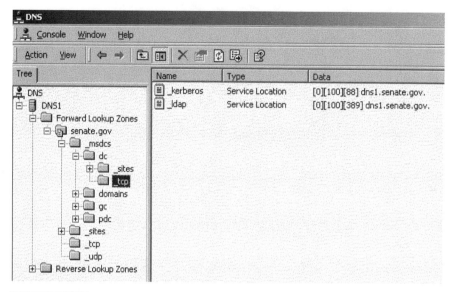

Name	Type	Data
_kerberos	Service Location	[0][100][88] dns1.senate.gov.
_ldap	Service Location	[0][100][389] dns1.senate.gov.

FIGURE 13–5   *Some of the SRV records for the senate.gov domain*

While the foregoing discussion showed how to automatically install a Windows 2000 DNS server to support the Active Directory, you could support your Windows 2000 domain with any DNS server that is at least Berkeley Internet Name Domain (BIND) 4.9.6 compatible. The server must support SRV records and, if you're not using the Windows 2000 DNS server, you'll likely need to create all those SRV records yourself. This is a daunting task considering the complexity of the record and the requirement to create several records for each network resource added to your domain. The Active Directory Installation Wizard, however, will actually create the initial SRV records for you. You can find them in the Netlogon.dns file (located in the %systemroot%\System32\config folder).

While BIND 4.9.6 will do the job, a server supporting at least BIND 8.2.2 is recommended, and the server should be dynamically updateable and should support incremental zone transfers (more on this a bit later).

Active Directory integrated zones can exist only on Windows 2000 domain controllers whose Directory Services contain the zone. We showed how DNS can be automatically installed and configured on a domain controller during Active Directory installation. You may wish, however, to have more than one DNS server servicing your domain (for load balancing and fault tolerance). You may add additional DNS servers to other domain controllers in your network using the procedures outlined in Chapter 12. Once the server is installed, you can add the Active Directory integrated zone by invoking the New Zone Wizard (as discussed in Chapter 12) and selecting *Active Directory-Integrated* (see Figure 13-6). The wizard will ask for the zone name (see Figure 13-7) and will automatically create the zone on the domain controller for you.

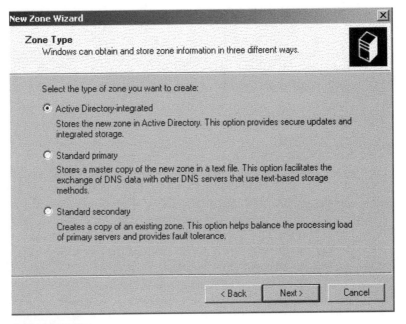

FIGURE 13–6   *New zone wizard*

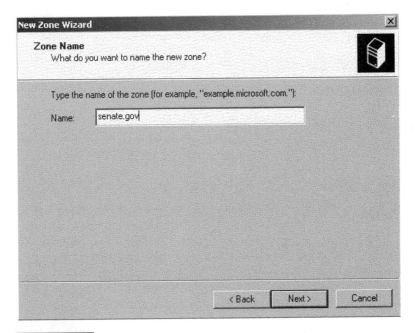

FIGURE 13–7   *Enter zone name*

Storage and Replication

As we're about to see, Active Directory integrated zones are stored differently and are replicated differently from conventional DNS zones. Having said that, it is still possible to perform a normal zone transfer with an Active Directory integrated zone to a conventional DNS server (or even a Windows 2000 DNS server with or without Active Directory-Integrated zones). This may be accomplished simply by adding the zone to the server as a conventional secondary zone.

While a standard DNS zone file is stored as a text file on the DNS server, the Active Directory integrated zone is stored within the Active Directory on the domain controller. Another key difference is how the zone information is replicated to other servers. Unlike conventional DNS replication where edits may be done only on the one primary server and changes are replicated secondary servers, Active Directory integrated zones use *multimaster replication*. Under multimaster replication, changes may be made to any DNS server servicing the zone. The DNS data is then replicated along with the rest of the Active Directory domain data, using the same connections and procedures. When conflicting changes have been made to two or more servers between replication cycles, the one with the latest time stamp is used. These features provide much better security, efficiency, and fault tolerance. This is critical in Windows 2000 because failure to obtain DNS services in that operating system means much more than not being able to find a desired website. It may result in failure to find the domain controller which can result in failure to be able to access any network resources or even the inability to log onto a workstation.

Active Directory Zone Objects

When DNS zones are stored in the Active Directory they are stored as "objects." This is simply a way of categorizing items in the Active Directory database. A resource is represented by an object that has attributes to define its particular characteristics. It is possible to view zone objects stored in the Active Directory:

- Click **Start**, point to **Programs and Administrative Tools**, and then click **Active Directory Users and Computers**.
- In the **View** menu, click **Advanced Features**.
- Double-click the **Domain object**, the **System object**, and then the **MicrosoftDNS object** to display the dnsZone objects (see Figure 13-8).
- Double-click the zone that you want to view.

Although you can see the zone objects from within the Active Directory Users and Computers component, the component cannot interpret the values

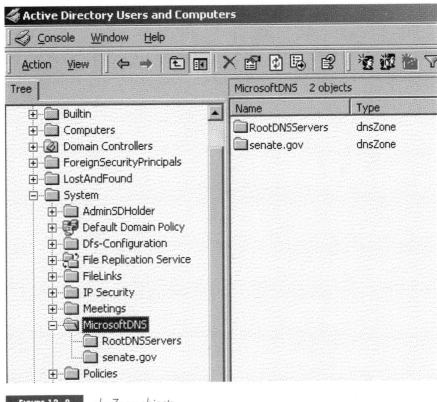

FIGURE 13-8	*dnsZone objects*	

of the dnsRecord attribute (visible when you expand the dnsZone object). If you want to view the DNS domain hierarchy and associated records, you do so from within the DNS console or by using *NSLOOKUP.*

INCREMENTAL ZONE TRANSFER

When we discussed zone transfers in Chapter 12 we were talking about *full zone transfer* (AXFR). This transfer method is the traditional DNS method where the entire zone file is replicated. While the concept is simple, a full zone transfer is inefficient and can be error-prone (because of the volume of information transferred). Another transfer method is incremental zone transfer (IXFR). The IXFR protocol is defined in RFC 1995.

IXFR is a zone transfer protocol that replicates only the zone's added (new) or changed records. IXFR can be used in both standard and Active Directory integrated zones. The Windows 2000 DNS server can manage both IXFR and AXFR when dealing with other servers.

When a change occurs in a zone an IXFR master server sends a NOTIFY packet telling its secondary servers that new information is available. If the secondary server is IXFR capable, it responds with the start of authority (SOA) serial number of its current zone copy. The master name server compares the secondary's serial number with its list of changes and serial numbers and sends just the information the secondary needs to get up-to-date.

The master server may resort to an AXFR when the sum of the changes would result in more data transfer than simply transferring the entire zone or if the secondary server has been off-line long enough to have a serial number that is no longer contained on the master server. If the secondary server is not IXFR capable, it will request an AXFR upon receiving the NOTIFY packet.

IXFR AND THE ACTIVE DIRECTORY

In an Active Directory integrated multimaster environment, zone changes can be made to any DNS server. This means different servers can contain zone changes applied in a different order. As long as the DNS master server that previously provided changes to the client is available, IXFR works well. If that server becomes unavailable, however, the client may miss some changes because of the difference in record order. When the secondary server detects this it requests AXFR. You'll remember we said that within the Active Directory domain, DNS data is simply replicated along with the rest of the Active Directory. It is important to remember this in the context of zone transfer. The entire discussion of IXFR and AXFR is valid only when talking about standard zone transfers. This may occur outside the active directory or when an Active Directory based DNS server is supported by nonactive directory secondary servers. (We'll see where this can occur at the end of this chapter when we discuss DNS planning for the Active Directory.)

MULTIMASTER REPLICATION

Active Directory supports multimaster replication. This allows any domain controller to send or receive updates of Active Directory information. Replication occurs on a per-property basis, which means that only relevant changes are forwarded. This differs from DNS full zone transfers, in which the entire zone is replicated. It is also a bit different from *incremental* zone transfers, in which the server forwards all changes made since the last update. With Active Directory replication only the final result of all changes to a record is sent.

CONVERTING AND DELETING ZONES

You can convert a standard zone to an Active Directory integrated zone and vice-versa with little difficulty. To do so, simply highlight the zone, and select *Properties* from the *Action* menu to reveal the zone properties dialog box shown in Figure 13-9.

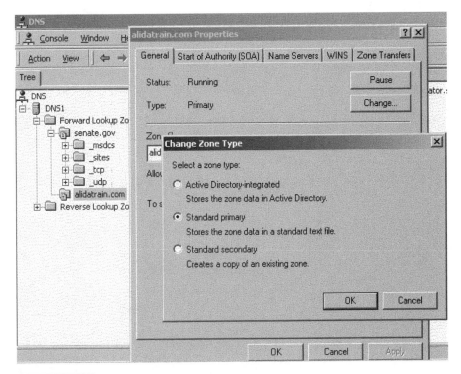

FIGURE 13-9   *Zone properties dialog box showing change zone type option*

By clicking **Change** you can open the **Change Zone Type** dialog box. Select the radio button that represents the zone type to which wish to convert and the DNS will do the rest. (Of course if you wish to convert to Active Directory-integrated, you must be using a server that is running Active Directory. If you wish to convert to a standard secondary zone, you will be asked for the address of a server that will be authoritative for the zone.) Now that we see how easy it is to convert zones, we need to consider the implications of doing so.

In converting a standard primary or secondary zone to an Active Directory integrated zone, remember:

- DNS servers hosting Active Directory integrated zones must be running on domain controllers.
- You cannot host Active Directory integrated zones from other domains. You can, however, load the foreign Active Directory integrated zone as a secondary zone.
- You can't create an Active Directory integrated secondary zone. In Active Directory, all domain controllers can update the zone.

- It is not possible to have both an Active Directory integrated zone and a standard primary copy of the same zone at the same time.

When you convert an Active Directory integrated zone to either a standard primary or standard secondary zone consider:

- When converting to a standard *secondary* zone, the zone is *copied* to the name server from which you initiated the conversion. The server will no longer load the zone from Active Directory, but will use the copy. It will request zone transfers from the server you specified as the primary server for the zone during the conversion process.
- When converting to a standard *primary* zone, the zone is copied to the server on which you initiated the conversion and is deleted from Active Directory. The zone ceases to function as an Active Directory integrated zone.

DELETING ZONES

If you delete an Active Directory integrated zone with **Load data on startup** set to **From Active Directory and registry**, the zone will be deleted from the entire domain. Before completing the deletion you are shown the dialog box in Figure 13-10 to make you aware of the impact of the deletion.

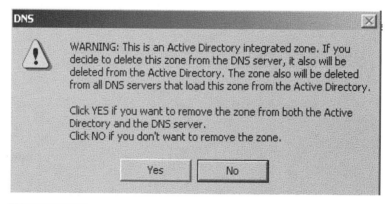

FIGURE 13–10   *Deleting Active Directory integrated zone with server set to registry and Active Directory*

If you attempt to delete an Active Directory integrated zone with **Load data on startup** set to **Registry**, you are asked if you want to delete the zone from Active Directory (see Figure 13-11).

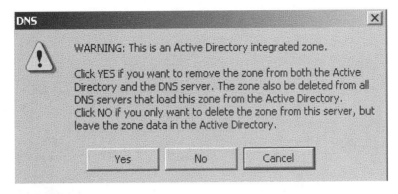

FIGURE 13–11   *Deleting Active Directory integrated zone with server set to Registry*

If you answer **Yes**, the zone is removed from Active Directory. If you select **No**, the zone is removed from the registry but remains in Active Directory. If **Load data on startup** is changed to **From Active Directory and registry**, the zone will reappear when the DNS server polls the Active Directory for changes. If **Load data on startup** remains set to **Registry**, the zone will not reappear.

If you delete a standard secondary zone from a DNS server operating on a domain controller, it is deleted from that server. If a corresponding Active Directory integrated zone exists, however, and you have configured the DNS server to **Load data on startup** from **Active Directory and registry**, the zone will reappear as an Active Directory integrated primary zone. You can delete the Active Directory integrated zone from the computer or from Active Directory as desired.

DNS Dynamic Update

Throughout this text we've alluded to the concept of automatic or *dynamic* updates for DNS. This is a significant advance in the DNS world because the previous requirement for "manual only" updates certainly took a lot of the fun out of DNS maintenance. As we're about to see, the Windows 2000 DNS permits both dynamic DNS updates and secure dynamic DNS updates. Dynamic DNS update is defined in RFC 2136 and secure DNS update is defined in the IETF Internet-Draft "GSS Algorithm for TSIG (GSS-TSIG)."

Dynamic update capable clients (including DHCP clients) can automatically register A and *pointer (PTR) resource records* with a primary server. DHCP servers are able to register A and PTR resource records on behalf of their clients who are not dynamic update capable. Additionally, the Active

Directory setup wizard can dynamically register the new domain controller's service (SRV) records during the installation process.

Under secure dynamic update, the authoritative name server accepts updates only from clients and servers that are authorized to make dynamic updates to the dnsZone and dnsNode objects. This protects zones and resource records from being modified by unauthorized users. Under secure dynamic update you may specify which users and groups can modify zones and resource records.

To configure the secure update status for an Active Directory integrated zone, select the **zone properties**. The **Allow Dynamic Updates** drop-down box on the General tab permits you to select **Only Secure Updates** (See figure 13-12). This option is the default for Active Directory integrated zones and is not available for conventional DNS zones. To allow nonsecure dynamic updates select **Yes** instead of **Only Secure Updates**.

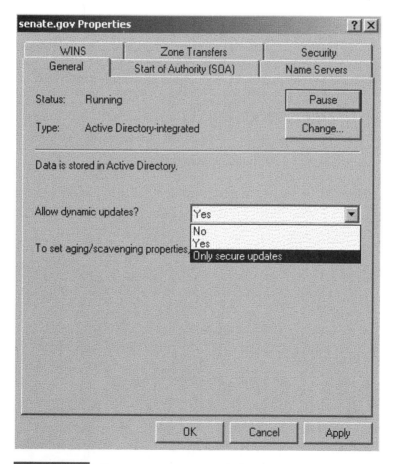

FIGURE 13–12   *Zone properties—General tab*

Note	While a primary zone can be configured for dynamic update, only Active Directory integrated zones can be configured for secure dynamic update.

To authorize users or groups to update the zone, select the **Security** tab from the zone properties dialog box. (This tab is available only for Active Directory integrated zones.) This will reveal a standard Windows 2000 security dialog box (see Figure 13-12). The default permissions permit system resources and administrative personnel to properly manage the zones. If you choose to delegate this authority to others you can change the permissions here.

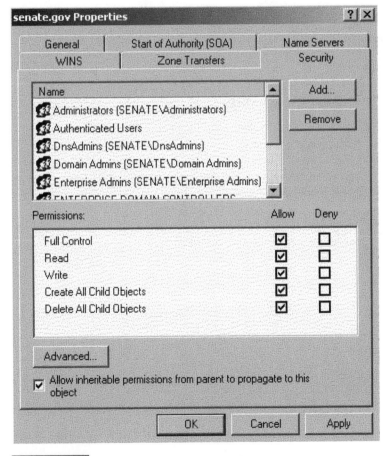

FIGURE 13-13   *Zone properties—Security tab*

By default, the dynamic update client assumes it can accomplish an unsecured dynamic update. If it fails (because the server requires secure updates), the client will negotiate a secure dynamic update.

Changing the Client's Update Procedure

You can configure a client to attempt only insecure dynamic update or secure dynamic updates by adding the **UpdateSecurityLevel** registry entry to the following subkey:

HKEY_LOCAL_MACHINE\SYSTEM\CurrentControlSet\Services\Tcpip\Parameters (REG_DWORD)

The value of **UpdateSecurityLevel** can be set to the decimal values 0, 16, or 256, which configure security as follows:

- *256*. Specifies the use of secure dynamic update only.

- *16*. Specifies the use of insecure dynamic update only.

- *0*. Specifies the use of secure dynamic update when an insecure dynamic update is refused. This is the default value.

If you disable secure dynamic update, the client is not able to perform updates on zones that have been configured for secure dynamic update.

Dynamic Update Process

Now that we're excited about dynamic updates, let's see how the process works in our Windows 2000 network. Dynamic updates can be sent on behalf of different services such as the DHCP client, the DHCP server, Netlogon, and cluster services. In this chapter we will describe only dynamic updates performed by the DHCP client and server.

In Windows 2000, clients can send dynamic updates for three different types of network adapters: DHCP adapters, statically configured adapters, and remote access adapters. Regardless of which adapter is used, the DHCP client service sends dynamic updates to the authoritative DNS server. The DHCP client service runs on all computers regardless of whether they are configured as DHCP clients.

Note   Don't let the term "adapter" confuse you. In this context, adapter refers to the way the system communicates. A DHCP adapter and a statically configured adapter, for instance, could be identical devices, one receiving its information from DHCP and the other configured at the machine. A remote access adapter could be a modem and/or code that permits access to a virtual private network.

By default, the dynamic update client dynamically registers its A resource records and possibly all of its PTR resource records every 24 hours or whenever any of the following events occur: (A *dynamic update client* is any client that can perform dynamic updates in accordance with RFC 2136.

For all intents and purposes, you may consider a dynamic update client to be a Windows 2000 computer.)

- The TCP/IP configuration is changed.
- The DHCP address is renewed or a new lease is obtained.
- A Plug and Play event occurs.
- An IP address is added or removed from the computer when the user changes or adds an IP address for a static adapter. (The user does not need to restart the computer for the dynamic update client to register the name–to–IP address mappings.)

The dynamic update client automatically deregisters name–to–IP address mappings (by default) whenever the DHCP lease expires. You can configure the client not to register its name and IP address in DNS. If you do, and the DHCP server is running Windows 2000 and is configured to **Enable Updates for DNS clients that do not support dynamic updates**, the DHCP server attempts to update the mappings for the client. The DHCP server displays the dynamic update status of each client with a distinctive icon (see Figure 13-14).

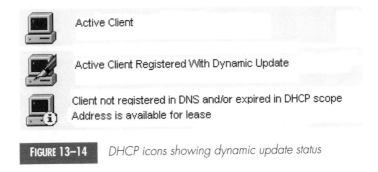

FIGURE 13–14   *DHCP icons showing dynamic update status*

To prevent the client from registering name–to–IP address mappings:

1. Double-click the **Network and Dial-up Connections** icon in **Control Panel**.
2. Right-click the icon for the connection on which you want to disable registration of name–to–IP address mappings, and then click **Properties**.
3. Click **Internet Protocol (TCP/IP)**, and then click **Properties**.
4. Click **Advanced**, and then click the **DNS** tab (see Figure 13-15).
5. Clear the check box **Register this connection's address in DNS**.

You can force a reregistration by using the command-line tool *ipconfig*. Type the following at the command prompt: **ipconfig /registerdns** (see Figure 13-16).

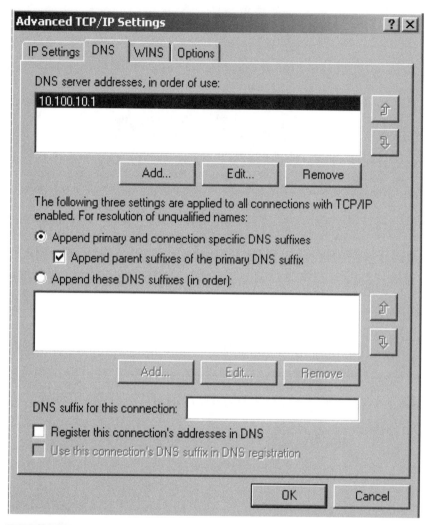

FIGURE 13–15 *Advanced TCP/IP settings*

```
C:\>ipconfig/registerdns

Windows 2000 IP Configuration

Registration of the DNS resource records for all adapters of this
computer
has been initiated. Any errors will be reported in the Event Viewer in
15 minutes.
```

FIGURE 13–16 *Ipconfig/registerdns results*

Dynamic Update Failure

Dynamic updates can fail. The most common reason is that the primary server that is authoritative for the name does not respond. This may be because the primary server is down or because the local name server has an incorrect or outdated name server listed in its SOA resource record. DNS servers with standard zones (including secondary servers for Active Directory integrated zones) can cause problems by sending incorrect or outdated SOA records when dynamic update clients request them. DNS servers for Active Directory–integrated zones, however, always include their name in the SOA records. It is unlikely, therefore, that an Active Directory integrated name server would have an incorrect or outdated SOA record. If the primary server does not respond but the zone is replicated through multimaster replication, the client attempts to register the name with the other primary DNS servers that are authoritative for the name. If the update fails because the server is not available, the client logs a message in the event log.

Other reasons for failure may be that the server is not accepting dynamic updates because the zone is being transferred, the server accepts only secure dynamic updates and the insecure dynamic update operation failed, or prerequisites have not been met. (For example, the dynamic update client might be trying to update a name for which no records currently exist).

Time to Live

Whenever a dynamic update client registers in DNS, the associated A and PTR resource records include the Time to Live (TTL), which by default is set to 20 minutes. You can change the default setting by creating or modifying the **DefaultRegistrationTTL** entry in the following registry subkey:

```
HKEY_LOCAL_MACHINE\SYSTEM\CurrentControlSet\Services\Tcpip\
Parameters
```

The entry has a DWORD value and lists the TTL in seconds. A small value causes cached entries to expire sooner, which increases DNS traffic but decreases the risk of entries becoming stale. Expiring entries quickly is useful for computers that frequently renew their DHCP leases. A large value causes cached entries to be retained longer, decreasing DNS traffic but increasing the risk of entries becoming stale. Long retention times are useful for computers that renew their DHCP leases infrequently.

Resolving Name Conflicts

What if during dynamic update registration a client determines that its name is already registered in DNS with an IP address that belongs to another computer? By default the client will attempt to replace the registration of the other computer's IP address with the new IP address. This means that for zones that are not configured for secure dynamic update, any user on the network can modify the IP address registration of any client computer. For zones that are configured for secure dynamic update, however, only authorized users are able to modify the resource record.

You can change the default setting so that instead of replacing the IP address, the client backs out of the registration process and writes the error to the Event Log. To do so, add the **DisableReplaceAddressesInConflicts** entry with a value of 1 (DWORD) to the following registry subkey:

```
HKEY_LOCAL_MACHINE\SYSTEM\CurrentControlSet\Services\Tcpip\
Parameters
```

Secure Dynamic Update

Active Directory–integrated zones can be configured for *secure* dynamic update. Only users or groups with permissions in the access control lists (ACL) will have authority to modify the zone and its records.

Note　　Secure dynamic update is available only on Active Directory–integrated zones.

CONFIGURING SECURE DYNAMIC UPDATE

Active Directory integrated zones are configured, by default, to permit only secure dynamic updates. A standard primary zone that is later converted to an Active Directory integrated zone will be configured for nonsecure dynamic updates or no dynamic updates, depending on how the primary zone was previously configured.

To manually configure a zone to use secure dynamic update, select **Only secure updates** in the **Allow dynamic updates?** drop-down box of the zone properties **General** tab (see Figure 13-17).

Under secure dynamic update, only computers and users with ACL permissions may update the zone's dnsNode objects. (The ACL is configured at the **Zone Properties dialog Security** tab as depicted in Figure 13-18.) The authenticated user group has, by default, ACL create permission. As a result, any authenticated user or computer is allowed to create a new object in the zone. The authenticated user who creates the object becomes the creator-owner and receives full control permission over the object he or she created. (The *Authenticated User Group* is the group of all authenticated computers and users in an Active Directory forest.)

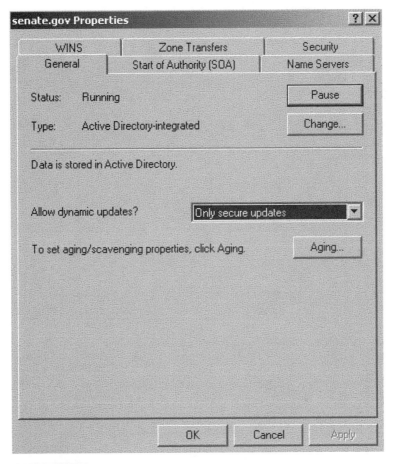

FIGURE 13–17   *Zone properties—General tab*

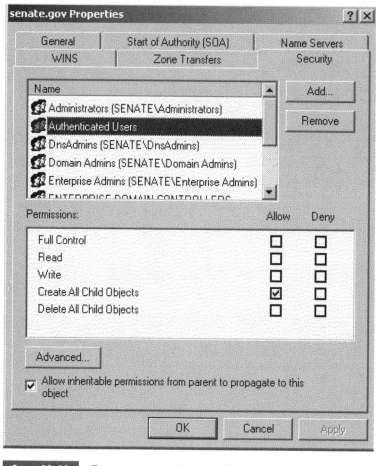

FIGURE 13–18   *Zone properties—Security tab*

DNS Strategies for the Windows 2000 Domain

As we've seen, DNS is absolutely critical to the operation of a Windows 2000 domain. While Active Directory installation and its attendant DNS implementation appeared straightforward in our examples, this may have been because our examples were placed in a fairly sterile environment. In the "real world," we need to concern ourselves with Internet presence, registered domain names, existing DNS servers, "political" considerations that dictate the use of non-Windows 2000 DNS servers in our enterprise network, and the degree of protection we need to provide to our network resources. A Windows 2000 installation needs to be done, therefore, in this real world context. To ensure a successful implementation, we'll need to formulate the best plan to permit our Windows 2000 DNS servers to function with registered names, existing servers, and Internet connectivity. We will detail four basic deployment strategies that will permit you to overcome most obstacles.

Use Your Registered DNS Domain Name for the Active Directory Root

This is perhaps the simplest DNS implementation. If you have a registered DNS name, simply use this for your active directory name. This solution presupposes you maintain and control the DNS servers authoritative for your domain. The advantages of this solution stem from simplicity. No names, zones, or DNS structures need be changed. You will need, of course, to ensure all your DNS servers support SRV records. Of course, if they all run on Windows 2000 computers, you can be sure they do. The biggest disadvantage of this strategy is security. If you'll use your DNS servers for both Active Directory and normal Internet name resolution, you'll need to expose a lot of network resources directly to the Internet. Modifying this installation to ensure the appropriate level of security may result in a more complex implementation than one of the other deployment strategies.

Use a Delegated DNS Subdomain for the Active Directory Root

Rather than exposing your domain to the Internet, you can create a DNS child domain to host your Windows 2000 domain. As depicted in Figure 13-19, we have installed our Windows 2000 domain as ad.senate.gov and placed it in its own zone (Zone 2 in the figure). The Zone 1 DNS servers continue to provide name resolution to the outside environment while the Zone 2 DNS servers support the Active Directory in the internal environment. Zone 2 would be delegated on the Zone 1 DNS servers, as described in Chapter 12. Using this strategy, the outside world sees no change in DNS support while the Windows 2000 domain may operate safely within the firewall. Name resolution for internal computers *may* be possible since the Zone 1 DNS servers can access the Zone 2 DNS servers to obtain information for the ad.senate.gov domain. (The word *may* was used in the previous sentence because the administrator can control access to the internal network through the firewall and it may or may not be prudent to allow external hosts to come in.)

In addition to permitting isolation of the internal network, this solution works without upgrading the existing (Zone 1) DNS servers. Except for the subdomain delegation, no modification of the current DNS function would be required. On the negative side, the internal domain name structure becomes longer and, perhaps, causes some confusion for internal users. This solution also requires the creation and maintenance of additional DNS servers to support only the internal network. (Since the Active Directory integrated DNS server must operate on a domain controller, however, this may not be such a bad thing. Using a domain controller for name resolution to the Internet may place an unnecessary burden on a machine that is already heavily tasked in supporting the Windows 2000 domain. The internal/external DNS server strategy may better distribute the workload.)

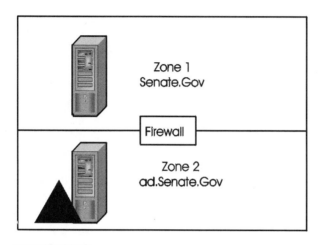

FIGURE 13-19   *Delegating a DNS subdomain for the Active Directory root*

Use a Single DNS Domain Name for the Internal and External Networks

You can get around the long domain name problem of the preceding strategy by using the same domain name on both sides of your firewall. As shown in Figure 13-20, DNS servers on each side of the firewall provide name resolution for senate.gov. DNS1 is visible to the external network and contains resolution information for resources outside the firewall. DNS2 maintains name resolution information for the Windows 2000 domain. As in the previous strategy, internal resources are protected from the outside world. While users from the Windows 2000 domain don't need to use longer domain names, additional configuration of both servers is required. Without additional configuration, for instance, users on the internal network will be able to find all internal resources but will be unable to find www.senate.gov. This is because internal users will go to DNS2 for mappings. Since DNS2 thinks it's authoritative for all of senate.gov, it won't query DNS2 for the address but will send a negative response to the resolver. Likewise, DNS1 will be able to provide a mapping for the web server but will be unable to provide information for DC1 to users outside the firewall. To correct these problems, the administrator must enter records on DNS2 for senate.gov resources outside the firewall and on DNS1 for senate.gov resources inside the firewall. Depending on how much access to the internal network is required, you may need to place SRV records on DNS1.

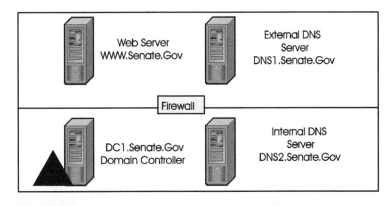

FIGURE 13-20 *Using a single DNS name on the internal and external networks*

An advantage of this strategy is that mappings may be entered selectively. That is, there is no need to enter information on DNS1 for resources you wish to hide from external users or to enter information on DNS2 for resources the internal network doesn't need to access. This solution may allow you to retain existing external DNS server resources (assuming the existing servers support SRV records or SRV records won't be required on them). Because you retain the same name there is no requirement to register a new name or teach your users new domain names. The only real disadvantage here is in the requirement to maintain some manual entries on servers inside and outside the firewall.

Use a Different DNS Domain Name for the Internal and External Networks

The fourth alternative is to use different domain names for internal and external resources. As shown in Figure 13-21, internal resources are isolated from external resources by their domain name. Internal users will be able to resolve external names because DNS2 can be configured to forward resolution requests to the outside world. An internal user attempting to contact www.senate.gov, for instance, would make a recursive request to DNS2, which would make an iterative request to find DNS1 to obtain a mapping. (Actually, as you'll remember, we could configure DNS2 to use DNS1 as a forwarder.)

This is a good strategy if you don't want internal resources accessible from the external network. (To permit name resolution from outside users, you would need to register the internal domain name and ensure outside users could find your internal servers. This, of course, would result in a solution similar to the first strategy we discussed, which would expose your internal servers to the outside.) This solution will require your users to learn a new domain name but will permit you to retain your current DNS server resources without modification.

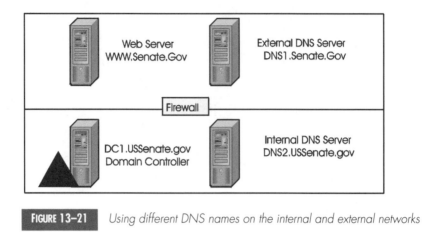

FIGURE 13–21   *Using different DNS names on the internal and external networks*

Summary

As we've seen, DNS is so important to Active Directory that a DNS server will be installed during the Active Directory installation process if a suitable one cannot be found within the environment. To support Active Directory, a DNS server must be at least BINSD 4.9.6 compliant and must support SRV records (dynamic update capability and incremental zone transfers are desirable).

The Windows 2000 DNS server supports Active Directory integrated zones. These zones function on DNS servers that are also Windows 2000 domain controllers. Unlike conventional zones, Active Directory integrated zones are stored in the Active Directory and benefit from multimaster replication. Under multimaster replication, changes may be made to any DNS server and will be replicated to the other servers based on a time stamp. Windows 2000 servers also support incremental zone transfer (IXFR). IXFR improves efficiency by transferring only changed information instead of the entire zone file.

Unlike previous versions of DNS, the Windows 2000 DNS server supports dynamic update. Using dynamic update, Windows 2000 clients can automatically register or update their DNS data without the need for administrator intervention. Clients that don't support DNS dynamic update can have their DNS data updated by their servicing the DHCP server. Windows 2000 DNS servers may be configured to allow only secure dynamic updates to ensure only authorized resources are allowed to alter DNS information.

Finally, there are several ways to employ DNS servers to support Windows 2000. It is important to select the appropriate strategy based on Internet presence, registered domain names, existing DNS servers, and the degree of protection from the outside world your network requires. We discussed four strategies: using the registered DNS domain name for the Active Directory root, using a delegated DNS subdomain for the Active Directory root, using a single DNS domain name for the internal and external network, and using a different DNS domain name for the internal and external network.

Test Yourself

1. Which of these CANNOT be performed on an Active Directory zone?
   A. Converting an Active Directory integrated zone to a standard zone
   B. Deleting zones
   C. Creating a secondary copy of an Active Directory integrated zone
   D. Converting an Active Directory integrated zone to a tertiary zone

2. By default, the dynamic update client dynamically registers its A resource records (choose all that apply):
   A. Every 24 hours
   B. When the TCP/IP configuration is changed
   C. When the DHCP address is renewed or a new lease is obtained
   D. When a Plug and Play event occurs

3. The automatic update may fail because (choose all that apply):
   A. The primary server that is authoritative for the name does not respond
   B. The zone is being transferred
   C. A large value causes cached entries to be retained longer
   D. The server accepts only secure dynamic updates, and the insecure dynamic update operation failed

4. DNS incremental zone transfer:
   A. Reduces network load by transferring zone information in small segments
   B. Is not available in the Windows 2000 DNS
   C. Is available only for Active Directory integrated zones
   D. Transfers only new or changed records

5. The operation of the Active Directory depends on _____ records.
   A. HINFO
   B. MX
   C. SRV
   D. PTR

IPSec and RRAS

This chapter covers two important Windows 2000 networking areas that will permit you to secure your network communications, perform a host of routing functions, and provide dial-in services and Virtual Private Networking to your users.

Internet Protocol Security (IPSec) permits you to encrypt your network transmissions to provide both local area network (LAN) and wide area network (WAN) security. The Routing and Remote Access Service (RRAS) permits you to configure your computer as a static or dynamic router, Dynamic Host Configuration Protocol (DHCP) relay agent; network address translation server, dial-in server or connection-sharing dial-out Internet gateway; or virtual private networking server. The skills you will learn in this chapter will enable you to support a myriad of wide area networking capabilities.

IPSec

Typically when we talk of network security, we think about threats from the external network (read Internet). We rarely think of our LANs being compromised from within. Unfortunately, anyone who can gain physical access to your LAN cable could use a protocol analyzer to capture your packets and extract the clear text from them.

Windows 2000 brings us a new technology, IPSec, which, when properly configured, authenticates computers and encrypts the data sent between them. IPSec can provide these services in WAN or LAN communication to include communication between networks and remote users and even between remote networks themselves. IPSec can use Kerberos Version 5 or preshared key support for authentication and features complete public key infrastructure support. Data is encrypted through the data encryption standard (DES) and uses standard IP packet formatting to permit devices such as routers to handle IPSec packets as they would any other transmission (in fact, these devices can't tell the difference between an IPSec and an unencrypted packet). IPSec operates at the network level, making it transparent to users and applications, and is configured through the Windows 2000 Group Policy, making it easy to centrally administer (it may also be configured at the local computer level to address any unique requirements).

Because IPSec features both encryption and authentication, it protects the network from a host of attacks and intrusions to include address spoofing, re-routing, and denial of service attacks. IPSec can provide packet filtering where communications from specific address ranges, protocols, or ports can be blocked. Automatic security negotiation permits computers without identical IPSec policies to communicate (provided there are enough common negotiation options to work with).

Common Security Attacks

Here are some of the attacks that IPSec can guard against:

Sniffing: Compromise of packets through use of a program or device such as the Microsoft Network Monitor.

Data modification: Data is modified, in transit, by a third party to gain access to secure information or to alter the transmitted message.

Address spoofing: An attacker creates packets that look as if they've come from a legitimate network host.

Application layer attack: Exploitation of weaknesses in the server operating system and its applications.

Man-in-the-middle: A third party intercepts and controls the data without network users knowledge. Data may be subtly altered or rerouted.

Denial-of-service: One or more techniques to flood the network with traffic to impede normal network operation.

IPSec Negotiation and Encryption Process

Negotiation and encryption are fairly straightforward but require that both sending and receiving computers be configured with the appropriate IPSec drivers. In the first step, the IPSec policies from the remote machine are delivered to the local machine's IPSec driver. Local and remote machine policies are compared to develop keys. The policies reside either at the local machine level or in the Active Directory group policy. In either case, the *Internet Security Association and Key Management Protocol* (ISAKMP), in conjunction with the Oakley Key Determination Protocol, oversees the negotiation to provide appropriate keys. Once key negotiation is complete, the IPSec drivers are able to monitor, filter, and secure traffic.

ISAKMP Negotiation

There are two steps in the negotiation process. In the first step, ISAKMP manages a user-identity negotiation where both hosts exchange session keys with which to communicate. In the second step, the hosts negotiate specific security settings they'll use to encrypt their communication.

Security Policies

In the preceding section we slipped the term *policy* right by you. Perhaps we should spend a line or two to try to define this concept. In the context of IPSec, *policies* are security rules that define parameters such as security level, encryption algorithm, and key length. They also define where to define the IPSec settings. This may be based on address, protocol, DNS name, subnet, and/or connection type.

As we indicated, IPSec policies may be configured at the local machine or through the Windows 2000 group policy. Windows 2000 provides default policies that may be applied directly or modified to meet specific requirements.

Configuring IPSec

Let's continue our IPSec discussion by configuring it to work between two machines. Since this is a book on Transport Control Protocol/Internet Protocol (TCP/IP) and not Windows 2000 group policy, we'll use local policies (rather than Active Directory group policy). If you plan to follow along by configuring a couple of computers on your local network, it's a good idea to verify you can ping between them before we start—this will ensure you have known network connectivity prior to implementing IPSec.

The first step in creating an IPSec policy is to select **Local Security Policy** from the **Administrative Tools**, as shown in Figure 14-1. This will launch the **Security Policies** console. Select **IP Security Policies** to reveal the dialog box shown in Figure 14-2.

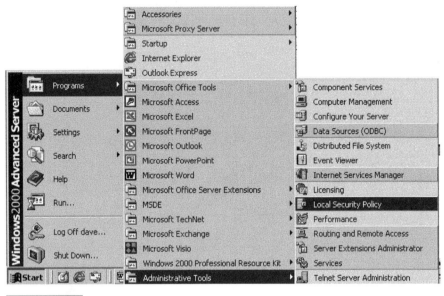

FIGURE 14-1   *Select local security policy*

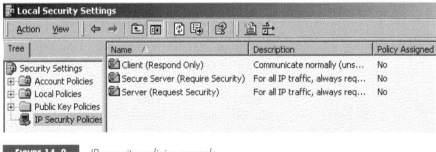

FIGURE 14-2   *IP security policies console*

The console displays three predefined policy entries that you may assign:

- *Client (respond only)*: This policy normally operates with clear text but is able to respond to an IPSec request for security and will attempt to negotiate a secure connection.
- *Server (request security)*: This policy will always attempt to use IPSec for outgoing communications and will respond to IPSec requests for incoming messages. For outgoing messages, the sender will revert to clear text if the target computer doesn't respond to the IPSec request.

- *Server (require security)*: This policy requires IPSec for all inbound and outbound communications. No clear text communication will be permitted.

To assign a policy, simply right-click the desired policy and select **Assign**. The policy is assigned and the **Policy Assigned** column in the IPSec console changes from **No** to **Yes** for that policy. While you may define several policies, you may assign only one to a computer at any given time. You may edit any of these default policies by right-clicking the policy and selecting **Properties**.

CREATING AN IPSEC POLICY

Rather than editing an existing policy, let's learn about editing by creating our own policy. The first step is to select **Create IP Security Policy** from the **Action** menu, as shown in Figure 14-3.

This launches the IPSec Policy Wizard. As you go through the wizard you're given an opportunity to enter a meaningful name and description of the policy (see Figure 14-4). You are next asked if you want to activate the **Default Response Rule** (see Figure 14-5). This feature permits the computer to respond if the incoming communication doesn't fit a specific rule defined for this policy. Next, you can select the authentication method (see Figure 14-6) for the default response rule. Since we're working in a Windows 2000 environment, we'll select the Kerboros V5 protocol.

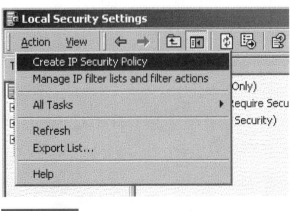

FIGURE 14–3   *Create IP security policy*

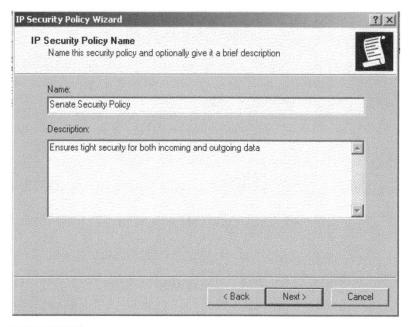

FIGURE 14–4 *Name the IPSec policy*

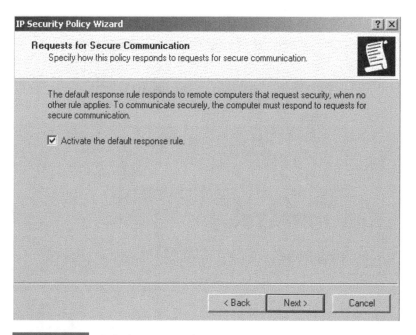

FIGURE 14–5 *Default response rule*

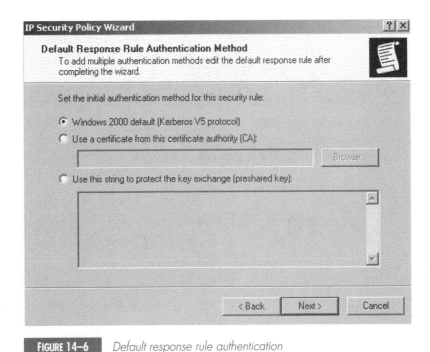

FIGURE 14-6 *Default response rule authentication*

This completes the creation of the policy. At this point, however, we've defined only the default response rule. If we want to define anything further (which is the whole idea of creating a policy), we'll need to edit the policy. By default the wizard leads us directly to the editor.

RULES

Before we create a rule, let's take a look at the six rule components:

- IP filter list: Identifies the type of traffic the rule applies to.
- Filter actions: Defines what actions to take when the traffic matches the IP filter. This may be to permit or block traffic or to negotiate security for a particular connection.
- Security methods: Prescribes the level of security to be used during communication.
- Tunnel settings: Permits you to specify a particular IP address with which to communicate. There must be two rules to support tunneling (one for each direction of communication).
- Authentication methods: Select the appropriate method to validate the remote computer. There are three authentication methods:
    - Kerberos Version 5—Kerberos V5 is the default protocol. This authentication method can be used for any trusted domain member capable of running the protocol. (The client does not need to be Windows based.)

- Certificates—Uses X.509 Version 3 certificates. Requires the configuration of at least one trusted certificate authority.
- Preshared key—This is a manual solution. Users must agree upon and configure such a key before use.
- Connection types: Select the connections the rule applies to (all, LAN, and/or remote access).

CONFIGURE A POLICY

Now that we understand a bit about rules, let's apply those rules to the policy we created earlier. If we double-click the policy, we reveal the **Security Policy Properties** dialog box shown in Figure 14-7. Note the default rule that the wizard helped us to create.

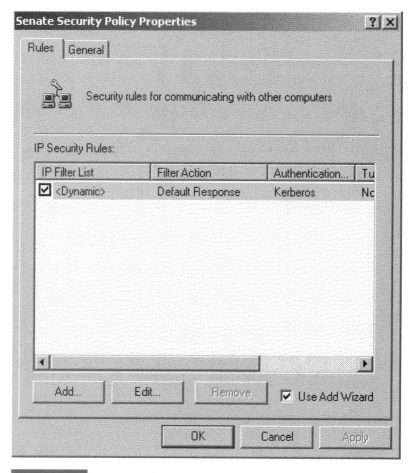

Senate Security Policy Properties

Rules | General

Security rules for communicating with other computers

IP Security Rules:

IP Filter List	Filter Action	Authentication...	Tu
☑ <Dynamic>	Default Response	Kerberos	Nc

Add...   Edit...   Remove   ☑ Use Add Wizard

OK   Cancel   Apply

FIGURE 14-7   *Security policy properties*

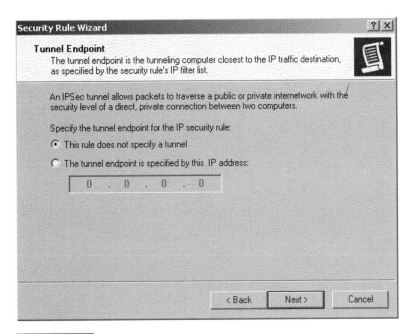

FIGURE 14–8   *Tunnel endpoint*

Click **Add** to open the **Create IP Security Rule** wizard. As we step through the wizard we are first asked if we wish to create a tunnel endpoint (see Figure 14-8). We do not, so we'll leave the default (*This rule does not specify a tunnel*) setting and continue.

Next, we can select network types to which the rule should apply; we'll set this for all connections (see Figure 14-9).

Now we need to select an authentication method. We'll use a preshared key, as depicted in Figure 14-10.

Since our rule should apply to all IP traffic, we select this option, as shown in Figure 14-11.

On the next screen, we determine the way this rule will function in the network. We want to ensure all of the server's IP traffic is controlled by this rule so we'll select **Require Security**, as shown in Figure 14-12.

We can now tell the wizard to **Finish**. Once the wizard is complete, double-clicking our new security policy shows the new rule (see Figure 14-13).

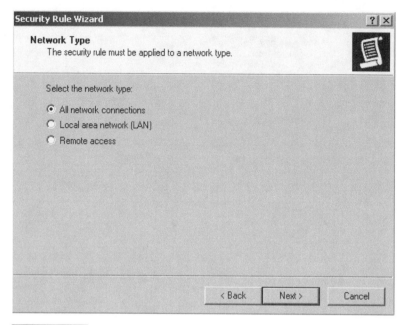

FIGURE 14–9 *Network type*

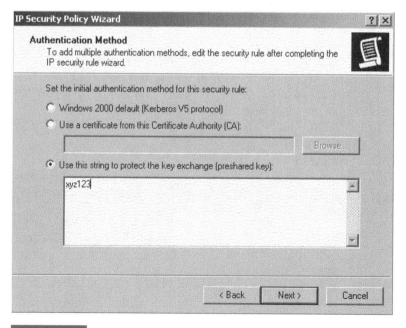

FIGURE 14–10 *Authentication method*

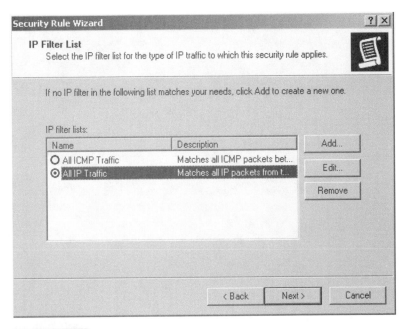

FIGURE 14-11   *IP filter list*

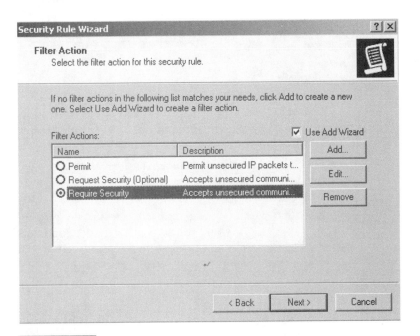

FIGURE 14-12   *Filter action*

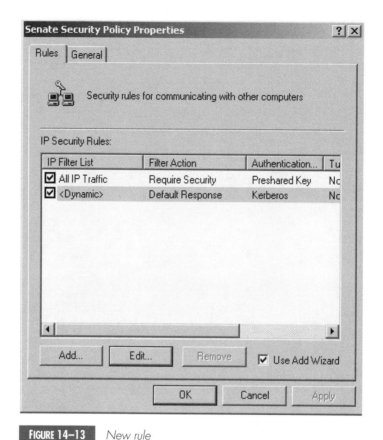

FIGURE 14-13   *New rule*

In order for the new policy to take effect, you must restart the **IPSEC Policy Agent**. This may be done through the **Local Computer Management** console, as shown in Figure 14-14.

Finally, we must assign the policy we created to the machine. In the **Security Settings** snap-in, right-click the new policy and select assign (see Figure 14-15.)

Now that our policy is in effect, let's test it. Try pinging another machine in your network. If your policy was properly configured, your machine should refuse to communicate with the other host. When the ping goes out, the system will attempt to negotiate a security policy. (Since the other machine is not configured for IPSec, negotiation will fail and no ping response will be received (see Figure 14-16.)

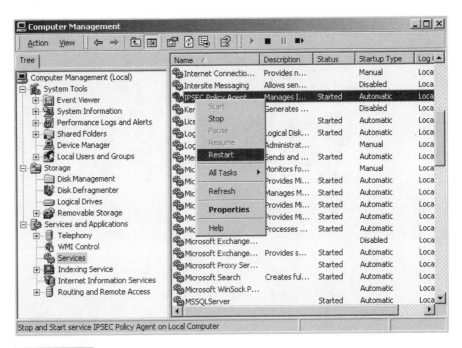

FIGURE 14–14   *Restart IPSEC policy agent*

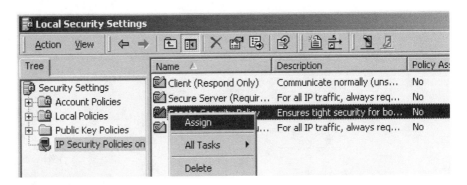

FIGURE 14–15   *Assign policy*

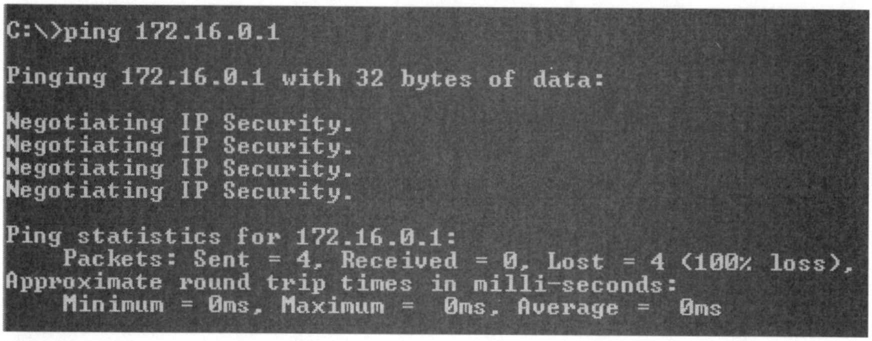

```
C:\>ping 172.16.0.1

Pinging 172.16.0.1 with 32 bytes of data:

Negotiating IP Security.
Negotiating IP Security.
Negotiating IP Security.
Negotiating IP Security.

Ping statistics for 172.16.0.1:
    Packets: Sent = 4, Received = 0, Lost = 4 (100% loss),
Approximate round trip times in milli-seconds:
    Minimum = 0ms, Maximum =  0ms, Average =  0ms
```

FIGURE 14–16   *Negotiating IPSec*

Next, go to the machine you were trying to ping and configure a security policy to work with the one we created. The new policy must use the same preshared key we used in the example. It does not, however, need to have a **Require Security** filter action. While this will certainly work, the lesser filter actions will also permit you to communicate with the other machine. Try pinging the machine you just configured. If you have successfully configured it, you should get a successful ping, as shown in Figure 14-17. It may require a number of attempts (two or three) to complete the security negotiation before the ping will work, but it will ultimately work and will then work every time without fail.

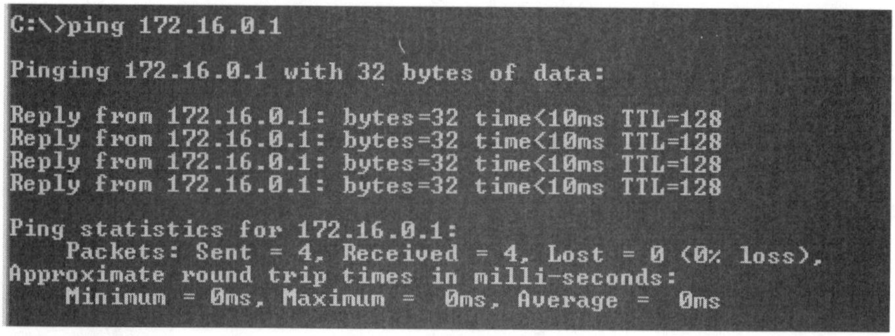

```
C:\>ping 172.16.0.1

Pinging 172.16.0.1 with 32 bytes of data:

Reply from 172.16.0.1: bytes=32 time<10ms TTL=128
Reply from 172.16.0.1: bytes=32 time<10ms TTL=128
Reply from 172.16.0.1: bytes=32 time<10ms TTL=128
Reply from 172.16.0.1: bytes=32 time<10ms TTL=128

Ping statistics for 172.16.0.1:
    Packets: Sent = 4, Received = 4, Lost = 0 (0% loss),
Approximate round trip times in milli-seconds:
    Minimum = 0ms, Maximum =  0ms, Average =  0ms
```

FIGURE 14–17   *Successful ping*

Finally, we need to return our server to normal operation (without IPSec). We could go back to the **Local Security Settings** snap-in, but let's look at another facility for controlling IPSec. Select the **Advanced** features of the **TCP/IP** properties for your server and click the **Options** tab. Clicking **Properties** reveals the IPSec dialog box shown in Figure 14-18. Here you can

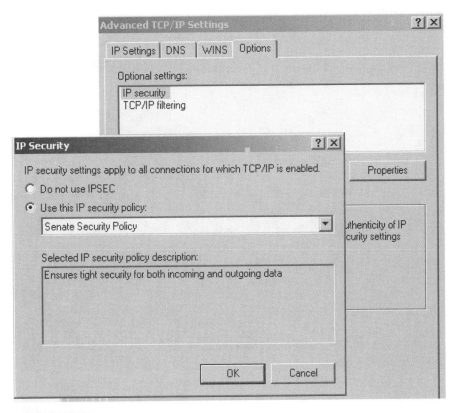

FIGURE 14-18 *IPSec dialog box*

select another available policy or disable IPSec altogether. Let's disable IPSec by clicking the radio button next to **Do Not Use IPSec**. This will disable IPSec on your machine and return it to regular operation—which you may verify by using ping.

Monitoring IPSec Activity

You can monitor the activity of IPSec on your machine by using the IPSec monitor. To execute it, go to the command line and type *ipsecmon*. This will execute the monitor shown in Figure 14-19. The IPSec monitor permits you to watch what goes on between the machines and shows the amount of encrypted and nonencrypted traffic between them.

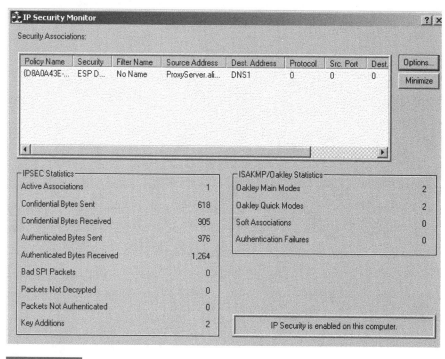

FIGURE 14–19   *IPSec monitor*

Routing and Remote Access Service—Routing

The Windows 2000 RRAS integrates with the Active Directory and provides a single location for configuring multiple networking needs. We'll look at RRAS capabilities for routing, network address translation, dial-up access, and virtual private networking.

Configure and Enable RRAS

Before we get very far with RRAS, we'll need to ensure it is installed and running on our server. When you activate the RRAS console from Administrative Tools or the RRAS snap-in from the management console, you'll find the service needs to be configured and enabled, as shown in Figure 14-20.

To start the RRAS configuration process, select **Configure and Enable Routing and Remote Access Service** from the **Action** menu, as shown in Figure 14-21.

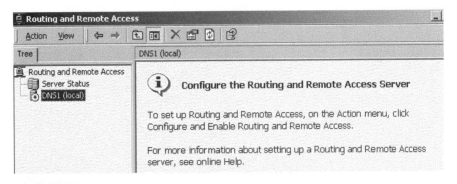

FIGURE 14—20   *Configure and enable RRAS*

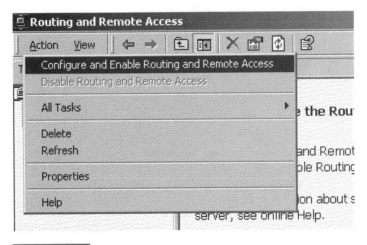

FIGURE 14—21   *Configuring RRAS*

This brings up the RRAS server setup wizard. As you can see in Figure 14-22, RRAS can be configured to perform a number of specific purposes by selecting the appropriate option. Once an option is configured, you may configure other options directly through the console. We'll configure all our RRAS options at the console, so we'll select **Manually configured server**.

Once the wizard has completed the installation steps, it affords you the opportunity to start the service (see Figure 14-23). Once the service starts, the RRAS console appears, as in Figure 14-24. Should you subsequently wish to disable RRAS on this machine, simply return to the **Action** menu and select **Disable Routing and Remote Access**.

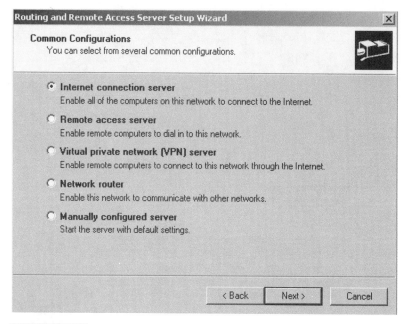

FIGURE 14—22 *Common configurations*

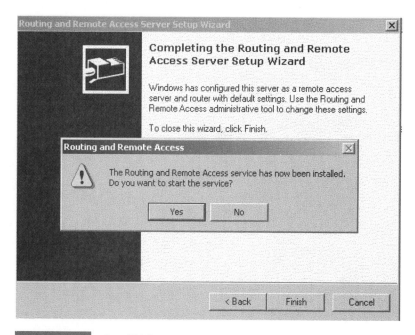

FIGURE 14—23 *Start RRAS*

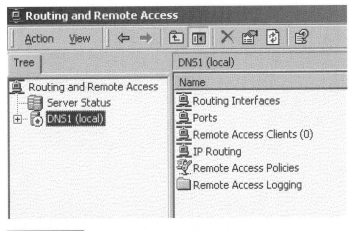

FIGURE 14–24   *Completed RRAS installation*

Configure a Static Router

Once installed, RRAS makes your computer behave as a full function router. Let's begin by configuring our machine to do simple static routing between interfaces. To permit our server to operate as a route we've installed a second network interface and renamed it "External Connection." The machine now uses two interfaces: *Local Area Connection* (172.16.0.1) and *External Connection* (172.18.0.1). The actual interface names aren't particularly important but they should represent the function of the card. In this case, we're assuming our router will route between our local network and other networks external to ours.

Our first task, then, is to get the two interfaces to pass packets between them destined for the other side. We'll first assume this router will route information only to specific networks on the external network, so we'll configure each interface only to route to the network on which the other operates.

The first step in configuring a static route is to expand **IP Routing**, right-click **Static Routes**, and select **New Static Route** (see Figure 14-25). This reveals the static route configuration dialog box shown in Figure 14-26.

For the Local Area Connection interface, we need to set the **Destination** network to the network on which the interface is currently operating (172.16.0.0). We need to include the appropriate subnet mask and, under **Gateway**, we need to **enter the IP address** of the Local Area Connection interface we wish to use. (Remember, it is possible to bind more than one IP address to a network interface; here we designate the actual IP address that clients will use as their default gateway.) Since our router has only two network connections we won't need to worry about selecting one gateway over the other, so we can leave the **Metric** field at 1.

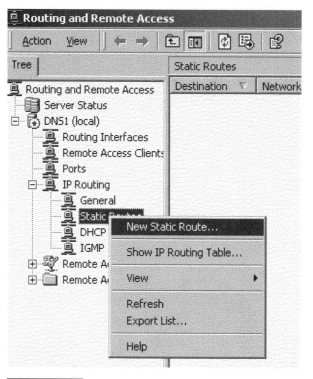

FIGURE 14–25 New static route

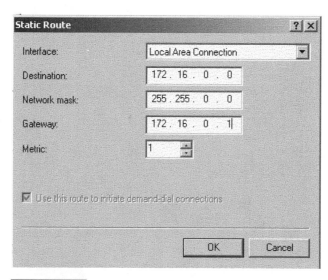

FIGURE 14–26 Configure static route

Using the same procedure, configure a static route for the External Connection. This should result in the routing depicted in Figure 14-27.

When machines on the 172.16.0.0 network are configured to use 172.16.0.1 as a default gateway, and machines on the 172.18.0.0 network use 172.18.0.1 as a default gateway, they will be able to communicate across the router with no difficulty.

What if our router were to route local network machines to the outside world instead of only to a single network? If this were the case, we'll need to use something other than 172.18.0.0 for the destination of the External Connection. You may remember that 0.0.0.0 was the destination for a default gateway. We can use the same principle for our router. To alter the information, right-click the route for the External Connection and select the properties. Enter 0.0.0.0 for both IP address and Network Mask to achieve the routing shown in Figure 14-28.

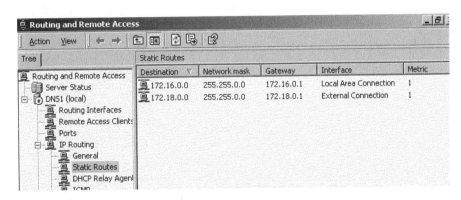

FIGURE 14–27   Static routes

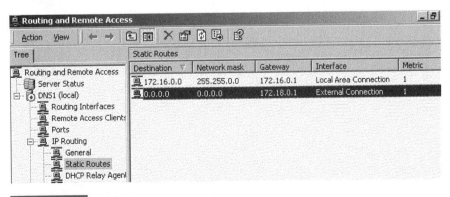

FIGURE 14–28   Default routing

Network Address Translation

Let's say that the computers on your LAN all use IP addresses from the private addressing space and you wish to use your router to allow them to access the Internet. This is known as Internet connection sharing and requires a *network address translation* (NAT) to convert our private addresses to one or more public addresses on the external network. Fortunately, RRAS features a NAT protocol that will accomplish just this function. Unfortunately, NAT doesn't work in all cases. Applications that place IP addresses in fields other than the standard TCP/IP header fields will fail when using NAT. Two protocols that are incompatible with NAT are IPSec and Kerberos. Additionally, since NAT provides name resolution components to provide DHCP and DNS services for private networks, the NAT computer shouldn't run DNS, DHCP, or the DHCP relay agent.

Note

The astute reader will notice all the IP addresses being used in this text are from private addressing. This is because we're undertaking all of these exercises off the Internet. We'll simulate, however, that the 172.18.0.0 network is Internet capable for the purposes of this book.

Now that we're excited about NAT, perhaps we should install and configure it. The first step is to expand **IP Routing**, right-click **General**, and select **New Routing Protocol** (see Figure 14-29) to reveal the **New Routing Protocol** dialog box displayed in Figure 14-30.

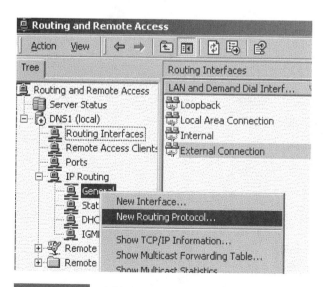

FIGURE 14–29   *Add new routing protocol*

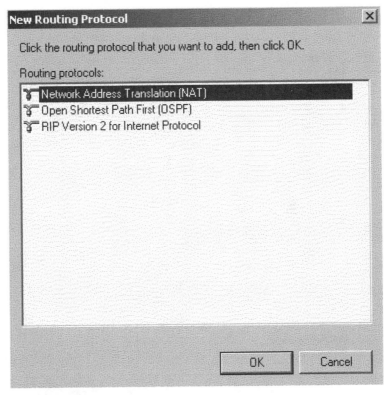

FIGURE 14–30 *New routing protocol dialog box*

Select **Network Address Translation** to install NAT. The protocol installs quickly and **Network Address Translation** appears in the console under IP routing. The first step in configuration is to add your interfaces to the protocol. Right-click **Network Address Translation** and select **New Interface**, as shown in Figure 14-31.

This reveals the **New Interface** dialog box (see Figure 14-32). We'll select the internal interface (**Local Area Connection**) first.

This will be our private interface; configuration requires only that we select the *Private interface connected to private network* radio button (see Figure 14-33).

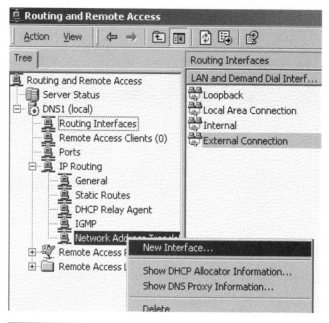

FIGURE 14–31   *Select new interface*

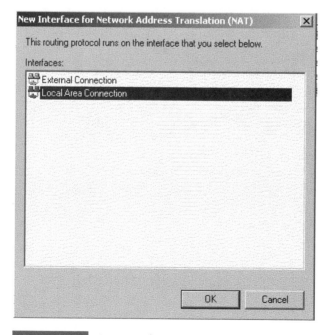

FIGURE 14–32   *New interface*

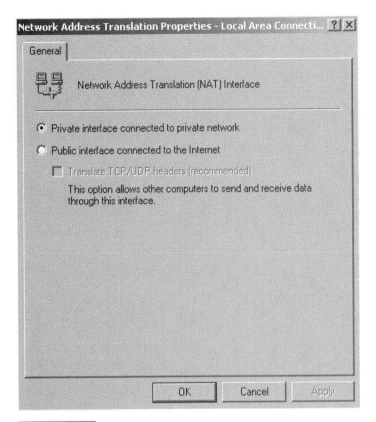

FIGURE 14–33   *Configure private interface*

In like manner, select the external interface (**External Connection**). Configuration of this one is a bit more involved (see Figure 14-34). We first select the **Public interface connected to the Internet** radio button. Since we're using only one IP address on the external interface, it is necessary to ensure the **Translate TCP/UDP headers** check box is checked. This feature allows you to translate all the traffic to the one address. In our simple NAT implementation, we can stop right here and we'll have a functional NAT server.

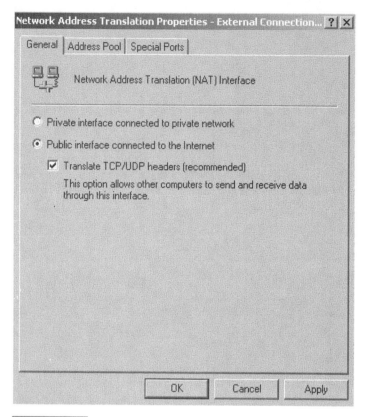

FIGURE 14–34   *Configure public interface*

Let's look at some other interface configuration options before we continue. The **Address Pool** tab (Figure 14-35) permits you to enter a pool of addresses to be used on the public interface. You may enter a range here and your internal computers will select one of the addresses in the list. (If this list is populated, the **Translate TCP/UDP headers** check box may be left unchecked on the **General** tab.)

So far, we've configured network address translation with the assumption that all communication would originate from inside our private network. While this is the typical use of NAT, what if we wanted to host a web server on the internal network? How would someone on the external network find a server on the internal network? The short answer is "they can't" and that's the beauty of NAT! A slightly longer answer would include the configuration of "special ports." When we select the **Special Ports** tab, we can access the dialog box shown in Figure 14-36. Here you can configure the service to forward inbound communications to other hosts based on the port address (either TCP or UDP) upon which the communication arrives. In the figure we have

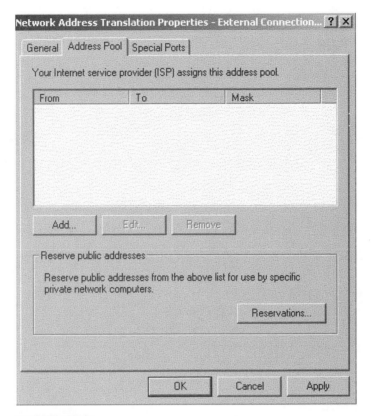

FIGURE 14-35   *Address pools*

told the service to forward TCP messages arriving on the external interface using Port 80 (the port used by HTTP) to the host 172.16.0.10 on the internal network, and to use port 80 on that machine also. This configuration would permit someone on the external network to send a World Wide Web request to the IP address of the external interface (if a range of IP addresses is selected, that range can be designated). The NAT server will then forward the request to the host on the private network. The external user will get a response from the internal machine without knowing (or caring) that it's really on the private network.

Once both interfaces are properly configured, NAT will function. If you now select the **Network Address Translation** feature, you can see the configured interfaces, as shown in Figure 14-37.

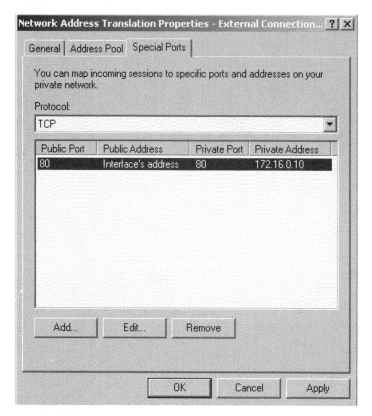

FIGURE 14–36 *Special ports*

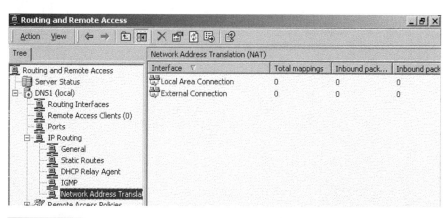

FIGURE 14–37 *NAT configuration complete*

GENERAL CONFIGURATION

Before we leave NAT, let's look at a few general configuration features. To select the NAT properties, right-click **Network Address Translation** and select **Properties**. This reveals the **General** tab of the properties dialog box as depicted in Figure 14-38. As you can see, this tab permits you to control the level of information sent to the Windows 2000 system log. The **Translation Tab** is shown in Figure 14-39. Here you can configure the TTL for TCP and UDP mappings between the internal and external networks. The *Applications* button permits you to define applications on the external network your internal users may run. To enter an application, you'll need to identify it by inbound and outbound protocol (TCP or UDP) and port number.

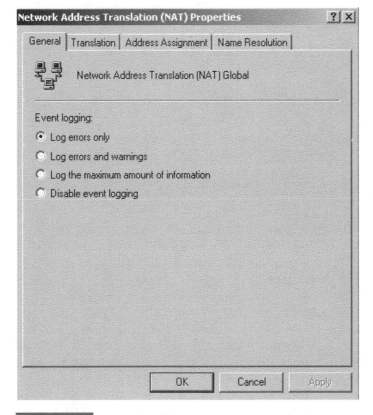

FIGURE 14–38   *Network address properties—General tab*

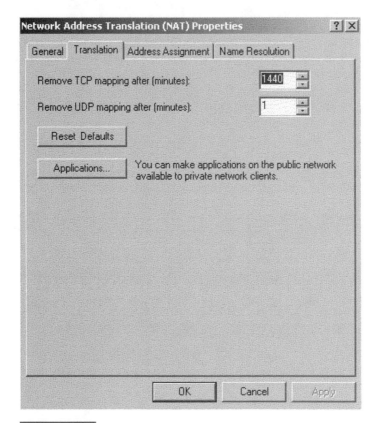

FIGURE 14-39 *Network address properties—Translation tab*

The **Address Assignment tab** (see Figure 14-40) permits you to enable the **DHCP Allocator** function of NAT. This provides a single scope "mini" DHCP server. When you check the **Automatically assign IP addresses by using DHCP** check box, you enable this feature. Ensure you have entered the appropriate network and mask in the **IP address** and **Mask** edit boxes. The selected network must have an IP address on the interface you selected as your private interface. Using the **Exclude** button, you can designate IP addresses (e.g., the address of your private interface) to be excluded from the list of those to be given to clients. Client machines should be configured as DHCP clients. The **DHCP Allocator** function will assign an IP address and subnet mask. It will use the IP address of the private interface as the default gateway and DHCP server address.

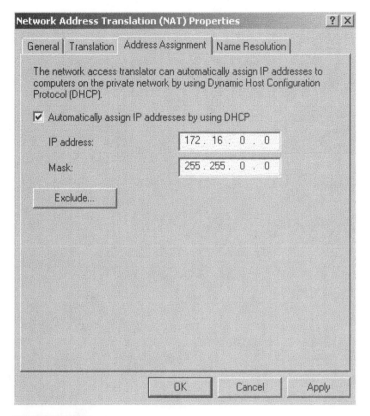

FIGURE 14–40   *Network address properties—Address Assignment tab*

The **Name Resolution** tab is shown in Figure 14-41. By checking the upper check box, you enable the **DNS Proxy Component**. Configured this way, computers on the private network send their DNS requests to the NAT server which relays them to the DNS server it—the NAT server—is configured to use. When this is activated along with the **DHCP Allocator Component**, the NAT server assigns its private interface address to the client as a DNS server address. The **Connect to the public network when a name needs to be resolved** check box permits you to designate a configured demand dial interface (covered later in this chapter) to dial out for DNS information.

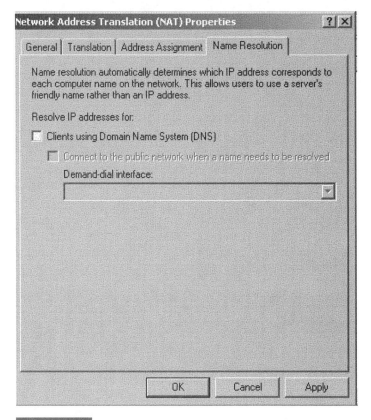

FIGURE 14—41 *Network address properties—Name Resolution tab*

Dynamic Routing

As you will likely remember, we spent a lot of time looking at routing in Chapter 6. One discovery we made was the concept of *dynamic routing*. You'll recall the benefit of such routing was that the routers discussed the network layout among themselves and updated their routing tables accordingly. RRAS allows us to configure our server as a dynamic router using the Routing Information Protocol (RIP) or Open Shortest Path First (OSPF) protocol we discussed in Chapter 6. Installation of these protocols is very similar to installation of the NAT protocol we worked on in the previous section. The configuration, on the other hand, provides many more options. While this section is not intended to be a primer on all aspects of dynamic routing, we'll briefly look at the configurations options which will present a good, if brief, overview of dynamic routing factors.

ROUTING INFORMATION PROTOCOL

To install RIP expand **IP Routing**, right-click **General**, and select **New Routing Protocol**, just as we did earlier to install NAT. This time, we select **RIP version 2 for Internet Protocol**. The RIP icon is now visible under **IP routing** in the RRAS console. Just as we did with NAT, we need to select the interfaces that will participate in routing. We'll add the External Connection interface first. As soon as we select an interface, we are presented with the RIP Properties dialog box shown in Figure 14-42. While RIP will work with the default configuration once the interfaces are added, let's look at the available configuration options.

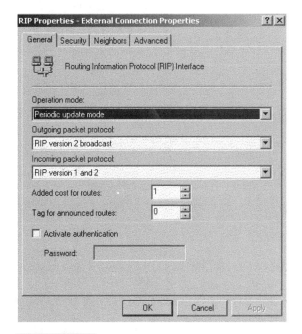

FIGURE 14–42   *RIP interface properties—General tab*

The **Operation mode** window permits you to select **Periodic update mode** or **Auto-static update mode**. The default for LAN interfaces is periodic update. This will force the router to send out RIP announcements at a fixed interval, as configured on the **Advanced** tab. The autostatic mode causes the router to announce only when another RIP router requests an update. Learned routes are stored in the routing table as static routes. Autostatic is the default for demand-dial interfaces.

Outgoing packet protocol provides a choice of how outgoing RIP announcements will be made. The default is **RIP version 2 broadcast**. This mode sends RIP version 2 announcements as broadcasts—this is the appropriate mode for a mixed version 1/version2 environment because RIP version 1 was designed for *forward* compatibility with RIP version 2. You may also select **RIP version 1 broadcast**—RIP version 1 doesn't support classless interdomain routing (supernetting) or custom subnetting because the subnet mask isn't transmitted with the IP address. If all RIP routers on the network support RIP version 2, you may select **RIP version 2 multicast** to enable multicast RIP routing. If you want your router to receive updates from other RIP routers but do not want it to announce its own routes, select **Silent RIP**.

The incoming packet protocol selection allows you to restrict incoming packets to RIP version 1, RIP version 2, or both. You may also select **Ignore incoming packets** to make your router reject all updates.

The **Added cost for routes** window permits you to increase the cost of traversing this interface. By default, this is set to 1, indicating the hop-count. If travel through the interface is at a greater cost, you may raise this value to indicate the increase.

The **Tag for announced routes** field allows you to enter a number that will appear in the interface's RIP version 2 announcements to more easily identify those originating from the interface.

If you want to restrict communications between routers, check the **Activate authentication** check box and enter a password in the **Password** field. This feature is available only on RIP version 2 and will restrict communications to only those routers configured with the same plain-text password. This option permits router identification and control but, because of the plain-text password, it should not be considered a security option.

The **Security** tab, depicted in Figures 14-43 and 14-44, permits you to accept (incoming) or announce (outgoing) all routes, to accept or announce from a specific range of routes, or to reject announcements to or from a specific range of routes. You'll note that Figure 14-43 shows this interface will accept all incoming announcements (the default for both incoming and outgoing announcements) but that we've decided to *announce* only a specific range of routes on this interface (as shown in Figure 14-44).

The **Neighbors** tab, shown in Figure 14-45, determines how the router interface will interact with other routers on its network. The default (**Use broadcast or multicast only**) setting ensures all announcements are sent in accordance with the **Outgoing packet protocol** selected on the **General** tab. By selecting **Use neighbors in addition to broadcast or multicast**, and specifying the neighboring router interface address(es) in the **IP address** window, you may add routers that wouldn't normally be accessed under the **Outgoing packet protocol**. If, on the other hand, you select **Use neighbors instead of broadcast or multicast**, and specify the neighboring router interface address(es) in the **IP address** window, the router(s) you specify will be the only one(s) accessed (the **Outgoing packet protocol** settings will be ignored).

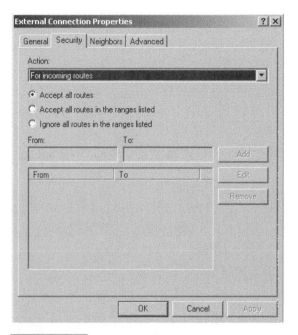

FIGURE 14–43   *RIP interface properties—Security tab: incoming*

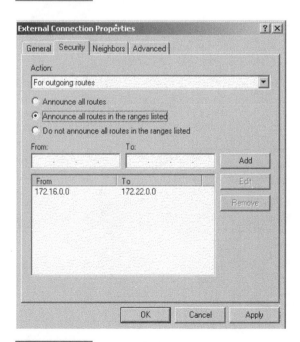

FIGURE 14–44   *RIP interface properties—Security tab: outgoing*

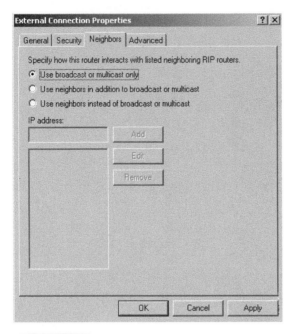

FIGURE 14-45 *RIP interface properties—Neighbors tab*

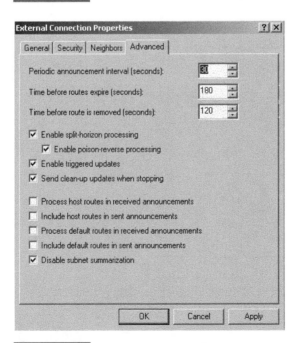

FIGURE 14-46 *RIP interface properties—Advanced tab*

The **Advanced** tab (see Figure 14-46) permits you to configure the announcements times and set a host of other options. The announcement time settings are valid only when the **Periodic update mode** is selected on the **General** tab. The **Periodic announcement interval** controls how often a RIP announcement is sent. You may set this (in seconds) to any value between 15 seconds and 24 hours. The **Time before routes expire** value controls the route's time to live. This may be set (in seconds) to any value between 15 seconds and 72 hours. **Time before route is removed** controls how long after a route's time to live has expired that it will actually be removed from the routing table. You may set this (in seconds) to any value between 15 seconds and 72 hours.

The rest of the advanced options are covered in Table 14.1.

TABLE 14.1   *RIP Interface Advanced Options*

Option	Description
Enable split-horizon processing	When checked (the default), routes learned on a particular network won't be announced on that network.
Enable poison-reverse processing	This option (available only when split-horizon processing is turned on) ensures routes learned on a particular network are announced as unreachable on that network (enabled by default).
Enable triggered updates	When selected, new routes and metric changes will trigger an immediate update. The update will include only the changes. This is enabled by default.
Send clean-up updates when stopping	When this is set (the default), the router, during shut down, advertises the routes through the selected interface as unavailable.
Process host routes in received announcements	When selected, host routes received in RIP announcements are accepted; this is off by default.
Include host routes in sent announcements	When selected, host routes are included in RIP announcements; this is off by default.
Process default routes in received announcements	When selected, default routes (0.0.0.0) received in RIP announcements are accepted; this is off by default.
Include default routes in sent announcements	When selected, default routes (0.0.0.0) are sent in RIP announcements; this is off by default.
Disable subnet summarization	When checked (the default), subnet routes are not summarized when announced on a network that is not a subnet of the class-based network that contains the subnet route. This option is available only when the *Outgoing packet protocol* is set *to RIP version 2 broadcast* or *RIP version 2 multicast.*

Now that we've gone through all the interface options, let's add our other interface (Local Area Connection) to complete configuration of our RIP router. Once complete, our RIP router console should look like that in Figure 14-47. Over time, the Responses Sent and Responses Received columns will show RIP router traffic.

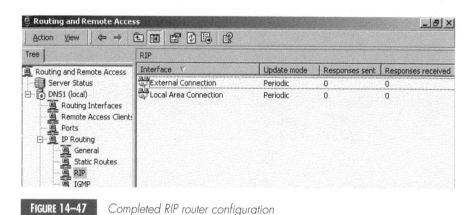

FIGURE 14-47   *Completed RIP router configuration*

Before we move on, let's look at the general RIP router properties. These are accessed by right-clicking the RIP icon and selecting **Properties** from the context menu. The RIP properties dialog box has two tabs. The General tab (see Figure 14-48) permits you to set the time the router will wait before sending a triggered update. This delay time ensures updates are delivered in groups and do not result in continuous streams of communication. The tab also permits you to select logging options.

The Security tab (see Figure 14-49) allows you to accept or ignore announcements from all or selected routers. This is similar to the Security function for the interface, but settings here apply to the entire router.

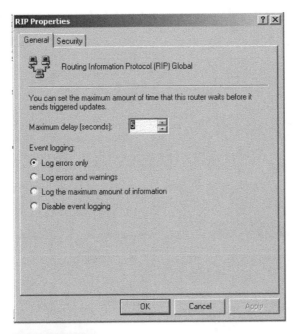

FIGURE 14–48   *RIP properties—General tab*

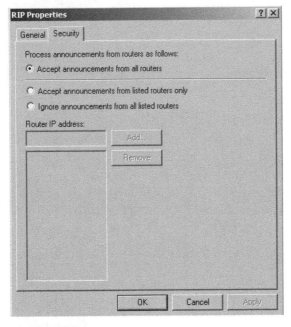

FIGURE 14–49   *RIP properties—Security tab*

OPEN SHORTEST PATH FIRST

You'll remember from Chapter 6 that RIP routers have some limitations, not the least of which is a maximum hop count of 15. If our network will require more than 15 hops, we'll need to configure our router to use OSPF routing, which is far less constrained than RIP.

OSPF is installed into RRAS in the same manner as RIP and NAT. Install OSPF and add your External Connection interface just as we did with RIP. As with RIP, your OSPF router will function with the default configuration, but we should spend some time looking at the interface and router configuration options available.

When you add each interface, the OSPF Interface Properties dialog box is revealed. The General tab depicted in Figure 14-50 is displayed by default.

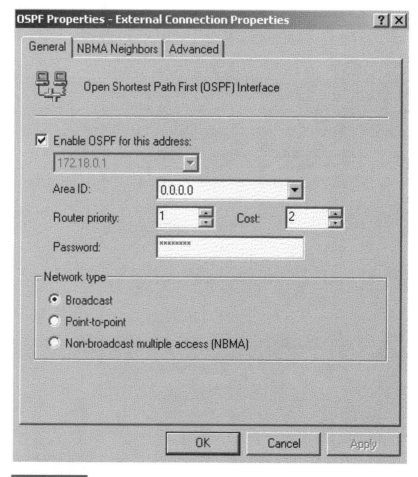

FIGURE 14-50   *OSPF interface properties—General tab*

The first setting on the tab permits you to enable or disable OSPF for a particular IP address. We've bound only one IP address to the interface so we aren't able to select a particular address in this case. If the interface had multiple addresses, and we wanted to configure routing for each, we'd need to select each address and complete the settings on each tab individually for each address.

The *Area ID* selection shows the area IDs available to the interface. Although an area ID looks like an IP address, it is *not*. OSPF routers are typically assigned to "areas." Routers within the area share a common link state database. Areas are connected by routers with interfaces in different areas—these routers are called *area border routers*. The displayed area ID (0.0.0.0) is reserved for the backbone route—we'll see how to create our own areas a bit later in this section.

The router priority setting determines if this router will be selected as the network's *designated router*. A designated router acts as a hub for the distribution of OSPF routing information to the network. The router with the highest router ID will take precedence. A router with a priority of zero will never become a designated router. (When a new router interface is configured, it will defer to an existing designated router without regard to the priority setting.)

The *Cost* setting permits you to establish a cost for this interface—this is similar to "costing" a RIP interface. The lower the cost, the more traffic will pass through this interface.

You can set a password for this router interface in the *Password* edit box. As in RIP routing, this is a plain-text password, which provides identification but not security for OSPF routers in the area. If passwords are enabled (they are by default), all interfaces in the same area on the same network must use identical passwords. The default password assigned to all interfaces at installation is '12345678.' We'll see how to enable or disable passwords for a particular area when we look at OSPF general configuration.

You must ensure the appropriate *Network type* is selected. *Broadcast* networks are Ethernet, Token Ring, and FDDI. *Point-to-point* networks are those between a single pair of points such as T1/E1, T3/E3, ISDN, and other dial-up links. A *nonbroadcast multiple access* (NBMA) network would be a network like X.25, Frame Relay, and Asynchronous Transfer Mode. When NBMA is selected, the options on the NBMA tab are activated.

The *NBMA Neighbors* tab provides a capability to configure how the interface will operate with neighboring nonbroadcast multiple access OSPF routers (see Figure 14-51). Unless the network type is set to NBMA, this dialog box will be disabled. As on the tab, we must first select the IP address that we wish to configure. Again, since our interface has only one IP address, we are unable to alter this setting. The rest of the dialog box permits you to enter the IP addresses for neighboring routers, along with a router priority. The priority entered determines the eligibility of the neighbors to become a designated

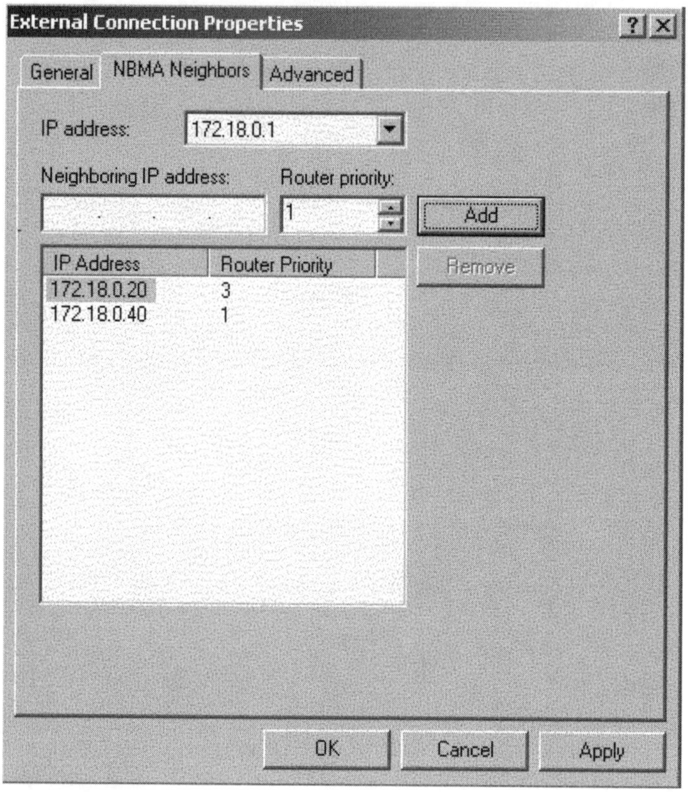

FIGURE 14–51   *OSPF interface properties—NBMA Neighbors tab*

router as explained above. The router currently being configured will use the priorities to determine the sequence for querying its neighbors to determine if they are designated routers.

The interface Advanced tab, once again, permits us to select the desired IP address and lets us configure the interface's timing and size properties. The default settings are shown in Figure 14-52, and the function of each setting is summarized in Table 14.2

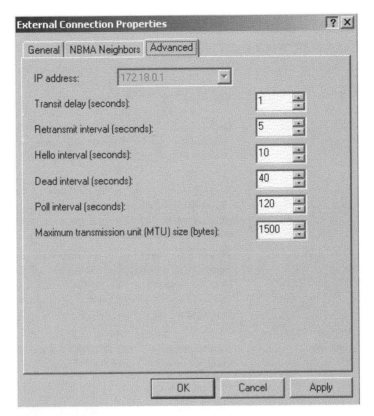

FIGURE 14–52   *OSPF interface properties—Advanced tab*

TABLE 14.2   *OSPF Interface Advanced Options*

Option	Description
Transit Delay	This is the estimated number of seconds to transmit an update packet over this interface.
Retransmit Interval	This represents the number of seconds the router will wait before retransmitting an announcement to an adjacent router. This should be greater than the expected round-trip time between two routers. Too large a value will result in needless retransmissions.

TABLE 14.2	OSPF Interface Advanced Options (continued)

Option	Description
Hello Interval	An OSPF router sends out a periodic OSPF Hello packet containing configuration information, such as the router ID and the list of neighboring routers for which the router has received a Hello packet. This sets the frequency with which those packets are sent. This must be the same for all OSPF router interfaces connected to the common network. (The default of 10 seconds works well for a LAN. An X.25 network would need about 30 seconds.)
Dead Interval	If a neighboring router doesn't receive a Hello packet within this interval, it will decide the router is down. This should be a multiple of the Hello Interval and must be the same for all OSPF router interfaces connected to the common network.
Poll Interval	This setting is only for NBMA interfaces. Once an NBMA interface has exceeded its Dead Interval, its neighbors send Hello packets at this interval to determine if it has come back on-line. This is typically set at twice the Dead Interval. (The default of 120 is the recommended value for an X.25 network.)
Maximum Transmission Unit Size	This is the maximum size of an IP datagram that can be sent without fragmentation. The 1,500 byte default is for an Ethernet network, while the MTU for a 100 MB FDDI network would be 4,352 bytes.

Now that we've gone through all the interface options, let's add our other interface (Local Area Connection) to complete configuration of our OSPF router. Once complete, our OSPF router console should look like that pictured in Figure 14-53.

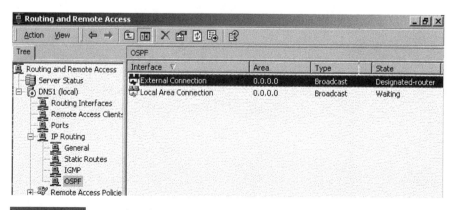

FIGURE 14–53	Completed OSPF router configuration

With our router interfaces configured, let's take a look at the general OSPF router properties. These are accessed by right-clicking the OSPF icon and selecting **Properties** from the context menu. The OSPF properties dialog box has four tabs. The General tab (Figure 14-54) permits you to set the router identification. This is a unique value that identifies the OSPF router to the network. It is conventionally the smallest IP address assigned to one of those router's interfaces. You may also designate the router as an *Autonomous System Boundary Router*. Such a router advertises external routing information from other route sources like RIP or static routers. Finally, this tab allows the same logging selections as the other functions we've examined.

As you may imagine, the **Areas** tab permits you to add and configure OSPF areas (see Figure 14-55). To add an area, click **Add** to reveal the dialog box shown in Figure 14-56. First, select an area ID and type it in the appropriate window. Next, decide if the plain-text password we discussed above should be enabled for this area (the default is to enable). A *stub area* is an OSPF area that does not consider external routes. If you select this as a stub area routing to external destinations will be through default routing only. You

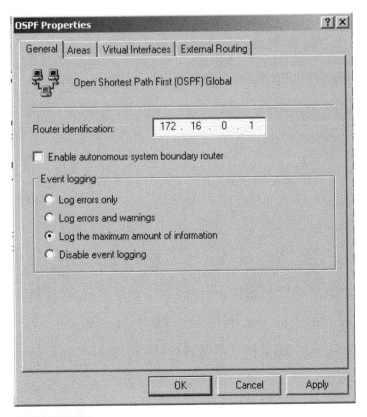

FIGURE 14—54   *OSPF properties—General tab*

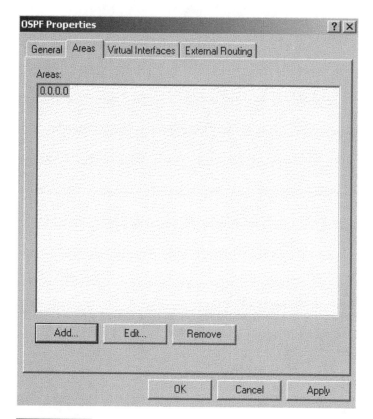

FIGURE 14–55   *OSPF properties—Areas tab*

cannot select this if this is the backbone (0.0.0.0) area. The *stub metric* is the cost of using the default route out of the area. If you select the Ranges tab, you can enter the IP address and mask pairs that belong in the area (see Figure 14-57.)

The Virtual Interfaces tab allows you to add virtual interfaces to create *virtual links* for this router. A virtual link is a connection between an area border router on the backbone network and an area border router not directly connected to the backbone. The link permits exchange of routing information between these routers. Addition and configuration procedures are similar to those covered earlier.

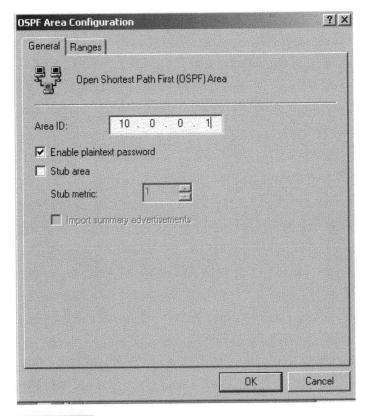

FIGURE 14–56 *OSPF properties—add areas: general*

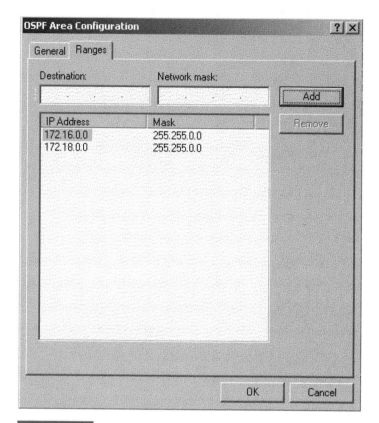

FIGURE 14–57   *OSPF properties—add areas: ranges*

The External Routing tab is used only when **Enable autonomous system boundary router** is checked on the General tab (see Figure 14-58.) Using this dialog box you may specify external routing sources to accept or reject from your OSPF announcements. Carefully note the verbiage used against the radio buttons at the top of the dialog box. The upper choice will accept all routes except those you check below under *Route sources*. The lower choice will accept *only* those you've checked under *Route sources*. If you click **Route Filters**, it will reveal the dialog box shown in Figure 14-59. This option permits you to accept or ignore specific external routes based on the destination interface.

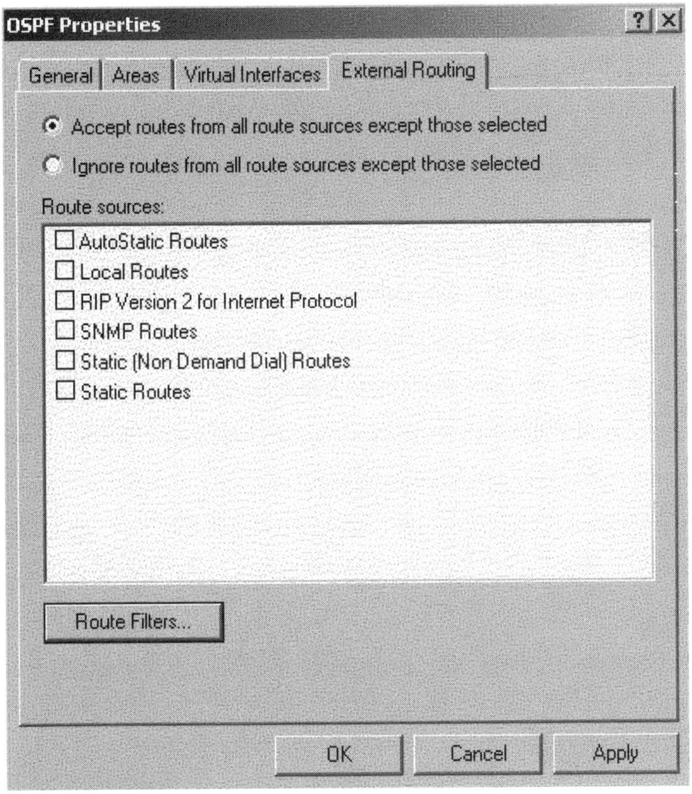

FIGURE 14–58 *OSPF properties—external routing*

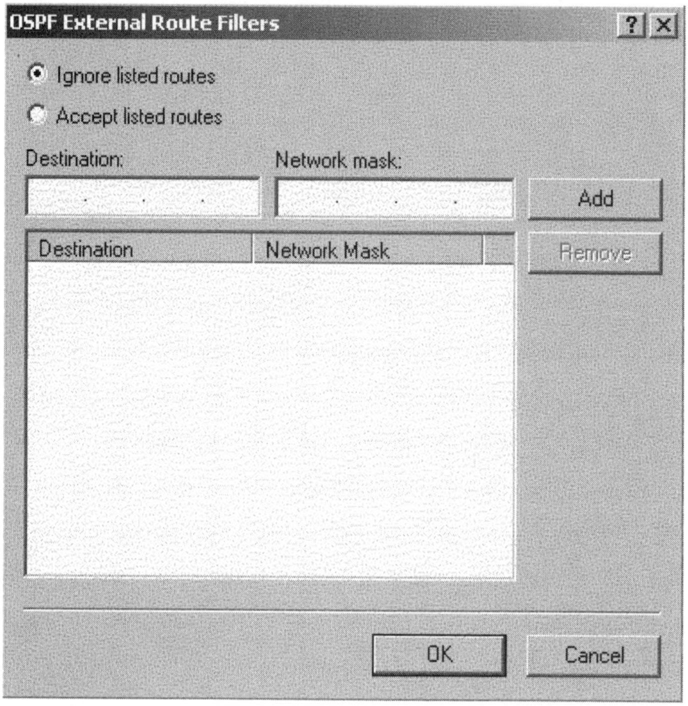

FIGURE 14-59 *OSPF properties—external route filters*

Multicast Routing

As you might imagine, multicast routing requires a multicast routing protocol. Windows 2000 doesn't come with one, but RRAS is an extensible platform, so third-party protocols could be developed and easily added to the system. Windows 2000 RRAS will support a multicast forwarding mode, which provides some limited routing between external and internal networks. Windows 2000 computers are fully multicast capable, so a Windows 2000 internal network will be able to participate in multicasting through the multicast forwarder.

RRAS' multicast capabilities come from its Internet Group Membership Protocol (IGMP). RRAS has an IGMP *proxy* mode and an IGMP *router* mode. The proxy mode is to be bound to interfaces that face the external, multicast capable, network. This mode permits the interface to connect to other router interfaces that are operating in IGMP router mode (or actual multicast capable routers). The router mode should be bound to the interfaces on the internal network that service the multicast capable listening hosts. In router mode, the interface listens for IGMP traffic from the hosts, updates the multicast forwarding table, and sends IGMP queries.

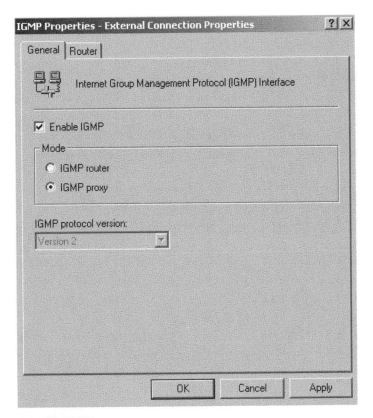

FIGURE 14–60   *Add IGMP proxy interface*

Configuration of IGMP forwarding is fairly simple. IGMP is installed in RRAS by default. To add interfaces, we simply right-click the **IGMP** icon under **IP Routing** and proceed as we have before. First, we'll add the external interface and designate it as an IGMP proxy, as shown in Figure 14-60. Next, we add our internal interface as an IGMP router (see Figure 14-61). When the interfaces are added, our IGMP forwarding capability is operating, as indicated in Figure 14-62.

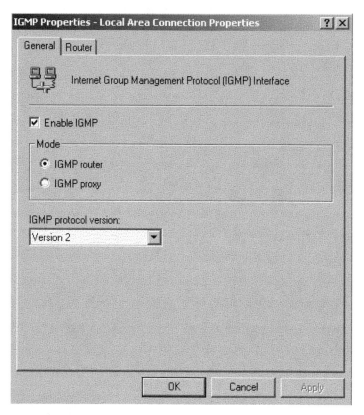

FIGURE 14-61 *Adding IGMP router interface*

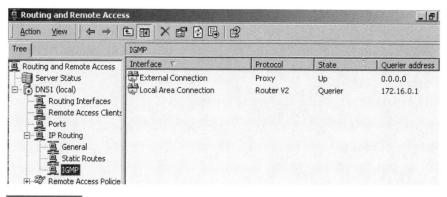

FIGURE 14-62 *Completed IGMP forwarder*

Routing and Remote Access Service— Virtual Private Networking

Today, many companies utilize the Internet not only for gaining access to the information it contains, but also to provide network connections to employees who are out of office or on the road. It has always been the case that utilizing the Internet is a much cheaper form of connecting remote locations than using dedicated direct links or long distance phone lines. However, there have always been concerns about transferring confidential or secret information though the public Internet. The solution to this problem is to create a virtual private network (VPN) based on encrypted tunnels provided by the Point-to-Point Tunneling Protocol (PPTP) or Layer Two Tunneling Protocol (L2TP).

The idea behind these encrypted tunnels is based on the encapsulation and encryption of IP packets into a secured tunnel. A tunnel is nothing more than an idea of sending streams of encapsulated packets in secured envelopes that cannot be easily decrypted. Even if somebody captures such an envelope during its travel through the Internet, its contents will not make sense.

How Does PPTP Work?

To better understand the tunneling concept, let's take a look at how the PPTP works. PPTP is a network protocol that provides a secure way to transfer data from a remote client to a private server or network by creating a VPN across TCP/IP-based data networks.

The networking technology of PPTP was created as an extension of the Point-to-Point Protocol (PPP) referred to in RFC 1171. PPTP is a network protocol that encapsulates PPP packets into IP datagrams for transmission over the Internet or other public TCP/IP-based networks. PPTP can also be used in private LAN-to-LAN networking. The PPTP encapsulation technique is based on the Internet standard GRE (generic routing encapsulation) which allows tunneling of protocols over the Internet. (For more information about this, review RFC 1701 and RFC 1702. You can find this and other RFCs at www.cis.ohio-state.edu/rfc/ or http://www.rfc-editor.org.)

A typical PPTP scenario assumes the remote client already has an Internet connection from its local Internet Service Provider (ISP). Clients may use computers running Windows NT Server or Workstation Version 4.0, Dial-Up Networking, and the remote access protocol PPP to connect to an ISP. Being connected to the Internet, the client makes a second Dial-Up Networking call over the Internet connection. Data sent using this second connection is in the form of IP datagrams that contain PPP packets. This second call actually creates a VPN connection to a PPTP server on the private enterprise LAN—this is referred to as a *tunnel*.

Let's see how the PPTP client creates a packet to send to the PPTP server. For the purpose of our discussion, let's assume that the PPTP client is connected to the Internet using a LAN adapter (the situation changes slightly if the PPTP client uses a communication device such as modem).

The process of encapsulating the data in the PPTP datagrams is illustrated in Figure 14-63.

As you can see, when the application on the PPTP client computer sends a packet to the PPTP server, the data is first encapsulated in the IP datagram using the private IP address—the one that was assigned when the PPTP connection was established. Then, the IP packet gets encapsulated into the PPP packet and is encrypted through the PPTP and GRE modules. The encrypted data is inserted, then, into the IP datagram once more. In this case the real, globally routable IP address is used. The packet is transmitted, then, over the Internet. On the receiving end, the PPTP server reverses the procedure. It receives the packet from the routing network and sends it across the private network to the destination computer. The PPTP server does this by processing the PPTP packet to obtain the private network computer name or address information in the encapsulated PPP packet.

The key point of this is that packets travel through the Internet in the PPTP tunnel—even if a third party computer in the Internet captures the packet, it will not be able to use the data inside it.

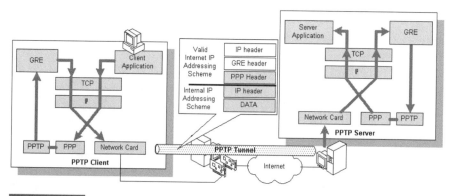

FIGURE 14–63   *PPTP concepts*

Layer Two Tunneling Protocol

Now that we understand PPTP we also understand the general concept of L2TP. Like PPTP, L2TP creates an encrypted tunnel and uses PPP. Unlike PPTP, which requires an IP-based network, L2TP can use IP, Frame Relay, X.25, or ATM. Using header compression, L2TP can operate with 4 bytes of overhead. PPTP does not use header compression and has a 6-byte per packet overhead. Unlike PPTP, L2TP features native tunnel authentication. Both PPTP and L2TP may be used, however, with IPSec. Since IPSec provides its own authentication tunnel, authentication is available under both protocols. PPTP, however, provides PPP authentication, which cannot be disabled. Using IPSec with PPTP will result, therefore, in "double encryption" which will significantly degrade performance. Unlike PPTP, L2TP has no native encryption scheme. L2TP encryption is available only through IPSec. To use L2TP, you must install machine certificates for machine-level authentication of VPN clients. This is accomplished through Windows 2000 Certificate Services and is beyond the scope of this book.

Configuring a VPN

Configuring a VPN with RRAS is remarkably easy. If you click on the Ports icon on the RRAS console, you'll discover that RRAS already has five PPTP and five L2TP ports installed (see Figure 14-64). You can add or subtract ports by right clicking the **Ports** icon and selecting **Properties**. The **Configure** button allows you to alter the total number of ports.

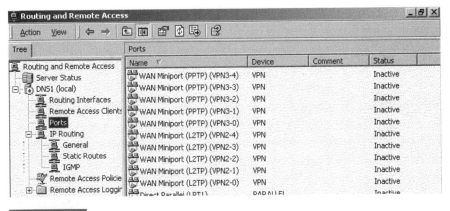

FIGURE 14-64   *VPN ports*

We'll configure a client to access the RRAS server and our internal network using a VPN. We'll assume the client machine has a routed connection to the Internet and will use the VPN connection to participate on our network. Since we're not going into Certificate Services, we'll complete our connection using PPTP. With the VPN ports already set up, we need to make only one more configuration to our RRAS server. When the PPTP client connects with the RRAS server, it will need a local IP address to use on the network. Since we'll configure the host we have operating on the External Connection interface (which is on the 172.18.0.0 network), we'll need to ensure our RRAS server has some IP addresses on the 172.16.0.0 (Local Area Connection) network to give out. To configure this, right-click the RRAS server icon, select **Properties**, and click on the **IP** tab to reveal the dialog box shown in Figure 14-65. By default, we expect to get our IP addresses from a DHCP server, as you can see in the figure. Since we don't have a DHCP server, we'll need to configure our own IP address pool.

Note

When RRAS requests IP addresses from DHCP, by default it reserves them in blocks of 10. This means if you configure RRAS to use DHCP for IP addressing, it will automatically take up 10 addresses. When the eleventh client needs an IP address, your RRAS server will allocate a total of 20 addresses. While this arrangement works well in a high-volume remote access network, if your DHCP server has only a few IP addresses to give out, it may create a problem. You can add the following registry key to set your own IP address blocking: \Hkey_Local_Machine\System\CurrentControlSet\Services\RemoteAccess\Parameters\Ip\InitialAddressPoolSize. This is a REG_DWORD entry. If you set it to three, for instance, RRAS will initially take only three DHCP addresses and when the fourth address is required, it will reserve a total of only six.

Select **Static Address pool** and click **Add** to enter a range of IP addresses (see Figure 14-66). VPN clients will be given an IP address between 172.16.0.20 and 172.16.0.29 when they connect with the server.

Letting the Client Pick Its Own IP Address

You may want to allow a client computer to designate its own IP address when it makes a VPN (or dial-up) connection. Although DHCP assigned addresses will get us on the network, if the client depends on a particular IP address to provide a specific function or support a unique application, it must designate the desired IP address when it connects. (The requested IP address must not be, of course, in any DHCP or RRAS address pool.) The configuration is easily done on the client side simply by entering a static IP address for the connection, just as we'd do for a normal LAN connection. Unfortunately, The RRAS server will reject the connection attempt unless you make a modification to the registry. Set HKEY_LOCL_MACHINE\System\CurrentControlSet\Services\RemoteAccess\Parameters\Ip\AllowClientIpAddresses (REG_DWORD) to 1 and the server will readily permit client-requested IP addresses.

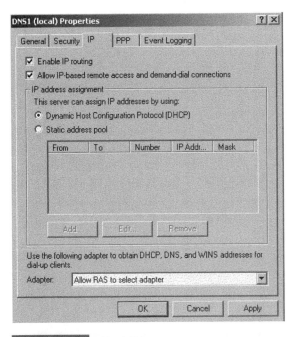

FIGURE 14-65   *RRAS IP properties*

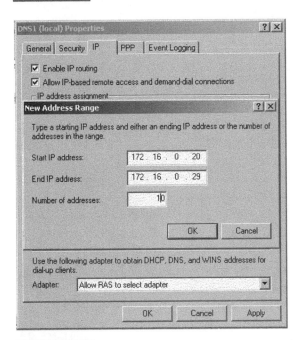

FIGURE 14-66   *Add new address range*

Now that our server is configured, we can turn our attention to configuring the client. This is a very easy wizard-based installation. To begin, go to **Start | Settings | Network and Dial Up Connections** and select **Make New Connection**. This will launch the **Network Connection Wizard**. As you step through the wizard, you are first asked what kind of network connection you wish to create. As indicated in Figure 14-67, we'll select **Connect to a private network through the Internet**.

Next, we need to indicate the address (server name or IP address) of the remote RRAS server we wish to use for VPN. In this case, we assume the IP address is not mapped in a DNS server but can be routed through the Internet so we've entered the server's IP address, as depicted in Figure 14-68. (Once again, you'll note the actual IP address we're using is from the private address space, which is not routable through the Internet. This is because we're simulating the Internet in our small academic network. If we were actually to use this on the Internet, the server would need a valid Internet IP address.)

Next, we are asked if the connection should be just for ourselves or for all machine users. (See Figure 14-69) If we elect to have a connection only for ourselves, the configuration information will be stored in our profile.

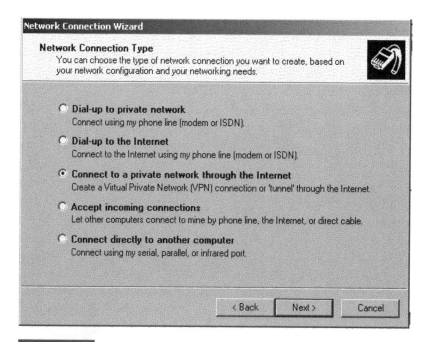

Connection availability

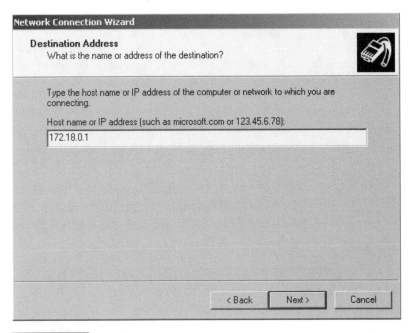

FIGURE 14–68   *Destination address*

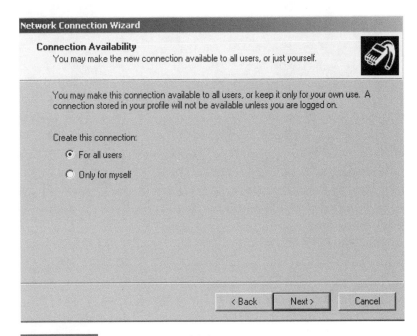

FIGURE 14–69   *Connection availability*

The next selection, depicted in Figure 14-70, asks us if we want to enable **Internet Connection Sharing**. This Windows 2000 feature provides a modem sharing capability to make your machine a minirouter between the network and the VPN connection you're creating. It's principally intended for small network modem sharing. It forces the network to use an IP address from the private addressing space on the internal network. Since we're going to use RRAS for our routing needs, we'll not take advantage of this option.

Once we complete the VPN installation, the wizard permits us to log onto the server, as shown in Figure 14-71. The account we use must be recognized on the VPN server and it must be allowed Dial-In access, as depicted in Figure 14-72. (Even though this is *not* a dial-in connection, Windows 2000 treats dial-in and VPN authentication in the same manner.)

Once you've logged on and been authenticated, the connection is established. Figure 14-73 shows the clients **Network and Dial-up Connections**. You'll note a new connection indicated for the VPN.

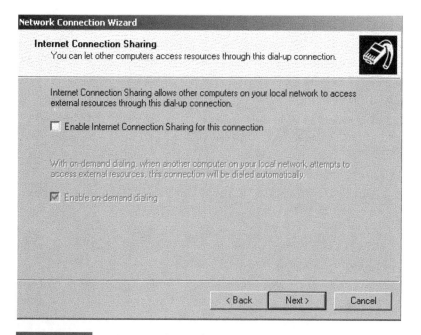

FIGURE 14-70 *Internet connection sharing*

FIGURE 14–71   *Log onto VPN*

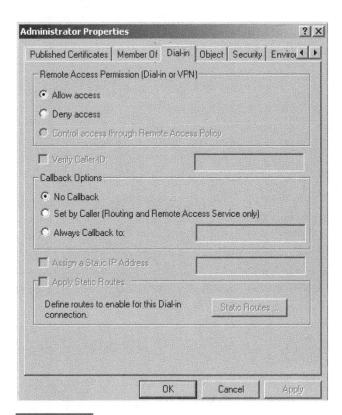

FIGURE 14–72   *Allow dial-in access*

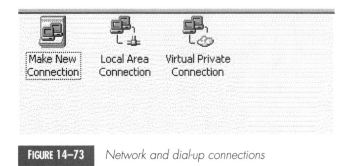

FIGURE 14–73   *Network and dial-up connections*

If we look at the ports on the RRAS server, we see that one of the PPTP ports is now active (see Figure 14-74). Double clicking the port reveals the dialog box shown in Figure 14-75. Looking at the dialog box, we see the connected user, the line speed, and how long the line has been connected. It also shows connection statistics and errors as well as the connection's IP address.

Note the connection has an IP address from the range we selected. If you have accomplished all the configuration steps, you'll be able to function in the 172.16.0.0 network even though your computer has a LAN card on the 172.18.0.0 network. This is because you have a virtual private network connection to the server that uses an IP address in the 172.16.0.0 network. Try pinging computers in the other network to prove to yourself it works. (Make sure you've removed all the other routing features form RRAS to prove you're actually routing through the VPN.)

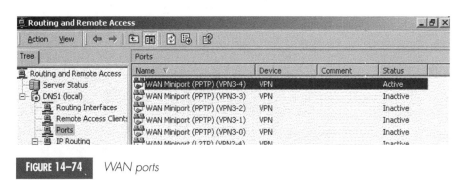

FIGURE 14–74   *WAN ports*

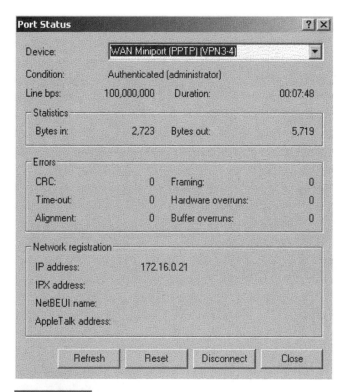

FIGURE 14–75 *Port status*

CONFIGURING VPN PROPERTIES

Installing VPN seemed pretty straightforward because we used the wizard. Once installed, however, we can still manipulate a number of important VPN properties. To access the properties, right-click on the connection and select Properties, just as with a regular LAN connection. This will reveal the dialog box shown in Figure 14-76.

The General tab permits us to change the RRAS server address. It also provides a *Dial another connection first* capability. This is intended for dial-up connections (which we will discuss later in this chapter). This option allows you to select a connection to dial out to make the actual physical connection before the system creates the virtual connection over the same line. In the present case, this is not an issue since we're using an existing LAN connection to go to the Internet (presumably through a router).

Except for the ability to include a domain in the logon box, the Options tab is used principally for dial-up networking—we'll discuss it later in the chapter. The Security tab is depicted in Figure 14-77. This configuration is used both for VPNs and dial-up connections. If you select the Typical settings, you can choose between *secured password* and *smart card* authentication.

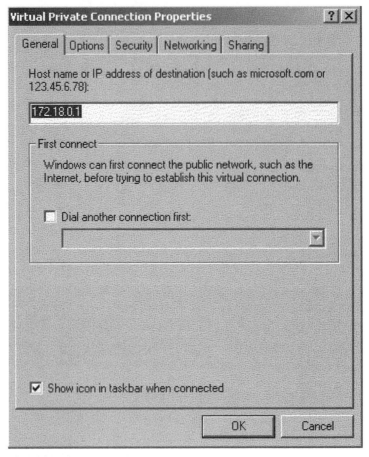

FIGURE 14–76   *VPN properties—General tab*

You may also have the connection automatically use your Windows logon information (this would work well if you had configured the connection as a personal connection). You can also require data encryption. (Since this is a VPN connection, it wouldn't make much sense to go through the trouble of creating a VPN and allowing unencrypted data.) You may also select the Advanced settings to control specific authentication protocols. The default is the Microsoft Challenge Authentication Protocol (MS-CHAP), but you can select other protocols, including unencrypted password and the Extensible Authentication Protocol.

Note   A smart card is a small hardware device that plugs into a system and acts as a security key for a particular user.

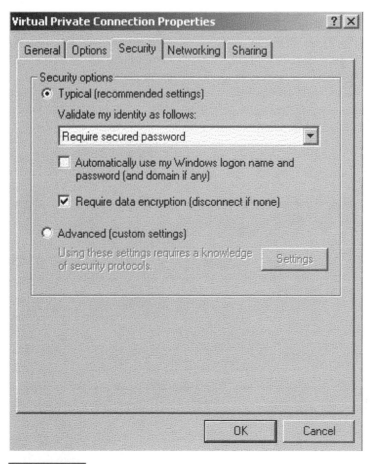

FIGURE 14-77   *VPN properties—Security tab*

Extensible Authentication Protocol

The Extensible Authentication Protocol (EAP) uses an arbitrary authentication mechanism negotiated by the remote access client and the server. It can be used to support a number of authentication schemes to include smart cards. When EAP is used with smart cards, the authenticator can obtain a name, PIN, and card token value from the client. Both the remote access client and the server must support the same EAP type.

The Networking tab allows you to configure the type of VPN connection you will use. You may remember we said we'd use PPTP instead of L2TP because we weren't going into Certificate Services. Did you wonder how we got the PPTP connection without configuring it? You'll notice the choices for *Type of VPN server I am calling* in Figure 14-78. We can select Automatic, PPTP, or L2TP. Automatic is selected by default. Under Automatic, L2TP is tried first and then PPTP if the L2TP connection is unsuccessful. If you want to see the effect of this setting, terminate your VPN connection, set this to L2TP, and try to reconnect. Unless your machines have installed certificates, the connection will fail. While on the Networking tab, you may also configure the other network components used by the VPN connection.

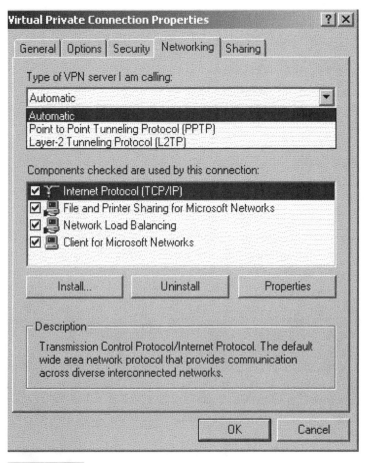

FIGURE 14–78   *VPN properties—Networking tab*

The Sharing tab permits you to configure *Internet Connection Sharing* as explained above.

ROUTER TO ROUTER VPNS

Up to now, we've looked at using a VPN between a client and a remote server. What if we want to use the Internet for connectivity between networks? In this case, we'll want to configure our router to connect to another router through a VPN. This is exactly the same concept as the one we outlined above, but the RRAS server becomes the client of another RRAS server. The first step in this procedure is to create a router interface for our RRAS server.

Open your RRAS console, right-click **Routing Interfaces**, and select **New Demand-dial Interface** (see Figure 14-79). This launches the **Demand Dial Interface Wizard**. (Although we're asking for a demand dial interface, we'll soon configure it as a VPN interface NOT a demand dial interface. I know this is confusing, but understanding these nuances is why IT professionals get the big bucks!) As you navigate through the wizard, the first screen asks you for the name of the interface. In Figure 14-80 you'll note we've provided a meaningful name.

Next, we designate the type of connection. Figure 14-81 shows that we'll connect with a VPN.

Next, we select the VPN type (Figure 14-82). The principle here is the same as we discussed for the client configuration. The next screen requests the IP address or name of the other VPN router. As you can see in Figure 14-83, we'll connect to a router on our other network segment. Next, we select the type of protocol we'll use (this *is* a TCP/IP book, so we'll stick with IP). You'll also notice that the wizard will help us create an account to enable another router to dial in. We already have an account to use so we won't select this option (see Figure 14-84).

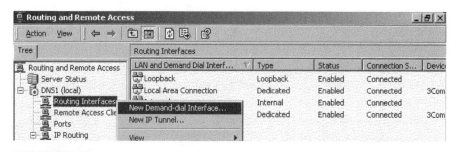

FIGURE 14-79 *Select interface*

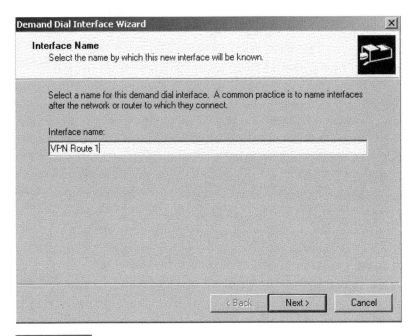

FIGURE 14-80   *Interface name*

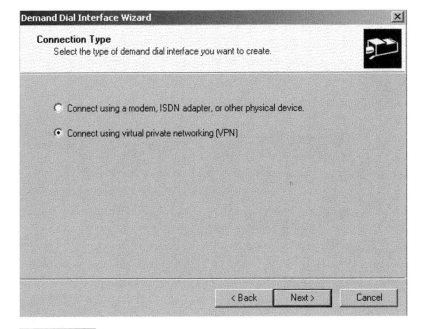

FIGURE 14-81   *Connection type*

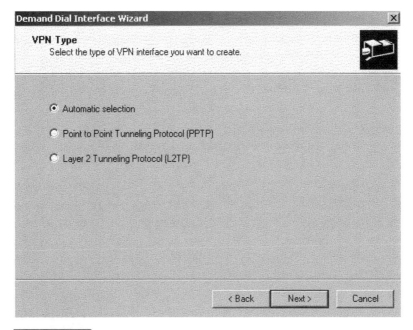

FIGURE 14–82   *VPN type*

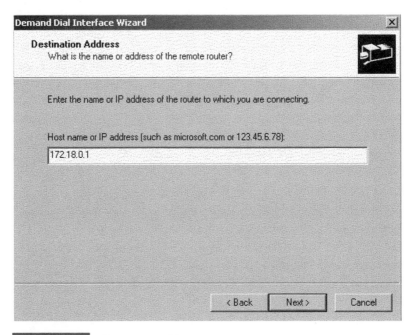

FIGURE 14–83   *Destination address*

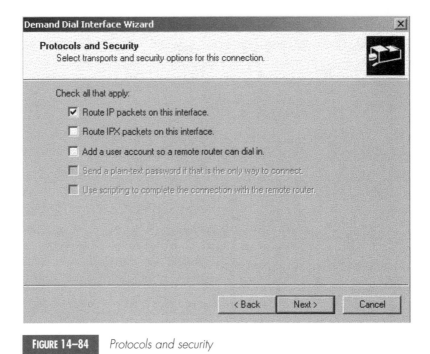

FIGURE 14–84   *Protocols and security*

The next screen asks for dial-out credentials (see Figure 14-85). This represents the account the router will use when dialing out to the other router. This account must have dial-in permission on the remote router just as the case with the individual client connection. If you omit the domain name in this box, it assumes the home domain of the remote router.

You can now complete the wizard; the new interface appears in the routing interfaces list shown in Figure 14-86. Our configuration is nearly complete but we've left out an important part. Right now, our RRAS server will easily communicate with the remote VPN server but our machine doesn't know that it should route clients over the connection. You'll remember we created a static router before by configuring Static Routes. We need to do this for our VPN interface. Using the procedures we outlined earlier we created the static route depicted in Figure 14-87. You'll notice the value for Gateway is None. This is because our VPN interface doesn't have an IP address to identify. Our route is configured as the default route (0.0.0.0). Any messages arriving at the RRAS server for a network outside the local network will be routed to the VPN interface and over our VPN connection. If this connection were for only a select number of networks, we'd use one or more specific routes instead of the default routing.

Demand Dial Interface Wizard   ⊠

Dial Out Credentials
Configure the user name and password to be used when connecting to the remote
router.

You need to set the dial out credentials that this interface will use when connecting to
the remote router. These credentials must match the dial in credentials configured on
the remote router.

User name:	administrator
Domain:	
Password:	✕✕✕✕✕✕✕✕
Confirm password:	✕✕✕✕✕✕✕✕

< Back   Next >   Cancel

FIGURE 14-85   *Dial-Out credentials*

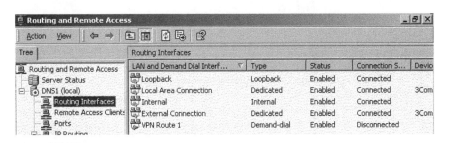

FIGURE 14-86   *New VPN interface*

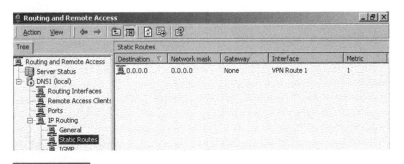

FIGURE 14-87   *VPN static route*

There is just one more step to completing our router-to-router connection. We need to connect to the remote server. To do this return to **Routing Interfaces**, right-click the **VPN interface**, and select **Connect**, as shown in Figure 14-88. Your VPN router is now up and running and will route messages using PPTP between networks.

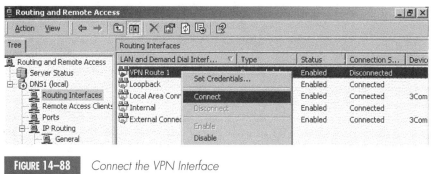

FIGURE 14-88   *Connect the VPN Interface*

Routing and Remote Access Service— Dial-Up Networking

When we speak of *remote access*, most people think about *dial-up* access. This is reasonable because the telephone line is the most ubiquitous data communication channel in the world today. Windows 2000 RRAS provides complete dial-up networking support. The Windows 2000 RRAS communicates over telephone lines using PPP. The Windows 2000 dial-up client is capable of both PPP and Serial Line Internet Protocol (SLIP).

Serial Line Internet Protocol

SLIP is an industry standard that dates back to 1984. SLIP was originally developed by students at the University of California-Berkeley as a protocol for transmitting TCP/IP packets between UNIX computers over serial lines (e.g., Public Switched Telephone Network—PSTN). SLIP is a small, efficient protocol but it offers no advanced features such as error checking or data compression (there is a separate version of the protocol called CSLIP that does provide some compression). CSLIP utilizes VanJacobsen compression. In some Microsoft implementations of SLIP, CSLIP is invoked through the VJ compression check box. For this to work properly, both sides of the communication must select compression.

SLIP supports only TCP/IP and cannot make automatic connections to the receiving host. SLIP network connections are typically automated by running a logon script once the client has accessed the remote server. (Without a script, the only option is to open a terminal window and perform the logon manually.) Limitations in the protocol prevent the use of encrypted authentication—all logons are conducted using clear text, a very insecure practice.

In addition to its other limitations, SLIP will not permit the client to receive any automatic protocol configuration information from the remote server. This information must be entered prior to attempting to access the server. The IP address and other information selected must be consistent with the LAN being accessed through SLIP. If an IP address that won't work on the LAN is used, communication likely will be impossible. This is a serious limitation in remote access because it means every remote called must be assigned a valid IP address whether they will use the network continuously or will only dial in periodically. There is rarely an excess of IP addresses in modern networks and this requirement can put an even greater constraint on that commodity.

Point-to-Point Protocol

PPP provides all the support found lacking under SLIP. Not constrained to serial lines like SLIP, PPP operates over a variety of media and can support a number of transport protocols. PPP supported protocols include AppleTalk, DECnet, NetBEUI, TCP/IP, and IPX.

PPP uses the Link Control Protocol (LCP) to manage and monitor the connection. LCP provides error checking and automatic configuration support between the client and server. PPP permits automated connection (no need to use a script) and encrypted authentication and features very sophisticated data compression.

Automatic protocol configuration can solve many of the problems associated with SLIP. The server may assign an IP address from a given pool of addresses or may use a DHCP server to provide the information.

Configuring a Dial-In Server

We already know a great deal about configuring our server for dial-in access. This is because most of the steps are very similar to making the machine a VPN server. You'll remember we discovered a number of PPTP and L2TP ports already configured on our RRAS computer. If your system had a modem installed this will show up as a port also (see Figure 14-89).

Unlike the PPTP and L2TP ports, your modem port is not automatically configured to send or receive calls. To configure your modem port, right-click **Ports** in the RRAS console, select **Properties**, select your modem, and click **Configure** to reveal the dialog box shown in Figure 14-90.

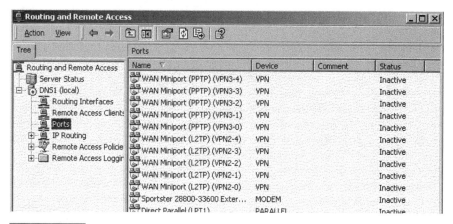

FIGURE 14–89 Modem port

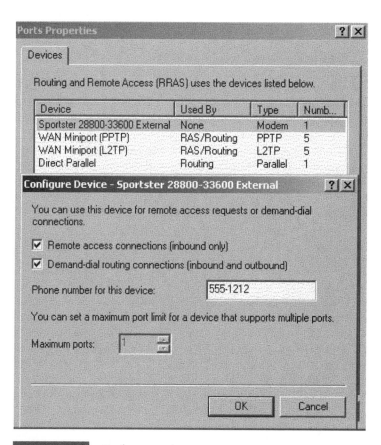

FIGURE 14–90 Configure modem port

We've selected the check boxes for both inbound remote access connections and inbound and outbound demand-dial routing connections because we'll use this modem for both functions. If you'll use only the dial-in or routing functions, check only the appropriate boxes. (The VPN ports have both checked by default. You may deconfigure either feature on them if desired.) The *Phone Number for this device* edit box should have the modem's telephone number. This provides the Called-Station-ID information to client software that requires it. (For VPN ports you can enter the IP address assigned to the port's interface if desired.) For simple dial-in access, we needed only to configure the port for *inbound remote access*. The configuration we've just completed will allow us to use this port for inbound remote access as well as inbound and outbound routing.

Note   Windows 2000 has a remote access policy that can be used to control remote access calls in a number of ways to include Called-Station-ID. The policy is part of the Active Directory and beyond the scope of this volume.

Configuring a Dial-Up Router

In the previous section we got our RRAS server to accept incoming calls. Although there are some general configuration issues we still need to look at, the server is ready to answer remote users who dial into the network. (You'll remember we configured some IP addresses for inbound clients back in the VPN section. We'll rely on them for the time being.) Let's make our RRAS server perform as a router. The procedure is essentially the same as the VPN router configuration we did earlier. The dial-up router configuration is very common and is frequently used to route an internal network to the Internet through a dial-up line to an ISP.

Our first step is to create a routing interface. Right-click **Routing Interfaces** and select **New Demand Dial Interface** to launch the **Demand Dial Interface Wizard**. You'll remember this procedure from the VPN router we installed previously. Working your way through the wizard will look essentially the same. We'll look at the exceptions in the following paragraphs.

The installation becomes a true demand-dial configuration when you select the **modem, ISDN adapter, or other physical device** radio button on the **Connection Type** dialog, as shown in Figure 14-91. The next screen asks for the interface type (See Figure 14-92). Notice you could actually use a cable between parallel ports to connect computers. We'll use our installed modem, however.

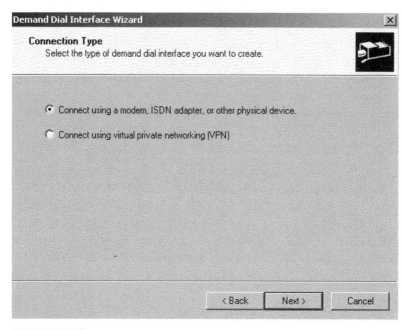

FIGURE 14–91 *Connection type*

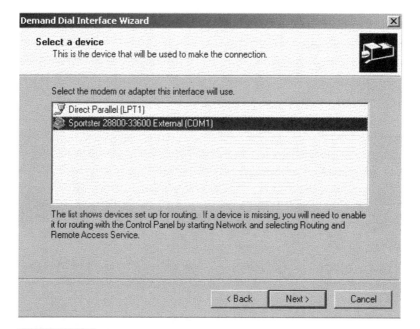

FIGURE 14–92 *Select device*

Finally, we're asked to enter a phone number (see Figure 14-93). This is the telephone number our router will call. This is typically the number given to us by our ISP. When we complete the wizard, we should see the new routing interface in the RRAS console. We named ours *Dial to ISP*; you can see it in Figure 14-94.

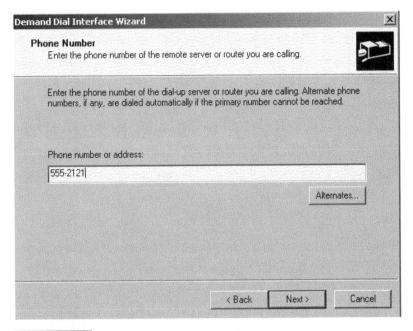

FIGURE 14-93 *Select phone number*

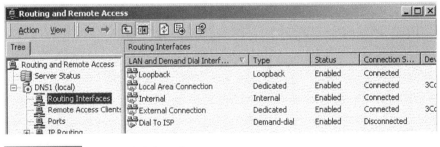

FIGURE 14-94 *Demand dial interface*

CONFIGURE THE PORT

Just as we did with our VPN router, we should take some time and look at the port configuration. Right-click your port and select Properties to reveal the dialog box shown in Figure 14-95.

Here we can change the modem configuration, change the phone number the port will dial out, or add alternate dial-out numbers to use if the primary number is unavailable. Clicking the **Options** tab opens the dialog box in Figure 14-96. The default connection type is **Demand dial**. This will cause the router to dial out when it needs to make a connection to the external network. The *idle time* configuration sets how long the connection will persist with no traffic before hanging up. If you have a dedicated line and wish to have your router connected all the time, select the **Persistent connection** radio button. The **Dialing policy** allows you to set up automatic redial in case the remote router doesn't answer the first time. If you click **Callback**, you can configure a phone number for the remote router to call back to. If the remote router is configured to offer to call back, it will hang up and dial the number you enter. The default is *No callback*.

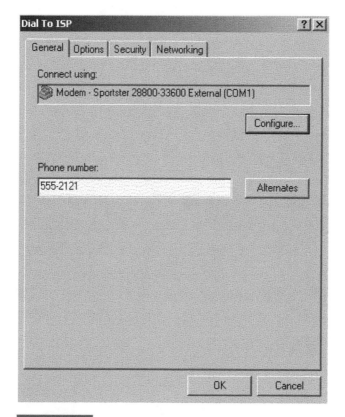

FIGURE 14–95   *Port properties—General tab*

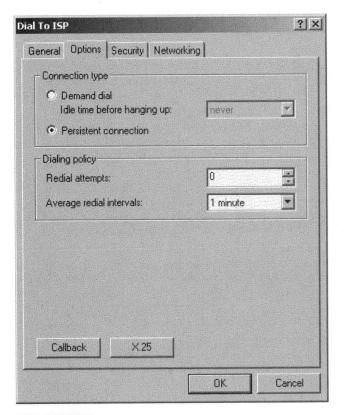

FIGURE 14–96   *Port properties—Options tab*

The Security tab (see Figure 14-97) provides essentially the same options we had when configuring VPN security. The validation settings allow you to require a secured (encrypted) password or allow an unsecured password. You may also designate a script file to run after the server dials in to the router.

The Networking tab permits you to configure your networking components, just as we saw in the VPN configuration. Looking at Figure 14-98, you'll notice PPP is selected as the **Type of dial-up server I am calling**. If you try to select another protocol, you'll discover this is the only option available—as we indicated at the start of this section.

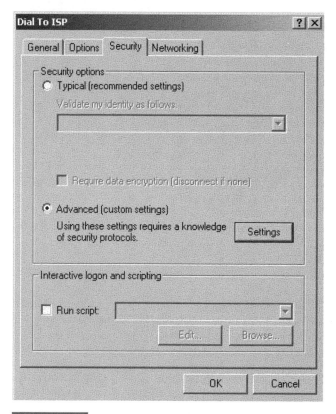

FIGURE 14-97 *Port properties—Security tab*

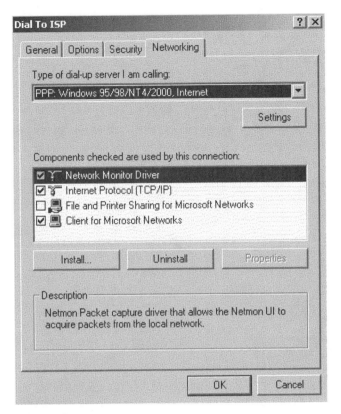

FIGURE 14-98 *Port properties—Networking tab*

COMPLETE THE INSTALLATION

Our router installation is nearly complete! The system will work as desired with only two more steps—steps we should know by now. We need to configure a static route to point our local network clients to the dial-out port. Finally, we need to select our interface and select **Connect**.

ADDITIONAL PORT CONFIGURATION

Before we complete our dial-up router discussion, let's look at additional port configurations available to dial-up and VPN ports. Right-clicking the port reveals the dialog box shown in Figure 14-99. The *Set Credentials* option allows you to change the account information used in connecting to the server. The *Dial-out hours* option enables us to control when the modem will dial out—this may be used to control what routers use a particular line at a given time.

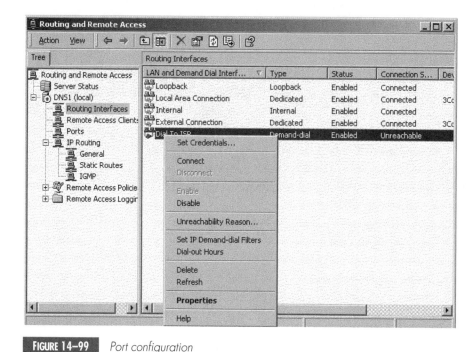

FIGURE 14-99   *Port configuration*

The *Set IP Demand-dial Filters* option permits us to control networks that will be routed to or accepted from this port by protocol. In Figure 14-100, we've designated the 172.20.0.0 network as the source and destination network for this filter for *any* protocol. This results in the filter entry shown in Figure 14-101. You'll notice that our filter will reject incoming and outgoing traffic for the network we just designated. We could also have configured filters to accept traffic from only the designated network by changing the radio button position at the top of the dialog box.

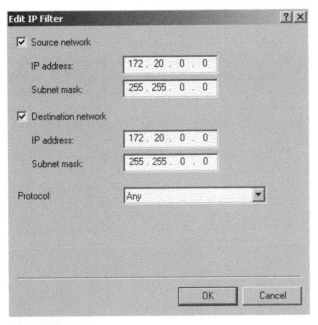

FIGURE 14—100   *Enter IP filter network addresses*

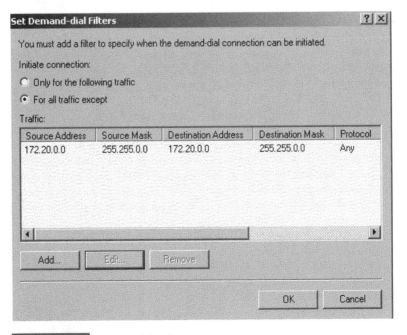

FIGURE 14—101   *Demand-dial filters*

Dial-Up Client Configuration

Now that our server is configured, let's look at how to configure a Windows 2000 client for dial-in access. Installing the dial-up connection requires a modem and the network connection wizard we used for our VPN connection. Select the **Dial-up to private network** option (see Figure 14-102) and run the wizard just as before.

When your connection is installed, right-click and select **Properties** to reveal the dialog box shown in Figure 14-103.

The General tab permits you to configure your modem or change/add phone numbers just as we did with the router interface. The Options tab (see Figure 14-104) allows you to configure the appearance and operation of the dial-in dialog box. If you will use this connection to connect to a Windows domain, check the *Include Windows logon domain* option. The *Redialing* options are the same as we discussed under the server options.

The Security tab allows you to decide if you'll permit authentication with an unsecured password, a secured password, or a smart card. If you require a secured password, you can configure the connection to automatically use the logon information you supplied when you logged onto the Windows 2000 network. You may also require that data sent to you from the server be encrypted. You may also configure the connection to show a terminal window or run a logon script after dialing (see Figure 14-105).

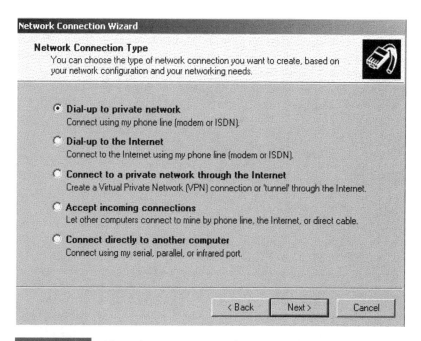

FIGURE 14-102   *Network connection wizard*

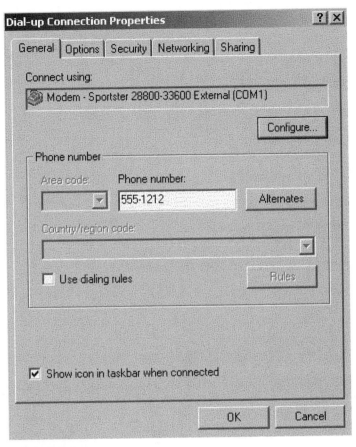

Dial-up connection properties—General tab

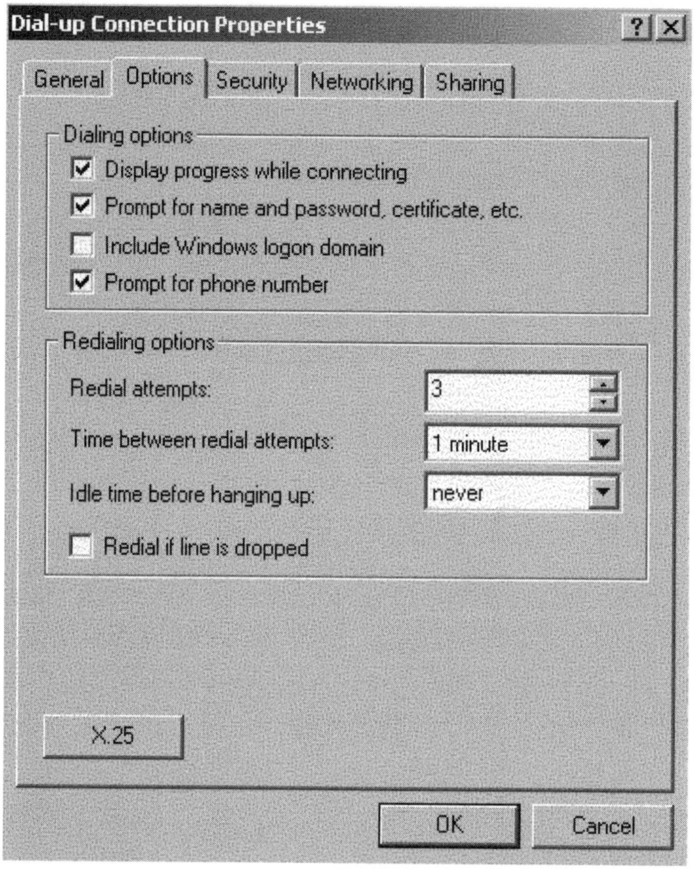

FIGURE 14–104 *Dial-up connection properties—Options tab*

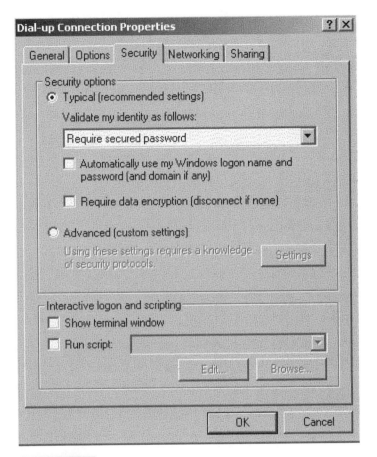

FIGURE 14–105 *Dial-up connection properties—Security tab*

The Networking tab shown in Figure 14-106 allows you to select either PPP or SLIP for your connection. Remember, if you're dialing in to an RRAS server, you must use PPP. You may configure the networking components in this dialog box also. If PPP is selected, you'll be able to select automatic IP address and DNS server configuration. The SLIP option does not permit automatic parameter assignment so you'll need to ensure information is correctly entered. The Sharing tab configures *Internet Connection Sharing* as we previously discussed.

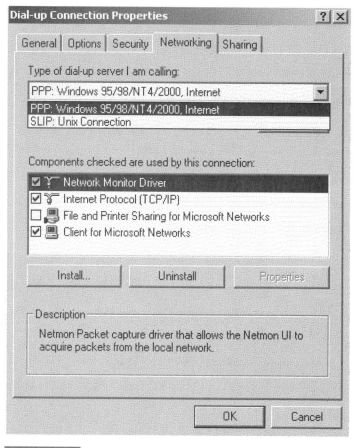

FIGURE 14-106 *Dial-up connection properties—Networking tab*

General RRAS Server Configuration

Now that we understand how RRAS works, let's look at the server's overall configuration options. Right-click the server in the RRAS console and select **Properties** to reveal the dialog box shown in Figure 14-107.

The General tab controls the server's capability. By default it is configured as both a router and remote access server. By enabling it as a router it will forward packets between interfaces. If you change the setting to LAN routing only, you effectively disable its demand-dial and VPN router capabilities. The **Remote access server** selection configures this machine to accept client VPN and dial-up connections. The Security tab (see Figure 14-108) allows you to chose between Windows and Remote Authentication Dial-In

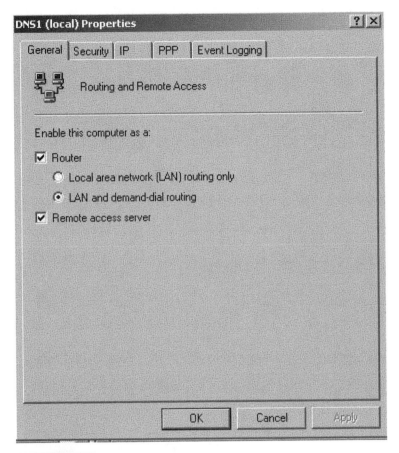

RRAS server properties—General tab

User Service (RADIUS) authentication and accounting. RADIUS is an industry-standard authentication protocol that can be used in place of the native Windows methods. It is a good selection when operating in a network with multiple platform types. It is also beyond the scope of this book. While *Authentication* should be self-explanatory, the *Accounting* selection determines which system will be used to log connection information.

We spent time on the IP tab when we configured a static address pool. Let's look at some of the other options available here. Looking at Figure 14-109 you'll notice the *Enable IP routing* and *Allow IP-based remote access and demand-dial connections* check boxes. At first this may seem confusing since we've already configured routing and remote access capabilities on the General tab. These selections, however, are for IP routing and remote access only. (Although we've limited our discussion to RRAS TCP/IP capabilities, remember RRAS is a multiprotocol router.) By disabling IP routing, your RRAS server

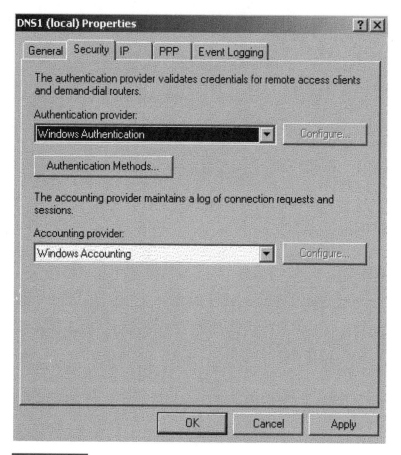

FIGURE 14–108 *RRAS server properties—Security tab*

will no longer forward IP packets from one interface to another. Disabling this feature would permit dial-in and VPN IP clients to access the server but not access machines on the rest of the network. You may also disable remote access for your IP clients. By doing so, you could allow your machine to operate as an IP router while denying IP remote access clients access to your network. We already know about the *IP server address assignment* option, but we didn't mention the adapter selection choice at the bottom of the dialog box. Since RRAS can supply DHCP, DNS, and WINS information to its dial-up clients, the adapter it uses to obtain the information may be an issue. The default is to let RAS select the adapter. This means the server will randomly select an adapter when the RRAS service starts. If your DNS, WINS, and DHCP data is available on a specific adapter, selecting it will permit more efficient distribution of these services.

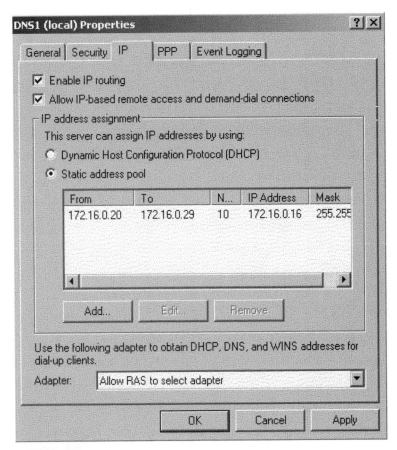

FIGURE 14-109   *RRAS server properties—IP tab*

The *PPP* tab (see Figure 14-110) allows you to configure options for PPP. All options are selected by default. *Multilink connections* permits you to combine multiple connections (e.g., two or more modems) into a single logical connection to increase bandwidth. You may also use the *Bandwidth Allocation Protocol* or *Bandwidth Allocation Control Protocol* to decide how many multilink connections to use for a particular connection. Disabling the *Link Control Protocol Extensions* will prevent the server from sending time-remaining and identification information and requesting callback during the connection process. Disabling *Software Compression* will prevent the server from using the *Microsoft Point-to-Point Compression Protocol* to compress remote access and demand-dial data.

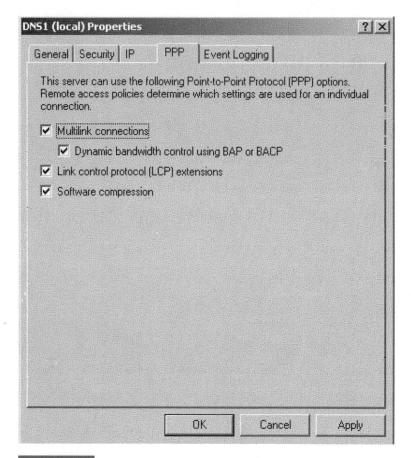

FIGURE 14–110   *RRAS server properties—PPP tab*

Finally, the Event Logging tab controls what, if any, information is sent to the Windows 2000-event log and controls if PPP information is logged to the ppp.log file.

BAP, BACP, LCP?

By now you may be a bit tired of learning about new protocols but we've just introduced three very important protocols in passing, so let's spend a moment to look at them in a bit greater depth.

You'll recall we mentioned the Link Control Protocol as the protocol that allows PPP to perform the functions missing in SLIP. LCP can verify if the line is of sufficient quality to support the connection. The LCP link precedes action by the Network Control Protocol (NCP) component, which negotiates the actual encapsulation and transport of PPP information. Extensions to LCP permit time-remaining indications and identification during connection and allow a server to request a callback.

The Bandwidth Allocation Protocol (BAP) enhances PPP's multilink efficiency by adding or dropping links consistent with current traffic. This is especially useful when you're paying for your connection based on bandwidth. Using BAP, you could, for example, configure the system to drop an extra connection when link utilization drops below 50 percent for more than 30 seconds or add a connection if utilization goes above 50 percent for more than a minute. BAP also supports a server callback request.

The Bandwidth Allocation Control Protocol (BACP) operates within the NCP to dynamically manage the links. It works to select a particular link (known as the favored peer) to add to the connection.

BAP and BACP are covered in RFC 2125.

Remote Access Policies and the Active Directory

The Windows 2000 RRAS package integrates completely with the Windows 2000 Active Directory to permit or deny access based on a host of considerations from the user's telephone number to the protocol being used to the time of day the connection is made. These policies are configured through RRAS Remote Access Policies and are enabled in the user account. Configuration and use of these policies is beyond the scope of this volume.

Summary

This chapter covered the real application of TCP/IP routing in Windows 2000. We began our discussion with IPSec and saw this to be an excellent way of securing our LAN and WAN communication. Based on a wide range of industry standard security protocols, IPSec is a robust feature that can support many computing platforms. IPSec is relatively transparent to a network and will route, in most cases, just as any other IP communication.

We then turned our attention to the multitude of routing and remote access features available from the Windows 2000 RRAS. We first looked at static routing and discovered we could configure routes in our RRAS server. Next, we learned about the RRAS NAT feature. We saw that the RRAS server could translate many internal private IP addresses to one or a few external IP addresses to permit our internal network to communicate with hosts on the Internet without assigning Internet-capable IP addresses to our local network.

We configured our RRAS server to perform dynamic routing using both the RIP and OSPF routing protocol. Next we saw that RRAS has some limited Multicast routing capabilities using the IGMP.

RRAS can provide an efficient Virtual Private Networking server using either PPTP or L2TP. RRAS configures five PPTP and five L2TP ports by default. PPTP can be used by most clients, while L2TP requires machine certificates for authentication. We configured RRAS as a remote access VPN server, where a remote client can access the network from a client machine, and a VPN router where RRAS can link to another VPN router to connect networks over a VPN link.

Similar to VPN support was dial-in support and we configured our RRAS server to be both a dial-in server, capable of supporting remote clients over a dial-in line, and a dial-in router to provide Internet connectivity for internal network users through a dial-up link. We saw that the dial-up client can use both SLIP and PPP. RRAS, however, will work only with PPP.

Finally, we looked at some of the overall RRAS configuration options. We saw that we could control whether RRAS functions as a router, remote access server, neither, or both. We learned how to configure IP options to permit RRAS to provide IP addresses for dial-in and VPN clients and saw we had good control over RRAS' use of PPP and error logging.

Test Yourself

1. IPSec provides:
   A. Data encryption
   B. Data authentication
   C. Packet filtering
   D. All of the above

2. To allow computers on an internal network with IP addresses from the private address space to operate on the Internet you should configure your RRAS server to use:
   A. PPP
   B. NAT
   C. PPTP
   D. SLIP

3. Dynamic Routing Protocols are (select all that apply):
   A. OSPF
   B. L2TP
   C. RIP
   D. PPP

4. Virtual private networking:
   A. Requires the use of IPSec
   B. Uses PPP or SLIP
   C. Permits users to "tunnel" through the Internet
   D. Cannot work with L2TP

5. RRAS Dial-Up Networking functions with the following protocols (select all that apply):
   A. PPP
   B. PPTP
   C. SLIP
   D. L2TP

Connectivity in Heterogeneous Environments

*C*hapter 1 introduced the Transport Control Protocol/Internet Protocol (TCP/IP) protocol suite as a tool to connect dissimilar systems such as UNIX and Windows platforms. In this chapter we'll explore the connectivity options for using Microsoft TCP/IP to interoperate in a heterogeneous environment. We will look more deeply into the Microsoft TCP/IP connectivity utilities, discuss how to use Remote Execution (REXEC) and telnet, and show the features of the built-in File Transfer Protocol (FTP) client. We'll also spend some time on TCP/IP printing support and configuring a Windows 2000 computer to act as a print server for UNIX clients.

Microsoft TCP/IP Connectivity Utilities

Now that you're familiar with how to plan, install, and configure the Microsoft TCP/IP protocol suite, you should have no problem in building a complex TCP/IP based network where computers can effectively share resources such as files and printers. But stop! The TCP/IP protocol only gives *connectivity* to foreign computers (such as UNIX, OS/2, or VMS) because it is a common *network* protocol. In order to actually access resources and accomplish something with these foreign machines, common utilities (usually client/server) must exist on both ends. In Chapter 1, we discovered that Microsoft TCP/IP includes useful TCP/IP utilities for data transfer, monitoring and printing. These utilities, however, are specific to the TCP/IP version (Microsoft, UNIX, OS/2, etc.) in use. The question is: can you use standard Microsoft networking commands and utilities (for example, NET USE and Windows 2000 Explorer) to connect to and access data on a remote non-Windows host? The answer is "Yes," if the following conditions are met:

- Both computers must be able to communicate using the same protocol. (This protocol doesn't have to be TCP/IP; protocols such as IPX or NetBEUI will work as long as all systems use the same protocol.) This is often referred to as *Transport Driver Connectivity.*
- The non-Microsoft host must support the SMB (server message blocks) protocol. (SMB is the file-sharing protocol used on all Microsoft network products.) This requirement is referred to as *SMB Connectivity.*
- If the two computers have the Network Basic Input/Output System (NetBIOS) scope parameter configured, the scope ID must be the same or they will not be able to establish a NetBIOS session. (You'll remember we covered NetBIOS scopes in Chapter 8.)

If these conditions are met, Microsoft-based clients can easily connect to non-Microsoft platforms and vice versa. Today, many vendors have implemented NetBIOS over TCP/IP and included SMB support in their operating systems. For example, LAN Manager for UNIX and DEC PATHWORKS on VMS both feature SMB support.

UNIX-based computers can also access Windows 2000 servers through the SMB protocol with the installation of an SMB-based client. Alternatively, UNIX clients can connect to Windows 2000 servers using their native NFS (network file system) protocol if a Windows 2000 server has an NFS service installed. (Although, the NFS service is not included in Windows 2000, it is part of Microsoft Services for UNIX Version 2.0, which is installed through the Windows installer. The package is available at additional cost. Third-party NFS servers are also available.)

Connectivity Using Microsoft TCP/IP Utilities

Although many third-party solutions exist, we will explore only the native Microsoft Windows 2000 TCP/IP utilities that allow you to integrate Windows 2000 systems into heterogeneous environments. Microsoft TCP/IP utilities provide several options for connecting to foreign TCP/IP based hosts (see Table 15.1):

TABLE 15.1	*Microsoft TCP/IP Connectivity Utilities*

Utility	Function
RCP (Remote Copy)	Allows you to copy files between a Windows 2000-based computer and a server running RCP daemon (or service) without logging on.
FTP (File Transfer Protocol)	Provides bidirectional file transfers between a Windows 2000-based computer and a TCP/IP host running FTP server software.
TFTP (Trivial File Transfer Protocol)	Provides bidirectional file transfers between a Windows 2000-based computer and a TCP/IP host running TFTP server software. A subset of FTP.
Microsoft Internet Explorer	Allows access to documents stored on World Wide Web servers.
REXEC	Allows you to run a process on a remote host. (Requires you to provide a valid username and password.)
RSH (Remote Shell)	Permits you to run a command on a remote host with RSH server software installed. (Does not require you to log onto the target host.)
Telnet	Provides terminal emulation to a TCP/IP host running Telnet server software.
LPR (Line Printer Remote)	Allows you to send a print job to the printer connected to a server with the LPD service.
LPD (Line Printer Daemon)	Services LPR requests and submits print jobs to the printing device.
LPQ (Line Printer Queue)	Provides the ability to view the print queue on the LPD server.

Most Microsoft TCP/IP utilities are styled after their UNIX counterparts with a command line interface. Some of the utilities, however, do utilize a graphical interface.

Data Transfer Utilities

Microsoft TCP/IP data transfer utilities allow you to obtain files from remote TCP/IP computers and even permit you to copy files between two remote computers. These utilities are: RCP, FTP, TFTP, and web browsers such as Microsoft Internet Explorer.

RCP

The *Remote Copy* command line connectivity command can be used to copy files between a Windows 2000 computer and a computer running *rshd* software (RSH service or daemon as it is called in UNIX). Since Windows 2000 does not use the RSH service, a Windows 2000-based computer can only participate as the computer from which RCP commands are issued.

The RCP command does not use passwords—authentication is provided by a special .rhosts file on the target computer. The .rhosts file specifies which computers and users can access a local account using RCP. The .rhosts file is a text file, each entry of which consists of a host name and possible username. The RCP command transmits the local username to the remote computer. The remote computer checks to see if the given user and the computer from which the communication was initiated are listed in its .rhosts file. If appropriate .rhosts information is found, the file transfer is granted.

The syntax for the Windows 2000 RCP command is:

```
RCP [-a | -b] [-h] [-r] [host[.user:]]source
[host[.user:]]destination
```

where:

-a	Specifies ASCII transfer mode. This mode converts end of line (EOL) characters to a carriage return for UNIX and a carriage return/line feed for personal computers. This is the default transfer mode.
-b	Specifies binary image (versus ASCII) transfer mode.
-h	Transfers hidden files.
-r	Copies the contents of all subdirectories (destination must be a directory).
host	.Host name of source or destination computer.
.user:	If the user portion is omitted, the currently logged-on Windows 2000 username is used. If a fully qualified host name is used, which contains the period (.) separators, then the [.user] must be included. Otherwise, the last part of the host name is interpreted as the username.
source	Specifies the files to copy.
destination	Specifies the destination path.

Note   Any file name that is not preceded with a forward slash (/) for UNIX computers or a backward slash (\) for Windows computers, is considered to be relative to the current working directory (the directory from which the command is issued for the Windows 2000 computer or the logon directory for the remote computer).

For example, the command:

```
rcp report.doc hpserv.johnm:/users/johnm/WinReport.doc
```

Copies the file `report.doc` from the Windows 2000 local directory to `/users/johnm/WinReport.doc` on the UNIX server `HPSERV`. In order for this operation to complete successfully, the appropriate .rhosts file must exist on the `HPSERV` computer.

When .rhosts files are properly configured, the RCP command can be issued from a Windows 2000 computer to copy files *between* two computers running rshd. For example, you can use the following syntax to copy a file from one UNIX computer to another:

```
rcp serv1.user1:report.doc serv2.user2:reportcopy.doc
```

FTP

FTP is a command line TCP/IP utility which transfers files between local and remote TCP/IP hosts. (FTP is defined in RFC 959.) In contrast to the RCP command, the FTP utility authenticates when a username and a password are supplied for the remote computer.

FTP was one of the earliest methods used to transfer files on TCP/IP–based networks and the Internet. Currently WWW has replaced most FTP functions, but FTP is still the only way to upload files from a client computer to a server over the Internet.

To use FTP to transfer files between computers, both computers must support their respective FTP roles. In other words, one needs to be an FTP client and the other an FTP server. The FTP client can issue commands to the server (commands to download files, upload files, and create or change directories on the server). In order for a Windows 2000-based FTP client to connect to a remote FTP host, the target (remote host) computer must have the FTP service running and the user account for the Windows 2000 user configured.

Table 15.2 describes the most common FTP commands.

TABLE 15.2	Common FTP Commands
Command	**Purpose**
open	Connects to the specified FTP server.
delete	Deletes files on the remote computer. (Requires appropriate permissions.)
dir	Lists the remote directory's files and directories.
get	Downloads a remote file to your computer.
help	Displays descriptions for FTP commands.
put	Uploads a file from your computer to the remote computer. (Requires appropriate permissions.)
mkdir	Creates a directory on the remote computer. (Requires appropriate permissions.)
bye	Ends the FTP session with the remote computer and exits FTP.

The following example illustrates a typical FTP session:

```
C:\>ftp
ftp> open hpserv
Connected to hpserv.traincert.com.
220 hpserv FTP server (Version 1.7.109.2 Tue Jul 28
23:32:34 GMT 1992) ready.
User (hpserv.traincert.com:(none)): johnm
331 Password required for johnm.
Password:********
230 User johnm logged in.
ftp> get library.cpp
200 PORT command successful.
150 Opening ASCII mode data connection for library.cpp
(12500 bytes).
226 Transfer complete.
12500 bytes received in 4,00 seconds (3,12 Kbytes/sec)
ftp> bye
221 Goodbye.
```

Note FTP transmits data in the ASCII mode by default. If you are transmitting program files or other binary data, you'll need to shift the utility into *binary* mode by typing **binary** at the **ftp>** prompt. To revert to ASCII mode, simply type **ascii** at the prompt.

An FTP connection can be also established by using third-party utilities. Cute-FTP, for example, is an FTP utility that permits you to issue FTP commands using graphical interface.

Do not confuse FTP with TFTP. TFTP is a fast, simple file transfer protocol that uses the User Datagram Protocol (UDP) transport but does not support any user authentication. Files need to be world-readable and writable (UNIX permissions) on the remote system in order to be used by TFTP. The TFTP protocol is described in RFC 1350.

Note FTP does not encrypt usernames and passwords during authentication. Using FTP through the Internet can cause a security gap.

In addition to FTP client software, Windows 2000 contains the FTP server software. Internet Information Services (IIS) installs by default on your Windows 2000 server. While FTP is part of IIS, it doesn't install by default. If you want FTP to function, you must select it specifically during the Windows 2000 installation or install it later through **Add/remove Programs | Add/ Remove Windows Components | Internet Information Services**. On Windows 2000 Professional, the FTP server service is included as a part of Peer

Web Services (PWS). Once you have installed an FTP server, you are able to publish documents on the Internet.

WEB BROWSERS

Web browsers can access documents stored on WWW servers using the Hypertext Transfer Protocol (HTTP). HTTP is an application level protocol that utilizes TCP to transfer data. More specifically, a web browser acting as a client sends an HTTP request to TCP port 80 of the web server. The HTTP request contains the name of the document to be sent as well as additional information, such as browser version and client language. Having received such a request, the web server responds with the status of the transaction (successful or failed) and the data for the request. The type of data varies: a client can accept text documents, images, sounds, and others. After the requested document is sent, the connection is closed. If an HTTP document consists of multiple objects (for example, inline images), a separate connection is opened for each object.

A good example of a web browser is Microsoft Internet Explorer (included with Windows 2000). For the latest version of Microsoft Internet Explorer visit `http://www.microsoft.com/windows/ie/`.

The advantages of using a web browser are the following:

- A web browser can download text and graphical files and automatically display them to the screen.
- A web browser can play sound and video clips.
- A web browser can launch helper applications for known file types. (For example, when downloading a Word document, a properly configured web browser can launch Word and open the file with it.)
- A web browser can save a file of unknown type to a local hard disk drive.
- Web browsers exist for nearly every operating system and hardware platform.
- Web browsers support multiple protocols including Gopher, Network News Transfer Protocol (NNTP), and FTP. (You can, for example, use Microsoft Internet Explorer as an FTP client.)

Using a web browser you can easily access documents on a web server running under different operating systems, such as UNIX, Novell Netware, or Windows 2000.

Remote Execution Utilities

Sometimes you don't need to download a file but only wish to execute a command on a remote host. For example, an administrator of a mixed UNIX and NT network might want to view a list of files on a UNIX computer while sitting at a Windows 2000 computer. This is a job for the *remote execution utilities*.

RSH (REMOTE SHELL)

The command line connectivity utility RSH runs commands on a remote host which is running the rshd daemon (a UNIX daemon is equivalent to a Windows 2000 service). For example, you can use the RSH command to remotely compile programs. A user does not have to log onto the UNIX host in order to run a command—RSH security is implemented using the .rhosts file.

Here is the syntax of the Windows 2000 RSH command:

```
RSH host [-l username] [-n] command
```

where:

host	Specifies the remote host on which to run the command.
-l username	Specifies the username to use on the remote host. If omitted, the logged on username is used. (The user must be listed in the .rhosts file.)
-n	Redirects the input of RSH to NULL.
Command	Specifies the command to run.

The following code fragment shows how to issue a command to a UNIX host from a Windows 2000 computer. This command sends the contents of the log file on the UNIX computer hpserv to the specified email address:

```
C:\>rsh hpserv cat logfile "|" mail root@traincert.com
```

Note

You must use quotation marks around redirection symbols (| , > , >>) for redirection to occur on the remote host. For example, `rsh hpserv file1 ">>" file2` appends *remote* file to *remote* file2 and `rsh hpserv file1 >> file2` appends *remote* file to *local* file2.

REXEC (REMOTE EXECUTION)

In contrast to RSH, the REXEC utility provides remote execution facilities based on a username and password. In order to use REXEC, a user must have a valid account on the TCP/IP host.

The syntax of the REXEC command is the following:

```
REXEC host [-l username] [-n] command
```

where:

host	Specifies the remote host on which to run the command.
-l username	Specifies the username to use on the remote host. If omitted, the logged on username is used.
-n	Redirects the input of REXEC to NULL.
Command	Specifies the command to run.

REXEC prompts the user for a password and authenticates the password on the remote host. If the authentication succeeds, the command is executed.

In the following example, we see how you could view a mailbox on a UNIX host from a Windows 2000 computer using an REXEC session.

```
C:\>rexec hpserv -l johnm mail
Password (hpserv.traincert.com:):*******
From Administrator@traincert.com Thu Nov 12 21:08 GMT 1998
Received: by mail.traincert.com
     (1.37.109.4/16.2) id AA23186; Thu, 12 Nov 98 21:08:39
-0300
Date: Thu, 12 Nov 98 21:08:39 -0300
From: Administrator <Administrator@traincert.com>
Subject: Log Files
Apparently-To: johnm@traincert.com

Don't forget to clear the log files today!!!
```

Note   You cannot run most interactive commands. For example, vi or emacs cannot be run using REXEC.

TELNET

This connectivity command starts terminal emulation with a remote host running a telnet server service. Telnet provides DEC VT 100, DEC VT 52, or TTY emulation. You can think of a telnet application as a utility that transfers a sequence of characters from your computer to a remote process.

When you install the TCP/IP protocol suite on Windows 2000, the telnet client utility is installed automatically. You can launch the telnet client by typing **telnet** at the command prompt. In order to connect to a remote computer using the telnet application, the remote host must be running a telnet daemon (or service). In addition, you must have a valid user account on the remote host. When you connect to a remote host you may be asked to input a username and password before you can issue commands.

When you launch the telnet client application from the command prompt, you can pass, as an argument, a host name or an IP address for the computer to which you want to connect. (You can also use the `Remote System` command from Connect menu if the telnet client is already running.) For example, to connect to computer `hpserv`, type the following at the Windows 2000 command prompt:

```
telnet hpserv
```

Note	In order for this command to work successfully, the host name resolution must be set up properly.

Note	A telnet server is included on both Windows 2000 server platforms and Windows 2000 Professional. The service is not configured to start by default.

You can enter a port number right after the host name. If you leave the port number out, you connect to TCP port 23 by default.

Using Telnet Client to Connect to the Remote Process

You can use the Windows 2000 telnet client application to connect to the remote TCP/IP service by specifying the port number, which is used by this service. You may want to do this when troubleshooting this service. Of course, you must know the commands which are used by the service. For example, to connect to the Simple Mail Transfer Protocol (SMTP) service (TCP port 25) on computer hpserv, type the following at the command prompt:

```
telnet hpserv 25
```

After issuing this command you can transfer commands directly to the SMTP service on computer hpserv (user input is marked bold):

```
220 hpserv.senate.gov ESMTP Server ready
HELO
250 OK
MAIL FROM: johnm@senate.gov
250 OK - mail from <johnm@senate.gov>
RCPT TO: admin@senate.gov
250 OK - Recipient <admin@senate.gov>DATA
354 Enter mail, end with "." on a line by itself
Mail server testing
.
250 Ok
```

Configuring a Windows 2000 Computer to Support TCP/IP Printing

One of the problems that the administrators face in a mixed network, is how to ensure that each client can print. Clients from different operating systems behave differently in creating print jobs and sending those jobs to a print server and on to print devices. If your network consists of only Microsoft clients, network printing is as easy as "point and print." If, on the other hand, you are also blessed with clients running other operating systems, printing becomes more complex. This is mainly because print server services (software modules on print servers that receive print jobs) support print jobs from clients of only one type. For example, if a UNIX client wants to print a document on a Windows 2000-based print server, a print service that understands UNIX-style print jobs must be installed on Windows 2000. As we're about to see, however, by using a Windows 2000 server as your network print server, you have a seamless way to print, no matter what operating systems your networked computers use.

Let's focus on TCP/IP printing and see how Windows 2000 supports it.

TCP/IP printing can be explained in terms of three applications: *Line Printer Remote* (LPR), *Line Printer Queue* (LPQ) and *Line Printer Daemon* (LPD). The LPR and LPQ are client applications that communicate with the LPD application on the print server.

TCP-IP Printing Utilities

For a Windows 2000 computer to accept jobs from LPR clients (such as UNIX computers), the Windows 2000 LPD service needs to be running.

When the TCP/IP printer server service is started it is ready to accept print jobs from LPR clients. (See Figure 15-1.) Of course, we're assuming the Windows 2000 computer has a print device attached with a properly installed printer driver.

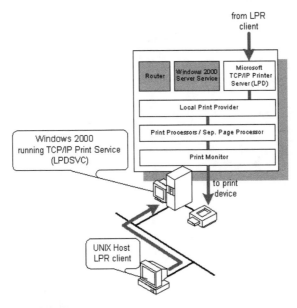

FIGURE 15-1   *Windows 2000 computer running TCP/IP print server service can accept print jobs from LPR clients*

Practical Application

After you have added a printer on a Windows 2000 print server, you need to set up clients to acccss it. For Windows 2000, Windows NT 4.0, Windows 95, and Windows 98 clients, you do not need to do anything further. However, you might need to manually install printing services for UNIX-based clients. Here is how it is done:

1. Insert the Windows 2000 installation CD-ROM into your CD-ROM drive.

2. Go to **Control Panel|Add/Remove Programs| Add/Remove Windows Components** and press **Components**.

3. Select **Other Network File and Print Services** and click **Details** (see Figure 15-2).

4. Select **Print Services for Unix** and press **Next** to install the necessary files.

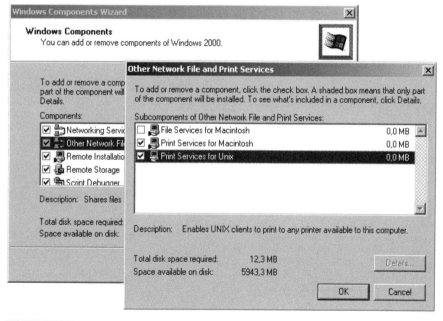

FIGURE 15–2   *Installing print services for Unix*

When LPD receives print jobs from LPR clients it submits them to the spooler. An LPR client always sends some control information within the print job. This control information contains administrative data. LPD uses that control information to assign a data type (TEXT or RAW) to the print job. For example, if the LPR client sends the f, o, or p control command, the LPD assigns the TEXT data type to the print job. This ensures that the spooler will alter this print job before printing. If the LPR client sends the 1 control command, the LPD assigns the RAW data type to the print job and the spooler does not modify it before printing.

The Microsoft TCP/IP printer server cannot be customized using a graphical user interface (GUI). You can, however, use registry editor to change configuration parameters in HKEY_LOCAL_MACHINE\SYSTEM\CurrentControlSet\Services\LPDSVC\Parameters. For example, you can control the maximum number of concurrent users by changing the MaxConcurrentUsers parameter.

Note   Most UNIX clients send the f control command within their print jobs. If your LPD print server is running, Windows 2000 treats these print jobs as the TEXT data type instead of the RAW data type (as they would be on UNIX). This could result in incorrect printing. To correct this problem, configure the LPR clients to send the 1 control command.

Submitting Print Jobs Using LPR

LPR is one of the protocols in the TCP/IP protocol suite. Defined in RFC 1179, LPR was originally developed as a standard for transmitting print jobs between computers running the UNIX operating system. Currently, LPR software exists for most operating systems, including Windows 2000. Using the Microsoft LPR utility you can issue print jobs to:

- UNIX computers
- Windows 2000 computers with the TCP/IP Print Server service installed
- Windows for Workgroups computers with a 3rd-party LPD
- Network printers, such as HP JetDirect or Emulex NetJet

Note   Some network-attached print devices that support TCP/IP are not fully compliant with RFC 1179: some do not implement the entire specification; others implement a proprietary specification. In these cases, the LPR utility may not print properly.

The LPR software is installed along with printing services. You can, now, submit print jobs to any computer running the LPD service (or daemon). You could, for example, submit a job to a UNIX host or another Windows 2000 computer, using the following syntax:

```
lpr -Sprint_server -Pprinter_name filename
```

where:

print_server	Specifies the name or IP address of the host providing LPD service
printer_name	Specifies the name of the printer queue ("printer" in Windows 2000 terminology)
filename	Specifies the name of the file to be printed

Note   The –S and –P options are case sensitive, and must be typed in upper case.

For example, the following command issued on the WKS computer submits a file c:\boot.ini to the printer queue LASER3D attached to the UNIX computer hpserv (see Figure 15-3).

```
lpr –Shpserv –PLASER3D c:\boot.ini
```

In order for this command to work successfully, host name resolution must work properly.

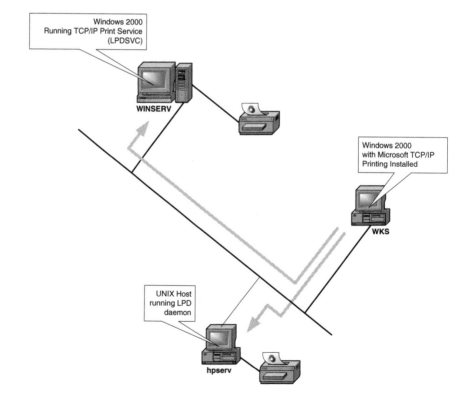

FIGURE 15–3   *Computer with LPR software can submit print jobs to LPD servers*

Additionally, computer WKS can issue a print job to the printer attached to computer WINSERV:

```
lpr -SWINSERV -PNTPrinter c:\boot.ini
```

Note   In order to send a print job, the LPR software under Windows 2000 makes a TCP connection to the LPD service using any available port between 512 and 1023. *Windows NT 3.5x sent all TCP/IP print jobs using TCP ports 721 through 731.*

Using LPR, you send a print job directly to the LPD service or print device and bypass the spooler. The print job is neither spooled nor modified. The LPR utility sends the control information along with the print job so that the server side LPD software knows how to handle the print job. By default, the LPR command sends the f control command. You can use the –o switch to override this behavior.

Unfortunately the LPR protocol does not support detailed error status information and therefore, if anything goes wrong, LPR reports only a generic error condition.

USING LPQ TO CHECK THE PRINT STATUS

Once a file has been sent to the printer using LPR, you can examine the status of the printer queue by using the LPQ command. The syntax of the LPQ command is the following:

```
lpq -Sprint_server -Pprinter_name [-l]
```

where:

-S server_name	Name or IP address of the host providing lpd service
-P printer_name	Name of the print queue
-l	Verbose output

The following sequence of commands submits a print job and then displays the status of the print queue (user input is in bold text):

```
C:\>lpr -SWINSERV -PW2kPrinter c:\boot.ini
C:\>lpq -SWINSERV -PW2kPrinter -l
              Windows 2000 LPD Server
        Printer \\172.16.0.20\W2kPrinter (Paused)
 Owner   Status   Jobname    Job-Id   Size   Pages    Priority
 ------------------------------------------------------------
 JOHNM   Waiting  c:\boot.ini   9      404      0        1
```

Configuring Print Manager with LPR

Although LPR works fine from the command line, you may want to take advantage of Windows applications. You may be wondering if you can print from Microsoft Word or Excel to a TCP/IP printer. The answer is: yes, you can! You simply configure the Windows 2000 print manager to use the LPD print server—known as the *LPR Print Monitor.*

The LPR print monitor redirects the spooled print job from the local computer to the LPD service running on another computer. To take advantage of the LPR print monitor, you must add an LPR port in the Add Printer Wizard. You will need to supply the name or IP address of the server running the LPD software as well as the name of the printer on that server.

Let's look at how Windows applications can print to the TCP/IP printer through the LPR print monitor (see Figure 15-4).

When a Windows-based application prints, the application calls the Graphical Device Interface (GDI). GDI renders the print job in the printer language of the print device. Then the print job gets passed to the spooler. The router, being part of the spooler, passes the print job to the local print pro-

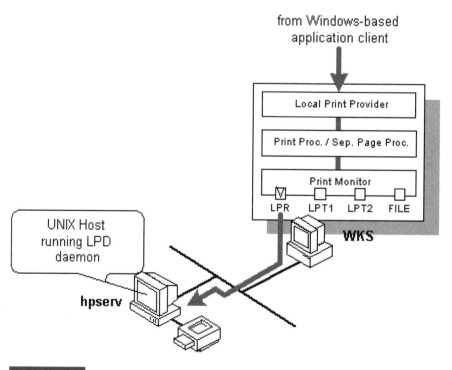

FIGURE 15-4   *Printing using the LPR print monitor*

vider, which spools it to disk. After being altered by the print processor and separator page processor, the job is despooled to the LPR print monitor which sends the print job to the TCP/IP host running the LPD service. The entire process is transparent to the application, which thinks that the printer is connected locally.

Note   If the target LPD server is Windows 2000 based, the printer should have the `Everyone/Print` permission so that the LPR clients could print.

Practical Application

To configure a Windows 2000 printer to use LPR software to submit print jobs to LPD, follow these guidelines:

1. In **Control Panel**, double-click **Printers** and launch the **Add Printer** wizard.

2. Click **Local printer**, clear the **Automatically detect my printer check box**, and then click **Next**.

3. Click **Create a new port**, and then click **Standard TCP/IP Port** (see Figure 15-5).

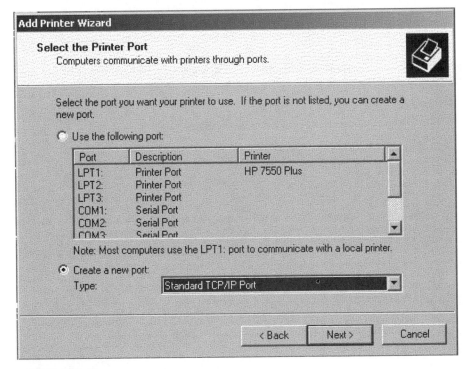

FIGURE 15–5   *Configuring print manager to use standard TCP/IP port*

Click **Next**, enter the DNS name or IP address of the print server under **Printer Name or IP Address** and enter a meaningful port name next to **Port Name** (see Figure 15-6).

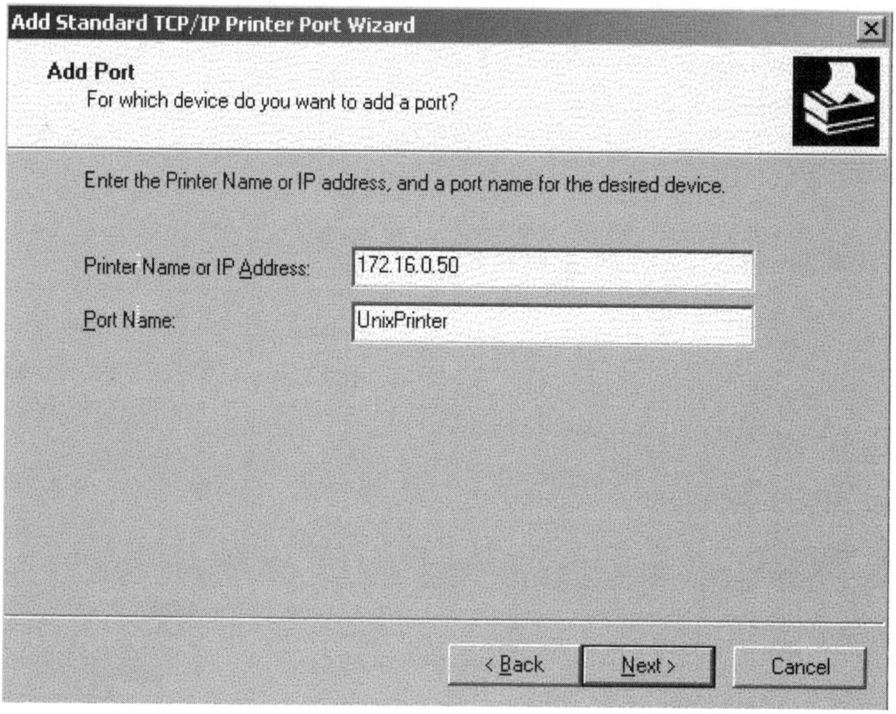

Add Standard TCP/IP Printer Port Wizard	✕

Add Port
For which device do you want to add a port?

Enter the Printer Name or IP address, and a port name for the desired device.

Printer Name or IP Address: `172.16.0.50`

Port Name: `UnixPrinter`

`< Back`   `Next >`   `Cancel`

FIGURE 15-6   *Enter print server and port identification*

4. Select **Custom** and click **Settings** on the **Additional Port Information Required** dialog box as shown in Figure 15-7.

5. The **Port Settings** page appears (Figure 15-8). You'll find the appropriate information entered for you under **Port Name** and **Printer Name or IP Address**. Ensure **LPR** is selected under **Protocol** and enter the printer name under **Queue Name**. This should be the same name you would use for the printer when using the LPR command. If your jobs print incompletely or not at all, try using the **LPR Byte Counting Enabled** selection. (This adds some nontrivial overhead but generally solves the problem.)

6. Follow the rest of the instructions in the wizard to complete the installation. This will include selecting a printer driver and the rest of the normal installation chores. When complete, your port will appear as a local printer (which may be shared out to other networked machines).

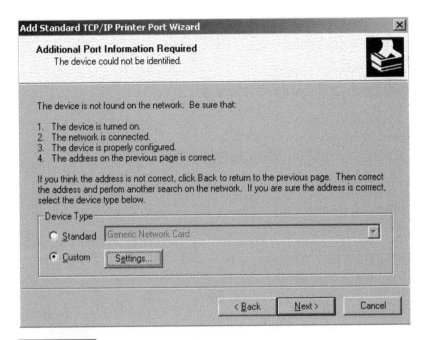

FIGURE 15–7   *Additional port information*

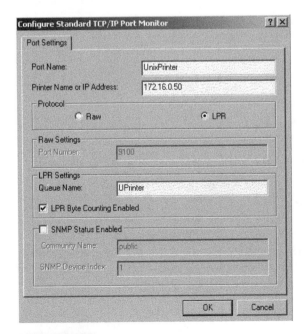

FIGURE 15–8   *Configure port settings*

Once you have created a printer that uses the LPR port, you can submit print jobs to this printer and they will be redirected automatically to the computer running the LPD service.

Using Windows 2000 as a Print Gateway

In some cases you may want to consider configuring a print gateway on a Windows 2000 computer. Windows 2000 with Microsoft TCP/IP print services installed can be configured to provide the following gateway functions:

1. Act as a gateway for Microsoft-based clients to forward their print jobs to print servers running LPD software.
2. Act as a gateway for LPR clients, such as UNIX-based computers, to automatically forward these print jobs to another printer.

PRINT GATEWAY FOR MICROSOFT-BASED CLIENTS

You can configure a Windows 2000 computer as a print gateway so that Microsoft-based clients can print documents on printers attached to computers running the LPD service. The entire printing process is transparent to Microsoft clients—client computers do not have to run LPR software or even the TCP/IP protocol (clients must use a protocol that is also in use on the print gateway server).

Practical Application

To enable your Windows 2000 computer to provide print gateway services for Microsoft-based clients, perform the following steps:

1. Using the **Add Printer** wizard, create a printer and add the **Standard TCP/IP Port** (as accomplished in the previous exercise).

2. Provide an address of the print server with LPD service and a name of the print queue on that server.

3. Once the LPR print monitor is configured, share this printer.

4. Connect your Microsoft-based clients to the shared printer.

Once you have completed the preceding steps, the printing process would be patterned after that shown in Figure 15-9. Microsoft-based clients connect to the shared printer and issue their print jobs as if the printer were attached directly to the Windows 2000-based print server. After receiving the print job from the network client, the print server spools it as a regular print job. In the final stage, however, when the print job gets to the print monitor, the print monitor transfers it to the UNIX host running LPD.

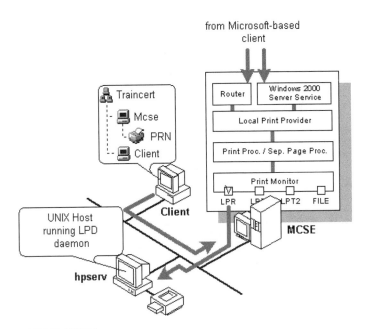

FIGURE 15-9 *Windows 2000 server as a print gateway for Microsoft-based clients*

PRINT GATEWAY FOR LPR CLIENTS

Suppose that you have several UNIX clients that need to print documents but all printers are attached to the Microsoft-based computer with no LPD software installed. A Windows 2000 server configured as a print gateway can solve this problem. In this situation, Windows 2000 LPD (TCP/IP printing server) receives a print job from a UNIX client and forwards it to any printer visible to the Windows 2000 computer.

Practical Application

In order for a Windows 2000 computer to provide print gateway services for LPR clients, perform the following steps:

1. Using the **Add Printer** wizard, create a local printer and add new local port.

2. Map the new local port to any visible network printer (see Figure 15-10).

3. Install the appropriate printer driver with the **Add Printer** wizard.

4. Give a name to the printer. (This name will also be used by the LPR clients.)

Now your Windows 2000 computer can accept the print jobs from LPR clients and automatically forward them to the network printer. The only requirement is that this network printer be visible to the Windows 2000 print gateway (see Figure 15-11).

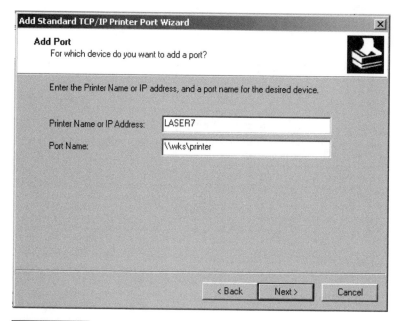

FIGURE 15–10   *Creating a local port and mapping it to the existing network printer*

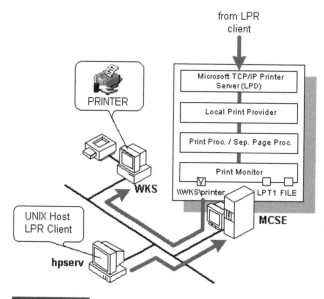

FIGURE 15–11   *Windows 2000 server as a print gateway for UNIX-based clients*

Summary

In this chapter we discussed Windows 2000 TCP/IP connectivity issues. We spoke about various connectivity utilities and identified when to use each. Data transfer utilities (RCP, FTP, TFTP, web browser) allow you to obtain files from remote TCP/IP computers. Remote execution utilities (RSH, REXEC, Telnet) allow you to execute a command or a program on a remote host. Some of the TCP/IP connectivity utilities require additional configuration on remote computers. UNIX hosts, for example, must maintain the .rhosts file in order for RSH and RCP to work.

We also explored TCP/IP printing and what is required to support it under Windows 2000. The LPR utility lets a Windows 2000 computer print on a printer attached to a UNIX host while LPQ allows you to view the status of the printer queue. Windows 2000 also provides the TCP/IP print server (also known as LPD) that allows a UNIX host to print on Windows 2000 printers. We also discovered that the Windows 2000 print monitor could be configured with an LPR port to permit Windows-based applications to take advantage of TCP/IP printing.

Test Yourself

1. What is NOT required for you to use standard Microsoft networking commands and utilities to connect to and access data on a remote non-Windows host?
   A. Both machines must communicate using TCP/IP
   B. Transport driver connectivity
   C. SMB connectivity
   D. The NetBIOS scope must be the same for both machines

2. LPR is used to:
   A. Receive print jobs and submit them to the spooler
   B. Transfer print jobs between computers
   C. Examine print status

3. LPQ is used to:
   A. Receive print jobs and submit them to the spooler
   B. Transfer print jobs between computers
   C. Examine print status

4. Which of the following is NOT a remote execution application?

   A. Telnet

   B. FTP

   C. RSH

   D. REXEC

   E. None of the above

5. A web browser may be used as an FTP client.

   A. True

   B. False

Simple Network Management Protocol

*I*n *this chapter we'll describe the Simple Network Management Protocol (SNMP), cover its terminology, and learn how to install and configure it on a Windows 2000 system.*

Defining SNMP

Before we get down to the work of installing and using SNMP, you are probably asking: "What is this SNMP thing, anyway?" Let's spend a few paragraphs looking at that very question.

While SNMP was originally designed to provide monitoring and trouble-shooting for network bridges and routers, the use of SNMP has expanded to most hardware and software in modern business communications. With SNMP you can monitor workstations and servers on your network, midrange systems which may be attached, and the routers, gateways, and other connection devices that are SNMP enabled.

SNMP uses a distributed system of network management systems and agents. The required components are SNMP managers (termed *management systems* in the RFCs) and SNMP agents. The Microsoft SNMP service consists of SNMP agent software that provides information to applications like Microsoft Systems Management Server, HP OpenView, and other third-party management systems.

Network management stations perform polling to collect information about network elements. They monitor and control network elements through the use of management applications. Network elements are devices such as hosts, gateways, terminal servers, and some software components. These elements have built-in management agents that are responsible for obtaining and reporting information required by the network management stations.

SNMP operates at the OSI application layer and uses Windows sockets and the User Datagram Protocol (UDP) to communicate between network management stations and the agents in the network elements. Figure 16-1 provides an overview of SNMP network architecture.

The SNMP management system directs SNMP agents to alter (`set`) or inspect and retrieve (`get`) variables present in the network elements. The management stations run specialized software not included in the Microsoft Transport Control Protocol/Internet Protocol (TCP/IP) suite to direct the agents' activities. To do this, the stations use three commands: `set`, `get`, `get-next`. The `set` command is not as widely used as `get` or `get-next` because most hardware does not provide a mechanism to set parameters remotely.

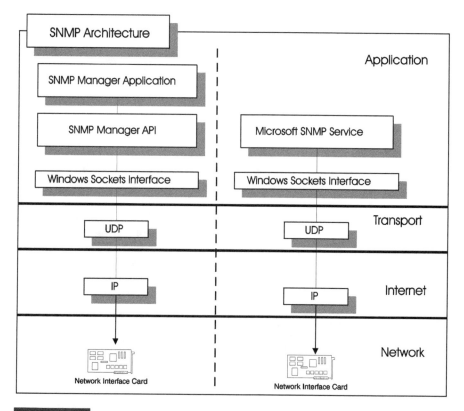

FIGURE 16–1   *SNMP network architecture*

The SNMP agent performs the work directed by the SNMP management stations. The SNMP agent can issue traps to provide the management system with information about unexpected events or error conditions on the SNMP agent's system. Password violations or exceeded threshold values would be likely candidates for an agent trap.

When installed on a Windows 2000 server, SNMP agent software permits you to use the Windows 2000 System Performance Monitor (known as *Performance Monitor* in previous versions) to chart TCP/IP values, such as packets sent and received or the number of TCP/IP transmission errors on a network.

SNMP Communities

SNMP communities are groupings of computers running SNMP services. The communities are given a community name which they use for primitive security and context checks to validate agents and managers in setting traps and issuing commands. Although an SNMP agent can be a member of more than one community, it will only respond to requests made by SNMP managers in its configured communities. Because SNMP managers can get sensitive information about your network, keeping communications within a community is a good thing. Communities help to prevent unauthorized people from installing their own SNMP managers and agents to compromise someone else's network. The default community name given during the installation of an SNMP agent is PUBLIC.

The SNMP Service on Microsoft Windows 2000

Any machine running Microsoft Windows 2000, with the SNMP service installed, can provide its status to an SNMP management system over TCP/IP. Microsoft's SNMP service is SNMP agent software that sends its status whenever it is polled by a management system or whenever the system handles some type of significant system event (such as running out of disk space). Microsoft's SNMP agent service is able to support requests from and report traps to multiple SNMP management systems. The service supports the use of IP address or host name to identify management hosts and provides for monitoring of the TCP/IP protocol in the Windows 2000 System Performance Monitor.

Management Information Base

A *management information base* (MIB) outlines what information can be collected on a particular network resource. An MIB is a database that contains a set of objects representing a wide variety of information about network devices. One example of this might be the version of the software that is running on a host computer. Another, more specific, example can be found in the LAN Manager MIB, which has objects to permit collection of user and logon statistics. Some MIB objects appear in the Windows 2000 System Performance Monitor.

In order to do their jobs efficiently, the SNMP management systems and management agents must share a common understanding of the MIB objects. The Windows 2000 SNMP service supports the Internet MIB II, LAN Manager MIB II, Host Resources MIB, and Microsoft proprietary MIBs. The Internet MIB II defines 171 objects that are required for fault or configuration analysis. (MIB II is an expansion of the earlier Internet MIB I standard and is defined in RFC 1212.)

MIB NAME SPACE

MIB objects are defined in a hierarchical tree, which has been compared to the Windows 2000 registry. Each of the manageable objects has a unique identifier that consists of a location in the tree and the object name. The InterNIC assigns authority for different parts of the name space to individual organizations so they can provide information and track their own objects. Each organization defines its own object names and does not have to register each new name or expanded function with the InterNIC. The name space represents a named value pair such that an object name and object number are paired in a MIB database. Any object can be identified in this way, either by its name or number. The information on standard MIB object types can be found in RFCs 1155, 1157, and 1213. Information on the Microsoft MIB object types can be found in the Microsoft Windows 2000 Server Resource Kit (TCP/IP Core Networking Guide).

To better understand MIB name space, refer to Figure 16-1 as we look at two examples. The first example is the MIB structure for an object called sysDescr (system description) taken from RFC 1155:

```
iso org dod internet mgmt mib system sysDescr
 1   3   6    1     2    1    1      1
```

The number for sysDescr becomes 1.3.6.1.2.1.1.1 and its full name is iso.org.dod.internet.mgmt.mib.system.sysDescr. Once sysDescr is registered, the owner can assign names to objects anywhere below it. For instance, 1.3.6.1.2.1.1.1.0 is the first object under sysDescr and returns information about the hardware and software used on the host. The object name would be: iso.org.dod.internet.mgmt.mib.system.sysDescr.0.

In another example, we see in Figure 16-2 that Microsoft has registered the LAN Manager MIB II as 1.3.6.1.4.1.77.

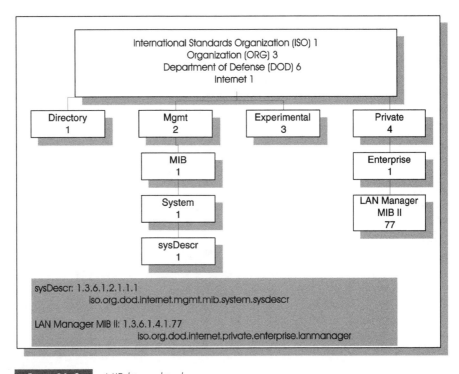

International Standards Organization (ISO) 1
Organization (ORG) 3
Department of Defense (DOD) 6
Internet 1

| Directory 1 | Mgmt 2 | Experimental 3 | Private 4 |

MIB 1

Enterprise 1

System 1

LAN Manager MIB II 77

sysDescr 1

sysDescr: 1.3.6.1.2.1.1.1
    iso.org.dod.internet.mgmt.mib.system.sysdescr

LAN Manager MIB II: 1.3.6.1.4.1.77
    iso.org.dod.internet.private.enterprise.lanmanager

FIGURE 16–2   *MIB hierarchical name space*

Warning   Don't confuse MIB names or numbers with fully qualified domain names or IP addresses. They may look similar, but they represent totally different things.

Installing and Configuring SNMP on Windows 2000

Microsoft's SNMP service can be installed on any Windows 2000-based system that is running the TCP/IP protocol. The Microsoft SNMP service is supported by the Windows sockets interface, which uses UDP to send and receive communications. It does not require authentication between managers and agents beyond the verification of the configured community names.

Before you install the Microsoft SNMP service, make sure you know the following information:

- Host name or IP address of the computer on which you will install the agent service
- Host name or IP address of the SNMP manager(s) your machine will report to

● Name of the community in which your computer will function

Once you have this information, you can install SNMP as a service:

1. Go to **Start|Settings|Control Panel|Add/Remove Programs**.
2. Select **Management and Monitoring Tools** and press **Details**.
3. Check **Simple Network Management Protocol** and click **OK** (see Figure 16-3).
4. Click **Next>** and **Finish** to complete the installation. (You will need to insert the Windows 2000 Installation CD or connect to the installation files over the network to complete this process.)
5. SNMP automatically starts after the installation is complete.

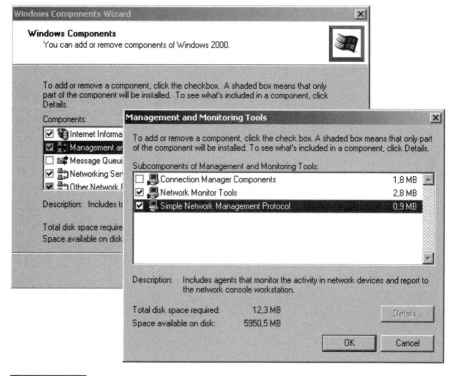

FIGURE 16-3 *Select the SNMP service*

With SNMP now installed and running, let's take a look at the configuration opportunities. We'll start with SNMP Trap:

1. Right-click **My Computer** and select **Manage**.
2. In the console tree under **Services and Applications**, select **Services**.
3. In the details pane, click **SNMP Service** (see Figure 16-4).

4. On the **Action** menu, click **Properties**.

5. On the **Traps** tab, under **Community name**, type the case-sensitive community name to which this computer will send trap messages, and then click **Add to list** (see Figure 16-5).

6. In **Trap destinations**, click **Add**.

7. In **Host name, IP or IPX address**, enter the host name or IP address of the machine(s) to which you want the SNMP service to send traps by clicking **Add**. (If you will use only SNMP to provide information to your machine's own system performance monitor, you may enter just the identification of your own computer, or may leave this blank.)

The SNMP Service Properties dialog box also allows you to configure SNMP security by selecting the Security tab, as shown in Figure 16-6.

1. Using Table 16.1 as a guide, you may set security as desired for the SNMP agent on your computer.

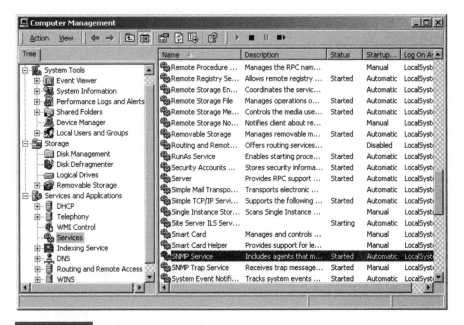

FIGURE 16–4   *Selecting SNMP service*

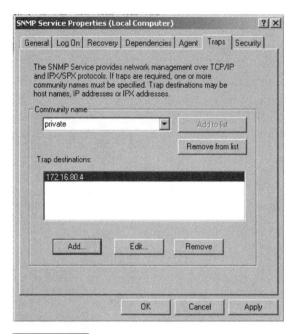

FIGURE 16-5   *SNMP properties—Traps tab*

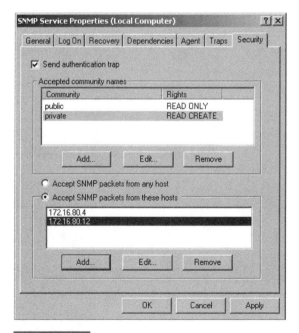

FIGURE 16-6   *SNMP properties—Security tab*

TABLE 16.1	*SNMP Security Configuration Options*

Parameter	Explanation
Send authentication trap	When the SNMP agent receives a request for information with an incorrect host or community name it can send a failed request trap to the SNMP manager.
Accepted community names	Permits configuration of one or more community names. By default, all managers and agents belong to the Public community. To enter new community names, click **Add** and enter the community name. You may assign the following permissions, which control how this host processes requests from the community indicated: None—do not process any SNMP requests; Notify—send only traps to the community; Read Only—prevent host from processing SNMP SET requests; Read Write—permit host to process SNMP SET requests; Read Create—permit host to create new entries in the SNMP tables.
Accept SNMP packets from any host	Enables this SNMP agent to accept SNMP manager requests from any SNMP manager in its community.
Accept SNMP packets from these hosts	Permits the agent to respond to only the specified SNMP managers. To specify hosts, click **Add** and enter the desired host name or IP address.

The SNMP properties dialog box also permits you to configure the agent services for SNMP by selecting the Agent tab (see Figure 16-7).

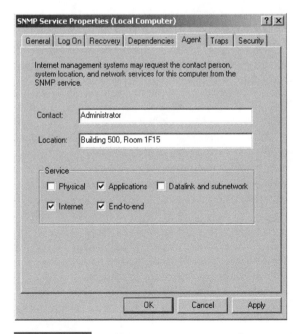

FIGURE 16–7	*SNMP properties—Agent tab*

1. You can enter the name of the person who uses the computer running the SNMP Agent in the Contact field of the SNMP agent dialog box.
2. In the Location field, enter the physical location of the computer.
3. You can configure the SNMP agent services in the Service area of the dialog box, as detailed in Table 16.2. This will control the services performed by the SNMP agent on the local computer.

| **TABLE 16.2** | *SNMP Agent Configuration Options* |

Parameter	Explanation
Physical	Used if host manages a *physical* device, such as a repeater or hub
Applications	Used if host uses any TCP/IP applications. (This should always be selected.)
Datalink and Subnetwork	Used if host is a bridge
Internet	Used if host is an IP router or gateway
End-to-End	Used if host is an IP host. (This should always be selected.)

Practical Application

In this exercise, we'll install SNMP and use it to provide an extension to the Windows 2000 System Performance Monitor. If you are on a large network, you may want to check with your network administrator to see if there is a machine in the environment running SNMP management software to permit you to set traps to monitor your machine.

Launch the Windows 2000 **System Performance Monitor** from the **Administrative Tools** program group. (Click **Performance** to launch this program.)

Press the **Add Counter** icon (appears as a button with a plus sign) to open the dialog window. Inspect the available objects in the **Performance** object list (see Figure 16-8). Can you find the ICMP, IP, TCP, or UDP object? (This exercise assumes SNMP has never run on your machine and that the listed objects are not available. If SNMP or some other service that installs those objects has previously run on your machine, the objects will be present. You can still accomplish the exercise but the results will be far less dramatic.)

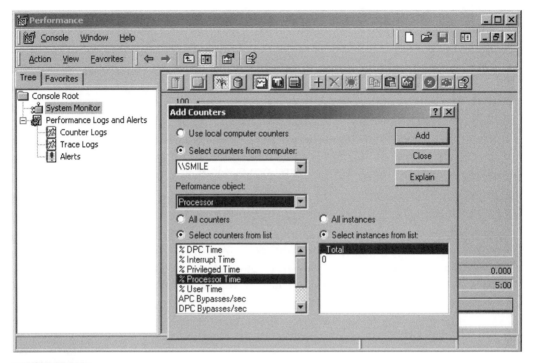

FIGURE 16—8 *System performance monitor: inspecting available objects*

Close **System Performance Monitor** and follow the steps at the start of this section to install and configure SNMP. (If you will use only **System Performance Monitor** in conjunction with the service, any configuration you accomplish after installation will be only for your training and experience.)

Once SNMP is installed, return to **System Performance Monitor** and check for the presence of the ICMP, IP, TCP, and UDP objects.

Select the **IP** object and add **Datagrams/Sec** in **System Performance Monitor**. Minimize **System Performance Monitor** and perform some network activity such as using **My Network Places**. Return to **System Performance Monitor** and note the activity caught by SNMP. (You may need to reduce the size of the **Vertical Maximum** in **System Performance Monitor** to easily view the activity.)

Summary

This chapter dealt with the facility for monitoring the activity of TCP/IP on the network: the Simple Network Management Protocol (SNMP). We saw that SNMP is used by both Windows and non-Windows systems and that it functions through *managers* and *agents*. The agent resides on the machine to be monitored and reports to the manager. Agents can set traps to detect unusual activity and report these traps to managers. We learned that Windows 2000 doesn't supply any SNMP management software but does have an installable SNMP agent which can report to third-party managers and which provides additional objects for the Windows 2000 System Performance Monitor.

We saw that SNMP security can be enhanced by placing SNMP systems within communities. Agents can be directed to report only to managers within their configured community.

We took a brief look at the construction of the *Management Information Base* (MIB), which stores the definitions of the objects used by SNMP to monitor network activity, and developed an understanding of the hierarchical MIB name space.

We discovered that SNMP is installed as a service, much as the other TCP/IP services, and that SNMP configuration permits us to select the communities and managers that will receive trap information and allows us to restrict responses to only specified managers. We can also enter identification information for the operator and the location of the agent machine and can configure the agent service for the particular role(s) our computer will function under.

Test Yourself

1. The default community name given during the installation of an SNMP agent is:
   A. PUBLIC
   B. PRIVATE
   C. WORKGROUP
   D. COMMUNITY

2. Each of the manageable MIB objects has a unique identifier that consists of:
   A. A port number and object name
   B. A location in the tree and the object name
   C. A location in the tree and the IP address
   D. The object name and the IP address

3. Before you install the Microsoft SNMP service you must know:
   A. Your host name or IP address
   B. The SNMP manager's host name or IP address
   C. The community name your agent will use
   D. All of the above

4. The Microsoft SNMP service uses:
   A. FTP
   B. SMTP
   C. UDP
   D. ICMP

5. Although Windows 2000 doesn't come with SNMP management software, the _____ will be able to provide some SNMP information once the SNMP service is added to the computer.
   A. Application log
   B. Network monitor
   C. System performance monitor
   D. System log

Troubleshooting Microsoft TCP/IP

*B*y now you should have learned how to plan and deploy Transport Control Protocol/Internet Protocol (TCP/IP) networks. You should also have discovered that TCP/IP services and parameters can be very error-prone. This chapter will help you determine what to do if something goes wrong. We will combine a review of the most important TCP/IP topics with some helpful troubleshooting guidelines. We will cover the major TCP/IP troubleshooting utilities and discuss how to use them most efficiently. Topics covered in this chapter summarize common TCP/IP-related problems, symptoms, and possible causes, as well as the concrete steps required to troubleshoot them.

General Considerations

When something goes wrong, we often try to choose a tool that can immediately solve our problem. Before deciding which utility to use, however, you should determine the source of the problem. A number of problems turn out not to be TCP/IP related (for example, a network interface card malfunction) and need to be solved by other methods. In this chapter, however, we will speak only of TCP/IP-related problems.

TCP/IP problems can be grouped by category, as shown in Table 17.1.

TABLE 17.1	*Major TCP/IP Related Problems*

Problem source	Symptoms
TCP/IP configuration	Host initialization fails, services fail to start, communication to all (some) other hosts is impossible.
Address resolution	Although you can ping your workstation, you cannot access some local or remote hosts.
NetBIOS name resolution	You can access a host by its IP address but cannot connect to it by its NetBIOS computer name.
Host name resolution	You can access a host by its IP address but cannot connect to it by its host name.

When a problem occurs, you might want to ask yourself these simple questions:

- What should work?
- What does work?
- What does not work?
- What has changed since it last worked?

Answering these questions will help you choose the right tool to isolate the problem. For example, suppose that Mary complains that she is unable to connect to remote Network Basic Input/Output System (NetBIOS) hosts by their computer name. After speaking with her you find out that recently she accidentally deleted some files from the %systemroot%\drivers\etc\ folder on her computer. Knowing what set of actions has resulted in this problem, you will not waste time in low-level connectivity checks but can go directly to the folder to check for an LMHOSTS file.

Windows 2000 Diagnostic Tools Overview

Microsoft Windows 2000 Server and Professional have many useful utilities to diagnose and troubleshoot TCP/IP. Many powerful utilities are included in the Windows 2000 Support Tools (installed from the distribution CD-ROM) and the Windows 2000 Resource Kit. Some examples of the resource kit tools include: *Browstat* (a command line utility that can be used to force the browser elections for a specified domain), *Browmon* (a graphical utility that can be used to view browsers for selected domains), *Netdiag* (a utility to help isolate networking and connectivity problems), and *Snmputilg* (a graphical utility to test and validate your simple network management protocol (SNMP) agent service). In addition, as you may already know, Microsoft systems management server includes an advanced version of Network Monitor—a great program to trace and monitor your network at the packet level. Table 17.2 lists common diagnostic utilities that are included in Microsoft TCP/IP.

TABLE 17.2	Microsoft TCP/IP Diagnostic Utilities

Utility	Function
Address Resolution Protocol (ARP)	Displays and modifies the cache of locally resolved IP addresses to media access control (MAC) addresses.
PING	Verifies the availability of the remote host by sending the echo request and analyzing replies.
TRACERT	Traces the route for packets from local hosts to the specified remote host.
IPCONFIG	Displays current TCP/IP configuration, including IP address(es), and DNS and WINS addresses.
ROUTE	Views and modifies the local routing table.
NBTSTAT	Displays protocol statistics and current TCP/IP connections using NetBIOS over TCP/IP. This utility is also used to determine the registered NetBIOS name and to view the local name cache.
NSLOOKUP	Displays information from Domain Name System (DNS) name servers about a particular host or domain. You can also use this utility to check the availability of the domain name across the Internet.
NETSTAT	Displays protocol statistics and current TCP/IP network connections.
Event Log	Standard Windows 2000 tool used to track events, warnings, and errors.
Network Monitor	Captures and displays packets.
Performance Monitor	Displays performance counters.
Microsoft SNMP Service	Supplies information to SNMP management systems.

Each utility may be used to diagnose only a portion of the problem. Unless your problem is very elementary, no single utility will likely solve the entire problem alone. Later in this chapter you will be introduced to how to use these utilities together to troubleshoot your network.

TCP/IP Troubleshooting Guidelines

There is no fixed sequence of steps to troubleshoot TCP/IP related problems—everything depends on the particular scenario. There are some basic guidelines, however, that fit most situations.

The first thing you should do is ensure the physical connection is functioning. It's useless to employ a host of troubleshooting utilities if the office hub is malfunctioning. When link reliability is in question, for example when the WAN link is malfunctioning, you may want to try a large number of *pings* to various remote hosts to check connectivity.

Once you're sure the links are functioning properly, you should start testing the local host's configuration parameters, then examine routing configurations, and finally check name resolution issues. The direction of troubleshooting steps is illustrated in Figure 17-1. Note that you test the lower layers of the TCP/IP stack first. Once the low-level TCP/IP functions are working correctly, you pass to the higher levels.

Identifying the TCP/IP Configuration

Checking the TCP/IP configuration is the most basic troubleshooting step. You might want to ensure the TCP/IP parameters have been entered without mistakes or that dynamic host configuration protocol (DHCP) has set them correctly. You should begin by checking the TCP/IP configuration on the computer that appears to be experiencing problems.

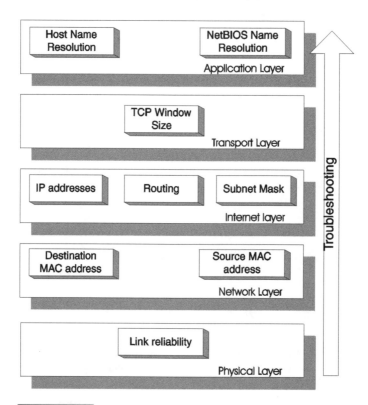

FIGURE 17-1   *TCP/IP troubleshooting guidelines*

A good starting point is the IPCONFIG command line utility. IPCONFIG displays the IP address, subnet mask, and default gateway, as well as other advanced TCP/IP parameters, such as the WINS server, IP address, and node type.

You should use the IPCONFIG utility with the /all switch because it produces a *detailed* report concerning the current TCP/IP configuration. The following is an example of the output from IPCONFIG:

```
C:\>ipconfig /all
Windows 2000 IP Configuration
        Host Name . . . . . . . . : mary
        Primary DNS Suffix. . . . . . : senate.gov
        Node Type . . . . . . . . . . : Hybrid
        IP Routing Enabled. . . . . . : Yes
        WINS Proxy Enabled. . . . . . : No
        DNS Suffix Search List. . . . . : senate.gov
Ethernet adapter External Connection:

        Connection-specific DNS Suffix. :
        Description . . . . . . . . . . : ELNK3 Ethernet Adapter
        Physical Address. . . . . . . . : 00-20-AF-AC-3A-76
        Autoconfiguration Enabled . . . : Yes
        DHCP Enabled. . . . . . . . . : Yes
        IP Address. . . . . . . . . : 172.20.0.10
        Subnet Mask . . . . . . . . : 255.255.255.0
        Default Gateway . . . . . . : 172.20.0.1
        DNS Servers . . . . . . . . . : 172.20.0.10 Primary WINS
Server . . . . : 172.20.0.20
        Lease Obtained. . . . . . . : Tuesday, 14 May 2000 1352:01
        Lease Expires . . . . . . . : Wednesday, 22 May 2000 1352:01
```

In some cases, just reviewing this report can resolve problem. For example, if the DHCP client could not obtain the IP address, running IPCONFIG returns an IP address and subnet mask of 0.0.0.0.

```
C:\>ipconfig
Windows 2000 IP Configuration
Ethernet adapter Local Area Connection:
        Connection-specific DNS Suffix . :
        IP Address . . . . . . . . . . . : 0.0.0.0
        Subnet Mask  . . . . . . . . . . : 0.0.0.0
        Default Gateway  . . . . . . . . :
```

This listing could indicate that the DHCP server is down or there are no free IP addresses in the DHCP server's scope.

IPCONFIG and Windows 2000

This book has covered the IPCONFIG arguments **/ALL**, **/Release**, and **/Renew**. Windows 2000 introduces several new IPCONFIG features which can be of help in configuring and troubleshooting your network:

/flushdns:	Purges the DNS resolver cache
/registerdns:	Refreshes all DHCP leases and re-registers DNS names
/displaydns:	Displays the contents of the DNS resolver cache
/showclassid:	Displays all the dhcp class IDs allowed for the adapter
/setclassid:	Modifies the dhcp class ID

If you can't remember these options or would like a refresher on their syntax, simply type **IPCONFIG /?** at the command line.

Incorrect IP Address Assignment

To determine if the computer has been assigned a valid IP address you can use the following guidelines:

- Check that the IP address is from the correct subnet
- Check that the IP address is not duplicated
- Check that the IP address is not a broadcast address for the given subnet (host ID is all-1s)
- Check that the IP address is not the subnet address (host ID is all-0s)

Figure 17-2 shows a network where computers have IP addressing problems. **Computer 1** and **Computer 3** have duplicate IP addresses. **Computer 2** has the IP address that is the broadcast address for subnet 172.20.0.0, mask 255.255.255.0. **Computer 4** has an IP address from another subnet.

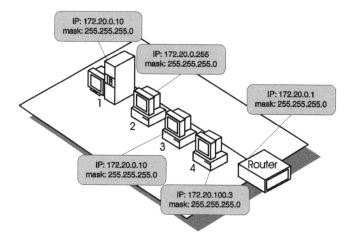

IP: 172.20.0.10
mask: 255.255.255.0

IP: 172.20.0.255
mask: 255.255.255.0

IP: 172.20.0.1
mask: 255.255.255.0

IP: 172.20.0.10
mask: 255.255.255.0

IP: 172.20.100.3
mask: 255.255.255.0

Router

FIGURE 17–2   *IP addressing problems*

Subnet Mask Problems

Subnet mask problems are very hard to diagnose and isolate. This is mainly because, depending on the actual numbers, an invalid subnet mask can have no negative impact or can make the entire network unreachable for a particular computer. In some cases an incorrect subnet mask could cause some computers to become unreachable, while the rest of network remains operational. In Figure 17-3, **Computer 2** has an incorrect subnet mask (displayed in bold). Although it can successfully establish a connection with **Computer 1**, **Computer 3**, and the **default gateway**, it fails to communicate with **Computer 4**.

There are two common problems with subnet masks:

- The configured subnet mask is shorter than needed (too many bits are reserved for network and subnet ID).
- The configured subnet mask is longer than needed (too few bits are reserved for network and subnet ID).

Improper subnet mask configuration is often the result of inaccurate planning. It may also be caused by mistyping the subnet mask during manual TCP/IP parameter assignment.

Let's look at some symptoms that can indicate these two problems. Suppose we have the Class C network 192.168.18.0. We divide it into 8 subnets using the subnet mask 255.255.255.224 (see Figure 17-4). Now, what happens if we assign a particular computer a shorter subnet mask: 255.255.255.192 (Arrow 1). That computer would think: "The shorter my subnet mask is, the greater number of other computers I recognize to be inside my subnet." If the subnet mask is 255.255.255.0, this computer will think the network is not divided into subnets at all.

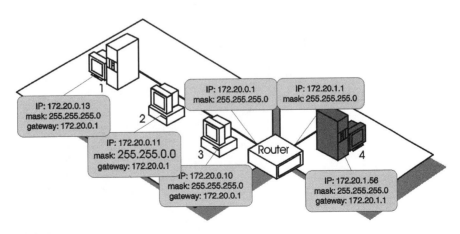

FIGURE 17–3 *An incorrect subnet mask may prevent your computer from communicating with one or more machines*

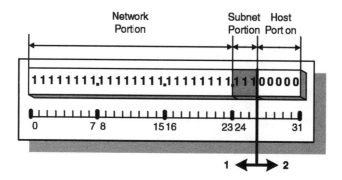

FIGURE 17-4   Subnet mask problems

On the other hand, if we assign the computer a longer subnet mask (Arrow 2), let's say 255.255.255.240, it will think some computers on the local network segment are outside its subnet.

The following example illustrates both of these subnet masking problems. Figure 17-5 shows a properly planned and configured network. Let's introduce some subnet masking errors to demonstrate how they affect network communication.

If we begin to enlarge the subnet mask of **Computer 6**, simulating a data entry error, the computer starts experiencing connectivity problems. Computers inaccessible to **Computer 6** hosts are dimmed in Figure 17-6.

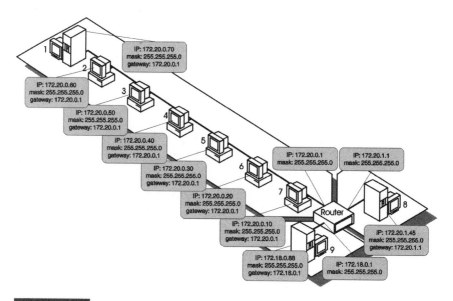

FIGURE 17-5   Network without subnet mask problems

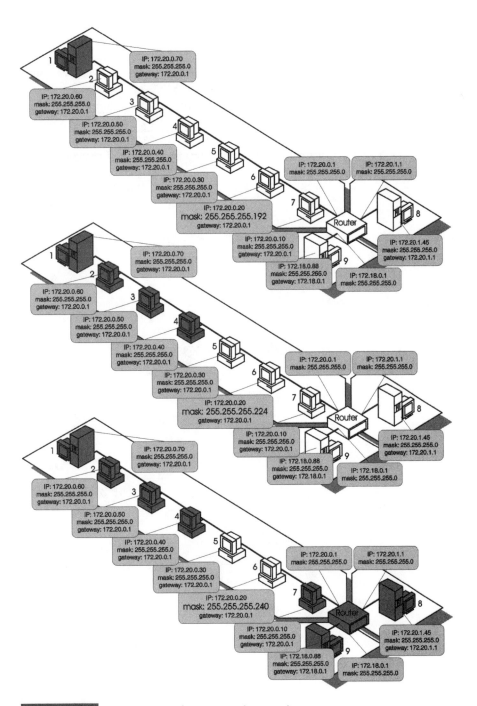

FIGURE 17-6 *Three stages of improper subnet masking*

With a subnet mask of 255.255.255.192, **Computer 6** thinks that **Server 1** is located on a remote network and sends all the packets for **Server 1** to the router instead of making a direct connection. The larger the subnet mask grows, the more computers jump out of reach of **Computer 6**. Finally, when Computer 6's subnet mask is 255.255.255.240, even the router is outside Computer 6's subnet, and communications to remote networks are impossible. Note that an incorrect subnet mask of 255.255.255.128 causes no apparent problem.

If the subnet mask is too short, we are likely to experience problems in trying to contact remote computers (see Figure 17-7). This is because the misconfigured computer expects many remote hosts to be within its local network and attempts to contact them directly and doesn't forward its communications to the default gateway.

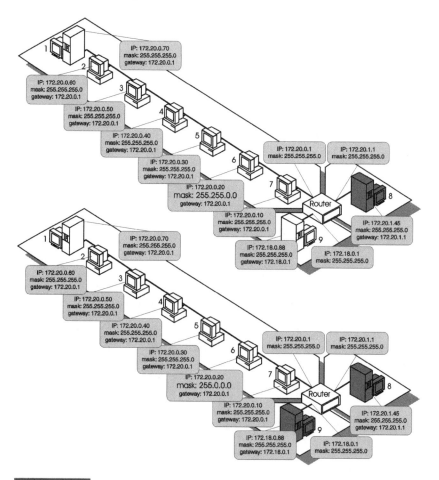

FIGURE 17-7   *Network with short subnet mask problems*

Testing IP Communications

Once your computer has obtained an IP address and a subnet mask, you should test the IP communications. PING is the utility that can be used for verifying the IP-level connectivity. As you may remember, PING sends the Internet Control Message Protocol (ICMP) echo request to the destination host and analyzes ICMP echo replies.

The recommended sequence of pings is the following:

1. Ping the loopback address.
2. Ping the IP address of the local computer.
   - If you cannot ping the local IP address, check to ensure your computer has a valid IP address that is not duplicated elsewhere on the network.
3. Ping the IP address of the default gateway.
   - If this step is unsuccessful, check the subnet mask on your computer.
4. Ping the IP address of the remote host.
   - If this step is unsuccessful, check the default gateway address configured on the local computer, the functionality of the link between routers, and the remote computer availability.
5. Ping the remote host by name.
   - If this step fails, check host name resolution

The PING utility has many switches that can be used to expand its functionality. To view the available command-line options, type PING -?

```
C:\>ping -?
Usage: ping [-t] [-a] [-n count] [-l size] [-f] [-i TTL] [-v TOS]
            [-r count] [-s count] [[-j host-list] | [-k host-list]]
            [-w timeout] destination-list
Options:
    -t              Ping the specified host until stopped.
                    To see statistics and continue - type Control-Break;
                    To stop - type Control-C.
    -a              Resolve addresses to hostnames.
    -n count        Number of echo requests to send.
    -l size         Send buffer size.
    -f              Set Don't Fragment flag in packet.
    -i TTL          Time To Live.
    -v TOS          Type Of Service.
    -r count        Record route for count hops.
    -s count        Timestamp for count hops.
    -j host-list    Loose source route along host-list.
    -k host-list    Strict source route along host-list.
    -w timeout      Timeout in milliseconds to wait for each reply.
```

For example, you can specify the size of the packets to use, how many packets to send, and how much time to wait for a response.

Routing Problems

Even when your computer is properly configured, a malfunctioning router can cause difficulties. An improperly configured route typically causes the problem (in this case, *improperly configured* could also mean *not configured*). Remember, if the Windows 2000 router does not have an interface on a given subnet, it will need a route to get there. You can do this by adding a static route or by using a multiprotocol router (MPR).

Note   Having multiple network adapters on a Windows 2000 computer allows you to add a default route for each network card. Although it will create several 0.0.0.0 routes, only one default route actually will be used. You should configure only one card to have a default gateway—this will reduce confusion and ensure the results you intended.

If you can ping across the router but cannot establish a session, check to see if the router is able to pass large packets. The PING utility sends its data in 74-byte blocks, but NET requests can be significantly larger. You can use the PING –l command to use a larger packet size. To correct this problem you may want to edit the registry to specify a smaller packet size.

Note   PING sends data in 74-byte blocks, but only indicates it's using 32 bytes of data. That's because PING reports only its data block length. The actual ICMP packet is 74 bytes: 32 byte data block + 14 bytes for the Ethernet header + 20 bytes for the IP header + 8 bytes for the ICMP header.

Editing the Registry to Specify a Smaller Packet Size

It's easy to say, "Edit the registry to specify a smaller packet size," but how do we actually accomplish this?

We'll need to add some keys to the registry values located under HKEY_LOCAL_MACHINE\SYSTEM\CurrentControlSet\Services \Tcpip\Parameters.

There are two registry entries that can affect the TCP/IP packet size. The first one is found in the TCPIP\Parameters subkey and is called *EnablePMTUDiscovery* (REG_DWORD). This entry can be set to 0 (false) or 1 (true); its default is 1. When set to 1, it directs TCP/IP to attempt to discover the Maximum Transmission Unit (MTU—largest packet size) over the path to a remote host. This permits TCP/IP to eliminate fragmentation at routers along the path that connect networks with different MTUs. If you set this value to 0, an MTU of 576 will be used for connections to all machines that are not on the local subnet.

The other registry entry is found in the TCPIP\Parameters\Interfaces\<*inteface name*>subkey and is called *MTU* (REG_DWORD). MTU can be set anywhere between 68 and the actual MTU of the underlying network. (The 68 minimum is required to provide space for the transport header—using a value less than this will result in an MTU of 68.) Setting this parameter overrides the default MTU for the network interface.

Neither of these registry entries appears in the registry by default. If you wish to use them, you must enter them yourself.

Testing TCP/IP Name Resolution

Once IP-level connectivity has been checked, you should examine name resolution. Most name resolution problems occur because the computer cannot resolve the host name or NetBIOS name to the IP address.

NetBIOS Name Resolution Problems

Because Windows 2000 operates well using host names and makes little distinction between NetBIOS names and host names, NetBIOS name resolution may not be a serious issue in a pure Windows 2000 environment. In a mixed Windows environment or one with applications that use NetBIOS, this becomes a very important issue and is worth understanding.

If you can ping the computer by its IP address, but not its NetBIOS name, you may want to check that the target host is NetBIOS enabled and ensure the scope ID on the source and target computers is the same. If scope IDs don't match, you probably have a NetBIOS name resolution problem.

Verify that the NetBIOS name-to-address mapping is available through broadcast, WINS, or the LMHOSTS file. If you have a WINS server, check that it is operational and that the local computer has been assigned the proper WINS server address.

If you suspect trouble with the LMHOSTS file, check that it is located in %systemroot%/system32/drivers/etc. Check that the file format matches the sample format originally installed with TCP/IP. Check for spelling errors, invalid addresses, and identifiers. Remember, the LMHOSTS file is parsed from the beginning, so if duplicate entries exist, only the first one is considered. Check for capitalization errors (although the NetBIOS names in the LMHOSTS file are not case sensitive, entries like #PRE and #DOM are).

Note   The LMHOSTS file does not support aliases for NetBIOS names. You must provide the actual NetBIOS name of each computer. Finally, ensure that the LMHOSTS file has no extension. It is easy to edit and save the LMHOSTS file with the default .txt extension (especially when using an editor like Notepad). If you do this, the file will NOT be recognized as an LMHOSTS file.

In some cases the NetBIOS name resolution works but is extremely slow. This could be caused by the large number of #INCLUDE tags and other entries in the LMHOSTS file. To correct the problem, place the most commonly used names closer to the beginning of the LMHOSTS file. Optionally, you can use the #PRE tag to force entries to be pre-cached.

You can use the NBTSTAT utility to check the state of current NetBIOS over TCP/IP connections, update the LMHOSTS cache, and determine the registered name and scope ID.

Host Name Resolution Problems

If you can ping a computer by its IP address, but not by its host name, you have a host name resolution problem. In this case, you should check that the host name-to-address resolution is possible by means of a DNS server, a HOSTS file, or through NetBIOS methods.

If a HOSTS file is your primary method of host name resolution, check that the entries use the proper sequence and delimiters. If you use DNS, verify that the DNS server is operational.

Note   Even if other methods of host name resolution are available, you should check that the DNS server is online and functioning. A DNS client (resolver) has a certain timeout before passing control to other methods. If the client is configured to use DNS, but the DNS server is unreachable, the client may experience long delays in host name resolution.

You can use NSLOOKUP to check records, domain host aliases, domain host services, and operating system information by querying the Internet domain name servers.

Another problem can occur when a TCP/IP connection to a remote system appears to be "hung." In this case you can use NETSTAT—a command to see the status of all activity on TCP and UDP ports on the local system. Good TCP connections usually appear with 0 bytes in queues. Large data blocks in either send or receive queues may indicate a connection problem or network delay.

Session Communications Problems

Sometimes you can ping the target computer by an IP address and by name but are unable to establish a session. For example, you are unable to FTP to the target host. Then you probably have a session problem. You may want to check that the correct services are running on the target computer and that you have the proper permissions to access it. Sometimes you are unable to connect because the maximum number of licenses is reached on the target computer. If the remote host is a UNIX-based machine, check that the appropriate daemon is configured and running.

EVENT VIEWER

You can use Windows 2000 Event Viewer to browse system information about TCP/IP. Important TCP/IP events, such as a duplicate IP address, are recorded to the event log.

NETWORK MONITOR

If you are unable to solve the problem using the above tools, you may want to try Network Monitor to capture the network traffic and analyze it at the packet level. If the problem is beyond your capability, you can send the capture to a network analyst or support organization.

Summary

This chapter summarized common TCP/IP related problems. We learned quite a bit about major TCP/IP faults and methods of correcting them. You learned to troubleshoot a TCP/IP network by first checking lower-level functions, such as link reliability, and then to progress to IP connectivity checks, and routing and name resolution tests. We discussed the typical symptoms of some TCP/IP related problems. Understanding the symptoms, you can frequently solve network problems without even touching a machine.

Test Yourself

1. Although network troubleshooting steps may depend on the scenario, what is generally accepted as the first troubleshooting step for network problems?
   A. Run TRACERT
   B. Launch IPCONFIG from the command prompt
   C. Check physical connectivity
   D. Check protocol properties

2. Where would you check if your computer can reach some but not all of the computers on your local network segment?
   A. Default gateway
   B. Subnet mask
   C. WINS server information
   D. DNS information

3. You try pinging machines on a remote network and find you can ping them by IP address but not by computer name. You suspect:
   A. Default gateway is down
   B. Subnet mask is wrong
   C. DHCP relay agent is not functioning
   D. Incorrect entry in the HOSTS file

4. What tool would you use to ensure your servicing DNS server is properly configured?
   A. NSLOOKUP
   B. TRACERT
   C. NETSTAT
   D. ROUTE

5. You can successfully ping the IP address of your configured default gateway but not the IP address of any remote host. You suspect:
   A. DNS servers on the remote network are down
   B. Wrong default gateway address is configured
   C. Bad subnet mask
   D. Your IP address is on the wrong network

Answers to Review Questions

Chapter 1

1. a; FTP: the File Transfer Protocol
2. b; Telnet
3. Ping verifies the availability of a remote host by sending an echo request and analyzing replies.
4. Network Monitor is used to capture network traffic on a packet-by-packet basis.

Chapter 2

1. Active Directory may be installed only on a Windows 2000 server computer. Installation of Active Directory on such a machine makes it a Domain Controller.
2. d; Scalability, interoperability, and extensibility are among the Active Directory's chief benefits!
3. d; A major part of network administration involves the management of users, groups, and computers.
4. b; With Active Directory authentication, a user can access resources throughout the network with only a single username and password.
5. Multimaster

Chapter 3

1. e; The OSI model has no Directory layer.
2. IP addressing is handled at the Network Layer.
3. c; Hardware addresses are resolved by the Address Resolution Protocol (ARP).

4. b; The Transmission Control Protocol (TCP) is a connection-oriented protocol and, as such, provides delivery verification to the sender.

5. b; A TCP/IP socket is the combination of an IP address and port number (e.g., 10.0.0.1:80).

Chapter 4

1. When they are on different network segments (and, therefore, have different network IDs).

2. a; The high order bit of a Class A address must be zero and the first octet may NOT be 127. The possible values under these constraints are 1-126.

3. An IP address that begins with 127 is a loop-back address.

4. a; Both Class B addresses have a network ID of 141.128 and both are in the 141.128.0.0 network.

5. b; IP address 22.254.255.255 is a Class A address. The host ID is 254.255.255. Although the 255s in the third and fourth octets may look suspicious, neither the network nor the host ID is comprised of all 1s!

Chapter 5

1. c; Current analysis and future planning is critical to network design. Unfortunately, TCP/IP won't permit hosts to share IP addresses on the same physical network.

2. 18; Six bits are required to create 40 subnets. Since an IP address contains 32 bits, 26 bits are left. We deduct the 8 bits (first octet) used to identify the Class A network and are left with 18 for host addressing.

3. 4; Although only 3 bits are needed to represent 7 networks, we must reject the all-1s and all-0s subnets. Three bits will make, at most, 6 subnets so we must go to 4 bits (which will actually create 14 usable networks).

4. d; The alternative designation specifies the number of bits in the subnet mask. A Class B subnet mask (255.255.0.0) has 16 bits in its subnet mask.

5. a; If you convert 192 to binary, you'll see the mask contains 2 bits. This is enough to represent 4 networks but, when the all-1s and all-0s networks are removed, we have 2 usable networks.

Chapter 6

1. The default gateway is the address of a router designated to forward traffic to external networks. The default gateway is used when a host has a message to send to a target host on an external network and when the host has no other routing information for the external network.
2. b; The "route print" command will show a computer's routing table.
3. b; A dynamic router will share routing information with other dynamic routers that use the same routing protocol. To communicate with static routers in the environment, the dynamic router must have manual entries in its routing table.
4. b; When multiple routes are available to the same network, the router will choose a functioning route with the lowest metric field entry.
5. b; The Routing Information Protocol is limited to 15 hops. Such a limitation would prevent many messages from ever arriving at their Internet destination.

Chapter 7

1. b; When a host receives a DHCPNACK message during a renewal attempt, it must negotiate a new lease.
2. b; A host obtains a DHCP lease from a broadcast. (Automatic IP configuration can also take place through Automatic Private IP Addressing, which requires no DHCP server at all.)
3. a; When an IP address cannot be obtained dynamically, the client will set its IP address to 0.0.0.0.
4. d; A client may access a DHCP server on an external network using a DHCP Relay Agent. If the external DHCP server has IP configuration information that will be valid on the client's network, it will offer an IP Configuration Lease.
5. a, b; Automatic Private IP Addressing will supply only an IP address and subnet mask. (The address will be in the 169.254.0.0/16 network.)

Chapter 8

1. b; NetBIOS operates at the application level and the session/transport level.
2. b; The first step is always to check the local cache. If resolution can't be obtained from the cache, the machine will broadcast and check the NetBIOS name server, depending on the name resolution node.
3. b; LMHOSTS files are not case sensitive.
4. a: A DNS server provides a fully qualified domain name (FQDN). If the FQDN exists and represents the NetBIOS name being sought, an IP address mapping will be returned.
5. c: Machines may have the same NetBIOS names if they are in different name scopes; they will be unable, however, to communicate with each other.

Chapter 9

1. a; WINS servers must have static addresses since clients seek them by IP address. They may obtain their addresses from a DHCP server as long as it's through a DHCP Address Reservation (so the IP address is guaranteed to remain static).
2. c; Static entries permit WINS clients to get resolution for non-WINS clients.
3. c; WINS proxy agents obtain/provide WINS resolution for non-WINS clients.
4. b; Since clients update data on only one WINS server, replication is critical to ensure each WINS server has mappings for all clients in the network.
5. d; Burst handling permits a WINS server to quickly respond to a heavy name registration workload by deferring name validation for a short, random period.

Chapter 10

1. d; All answers are applicable to the domain announcement datagram.
2. b; It is possible that a computer will appear in the browse list as long as 51 minutes after it is no longer available to the network.
3. b; Browsers are selected through browser elections.

4. b; The domain master browser is always the PDC Emulator and can be found across network segments.

5. d; The domain master browser can be located by using WINS, LMHosts, or DNS.

Chapter 11

1. b; TCP/IP utilities can obtain host name resolution. Because it eliminates the host name resolution step, however, the use of IP addresses is more efficient.

2. b; The Address Resolution Protocol (ARP) resolves hardware (MAC) addresses.

3. c; A simple text file, HOSTS provides host name IP address mappings.

4. c; UNIX hosts are very concerned about case sensitivity.

5. d; The first step in host name resolution is to check to see if the host name being sought is the same as the local host name.

Chapter 12

1. d; Slave servers must use forwarders to access other DNS servers on the external network.

2. a; The name server (NS) record contains a reference to each name server that can be used to look up hosts in the domain.

3. a; You'll need to register with the DNS server that is immediately above you in the Domain Name Space. If your DNS servers are on the second level, you'll need to contact the InterNIC; otherwise, you can contact the administrator for the level above you.

4. b; By configuring your DNS server to use WINS, you can enable it to obtain mappings from the WINS server even when they haven't been manually added to the DNS database.

5. d; Records in the Reverse Lookup Zone permit you to determine a fully qualified domain name when you know the IP address.

Chapter 13

1. d; You can perform options a, b, and c on an Active Directory integrated zone. DNS doesn't use a tertiary zone—we made it up!

2. a, b, c, d; These are all default update criteria.

3. a, b, d

4. d; Incremental zone transfer (IXFR) is a zone transfer protocol that replicates only the zone's added (new) or changed records.

5. c; A Windows 2000 Active Directory domain depends on SRV records for its operation.

Chapter 14

1. d; IPSec provides all these benefits.

2. b; Network address translation (NAT) translates IP addresses on the internal network to an IP address that will function on the external network.

3. a, c; Open Shortest Path First (OSPF) and Routing Information Protocol (RIP) are both dynamic routing protocols.

4. c; Virtual private networking permits users to create a virtual connection through the Internet that is secure and appears to the user as if it goes from the user straight to the target computer or network.

5. a, b, d; RRAS Dial-up networking relies on the Point-to-Point Protocol (PPP) for data communication. It supports Virtual Private Networking through Point-to-Point Tunneling Protocol (PPTP) and Layer Two Tunneling Protocol (L2TP). RRAS does not support the Serial Line Internet Protocol (SLIP).

Chapter 15

1. a; Although this IS a TCP/IP book, as long as the criteria in choices b, c, and d are met, any common transport protocol will do.

2. b; The Line Printer Remote (LPR) utility permits you to send a print job to the printer connected to a server running the Line Printer Daemon (LPD) service.

3. c; The Line Printer Queue (LPQ) utility permits you to view the print queue on an LPD server.

4. b; All listed utilities support remote execution except for FTP, which is a file transfer utility.

5. a; Web browsers support multiple protocols including Gopher, Network News Transfer Protocol (NNTP), and FTP.

Chapter 16

1. a; The default community name given during the installation of an SNMP agent is "PUBLIC."
2. b; Each of the manageable objects has a unique identifier that consists of a location in the tree and the object name.
3. d; All of these are required during installation.
4. c; The Microsoft SNMP service is supported by the Windows sockets interface, which uses UDP to send and receive communications.
5. c; When installed on a Windows 2000 server, SNMP agent software permits you to use the Windows 2000 System Performance Monitor (known as *Performance Monitor* in previous versions) to chart TCP/IP values, such as packets sent and received, or the number of TCP/IP transmission errors on a network.

Chapter 17

1. c; The first thing you should do is to ensure the physical connection is functioning. It's useless to employ a host of troubleshooting utilities if the office hub is malfunctioning.
2. b; In some cases an incorrect subnet mask could cause some computers to become unreachable, while the rest of network remains operational.
3. d; If you can ping by IP address but not name, the problem is in name resolution. The only name resolution related choice in this question has to do with the HOSTS file.
4. a; You can use NSLOOKUP to check records, domain host aliases, domain host services, and operating system information by querying the Internet domain name servers.
5. b; Since you're working with IP addresses, you can discount name resolution problems for now. You can successfully ping the address of your configured default gateway so your machine must be properly configured for the local network. Since you can't get to hosts in remote networks, the problem must be at the default gateway. In this case, the address you were using for a default gateway didn't represent a machine that was configured to route to the external network.

INDEX

485